CONFRONTING ARISTOTLE'S ETHICS

# CONFRONTING ARISTOTLE'S ETHICS

Ancient and Modern Morality

Eugene Garver

The University of Chicago Press

Chicago & London

Eugene Garver is Regents Professor of Philosophy at St. John's University in Minnesota. He is the author of three previous books, including, most recently, *For the Sake of Argument: Practical Reasoning, Character, and the Ethics of Belief,* also published by the University of Chicago Press.

The University of Chicago Press, Chicago 60637
The University of Chicago Press, Ltd., London
© 2006 by The University of Chicago
All rights reserved. Published 2006
Printed in the United States of America
15  14  13  12  11  10  09  08  07  06      5  4  3  2  1

ISBN-13 (cloth): 978-0-226-28398-2
ISBN-10 (cloth): 0-226-28398-4

Library of Congress Cataloging-in-Publication Data

Garver, Eugene.
    Confronting Aristotle's Ethics : ancient and modern morality / Eugene Garver.
        p.      cm.
    Includes bibliographical references (p.      ) and index.
    ISBN-13: 978-0-226-28398-2 (cloth : alk. paper)
    ISBN-10: 0-226-28398-4 (cloth : alk. paper)
    1. Aristotle. Nicomachean ethics.   2. Ethics.   I. Title.
    B430.G37   2006
    171'.3—dc22

                                                                    2006009141

# CONTENTS

## ACKNOWLEDGMENTS

If I were to give a complete accounting of all the debts I've acquired in writing this book, I would have to produce an intellectual autobiography. Although I don't want to do that, I do need to start by acknowledging discussions and friendships with teachers, colleagues, and students at the University of Chicago. My earliest teachers about Aristotle and the *Ethics,* Richard McKeon, David Smigelskis, Charles Wegener, and Warner Wick. I regret that only Smigelskis has lived long enough to see this final product. David Luban, Ed Halper, Doug Mitchell, Wendy Olmsted, David Reed are former colleagues and students who have given helpful advice, detailed criticism, and great support over the years. My current colleague Jim Read read a complete draft a few years ago.

One intense period of rewriting was spent enjoying the hospitality of the Tantur Ecumenical Institute in Jerusalem. I thank Tantur, and hope that Jerusalem may once again be a place peaceful enough for endeavors like this, which must look frivolous in the context of its current problems. While we were at Tantur, David Burrell read the entire manuscript and gave extensive and highly useful comments.

Lenn Goodman and David O'Connor have helped with conversations and comments over the last decade. David Depew and Charles Young have been extraordinary conversation partners over many more years than that. Young's written comments on a series of iterations of the manuscript have seriously delayed this publication, and I think improved the final version proportionately.

A Summer Stipend and then a Fellowship for College Teachers from NEH gave me the time to work without the usual interruptions. I'm grateful to the Endowment, and to Alasdair MacIntyre, Amélie Rorty, and Michael Stocker for their letters of support, as well as provoking conversations—in MacIntyre's case, many years of very fruitful conversations for me.

I owe a large debt to my colleagues in ancient philosophy at the Univer-

sity of Minnesota, Betty Belfiore, Norman Dahl, and Sandra Peterson, along
with the other members of our long-running discussion group. Their conversation has provided great stimulation and support over the years. Belfiore and Dahl helped immensely, and in their own very different ways, with
meticulous and spirited criticism of multiple drafts. It is not easy to be
simultaneously supportive and challenging, and I am lucky to have such
friends.

Over the years, I've read papers on the *Ethics,* and audiences have supplied different forms of useful criticism. I've given talks that in one way or
another led up to this book at the Society for Ancient Greek Philosophy
and the Minnesota Ancient Philosophy Conference, Berry College, Bucknell University, Cal State Fullerton, Claremont Graduate School, the University of Georgia, Marquette University, and Skidmore College.

Finally, I must thank again one of my former fellow-students who has
now been an extremely helpful editor for three books. I'm gradually learning what an editor does, and how excellent Doug Mitchell has been in this
very self-effacing function. The entire staff at the University of Chicago
Press has been exemplary.

Writing about the *Ethics* is a very different experience from writing about
the *Rhetoric,* or for that matter Machiavelli's *Prince.* I found very little of
the secondary literature about *Rhetoric* at all helpful. There is such a rich
tradition of consideration of the *Ethics,* though, producing a large body of
work of high quality, that it would be irresponsible to ignore it. I've written this book over so many years that some of the secondary literature that
influenced the most no longer appears in the final version. I have tried to
cite only materials that may help the reader orient himself or herself to my
project in relation to others that may be more familiar. Readers should not
assume that approbation attaches to the works I mention, or that works unmentioned are in my judgment inferior.

| | |
|---|---|
| *An. Post.* | *Posterior Analytics* |
| *An. Pr.* | *Prior Analytics* |
| *Caelo* | *On the Heavens [De Caelo]* |
| *Cat.* | *Categories* |
| *De An.* | *De Anima* |
| *EE* | *Eudaimonian Ethics* |
| *Gen. An.* | *Generation of Animals* |
| *Gen. Corr.* | *De Generatione et Corruptione* |
| *Hist. An.* | *History of Animals* |
| *IA* | *Progression of Animals [De Incessu Animalium]* |
| *Int.* | *De Interpretatione* |
| *Mag. Mor.* | *Magna Moralia* |
| *Met.* | *Metaphysics* |
| *NE* | *Nicomachean Ethics* |
| *Part. An.* | *Parts of Animals* |
| *Poet.* | *Poetics* |
| *Pol.* | *Politics* |
| *Ph.* | *Physics* |
| *Rh.* | *Rhetoric* |
| *Soph. El.* | *Sophistical Refutations* |
| *Top.* | *Topics* |

In writing about ethics and about Aristotle's *Ethics,* I see myself in the same position as the medieval Arab commentators on the *Poetics.* With no examples of the tragedies Aristotle was talking about to look at, their understanding of the *Poetics* was often comically distorted. I cannot write about Aristotle's virtues from personal experience. I have never had the opportunity to show courage in battle or make magnificent decisions about great displays of wealth. My opportunities for choosing the mean about anger have to do more with freeway driving than with insults to political honor. And if, as I argue, Aristotle's moral virtues are the virtues of citizens engaged in political activities of ruling, then even my experiences of temperance, liberality, and wittiness are only partial, since, apart from two weeks of jury duty and a day as a deposed witness, I lack the political experience that Aristotle makes central to living well. Many of my examples come from the limited experience of an academic facing challenges and making decisions concerning colleagues, students, and administrators. At one point I even appeal to the analogy of my experience with bicycle time-trials. Aristotle would not be pleased.

I went through one stage of rewriting this work as the only Jew living at Tantur, a Christian ecumenical center in Jerusalem, and an analogy struck me between my studying comparative religion and my studying Aristotle. In both cases I tried imaginatively to enter into an alien world. I didn't study Christianity in order to convert. It was not to add some Christian wisdom to my Judaism to make it better, or to show where Christianity went wrong. I wanted to understand something that I both admired and found incompatible with my own deeper commitments. In Jerusalem, I heard this called theological envy.

Aristotle's *Ethics* is not the ethical part of a religious faith called Aristotelianism. It contains nothing to take on faith or authority but rather presents a deep and rich exhibition of principles and consequences connecting souls, virtues, and happiness in a world that I cannot live in. The *Ethics* thus offers subjects for reflection, not options for action. I don't see it as an opportunity for nostalgia, or envy, or jealousy, but as an invitation to practical reflection. The more I think I understand Aristotle, the more attractive he seems. At the same time, the better I understand him, the more unavailable he seems, just as Christianity seems both attractive and impossible for me. By unavailable, I do not mean unintelligible: my hope is that this book makes the *Ethics* quite intelligible. But I do not see the vision of living well that Aristotle presents in the *Ethics* as something we can regard as an option we can choose, like the array of regimes Socrates says that democracy offers (*Republic* 557d). The experience of confronting the *Ethics* cannot result in being convinced that Aristotle is right and that therefore I should choose to live or think as he does. In the *Ethics*, some of the features that I find most attractive are unavailable, some are literally unthinkable, and, even more, some are repellent. Here is a short and personal list of such aspects of the *Ethics:*

- the political nature of ethics and the good life,
- the tie between ethics and the lawful,
- the unity of the virtues,
- the intimate connection between virtue and happiness,
- the connection between happiness and the philosophical life,
- the unbridgeable gap between art (*technē*) and virtue,
- the lack of a function for *phronēsis*—practical wisdom—independent of the moral virtues,
- the *phronimos*—the person with practical wisdom—as the ultimate judge without room for appeal to truly external criticism,
- the independence of practical knowledge from most results of the theoretical sciences,
- a moral psychology that includes not only reason and desire but reason, appetite, and spirit.

Some of the items on my list attract others to Aristotle. But the more I think I understand Aristotle, the more repugnant they are, in ways I will have to detail as this inquiry proceeds, as I try to show the price one must pay for taking seriously the facets of Aristotle's thought that one might regard as compelling. Part of their attraction comes from their central place in a systematic examination; they are appealing just because we encounter them while engaging with a great mind at work. And yet when I step back from the *Ethics,* they seem distant from anything within my own practical horizons. If Aristotle shows that living well is an essentially political activity, I can't convert and decide to live politically. The same applies to the rest of my list. Others may disagree about how attractive or repellent these features of the *Ethics* are to them, but, as I will show, they are all central to Aristotle's thought.

Those who see a strong continuity between Aristotle's ethics and ours are like those Christians who see the Hebrew Bible prefiguring the New Testament. Aristotle was really a social democrat or a communitarian *avant la lettre.* Such readers can dispose of inconvenient passages in the "Old Testament" by labeling them historical, laws adapted to the circumstances and customs of ancient Israelites, rather than eternal law, the things that Jews and Christians share. I reject the parallel domesticating of Aristotle's thought. Indeed, the more seriously we take the *Rhetoric* and the *Politics* as integrated with the *Ethics,* the more embarrassments we would have to discard. I situate the *Ethics* within Aristotle's practical world and his cosmos; the more embedded it appears, the more remote from us. We live in a different world and cannot will ourselves back to a better place, if indeed it was better. When interpretative charity makes Aristotle speak the truth by saying what we say, charity becomes condescension.[1]

Just as Machiavelli shows that being a pagan after Christianity is not simply to return to pagan virtues but to be a pagan *against* Christianity, so an Aristotelian today would not be thinking with Aristotle but thinking with Aristotle *against* contemporary science and morality. Practical self-understanding is increased by seeing something both attractive and impossible. The small size of Aristotle's polis does not imply that we should prefer more powerful local governments to a strong central state. His nomination of courage as a virtue is not an argument for compulsory military service. Giving advice of that sort is not the only practical value of a work like Aristotle's.

The subject of the *Ethics* is the best life. We can begin to focus on the uniqueness of the *Ethics* by imagining a sociological approach to questions of the best way to live. It would begin by looking at the kinds of behavior that people admire or recommend, and at the results that people think good action aims at. Staying as empirical as possible, the sociologist might eventually discover traits and abilities that were generally useful in bringing about good results and call these the virtues.

Imagine now a more psychological approach. It would begin with the human psyche and try to discover, equally empirically, the ways of living that are usually associated with souls that are content, satisfied, well-balanced, and organized. And the psychologist could call these things the virtues.

Is there any reason at all to think that the results of these two inquiries would coincide? Any reason to expect that the abilities most useful in doing good in the world would be exactly the abilities that brought psychic peace, harmony, and pleasure? There are far too many character types, and I will look at several in what follows, that succeed in one dimension at the cost of major distortions and failures in the other. A Social Security administrator might have a job that requires nothing but following the rules without any ethical or intellectual engagement, and yet she might do far more good in the world than the attorney whose work requires full maximization of all his ethical and intellectual powers, yet who does nothing more than move money from one giant corporation to another. Getting the results of the psychological and sociological inquiries to coincide by anything other than wishful thinking will take a lot of work.

What if the sociologist became more reflective and less empirical? She has read Machiavelli and knows that sometimes breaking one's word or acting with cruelty can do more good in the world than the virtues that people praise. Of the actions that have good outcomes, some are chosen and valued only because of those outcomes. But among the modes of action that we choose in the first place because of those benefits, we choose and do some of them for their own sakes. We admire, praise, and try to emulate courage, liberality, and justice not only because we think their practices are usually beneficial but also because we want to *be* courageous, liberal, and just. Therefore in this more sophisticated inquiry, we will call these things virtues.

Imagine that the psychologist gets a little more sophisticated too. He has read Montaigne and learned that psychic conditions have complicated connections to how people act and live. He realizes that the best way to live is not simply a matter of feeling good but has to do with a good way to *live*. Psychology would then know, still empirically but now more reflectively, ways of living associated with satisfied and well-balanced souls. And it would call these things the virtues.

It would still be wishful thinking to assert that the virtues picked out by the improved sociological and the psychological accounts would coincide. Yet the *Ethics* revolves around the idea that the abilities that let us choose actions that are their own end are precisely the abilities that bring the soul into the best condition. To elaborate the point a little more slowly: of the actions that produce valuable results, there are some which we value for their own sake. These, for Aristotle's project to make sense, must coincide with the exercise of powers that have brought the soul into the best possible shape. That coincidence of the two dimensions of goodness is the radical thesis that lies at the center of the *Ethics*. Aristotle's great gamble is that being good and doing good coincide. I devote this book to laying bare the meaning of that thesis, how Aristotle argues for it, the conditions under which it could be true, and the implications of realizing that it is true. This book, then, does not try to be a complete commentary on the *Ethics*. Instead it concentrates on this central and centrally important idea of the identity of being good and doing good. That will be challenging enough.

Since this problem seems to me the crux of the *Ethics*, I wonder why more commentators don't worry about it more than they do. Here I choose three among the most thoughtful contemporary commentators. Terence Irwin sees the problem and so begins his discussion of the virtues of character by "distinguishing eudaimonic virtues—those that promote the agent's self-realization—from moral virtues—those that promote the good of others."[2] Posing the issue in terms of altruism and a contrast between eudaimonistic and moral virtues is less faithful to the spirit of Aristotle's own thinking than my distinction of the two dimensions of virtue. But Irwin does observe that "Aristotle believes that these are not two separate lists of virtues, and that the moral virtues are eudaimonistic virtues also," just what I propose to prove.

Sarah Broadie, by contrast, seems to think this crucial problem not worth much worry:

> Once philosophers have made clear the analytic truth that the excellence of an F, for whatever F, is the quality by which something functions well as an F, and that functioning well is nothing other than functioning which reflects the excellence, we automatically find our own way to the substantial conclusion that functioning well as a human being is living the life of a just, courageous, temperate, and in all familiar respects decent person and citizen according to the standards we absorbed before ever starting to do academic philosophy.[3]

I reject the idea that we can move so easily from "analytic truth" to "substantial conclusion." If these are automatic moves, they are fallacious. Starting in chapter 2, I will look at a few of the crucial places where Aristotle makes such a move and worry about whether it can be licit; here I just want to emphasize how crucial that move is.

Richard Kraut sees more of the problem. Speaking, like Broadie of the "ergon" or function argument of *NE* I.7, he states:

> I agree that the function argument does not by itself show that temperance (for example), as Aristotle conceives of it, is a virtue. But we would be impatient students of the NE if we expected it to present the whole of its argument at once. Instead of regarding the function argument as a complete but defective argument on behalf of the ethical virtues, we should treat it as the foundation for a defense that Aristotle continues to develop throughout the rest of the work. . . . What we can legitimately demand of Aristotle is this: once he has finished his treatment of the practical virtues, he should be able to connect them with the conception of happiness put forward in the function argument, and in light of that connection, we should be able to see why happiness consists in exercising precisely those skills.[4]

But Kraut's own solution is slight:

> Suppose one's end is excellent practical reasoning, and one seeks to exercise this virtue on a grand scale, in the political arena. It will suit one's purposes best if one has a temperate person's moderate desire for physical pleasure. Too little appetite endangers one's health, whereas too much disrupts one's reasoning.[5]

The problem deserves more serious argument, especially since the criteria for "excellent" practical reasoning are themselves in question: should our goal be to secure our goals through reasoning, or should reason tell us what our goals ought to be, or should practical thinking bring the soul into harmony, or something else?[6]

The radical nature of Aristotle's thesis that being good and doing well intersect can be seen in Kant's vigorous denial:

> The principle of *personal happiness* is . . . most objectionable, not merely because it is false and because its pretense that *well-being always adjusts itself to well-doing* is contradicted by experience; not merely because it contributes nothing whatever towards establishing morality, since making a man happy is quite different from making him good and making him prudent or astute in seeing his advantage quite different from making him virtuous.[7]

Happiness and goodness, prudence and virtue—Kant sees oppositions where Aristotle sees harmony. Kant seems to have the advantage over Aristotle because he sees a problem where Aristotle seems to find a preestablished harmony between doing well and being good so obvious that he doesn't even worry about it. Maybe the other commentators on Aristotle are more faithful to his spirit when they don't take the problem seriously.

The connection between happiness and goodness, between virtues as the best development of the soul and as powers to choose actions worth doing for their own sake, seems to me a perennial and urgent ethical problem. Yet Aristotle might seem an odd place to look for help. Since he doesn't act as though he feels the force of my problem, he looks naïve, or perhaps looks as though he lived in a simpler age. He seems to have no interest in the ethical challenges already posed by Thrasymachus and Callicles. He thinks that good laws and the common practices of praise and blame give reliable information about which habits and actions are virtuous. This is why he is thought to be conservative, on the questionable side of several of the features of the *Ethics* I listed as simultaneously attractive and repellent.

The *Ethics* is a meditation on how to lead an active life. It locates human beings and human goods in a world made up of activities and the potentialities that make those activities possible. To be is to be active. We realize our nature by being as active as possible. Effective human action embodies the metaphysical urge to convert incomplete processes into complete activities, a metaphysical imperative Aristotle calls the love for the noble. While some ends are given to us by desire, we also try to decide which things to desire and value. This metaphysical urge is a desire to move from those given ends to ends that are activities we choose for their own sake.

What is the active life appropriate for a human, practical being? Aristotle will show that acting virtuously is more active than acting viciously, that the virtues more fully realize the potentialities of the soul than the vices. One person is happier than another by being more active and more virtuous. Since virtue is a rational condition, one person is happier than another by being more rational as well. We are more active when engaged in virtuous activity than in practicing any craft. Ruling over fellow citizens is more active than despotic rule and the apparently active life of conquest. The philosophical life, finally, is more active than the political life.

The key elements of the good life, virtue, happiness, choice, praxis, all need to be understood as activities. As fundamental as the idea of activity is to Aristotle's thought, he never defines it. There is an explicit discussion of activity in the *Metaphysics*, but, as we will see, it is a mixed blessing. It offers a condensed, abstract clarity with the accompanying risk of remoteness from the ethical concerns we started with. *Metaphysics* IX tells us to understand *energeiai*, activities, through contrast to its two contraries. First, *energeiai* complete and actualize *kinēseis*, motions or processes. This is a condensed and metaphysical way of putting my sociological understanding of virtue, knowing what virtue, the activity, is by starting with actions thought to be useful and admirable, which are on Aristotle's understanding processes rather than activities, *kinēseis* rather than *energeiai*. Saving one's comrade in battle is a good result; risking one's life for a noble end is worth doing for its own sake.

Second, *energeiai* perfect and realize *dynameis*, capacities or powers; we come to understand virtue through seeing what ways of living fulfill the soul. I am fully alive when risking my life for a noble end. The *Ethics* shows what virtuous action and the good life are both through contrasts between *energeiai* and *kinēsis* and through the relation of *energeiai* to *dynameis*. What I see as the crux of the *Ethics*, the identity between a person being good and doing good, is the identity of the best human activities considered as the realization of the soul—*energeia* as the perfection of a *dynamis*—and the best activities considered as securing the most desirable goods—*energeia* as the perfection of *kinēsis*.

*Energeia, kinēsis, dynamis:* these are all Greek words that resist translation. They also sound like the deepest, most ontologically basic ways of describing reality. To say in an introduction that to understand Aristotle's *Ethics* we have think in terms of *energeia, kinēsis, dynamis* might sound like I am claiming that one has to study metaphysics in order to understand ethics. The more we have to embed the *Ethics* in the context of the rest of Aristotle's works, the farther we will be from using the *Ethics* as a way of understanding our own practical concerns.

Fortunately, I think that's a misapprehension. I start my argument with the *Rhetoric* just because the goods of activity are omnipresent in the practical world, not to be located in the arcana of metaphysics. The *Rhetoric*, and the *Ethics*, don't depend on an esoteric doctrine about *energeia* and *entelechia*. Instead, Aristotle exhibits the same pattern of thought, the same drive to see the autonomous values in the world, throughout his range of inquiry. We will be more faithful to Aristotle's own way of thinking if we concentrate not on *energeia* as a term but on perfection, completion, realization, actualization as patterns enacted in Aristotle's inquiries. In the *Rhetoric* we see it in the definition of rhetoric. In the *Ethics*, we see it in actions that are chosen for their own sake. In the *Politics*, we find it in the self-sufficient community that aims at living well, in the *Physics* in the definition of nature as an internal principle of motion, and in the *De Anima* in the definition of soul as the first activity (*energeia*) of an organic body. When the *Ethics* talks about activity, it refers to things that we can easily recognize as activities, *praxeis*, things that people do, and not something that passes metaphysical tests. The *Rhetoric* presents the most down-to-earth opportunity to see this pattern of Aristotle's thought in action.

Here is a quick preview of the seven chapters to come.

**Chapter 1.** Like Plato, Aristotle frequently explicates the nature of virtue through comparisons to the arts. Rhetoric is the one art that Aristotle treats in detail, and rhetorical power has such intimate relations with virtue and practical wisdom that people, then and now, often confuse them. In fact, the *Ethics* ends by criticizing that confusion.[8] Yet neither in the *Rhetoric* nor in the *Ethics* does Aristotle offer any detailed comparison between rhetorical and virtuous activity. Seeing what is rational about an art of rhetoric helps to understand in a new way what is rational about virtue.

My first chapter, "What Aristotle's *Rhetoric* Can Tell Us about the Rationality of Virtue," exploits the comparison between rhetoric and virtue. The *Rhetoric* shows that the art of rhetoric aims at more than practical success because it is limited to rational persuasion. That limitation, we will see, comes from developing an art of persuasion and not from some external moral considerations. The emergence of actions that are their own end out of actions initially chosen to achieve some end distinct from themselves is what I called the sociological dimension of practical rationality. Even in rhetoric, there are values not reducible to success, and so intimations of actions that are their own end.

The *Ethics* finds in the virtues the same development of internal ends and actions chosen for their own sakes out of actions initially valued because of the external ends they achieve. For example, helping friends is a good. The virtue of liberality is a habit of choosing for its own sake to do what we can to help our friends. We choose to practice this virtue for its own sake. Where the external end is good, engaging in the internal end is noble. Aiming at the noble, we do not stop aiming at the useful. Virtuous actions have both internal and external ends, and the internal ends, such as engaging in the noble practice of helping friends financially, internalize the external and given end of our friends being helped. My comparison to the *Rhetoric* shows that ends become more rational as they become more practical, more within what the agent can do. Rationality and practicality grow together. The active life is the rational life.

**Chapter 2.** The first chapter develops the idea of action as its own end by stressing the similarities between virtuous activity and the activity of rhetorical persuasion. They both develop internal ends out of given ends. Chapter 2 highlights the contrast between rhetoric and virtue. Unlike the arts, the virtues bring the soul into good condition and so are psychologically satisfying. This dimension of virtue relates activities not to the processes they complete but to the powers they realize, corresponding to what I earlier called the psychological. The relation of virtue to soul makes the virtues rational in a different way from the rationality of art. The arts, including rhetoric, do not bring the soul into good condition, and so the arts, unlike the virtues, are not a constituent part of the good life. The rationality of virtue is a development, an *energeia,* of the irrational, desiring soul, while art is not. Here is a mode of practical rationality that does not exclude passion.

***Chapter 3.*** The first two chapters explore what it means to lead an active life by defining human activity first in contrast to incomplete activities or motions—*energeia* vs. *kinēsis*—and then in contrast to potentialities—*energeia* vs. *dynamis.* The two sides of *energeia* and of virtue are practical activity as doing good and as being in good condition. The connection between these two dimensions of activity occupies the rest of my book. Chapter 3 explores the background assumptions against which the theses of the *Ethics* make sense by raising the following questions:

- What are the background assumptions, psychological and sociological, that make it plausible to identify doing good and being in good condition?
- *When* can happiness be defined as virtuous activity, *energeia kat'aretēn?*
- When, that is, is virtue the principal cause of happiness, while the factors that support the clause "in a complete life," fortune and resources, are subsidiary?
- When is virtue rewarded?
- When is the subordination of the crafts to the virtues not only a philosophical thesis but a fact of life?
- Finally, what price does Aristotle pay for the exclusion of the crafts from happiness?

These questions seem especially urgent in a world in which the advantages of virtue, and the superiority of virtue to skill, are not so apparent. We know today that the best way to insure a long life is to pick long-lived parents. Can Aristotle be confident that the best way to lead a good life isn't similarly a function of luck?

***Chapter 4.*** The next three chapters explore and deepen my central thesis. Activity viewed as the completion of instrumental processes is the same human activity that fully realizes the soul and so makes us happy. The happy man is both practically successful and psychically fulfilled. A noble act and a noble person are excellent in both these ways. Chapter 4 contains the proof of my thesis, while the following two respectively explore its political and metaphysical conditions and consequences.

Virtues belong to the person in a way skills do not. Being courageous is part of being a good person, while being a good physician is not. Chapter 4 shows that virtue, the good condition of the soul, is the power to perform for their own sake virtuous actions, which have the right relation to both internal and external goods. We always deliberate about what to do. But figuring out what to do puts our souls in the best shape. The rationality of deliberating about what to do explicates how rationally to persuade the passions and so it is the rationality of practical deliberation that defines the right amount of the passions.

*Chapter 5.* Hand-in-hand with the separations of reason from emotion and rationality from goodness goes the modern separation of the ethical from the political, which makes politics a matter of amoral cleverness and cunning, and the corresponding morality apolitical and, usually, sentimental. As long as ethics is apolitical, it will be hard to integrate goodness and intelligence. Aristotle's moral life, instead, is a political life, a life led by citizens carrying out civic activities.

Aristotle's relation between ethics and politics differs so strongly from ours that it is hard to keep in mind how political the *Ethics* is. Virtue consists in doing for their own sake things that are first worth doing because of their results. But those initial results must be defined in and by the polis. Similarly, virtue brings the soul into good condition. The particular ethical virtues bring the entire desiring soul into good condition only if the souls realized in the virtues are the souls of citizens. The given external goods that are the starting points of deliberation are the goods of political practices. The souls whose good functioning are the virtues are the souls of citizens.

*Chapter 6.* Chapter 5 shows that political souls are realized in ethical virtues that are the perfection of politically good, useful, and praiseworthy acts. Chapter 6 shows the profound metaphysical character of the idea that the moral virtues are political virtues, since we are forced to think about human nature and activity and the place of humans in the cosmos. Happiness and virtue create their own enabling conditions, the conditions under which they can be successful. Since virtues become second natures, we need to know about their mode of reproduction. The virtuous person replicates himself through political activity, through developing conditions in which virtues can flourish.

Leading a good life therefore depends on knowing the place of people in the universe. A sign of the distance between Aristotle's world and ours is that readers today impute to Aristotle such anachronisms as natural law or metaphysical biology. Instead, the examples of perfect activity at *Metaphysics* IX.6.1048b23–25—seeing, understanding, thinking, living well, and being happy—are all either uniquely human or shared between people and gods. Human *practical* activity completes the *Metaphysics* and the cosmos.

Chapter 6 confronts a paradox. Other substances realize their potential far more often and regularly than humans. On the other hand, only humans (and gods) engage in perfect activity. Virtuous activity not only achieves external goods but also establishes conditions in which virtues can flourish. Other moral theories try to make it easier to become good, for example by postulating a moral sense or a universal moral capacity. The trouble is that, the more universal and natural morality is, the harder virtuous activity—as opposed to its capacity—becomes, the more luck can intervene, the more moral conflicts make it hard to act well. For Aristotle, on the contrary, while few can be virtuous, virtuous habits lead reliably and smoothly to virtuous action and happiness. While fewer people are happy than naturally heavy stones fall, the virtuous are happy with a natural regularity. Aristotle's "elitist" picture, in which a few men, only citizens of poleis, can lead ethical lives, is not a prejudice but an integral part of his picture of the cosmos. The attractive and repellent sides of Aristotle's thought are inseparable.

**Chapter 7.** Aristotle notoriously ends the *Ethics* by asking about whether the political or the philosophical life is the best life. Instead of presenting a contest between the active and contemplative lives, Aristotle shows how the philosophical life completes the political and practical life. The philosophical life is not an alternative to the practical life but its fulfillment. It is the good person, and not the theologian, who truly understands the assertion that people are not the best thing in the universe (*NE* VI.7.1141a20–21), because only the good person can understand and act on that thesis as a practical truth.

These final questions about the best life revive questions I raise in chapter 3 about the relation between virtue and happiness. The virtues, as good conditions of the soul, are what Aristotle in the *De Anima* calls first *energeiai,* powerful structures that make possible virtuous activities. Both virtuous activity and happiness are *energeiai* of the virtues. Therefore the question: How are individual acts of virtue integrated into a virtuous and happy *life?* He sees two possibilities for unification, the political life and the philosophical life. In Aristotle's argument, we never choose between

them—we never face the two as alternative options for a practical decision—yet we can see the superiority of the life of contemplation. Both
happiness and contemplation are subjects Aristotle raises in Book I but
does not discuss until the end of Book X. If the only route to both happiness and *theōria* is through the political life of actively exercising the ethical virtues, then we can see why the argument of the *Ethics* takes the form
it does.

Let me end the Introduction by returning to my experience in Jerusalem. I went to a seminar at Rattisbone Institute where the format was as
follows: a Jew presented what he thought it was most important that non-
Jews know about Judaism, followed by a Christian and a Moslem response;
next, a Christian said what he thought non-Christians should know about
Christianity, followed by a Jewish and Moslem response; finally, a Moslem
scholar explained what he thought others should know about Islam, with
Jewish and Christian response. I learned a lot, but one of the things I learned
was that what a Christian thought, maybe rightly, that non-Christians
should know about Christianity did not at all coincide with what a non-
Christian most wanted to know about Christianity. That too reflects my experience with Aristotle. He goes into great detail about the features of his
vision that he thinks most need and deserve careful exposition and glosses
over properties that are either too obvious or too unimportant for elaborate development. Unfortunately, his judgment and that of most readers
rarely coincide.

If the central question of the *Ethics* is how to live the active and rational
life, we can see a little better why Aristotle worries about what he does, apparently belaboring some issues and glossing over others. I have lived with
Aristotle's *Ethics* for most of my adult life. The more intimately I think I
understand it, the more alien it seems. I want this book to give the impression of immersion in a close relationship with a great mind at work, someone who thinks through hard and important ethical problems in a way that
is both accessible and strange. Aristotle thinks with such depth and individuality that he constantly frustrates our expectations; a frequent part of my
experience of reading Aristotle is surprise. Yet his individuality is never idio-
syncrasy. The reader is confronted by someone who at first seems to be worrying about side issues, but, as the experience of living with this mind
continues, his preoccupations make sense after all. Neither ethical life nor
thinking about ethics is an esoteric activity. Where Kant's *Fundamental
Principles of the Metaphysics of Morals* starts: "The only thing in the world, or
indeed outside it, that is good without qualification is a good will," the *Ethics*
begins with people trying intelligently to satisfy desires and secure goods:
"Every craft and every method, and likewise every action and decision, seems

to aim at some good." I try to show how the *Ethics* unfolds from that innocent beginning. Aristotle ends his inquiry first with an account of the philosophical life and then with a transition to the study of politics. And so my study ranges from the apparently low details of rhetorical persuasion to the heights of metaphysics. I aim to show Aristotle's mind at work struggling hard to show how to live an active and thoughtful life.

## CHAPTER 1

# What Aristotle's *Rhetoric* Can Tell Us
# about the Rationality of Virtue

> On any important decision we deliberate together because we do not trust
> ourselves. (*NE* III.3.1112b10–11)

Aristotle missed a great opportunity. The *Ethics* frequently compares
ethical virtue to art, but very rarely to the art of rhetoric in particular.
He knows that people often confuse rhetoric with ethical virtue, because
"rhetoric dresses itself up in the form of politics, as do those who pretend
to a knowledge of it, sometimes through lack of education, sometimes
through boastfulness and other human causes" (*Rh.* I.2.1356a27–30; see
*Poet.* 25.1460b13–28, *NE* IV.7.1127b20–22).[1] Rhetoric and virtue have
the same subject-matter—human actions and things that can be otherwise.
Both concern questions for which there is no method or settled body of
knowledge (*NE* II.2.1104a7–10, VI.51140a28–30 *Rh.* I.1.1354a1–3).
There are three kinds of rhetoric, deliberative, judicial, and demonstrative,
and the most important of the three is deliberative oratory (*Rh.* I.1.
1354b22–1355a3). In the same way deliberation is also the center of virtue, of living well and living together.

> To deliberate well is the most characteristic function of the prudent man; no
> one deliberates about things that cannot vary nor yet about variable things that
> are not a means to some end, and that end a good attainable by action. A good
> deliberator in general is someone who can arrive by calculation at the best of
> goods attainable by man. (*NE* VI.7.1141b9–13)

Aristotle's failure to use the *Rhetoric* to explicate the *Ethics* is a missed opportunity not only because the *Ethics* frequently compares virtue and art, and not only because people often confuse rhetoric with virtue and practical wisdom; the *Rhetoric* looks in detail at some of the most frustratingly brief and crucial claims in the *Ethics:*

- We deliberate about means (*pros ta telē,* literally things that are related to the end or conduce to the end) and not ends (*NE* III.3.1112b11–19, III.5.1113b3–4, VI.12.1144a7–9, 20–21, *Rh.* I.8.1366a3, 14–16).
- *Phronēsis* (or practical wisdom) is about means, ethical virtue about ends (*NE* VI.12.1144a8–9, 1144a20, VI.13.1145a4–6, X.8.1178a16).
- Knowing the highest good gives our deliberations a target to aim at (*EE* I.2.1214b6–11).
- Virtue is the target which makes our decisions correct (*NE* VI.12.1144a7–9, *EE* VIII.3.1249a22–24, cf. *Rh.* III.1417a17–28).
- Virtue and vice respectively preserve and destroy ethical principles (*NE* VI.12.1144a11–b1, VII.8.1151a15–19, *EE* II.11.1227b35–36).
- The young cannot profit from lectures on ethics—implying that someone else can (*NE* I.3.1095a6–14, X.1.1172a34–b7, X.9.1179b23–1180a4, *EE* I.3.1214b28–1215a3).
- Virtue apprehends the ultimates in both directions, both the most universal first principle and the particular thing to be done (*NE* VI.7.1141b14–16, VI.10.1143a28–b6).

It is a sign of the difference between Aristotle's interests and ours that none of these dicta seems to be a crucial or critical thesis for Aristotle in the *Ethics.* He presents each as uncontroversial, while they are at the center both of modern commentaries on Aristotle and of current discussions of practical reason. Using the *Rhetoric* to clarify these dicta will show us the relation between rationality and ethics, how to live with thought.

But isn't it perverse to explicate the *Ethics* by referring to the *Rhetoric*? The *Rhetoric* is almost by definition amoral and so can't be a guide to morals. On the contrary: I see that as a strong reason to turn to the *Rhetoric*. Explicit comparisons to the *Rhetoric* will let us avoid question-begging assumptions about morality; we can ask what is specifically ethical about the *Ethics.* It is too easy to assume that virtue, the subject of most of the *Ethics,* must have to do with ethics.

There is another reason to doubt that rhetoric can shed much light on ethics. The art of rhetoric is not only amoral; it is instrumental. Rhetoric is therefore the last place to look for actions chosen for their own sake, since no one engages in persuasion except to persuade someone. But even in rhetoric we can find goods internal to practices. As I mentioned in the introduction, Aristotle's world is full of *energeiai*. On this count too, looking at the *Rhetoric* will help us avoid begging questions by smuggling moral content into the idea of acts that are their own end.

### Rhetoric, Although an Instrumental Activity, Has Internal Ends

> The function of rhetoric is not to persuade but to see the available means of persuasion in each case. (*Rh.* I.1.1355b10–12)

Aristotle defines the art of rhetoric by a contrast to competing sophistic theories and practices, which, he says, have no art. Aristotle says that only *pisteis*—often translated as proofs; the most literal English would be "credibles"—are part of the art of rhetoric (*Rh.* I.1.1354a13), while the sophists concern themselves with everything but such things. Rhetoric is a rational activity not only because the rhetorician calculates how to persuade an audience but also because the substance of persuasion is reasoning.

Wrongly identifying rhetoric's means and resources, sophists also misidentify the end of rhetoric. How we think about means has consequences for how we think about ends. Sophists aim at persuading, but the true end of the art of rhetoric is "seeing in each case the available means of persuasion" (*ta huparchonta pithana*): "finding in each case the available means of persuasion" (*to endechomenon pithanon*) (*Rh.* I.1.1355b10–12, I.2. 1355b25–27). The difference between persuading and finding the available means of persuasion might seem slight, but it is a distinction that makes all the difference.

The Aristotelian rhetorician has two ends. She wants to win the argument but also aims at the internal and active end—which the sophist does not have—of finding the available means of persuasion. Internal, guiding, ends develop from external, given ones. This, as I will explain, is *energeia* as the perfection of *kinēsis*. Not everything that tends to achieve the given end of persuading counts as an "available means," which is why it sometimes seems almost irresistible to translate *endechomenon* as "appropriate means":

> Those who have composed *Arts of Speech* have worked on a small part of the subject; for only *pisteis* are artistic (other things are supplementary), and these writers say nothing about enthymemes, which is the 'body' of persuasion, while they give most of their attention to matters external to the subject; for verbal attack and pity and anger and such emotions do not relate to fact but are

appeals to the juryman. As a result, if all trials were concluded as they are in some present-day states and especially in those well governed, [the handbook writers] would have nothing to say. (*Rh.* I.1.1354a11–20)

The *Ethics* displays something similar to this apparent elision between *endechomenon* as "available" and as "appropriate." There Aristotle moves from conceiving of the mean as something moderate lying between two extremes and the mean as what is appropriate to a situation, the "mean relative to us." Only when the available is defined as what is rational, connected to the enthymeme or rhetorical syllogism, is the inference from *endechomenon* as available to *endechomenon* as appropriate licit. Rationality is the middle term that connects the available to the appropriate, and we will find that rationality will also allow the inference for the ethical virtues from what is moderate to what is appropriate.

Aristotle is not naïve in limiting the available means of persuasion to argument. He knows that more people are moved by emotional than by rational appeals and that arrangement, style, and delivery can be more persuasive than evidence (*Rh.* III.1.1403b36–1404a8). The limitation to argument must have some other basis than a judgment of what works. What is exciting about the *Rhetoric* is that these limits come from the demands of art itself, and not from extrinsic moral considerations.[2] That will make the *Rhetoric* more, not less, useful for the *Ethics*.

Through an analogy with the art of medicine, he points to the internal end which specifies the faculty and function:

> [Rhetoric's] function is not so much to persuade, as to find out in each case the existing means of persuasion. The same holds good in respect to all the other arts. For instance, it is not the function of medicine to restore a patient to health, but only to promote this end as far as possible; for even those whose recovery is impossible may be properly treated. (*Rh.* I.1.1355b10–14; but see *EE* II.1.1219a13–16)

If "even those whose recovery is impossible may be properly treated," then rhetoric and healing have values and standards of excellence that are not defined by an external end but that rather are located in the practices themselves. Doctors can succeed at saving the patient and can succeed at exercising this faculty well. With two kinds of success come two kinds of failure. One can either not achieve one's end or one can fail to follow the precepts of one's art. All four combinations of internal and external success and failure are possible.[3]

Since "internal" and "external" are ambiguous, I should note that at this point in my argument, internal ends are internal to practices, and to the art of rhetoric in particular. Whether they are also internal to the practitioner is another question. These particular internal standards of success and failure would not make sense unless one also had an external purpose: doing everything possible to save a patient could not be a value if a saved patient weren't already valued. We can find goods in the doing only when the purpose of the practice is some already valued end. Internal goods do not come from some separate faculty, of morality or conscience, as they do in many ethical theories, and in many readings of Aristotle. These new internal goods do not replace external goods, although they do come to have authority over them, an ethical advance from what is better known to us to *what* is better known as such.

At least in rhetoric and medicine, these internal goods are artistic standards. Aristotle discusses the limitation to available means explicitly in the *Topics:*

> We shall possess the method [of dialectic] completely when we are in a position similar to that in which we are with regard to rhetoric and medicine and other such faculties; that is to say, when we carry out our purpose with every available means (*ek tōn endechomenōn*). For neither will the rhetorician seek to persuade nor the physician to heal by every expedient (*ek pantos tropou*); but if he omits none of the available means (*tōn endechomenōn*) we shall say that he possesses the science sufficiently. (*Rh.* I.3.101b5)

Within the arts, the elision between "available" and "appropriate" becomes legitimate, because we can draw a distinction between *ek tōn endechomenōn*, everything possible or available, and other ways of accomplishing an end:

> Of the *pisteis,* some are inartificial, some artful. I call inartificial those that are not provided by us [i.e., the potential speaker] but are preexisting; for example, witnesses, testimony of slaves taken under torture, contracts, and such like; and artistic whatever can be prepared by method and by us; thus, one must *use* the former and *invent* (*heurein*) the latter. (*Rh.* I.2.1355b35–39)

Appeals not sanctioned by the art of rhetoric might succeed, but they have nothing rational about them. They are irrational because they are external to the art of rhetoric. Aristotle never promises that a practitioner of the art of rhetoric will be more persuasive, more successful at achieving the external end, than someone who argues through mere experience or even someone who learns from the sophists. Since reasoning is not clearly more effective at achieving the external end, he needs some other way of claiming that rational argument is *better* than other means of aiming at the same external end. Why not say, "So much the worse for rationality. I am going to choose what works"? How can limiting the *means* of accomplishing a given end become a new *end*? The challenge is to understand why this limitation is not arbitrary or moral in some external, adventitious sense. If we succeed, we will have a non-question-begging connection between rationality and goodness.

Aristotle limits the available *means* to argument and thereby constructs a new, internal *end* for the art of rhetoric. Here is the first surprising conclusion to draw from the *Rhetoric* to apply to the *Ethics:* internal ends emerge out of *limiting* the *available means* for achieving a given, external end. All kinds of factors might contribute to good and bad health, but not all of them count as part of the art of healing. I would guess, for example, that the amount of envy in a person's life is strongly and inversely correlated with that person's well-being, but unless someone comes up with an envy-reducing drug, or a medical explanation for the connection between envy and health, it lies outside the meaning of health for most contemporary medicine. I will argue that what I just asserted for rhetoric is true for ethics as well: the internal *ends* of actions chosen for their own sake emerge out of *limitations* of the available *means* for achieving given, external ends. We become better rhetoricians by attending to our means more than our ends. If I can argue for the analogy between rhetoric and virtue, we will become better people by attending to our means more than our ends.

Nothing can be part of the first sentence of the *Ethics*—"Every craft (*technē*) and every method (*methodos*), and likewise every action (*praxis*) and decision (*prohairesis*), seems to aim at some good" (I.1.1094a1–2)— without such a pair of ends. Nothing can have a function, an *ergon*, without these two ends. As I will show, the only way to aim *rationally* at external ends is through commitment to the internal ends that are properly associated with them. In other words, when we have an internal end, we "aim" at it rationally as we aim to gain mastery of the practice it involves. In that way we do all we can to secure the external end. Practices—using that term as to include everything in the *Ethics'* first sentence—must have internal ends to be rational.

I will look in more detail at the relation between internal and external ends in chapter 3, but I can elaborate a little here on the thesis that practices must have both internal and external ends. In the practice of a science, we follow rules of inference, experimental methods, etc. These are the internal standards of performance for knowing. If we do everything in accordance with the rules and canons of a science, we achieve the internal end of the practice. When sciences are in good shape, achieving the internal end defined by the canons of scientific method will also achieve the external end of contributing to scientific knowledge. The accuracy in which theoretical knowledge exceeds practical and productive knowledge comes from the unproblematic relation between internal and external end. Only rarely do we distinguish between following the rules and arriving at the truth: Is the computer-generated proof for the four-color problem really a proof? Is the "life" that medicine can now prolong the life we go to doctors to preserve?

The connection between internal and external ends becomes uncertain when achievement of the external end is influenced by factors that lie beyond the domain of the practice. As a physician, I can achieve the internal end of acting according to the norms of medical practice and yet see my patient die. As an architect, I may design a beautiful, energy-efficient building, which my client then decides not to build because there is now a glut of office buildings. My arguments for evolution are cogent and compelling, but the audience has too big a stake in creationism to give it up.

Finally, for practices that aim at ethical action, the internal standards of success have a more authoritative connection to external ends. "Virtue, like nature, is more accurate and better than art" (*NE* II.6.1106b14–15; see too *NE* V.11.1138a35–b5, VI.5.1140b22–24, *An. Post.* 100b5–12), because the internal ends of the virtues have more authority over their external ends than similar internal ends have in productive activities such as medicine and architecture. Having decided that my building design represents too great a financial risk, my client may request a redesign that cuts costs by eliminating much of the building's energy efficiency and most of its beauty. In such a situation, I would have no ethical duty insist on craft values at the price of losing the contract. Similarly, it is not clear that I would have an ethical duty to stay with purely scientific arguments about evolution, if my audience were a school board considering adding "intelligent design" to the high school curriculum. Situations calling for ethical choice, as we will see, are different: the choice between internal and external end is more complicated, because of the authority of the internal ends.

"It is visibly true of law that a really high technical proficiency liberates instead of binds—and this is one of the surest diagnostic signs of art."[4] So says Charles Black about the "art" of legal thinking. His point applies to the virtues and to the arts: for both virtue and art, what may seem from the outside to be an unfair limitation on what one can do to secure an external end becomes liberating. By restricting the range of decisions, rhetoric or any art makes the end more determinate and more connected to action. If I'm trying to persuade an audience, unless I see them as unusually corrupt, the art of rhetoric allows me not to devote much energy to my gestures and other aspects of delivery and to concentrate instead on reasoning. The restriction on means becomes an internal end. The internal end is not just somehow "inside" the person or the practice. It is more rational and active than any external end can be. Acts oriented toward the internal end are *energeiai,* activities.[5]

Now we can formulate Aristotle's important discovery: *The art of rhetoric is instrumental by having its own internal end.* The art of rhetoric can be used for good or bad ends outside itself. Good instruments, one might think, cannot have ends of their own, just as a slave only serves his master if he has no ends of his own. A good instrument is like a sterile medium in which all sorts of things can grow. The eye can see many colors because it is itself not colored but transparent. The *Rhetoric* has a different message. While the doctor can use his knowledge to kill or cure, medicine still has its own internal end, healing, without which he could neither kill nor cure. While we wouldn't develop an art without wanting first to achieve some external end, possessing an internal end is the condition for a practitioner adopting further, external ends.

The problem for virtue is structurally the same, although much more acute, as the problem for art. If I can accomplish the external end better through ignoring the internal ends of rhetoric or virtue, why should I not? The United States strategy of using high-altitude B-52s to bomb Serbia and avoid casualties to its own military was not courageous. Odysseus is not temperate in his resistance to the Sirens. The rich man who delegates the distribution of his wealth to someone else is not deciding to whom to give the money, under what circumstances, etc. But if these things bring better results than acting virtuously, why should I be moral?

Rather than a global, skeptical challenge to virtue of the form, Why should I be moral?, Aristotle invites the more particular question, Why not achieve external ends more easily and with more security through non-virtuous action? None of the virtue-avoiding strategies I just listed is vicious. None is wrong in all circumstances. Aristotle praises the mother who "gives her child away to be brought up" (*NE* VIII.8.1159a28–33, *EE* VII.12.1245b28–32), because she chooses a better result instead of doing something worse by herself. Yet he criticizes a state that builds walls: "Against those who are one's match and not very superior numerically it is not noble to try to defend oneself through the security provided by walls" (*Pol.* VII.11.1330b35–37). It may not be noble, but how strong a reason is that not to use walls instead of risking lives?

Legal scholars have often asked questions similar to the one I have posed for rhetoric and virtue, wondering whether there is something unique about law as opposed to other methods of obtaining peace and security.

The similarity between Aristotelian practical rationality focusing on the means and Lon Fuller's idea of the internal morality of law is especially strong. The challenge for both is to see how a limitation on means can become an internal end. Fuller finds an internal morality of the law distinct from an external morality concerned with the consequences of acting lawfully. He offers a series of constitutive conditions—generality, publicity, prospectivity, clarity, noncontradiction, practicability, constancy, consistency between a rule and actual official actions—that both make law possible and make it possible for law to achieve its external purposes. For law, "the enterprise of subjecting human conduct to the governance of rules," to be law, it must fulfill its own internal morality.[6]

But it is fair to ask Fuller whether the law is anything more than just an especially efficacious means for securing truer human ends such as freedom or lack of conflict. If not, then any allegiance to the rule of law must be derivative from these more basic motivations. The internal morality of law would have value only if it serves some external moral goods. In the same way, if rhetorical argument is nothing but an unusually effective and teachable means of securing persuasion, and if virtue is nothing but an effective means of securing our human ends, then there would be no reason to feel allegiance to either the art of rhetoric or to virtue. Then there are no goods internal to practices.

Law, on Fuller's understanding, must be more than just a particularly powerful means for achieving given ends of freedom or peace. If it were just that, then law would always be open to comparison to alternative means, such as military rule or administrative expertise. Similarly, rational persuasion would need constant testing against sophistic alternatives of style or emotional appeals to see which was more persuasive. We would have continually to confront the question, Why should I be moral?—that is, ask ourselves whether there aren't less demanding alternatives to morality that achieve happiness equally well. But according to Fuller, living lawfully becomes part of the meaning of living freely. Arguing rationally becomes part of the meaning of persuasion, in contrast to intoxication or manipulation. Living virtuously is part of what living a happy life consists in.

Whether these internal ends—the internal morality of the rule of law, the internal ends of rational persuasion, and the internal ends of the virtues—really are ends and not simply generally useful means to secure external ends is the issue I earlier expressed by asking how rational argument could be *better* than other means of securing the same external end.[7] Everything turns on the meaning of "best" when Aristotle says that deliberators "assume the end and consider how and by what means it is to be attained; and if it seems to be produced by several means they consider by which it is most easily and best (*kallista*) produced" (*NE* III.3.1112b16–17). Deliberation's considering the best means is not simply reducible to the easiest means. The magnificent person "will think more about the finest and most fitting way (*kalliston kai prepōdstaton*) to spend than about the cost or about the cheapest way to do it" (*NE* IV.2.1122b8–10). If there is a cheaper way of achieving the same end, why not do it?

Why aiming at the internal end is *better* than trying for the external end begs for explication in rhetoric. We may be tempted to think that there is no such explication needed in ethics—we know what "better" means in ethics. But the rhetorical parallel can help avoid begging the question. The sophists distinguish good and bad rhetoric by the ends different practices of rhetoric serve. Which ends are good and which are bad depends on moral evaluations external to rhetoric. Thus Gorgias offers to teach virtue, to give good ends, to any pupil who shows up wanting to learn rhetoric without those ends (Plato, *Gorgias* 459d–e). The good rhetorician is like the physician; the bad rhetorician is like the poisoner using the same power for bad ends (460d). Apart from their ends, they share the same craft. They know the same things. They deliberate in the same way. Sophistic seeks to change the agents while leaving the agency the same. Good and bad rhetoric are equally rational. Therefore the good and the rational are independent of each other.

Aristotle, though, distinguishes artful rhetoric from sophistic not by artful rhetoric's having a good end and sophistic's having a bad one, but by the presence and absence of an internal end and the limitation of means. Instead of leaving the practice of rhetoric untouched and simply moralizing its practitioners, Aristotle sees a difference between artful and sophistic *practice,* based on the difference between finding the available means of persuasion and simply aiming at persuading. Better rhetoric is more rational rhetoric.

The same holds in ethics. There too it will be fatal to find morality in the ends of action and rationality in the means. There too the end internal to the practice of virtue will be the source of both morality and rationality. Acting well consists in concentrating on internal ends, acting for the noble (e.g., *NE* III.7.1115b13, III.12.1119b16, IV.1.1120a24, 1122b6–7, *EE* III.1.1229a4, 1230a26–33). Whatever Aristotle means by saying that practical wisdom is about means and ethical virtue about ends—and I will look at those passages in detail—it cannot mean that deliberation about means is rational and amoral and the apprehension of ends moral but irrational.

The end of sophistic rhetoric is winning. Because it is externally related to any end for which it might be used, sophistic is defined by its motives while rhetoric is defined by its power, its *dynamis*. "Sophistry is not a matter of ability (*dynamis*) but of deliberate decision (*prohairesis*)" (*Rh.* I.1. 1355b17–18; see 1371a6–8, *Top.* I.1.100a19–101a4, *NE* II.2.1103a5, IV.7.1127b9–20). Sophistic is defined by its ends because there is nothing else left to define it.

By contrast, Aristotle's rhetorician tries to accomplish the given, external end by aiming at an internal end. She *wants* to persuade, but *aims at* finding the available means of persuasion. Therefore the exercise of rhetoric's function, aiming at the internal good, explains as much of its performance as the external end. Rhetoric can only exercise its function when the rhetorician has a case to win, but doing everything in one's power to win requires deliberating toward the internal end. Internal ends have value because they are rational ways of achieving external ends: the architect who builds beautiful edifices that no one wants to live in is not much of an architect. The physician might fulfill her function although the patient dies, but the point of the art of medicine is actually to cure people. To have an internal end is to have a form, and that form will be a power to achieve the external end. That sense of function and form as power will be important in subsequent chapters. Sophistic rhetoric has no form, and so its operations have to be explained by its motives. Sophistic might have a role, but it has no function.

### Locating the Rationality of Rhetoric

We most believe when we suppose something to have been demonstrated (*pisteoumen malista hotan apodedeichthai hypolabōmen*). (*Rh.* I.1.1355a5–6)

Starting with Plato, people have tried to understand practical rationality by comparing it to the rationality of the arts. Aristotle finds the rationality of the arts in an unexpected place, with surprising implications for the rationality of virtue. This is the second feature of the *Rhetoric* I want to use to understand the *Ethics,* beyond its focus on means. What is special about *reasoning* as a means toward persuasion that makes it worth singling out as *the* available means of persuasion? Why should reasoning be a *better* way of securing agreement than other inducements?[8]

All the arts are rational powers for making (*NE* VI.4.1140a20–21), but rhetoric and dialectic are rational in a further sense. They limit the artistic side of these activities to rational considerations: "Only *pisteis* are artistic (other things are supplementary [*prosthekai*],) and enthymemes [are] the 'body' of persuasion" (*Rh.* I.1.1354a13–15). Even emotional and ethical appeals are part of the art of rhetoric only to the extent that they too are rational (1356a8–9). I don't know what the limitations on the art of medicine are, but they would not be limited to reasoning with the patient. (On some accounts of medicine, reasoning with the patient could be barred and the physician limited to drugs, discounting talking to the patient as a placebo effect.) The reason for limiting rhetoric to rationality cannot be that argument is more efficacious in reaching the external end, since it isn't more efficacious. That would be like recommending virtue because of its ability to secure the objects of our antecedent desires for money, pleasure, and honor. Instead Aristotle asserts an internal connection between rationality and persuasion, and not between other means and persuasion:

> All opinion (*doxa*) requires conviction (*pistis*), conviction implies being persuaded (*pepeithai*), and persuasion implies discourse (*logos*). Conviction (*pistis*) belongs to no beasts, whereas appearance (*phantasia*) belongs to many of them. Every belief follows conviction, conviction follows being persuaded, persuasion follows reason. . . . There are beasts who have the possibility of imagination, but none are disposed to reason. (*De An.* III.3.428a19–24; see *An. Post.* I.10.76b24–25)

Artistic method is concerned with *pisteis,* and "*pistis* is a sort of demonstration (for we most believe when we suppose something to have been demonstrated) and rhetorical demonstration is the enthymeme (and this is, generally speaking, the strongest of the *pisteis*)" (*Rh.* I.1.1355a7).[9] Only argument supplies an internal connection between what the speaker does and what happens to the audience. *Pistis* refers equally to the effect aimed at, to the process of proof that brings persuasion about, and to the person who is most credible. The internal end of rhetorical deliberation, finding the available means of persuasion, makes deliberating concerning these means a rational procedure that constructs internal connections between what the speaker does, the argument, and what happens to the audience.

Rhetoric, like dialectic, is doubly rational. Rhetoric is a fundamentally rational activity, not only because, like any art, it is a rational faculty for making but because the connection between speaker and hearer, the substance of rhetoric, is logos, argument. That argument is the center of the art of rhetoric is as amazing as the discovery that even an activity as instrumental as rhetoric has internal values. What is persuasive is always persuasive to someone (*Rh.* I.2.1356b26), and so persuasion might appear to be a purely contingent and irrational event, having nothing to do with argument or reasoning. We should be surprised to find that if one looks at persuasive appeals in terms of their persuasiveness, one sees logical structure and form, but that is exactly what the *Rhetoric* teaches. Limiting the means the artful rhetorician uses to rational appeals provides a sense of art, and so of good and bad rhetoric, that does not depend on external moral criteria. We *ought* to be persuaded by reasoning and not by style and images. Better states bar purely emotional appeals (*Rh.* I.1.1354a18–20). Decent people are persuaded by reasons. We are a better audience for being persuaded rationally, and we are better speakers for treating our audiences this way. The internal end creates a normative "ought" within rhetoric itself. Reasoning should persuade. Achieving the internal end should be enough to accomplish the external end. The best argument defines what ought to be persuasive. The standards of practices then become ends and not simply especially powerful means for accomplishing the external ends.[10]

When "is" and "ought" come together in persuasion, this normative criterion may still be far from the ethical standards of the virtues, but at least the artful rhetorician gives the audience reasons to be persuaded. The relation between the instrumental and the rational values of rhetoric, which has such evident parallels for the rationality of praxis, is nicely captured by Charles Fried. Like Black's test of whether a rule is confining or liberating, Fried's "constitutive rationality" is a variation on Fuller's internal morality of the law:

> I call the rationality implicit in all these structures [of narrative and argument] constitutive, as opposed to instrumental or means-end, rationality. In instrumental rationality an end or value is posited, and all other elements in the argument are judged by whether they best lead to that end or maximize that value. Constitutive rationality proposes complex structures in which elements are related according to rules or principles, and it is the resultant whole that satisfies the conditions of this kind of rationality. An activity to which this concept applies I call rationally constituted. Thus, although *following* an argument may be— and, to the extent that it is done for its own sake, clearly is—an example of a rationally constituted activity, the argument itself may express nothing but instrumental reason. The argument that says: if you want to do *X*, you must do *A*, unless *B*, and if *B*, then *C* . . . , is purely instrumental for the goal *X*. So, to the extent that it is like a recipe for *X*, following the argument is not a rationally constituted activity—although it is certainly quite rational. But if getting to *X* by *following the argument* is the point of the activity, then that activity is rationally constituted. It is the difference between removing your opponent's pieces from the board by capturing them and just putting them in your pocket.[11]

The relation between rhetoric and ethics has become more complex. Rhetoric, while always instrumental and always done to achieve some external end, turns out to have internal standards of excellence. Virtue, while it consists in action that is its own end, is always done for the sake of achieving some external good.[12] The difference between making and doing, so crucial to Aristotle's conception of virtue and practical wisdom, is not so easy to draw.

### Internal and External Goods in Rhetoric and Ethics

> Even the things that are not noble by nature, but are good by nature, are noble for [virtuous people]. For these things are noble when that for the sake of which they act and choose is noble. Therefore for the good and noble person the things good by nature are noble. (*EE* VIII.3.1249a4–7)

> What sort of things should one place among [things good] in themselves? Is it just those that are pursued even all alone, such as thinking (*phronein*) and seeing and some pleasures and honors? For even if we also pursue these for the sake of something else, nevertheless one would place them among things good in themselves. (*NE* I.6.1096b16–19)

The rationality of rhetoric, we now see, like the rationality of any art or practice, comes from having an internal end. We know that the internal object is rational in a second sense, supplying a rational and internal connection between what the rhetorician does and what happens to the audience. In both rhetoric and the virtues, next, the internal end is the internalization of the external end, and not some distinct internal value, such as craft value or psychic satisfaction. The internal end consists in those aspects of achieving the external end which are within the agent's power, which are practical. Instead of aiming at health as a condition of the patient, the doctor aims at healing as an activity of her own. She deliberates about how to engage in healing, not in how to produce health, except as health is the result of her healing.

Deliberation never loses sight of its external, given end. But arts and virtues limit the means they consider. Broadie makes my point perfectly:

> Health as ordinarily conceived is the starting-point of medical deliberation about how to treat a patient, in the sense of being the raison d'être of all steps taken with a view to treatment, including the deliberation; but the technical goal presented in the leading premise is the starting-point that guides the physician to one conclusion rather than another. The former starting-point is what justifies engaging at all in the deliberation with a view to taking whatever action it will indicate; the latter explains why *this* conclusion was reached and *this* action taken.[13]

Broadie's "technical goal" is my internal end. We now have to understand more precisely how such internal ends emerge out of deliberating about how to achieve the given end. Why isn't poisoning the enemy's food as within my power as courageously withstanding fear and staying in line? Maybe in medicine the answer is simply that the technical goal is a target that usually or reliably lets us achieve "health as ordinarily conceived," and Fried can make things easy by pointing to chess as an example where the difference between "removing your opponent's pieces from the board by capturing them and just putting them in your pocket" is simple; in virtue the problem is more acute.

I want to make sense of the way the internal end internalizes the external end for ethics by denying David Pears's influential account which makes internal and external ends totally independent. He says courage, and the other virtues, have a "behavioral sense" and an emotional one. My genealogical approach, in which internal ends emerge out of external ones, and the account of habituation that Aristotle himself uses to show how being virtuous emerges out of acting virtuously, tell against the independence of internal and external ends. Such independence requires that morality have a source distinct from the reasons and incentives at work in the rest of our lives, separating morality from rationality. Answers to the questions Pears raises are easy once one changes the meaning of internal ends to the goods internal to practices:

> True Aristotelian courageous actions are performed on the field of battle by citizen-soldiers both for victory and for the nobility of the actions themselves. How are these two goals related to one another? Must there be an external goal, such as victory, or could a man cultivate courage purely for its nobility, like Hemingway, or, to take a passive case, like a prisoner waiting helplessly in a cell for his own execution? When there is an external goal, why must it be victory? There certainly seem to be other good things for the sake of which an agent might exhibit courage. Does the external goal even have to be good in order that courage may be exhibited? If so, this ought not to be a trivial matter of labels but a consequence of the structure of courage.[14]

Here the internal end—nobility—has its being and worth apart from achieving of external goals such as victory. This line of argument finds nobility in the absence of consequences, as Socrates stipulates that the truly just man will be so indifferent to appearances that he will appear unjust, exhibiting what MacIntyre calls "aristocratic carelessness about consequences."[15]

Recognizing courage as an act valuable in its own right does not devalue the external end; it does not mean that winning the battle now becomes unimportant, as with Pears's gesture toward Hemingway's "cultivat[ing] courage purely for its nobility." Aristotle would deny that there is anything noble about courage in the absence of a valuable external end. Virtue becomes virtuosity, pride in the achievement of internal ends of craft values detached from the external ends that made them initially attractive and intelligible. Without wars for testing themselves and acting courageously, young men devise exploits like antarctic exploration. Scott was an admirable, even heroic, character, but his actions in racing Amundsen were not, in an Aristotelian sense, courage but bravado. They looked glorious, but once the World War started, their hollow nature became evident.

Acting courageously is its own end because we not only want that the battle be won, but we want to win the battle. In the Introduction I called this the metaphysical urge to convert incomplete processes into complete activities. Courageous action is its own end, valued in its own right, not because one is no longer interested in victory but because the end—engaging the enemy through courageous action—is now defined by the actions that bring it about.[16]

As persuasion becomes more rational, it becomes more ethical. The rational connection between persuading and being persuaded draws a connection between how rationally one is persuaded and how much one *ought* to be persuaded. There are no guarantees. The sophist might defeat a rhetorician in a particular case, and the courageous man might be less successful in battle than the experienced soldier or the worthless man with nothing to lose (*NE* III.9.1117b17–20; see III.8.1116b13–15). But in another way courage redefines what military success means. In general, the internal end is the internalization of an external end that is by itself vague and impractical. External ends gain richness of content by being the externalization of the goods internal to a practice. One can act courageously even in defeat. Acting as the courageous person would act becomes the criterion for courageous action, and the same holds for the other virtues too (*NE* IV.1. 1120b7–9, IV.1.1121a4–7, *EE* VII.2.1237b30).[17] The end of virtue is conformity to the corresponding state of character (*NE* III.7.1115b20–22); virtuous action is its own end because it is the source and measure of its own value.

Aristotle emphasizes the fact that the end of courage is an internalized and practical form of the original end, and not an independent internal end. He carefully begins his treatment of courage by refusing to define courage simply as the mastery of fears and asks, instead, toward "which fearful things courage is displayed?" (*NE* III.6.1115a25). Fear's object— the noblest form of death—is built into courage's definition. The original external end becomes part of the internalized end. There is a difference between poisoning the enemy's food supply and mastering one's fears as means to military victory, just as there is a difference between persuading through trickery and through argument. If I act courageously, I *ought* to win, just as, if I reason well, I should be persuasive. I may not win, and I may not persuade my judges, but if I don't succeed, something went wrong. Poisoning the enemy's food supply carries no such normative connotations. If I poisoned the food and the enemy still won, there's no sense in saying that I should have won. Poisoning the enemy's food supply may be a means to victory, but it does not internalize that external end. It is not part of a practice, and so the normative inference is absent.

Because he separates internal and external ends, Pears calls courage an "executive virtue." For him, the internal goal is successfully withstanding fears, while the external end varies over situations. Thus, he says:

> If a brave man simply reflects on the risk of death, there is no reason for him to expose himself to it. It is true that on the field of battle he will decide in the end, all things considered, to expose himself to it. But that is because the things that he considers include the external goal, victory. He may also consider the internal goal, courageous action for its own sake, but that cannot be his only reason for exposing himself to the risk of death.[18]

Pears's understanding of the relation of internal to external ends is much more suited to games as a model for praxis than, as Aristotle has it, medicine as the paradigm. The internal ends of games, like the internal ends of the virtues as Pears described them, have nothing to do with external ends: playing chess well according to the rules has nothing to do with the reasons I might want to play chess, such as wanting to spend time with my son, while the internal good of the art of medicine is designed to contribute to health as ordinarily conceived.

A practice, whether an art or a virtue, is rational because it has an internal end. I now want to assert a much stronger thesis: *An end is rational in proportion as pursuing it is an activity.* Exercising reason is a human being's way of being active and fully human (*NE* I.7.1098a7, I.13.1102b31–1103a1, IX.9.1170a29–37). Our desire to achieve some good becomes complete by being realized in activities that are their own end. As our acts become more *energeia*-like and less *kinēsis*-like, they become more rational. Separating the internal and external goods of virtues destroys any rationality they might have. To be as explicit as possible about the rationality of virtue, I want in the next section to exhibit the rationality of rhetoric and then show, in section that follows, the rationality of praxis.

## Virtuous Knowledge as Self-Knowledge

> It is our decisions to do what is good or bad, not our beliefs, that make the characters we have. (*NE* III.2.1112a1–3)

> Generally speaking, the proof of a man's knowledge or ignorance is his ability or inability to teach. (*Met.* I.1.981b7–10; see *NE* X.9.1180b32–34)

Although the definition of ethical virtue contains a reference to right reason, Aristotle refuses to follow Socrates and Plato in assimilating virtue to knowledge. While knowledge is present in both virtue and the arts, it is all that is required for *technē*, while knowledge is less significant than the ethical factors in virtue (*NE* II.4.1105a26–b10;. see *EE* I.5.1216b3–25), which makes virtue more accurate than art (*NE* II.6.1106b14–15). Aristotle needs to explicate virtue as a mode of rationality distinct from both theoretical knowledge and from art.[19]

While virtue takes more than knowledge, the virtues are *more rational* than the arts. The virtuous person, unlike the rhetorician or other artisan, knows himself (*NE* II.2.1103b26–31). He knows himself as an agent, as the cause which connects the ultimate principles with ultimate things to be done (*NE* III.3.1112b31–32, VI.2.1139b4–5, IX.9.1168b28–33, *De An.* 433b28, *Met.* VI.1.1025b18–28, XI.1064a10–11, *EE* II.6.1223a5). When our internal goods are objects of decision, knowing them we know ourselves. "Every activity aims at the end that corresponds to the habit of which it is the manifestation (*telos de pasēs energeias esti to kata tēn hexin*). So it is with the activity of the courageous man: his courage is noble; therefore its end is nobility, for a thing is defined by its end" (*NE* III.7.1115b20–22; see too III.7.1115b23–4, III.9.1117b7–9, IV.2. 1122b6–7).[20]

When the virtuous person recognizes his actions as *energeiai* and so worth doing for their own sake, he knows himself as the cause of his actions and so understands how those actions contribute to *eudaimōnia*. The liberal person sees herself as an agent and money as a resource, while both the miser and the profligate make money the cause of what they take to be happiness, and therefore are ignorant of the self as its practical cause. The miser cannot bring himself to spend money to help a friend because he never wants to put himself in a position where she might be forced by poverty to do something shameful: "There are those who seem to keep what they have, or at any rate say they do, in order to prevent their ever being compelled to do something shameful" (*NE* IV.1. 1121b25–28).

But what sort of ignorance is this? Of what is the miser ignorant? His ignorance cannot be corrected by showing him actuarial tables that show that he has money to spare and can safely give money to a friend without risking his own poverty, as the art of measurement in the *Protagoras* suggests. He lacks self-knowledge, fails know himself as an agent. Someone who aimed at life, rather than the good life, could rely on a theoretical science of economics to determine how much money he could afford to give away. But how much one needs for living well is not calculable; the "costs" of liberality do not detract from living well as they might detract from living. If I aim at nobly helping others, I could still exhaust my resources, but calculating how much I should give is not an economic question but an ethical one about the place of good acts in a noble life.

Thus, the courageous person's confidence is truly *self*-confidence, confidence in himself, not confidence *that* the balance of forces is on his side.[21] The professional soldier, relying on *technē*, knows the odds of success and how to get it. The courageous person knows something quite different, the true value of the life he risks and of the noble end for which he risks it. "The more completely virtuous and happy a man is, the more he will be pained at the thought of death, for life is best worth living for such a man, and he knows that he is losing the greatest goods" (*NE* III.9.1117b9–11). In the same way, the person virtuously disposed toward anger knows himself, while, the inirascible man foolishly and slavishly doesn't realize that he or his family is insulted (*NE* IV.5.1126a3–8). Such ignorance is not an ignorance that could be set right by a detached theoretical investigation. Just as all friendship is rooted in self-love, so all practical knowledge is rooted in practical self-knowledge, knowledge of self as agent (*NE* IX.8. 1169a11–18).[22]

Ethical knowledge is knowledge of the self as the locus of good (*NE* II.2.1103b26–31, X.9.1179a33–b12). The agent is identified with his ends: a person's ends reveal his *ēthos* and who he is (*NE* III.2.1111b4– 6, III.4.1113a21–22, IX.5.1166a13–17, *EE* II.10.1226a11–13, II.11. 1227b34–1228a4, *Rh.* I.9.1367b21–27). The man of honor, by contrast, hopes to be honored because he does not himself believe in his own worth: "People pursue honor to convince themselves of their own merit" (*NE* I.3. 1095b26–28, VIII.8.1159a23–24). The small-souled man is not foolish but rather too retiring or timid, "for men's ambitions show what they are worth, and if they hold aloof from noble enterprises and pursuits, and forgo the good things of life, presumably they think they are not worthy of them." On the other hand, "vain people are foolish and do not know themselves" (*NE* IV.3.1125a24–29). Lying between these two, the great-souled man, by theoretical standards, may lack self-knowledge. He overlooks wrongs done to him (*NE* IV.3.1125a3–5) and forgets benefits he has received, while remembering the times he has helped others (1124b9–15). He knows himself practically. Only the virtuous person is active enough to have a knowable self.

### Self-knowledge and the Practice of Activity

> Existing is, for everyone, worth choosing and lovable; but it is by our actuality that we exist, since we exist by living and acting; but the work is, in some sense, its maker in actuality; hence he is fond of his work—for the reason that he loves existing. And this is natural, because what he is potentially, his work reveals in actuality. (*NE* IX.7.1168a5–9)

Because only the virtuous can practically know themselves, most people think that life and action are series of movements designed to end in states outside themselves, whether pleasure, honor, or wealth. To live well, one must practice the metaphysical truths that the basic substances in the world are defined by their activities, that activities are complete motions and complete realizations of our psychic powers. Living well means organizing one's life around the perfect *energeiai* listed at *Metaphysics* IX.6.1048b23–25— seeing, understanding, thinking, living well, and being happy. You don't have to read the *Metaphysics* to live well, but you do have to live by its truths. Alternative metaphysics, such as fatalism or the errors of *Metaphysics* IX.3 and 4, are ethical mistakes. Most people, then and now, organize their lives around a metaphysical mistake because of their lack of practical self-knowledge.

People without adequate practical self-knowledge make two mistakes. They misunderstand the nature of agency and so of the practical, and they identify the wrong highest goods. Eliminate the goods of activity, and practical reasoning becomes deliberation toward external goods, and external goods must be the highest goods, since they're the only goods. Locating goodness in external things, the vicious lack self-knowledge (*NE* VII.8. 1150b36).

The sophist, with his eye on victory, may seem more practical than the Aristotelian rhetorician who concentrates on argument. Because the art of rhetoric is limited to argument, the sophist seems to have an advantage in practical competition because he can use all sorts of nonartistic, even nonverbal, means of persuasion, displaying his weeping wife and children before the jury and talking about his years of military service. Seeing only evidence seems to put one at a practical disadvantage.

The sophist's activity is an unmethodical search for what might work. The sophist constantly makes *post hoc, ergo propter hoc* inferences, because he has nothing else to go on. For example, someone who does not know what he is talking about, or who knows she has a losing case, will frequently betray weakness through body language. Therefore, the sophist will teach people how to use gestures properly. The sophist might grasp some probable causes of success, but, without any understanding of the connection between cause and effect, his "art" will not count as knowledge. The sophist cannot say anything about what *should* persuade. The sophist does not know anything and certainly does not know what should be done (*Soph. El.* 34. 183b37–184a7). Since there is nothing to know, there is nothing to do but imitate success. The openness and opportunism of the sophist is not such an advantage after all. Concentrating on the external end and on winning turns out to be impractical.

Just as the sophist seemed more practical and more resourceful than the Aristotelian rhetorician, a chief good like money or honor seems more practical than the good expressed by Aristotle's formula that happiness is *energeia kat'aretēn* (*NE* I.7.1098a16). Under common understandings of what it is to be practical, knowing that happiness is virtuous activity is not practical. But that is less a criticism of this definition than grounds to reconsider the meaning of the practical. It is a mistake to try to derive what to do directly from a definition of the highest good. We understand happiness through understanding virtue; we don't deduce the virtues from happiness.[23]

The focus of attention in the *Ethics,* from the end of Book I until the end of Book X, is virtue, not happiness. The nonvirtuous focus their attention on the immediate ends of action, and they think that they also aim at a highest good such as pleasure, but these targets make invisible the true objects of practical knowledge, the internal goods of virtuous practices. Without internal ends, practice becomes irrational. Thus the definition of happiness as *energeia kat'aretēn* does not compete with the candidates for happiness Aristotle derives from common opinion. Virtuous activity is not a further end alongside honor and money. The person acting virtuously reorients his attention from external ends to the internal good of praxis. The virtuous person knows something others do not: the internal ends of praxis are the objects of practical knowledge and decision.

The virtuous person knows that there are two kinds of goodness in the world. "There are two things above all which make human beings cherish and feel affection, what is one's own and what is dear" (*kēdesthai kai philein, to te idion kai to agapēton*) (*Pol.* II.4.1262b22–23).[24] External goods such as wealth, honor, and health really are good, but not as good as the goods of virtuous activity.[25] Were external goods not worth having, it would be much easier to concentrate on internal goods. The stoics, thus, revalued external goods as indifferents and therefore were able to see internal goods as the only true goods; Pears's account of courage moves in that direction. But those internal goods aren't the goods of *activity* any longer. Aristotelian activities perfect *kinēseis*. They are activities oriented toward achieving external goods.

### Internal Ends as Actions Chosen for Their Own Sakes

> Production has its end beyond itself; but action does not, since its end is doing well itself (*esti gar autē hē eupraxis telos*). (*NE* VI.5.1140b6–7)

> Learning proceeds in this way—through that which is less knowable by nature to that which is more knowable; and just as in conduct our task is to start from what is good for each and make what is without qualification good good for each, so it is our task to start from what is more knowable to oneself and make what is knowable by nature knowable to oneself. (*Met.* VII.3.1029b3–8)

The contrast between the internal ends of the arts and the virtues puts us in a position to understand how an action can be its own end and see why that idea is fundamental to the *Ethics*. We can draw four consequences. In each case, we will see how the ethical virtues are more rational than any craft, including rhetoric, and so understand why virtuous activities are more rational and active than other things people do.

### We Deliberate about Means, Not Ends

> The noble is that which, being good, is pleasant because it is good (*kalon men oun estin d an di'hauto haireton on epaineton ē, ē de an agathon on hēduē, hoti agathon*) (*Rh.* I.8.1366a33–34; *EE* VIII.3.1249a18–19; see *Top.* II.11.115b29–35)

Aristotle's insistence that we deliberate about means and not ends (*NE* III.3.1112b11–12, b32–33) has provoked so much commentary that I will approach the subject several times as my argument progresses.[26] The comparison with rhetoric allows us to see what Aristotle means. People have tried to soften Aristotle's claim by pointing out that "means" is too limited a translation of *pros to telos,* things that are toward an end, but the real problem is trying to fit a means/end model—Aristotle explicates the nature of deliberation by analogy to a geometric construction—to activities that are their own end.[27] Praxeis don't have separate means the way makings have, and it is hard to see how deliberation works in such a case. The example of rhetoric shows internal ends emerging through limiting the available means for achieving a given, external end. Unlike many other versions of ethics, then, Aristotelian ethics has no room for an independent, critical function of reason in deliberating about and choosing among ends, one of the features I find both a strength and a weakness. The rationality of ends comes from their being chosen for their own sakes, through the internalization of given external ends.[28] By making practical ends into *energeiai,*[29] Aristotle avoids the implication that unless there is deliberation about ends, ends are irrational.

Initially, we cannot deliberate about ends because they are given. These are ends *pros ti,* ends because we desire them and deliberate toward them. With the internal ends of practices, we deliberate about means and not ends because ends are *known* to be good, and so not up to us. These are ends *haplōs.* And just as in the sciences, when we know the principles of the sciences, we still do not prove them, so here when we know the ends of good action and the good life, we still do not choose them. Restricting deliberation to means is of a piece with Aristotle's distinguishing the inferential powers of science from the capacity to know principles.[30] "Scientific knowledge (*epistēmē*) is a demonstrative state. . . . One has scientific knowledge whenever one has the appropriate sort of confidence, and knows the principles; for if one does not know them better than the conclusion, one will have scientific knowledge only coincidentally" (*NE* VI.3.1139b31–35). "We have *nous* about principles" (*NE* VI.6.1141a7–8). It is no denigration of *epistēmē* that it does not know principles; it is no denigration of deliberation and choice that they are limited to means.

We don't deliberate about external ends; they are simply given. Given ends function as postulates do in science. The clever person, no matter how rational his means, makes his ends no more rational by deliberating about how to get them. We deliberate toward external ends without being committed to thinking they are good in any sense beyond the fact that we desire them, as we derive consequences from postulates without worrying about the truth of our premises. The person of practical wisdom redefines the given external ends into things that can be chosen and done for their own sake. Thus we make our ends more rational by concentrating on rational means of attaining them. Scientific principles are known without being proven, and the ends of good action—virtue and happiness—are known and decided on without being subject to deliberation. We don't deliberate about ends, but if our ends are activities, they are rational.

Rationality enters praxis at the same place where it enters the arts such as rhetoric, not by having better ends but by having more thoughtful, rational, and fully chosen means. When we have rational means, decision makes our wishes determinate, because we wish for an achievement inseparable from the actions chosen. It is quite a remarkable achievement of Aristotle in the *Rhetoric* to be able to show the limitation of the art of rhetoric to reasoning without importing any external moral standards. It is an even greater achievement in the *Ethics* to show how rationality enters praxis not by having better ends but more rationally and fully chosen means. Rationally understood external ends are conceived as the manifestations of internal ends.

But the question remains: if we do not deliberate about ends, how do we rationally relate to them? Sometimes we question our given ends and seem to adopt new ones. I have chosen a modest rather than a wealthy life in order to teach philosophy. Isn't this a choice of ends, choosing a more pleasant activity over more money and possibly over a more productive activity? In the final chapter, I will look at Aristotle's comparison of the political and the philosophical life, and argue that he never poses the comparison as a choice of lives, but what about the more modest apparent choices of ends that we engage in all the time?

Instead of choosing our ends, we discover what is rational and intelligible about given ends. Finding what is rational about them means learning what is final about them, how they are really ends, what is good about them beyond the fact that we desire them. We start with a given end and deliberate about how to achieve it. The *Rhetoric* provides a model of such deliberation. Through that process, we discover that some aspects of that end can be achieved *in* good action and not merely *by* action. Those aspects are objects of decision and knowledge.

Sometimes, at an extreme, this process can show us that nothing in the given end can be internalized, actualized, and rationalized in this way. We abandon that end. When we see that an external end cannot be made determinate, it is seen as empty, and so we discard it. A life of pure pleasure and self-indulgence, the single-minded life of a committed miser, the life of endless acquisition governed by envy and jealousy, these ends have no rational aspect. More usually, though, we find through deliberation that some parts of a given end are activities and others are end-products. The soldier who takes as given that his job is to fight and defend his city discovers that he not only wants the result that his city win but also desires to act courageously in defending the city. When he comes to value the internal end, he is committed to it, and the commitment is the outcome of a rational deliberation. But he never chooses an end.[31]

### Only Virtuous, Not Artistic, Action, Aims at True Ends

> Although he who makes, makes for an end, what is made is not an end as such (*haplōs*), but only relatively (*pros ti*), as the end of a particular production; only what is done is an end as such, for good action itself is an end, and desire aims at this. (*NE* VI.2.1139b1–4)

Although we deliberate about means and not ends both in the arts and in praxis, there is a difference. If an act is done for some external end, not only is the process imperfect (*Met.* IX.6.1048b18–22), but the end is imperfect too. It is an end because someone aims at it, not because of some property of its own. An end of an instrumental process is an end because it happens to be the object of desire. It is an end because it is desired; it is not desired because it is an end. The internal ends of the arts remain in service to the given ends in a way that is not true for the virtues.

It is the nature of ends to be rational, so only the good man—not the vicious man and not the artisan—aims at true ends, ends that are ends because of their nature and not because they are aimed at. Virtuous activities have no existence apart from their being done as ends. Such is the meaning of Aristotle's claim that I use to head this section. Even if rhetoric and other crafts have internal ends, and even if they are enjoyable and fulfilling, these practices are not their own end. The internal ends of the arts are objects of knowledge; the internal ends of the virtues are objects of decision.

Because the virtues and not the arts aim at true ends, the internal end of rhetoric—finding the available means of persuasion—isn't much of a constraint on the external ends for which it can be used. The rhetorician can argue both sides of almost any question. Only constraints external to the art of dialectic stop the dialectician from arguing about whether there are gods and whether one should honor one's parents (*Top.* I.11.105a3–7). On the other hand, the internal end of the virtues—doing what is within one's power to achieve given goods—narrows the external ends toward which it can aim. Mastering my fears of death in noble circumstances will allow me better to serve my country, and not to become a mercenary. As I will show more in chapters 3 and 5, Aristotle's ethical virtues are so essentially political that using them for nonpolitical purposes is barred. True ends are necessarily political ends.

## Moral Progress Consists in the Gain in Rationality
## that Occurs when Actions Become Ends,
## Acts Chosen for Their Own Sakes

People think it takes no wisdom to know the things that are just and unjust, because it is not hard to comprehend what the laws speak of. But these are not the things that are just, except coincidentally. Knowing how actions must be done, and how distributions must be made, if they are to be just, takes more work than it takes to know about healthy things. (*NE* V.9.1137a9–14; see too V.8.1135b27–1136a1, *Rh.* I.13.1374a9–12)

We can act courageously only when confronted by an enemy. The judge needs cases to decide justly. The external end is always given, never chosen. That is part of the truth that we deliberate about means, not ends. We choose the internal end, facing the enemy because it is noble to do so, as a means toward accomplishing that external end, and then come to value it for its own sake. I want to return to my analogy to Lon Fuller's internal morality of law to see how virtuous actions are chosen for their own sake, while still being valued also because of the good results they bring. After presenting his conception of the internal morality of law, Fuller then asks whether it "represent[s] some variety of natural law." He rejects that possibility, since to conceive of the morality of law as higher natural law is like saying that orientation to the right ends makes an action good. Instead, the internal morality of law is a perfection of its means. "They are like the natural laws of carpentry, or at least those laws respected by a carpenter who wants the house he builds to remain standing and serve the purpose of those who live in it."

Because the internal morality of law is concerned with means, it is reasonable to think of it as procedural, "as indicating that we are concerned, not with the substantive aims of legal rules, but with the ways in which a system of rules for governing human conduct must be constructed and administered if it is to be efficacious and at the same time remain what it purports to be."[32] If anything, one should consider this sort of natural law not as "higher laws" but lower laws. The difference between a natural law that looks at procedures and one that is substantive is the difference between Aristotle's strategy of making praxis rational by making the means into acts that are chosen for their own sakes and the alternative strategy of making praxis rational by orienting it to a better set of ends. But calling the internal morality of law procedural makes it into a systematic and effective means to the end of governing human conduct, not something valued in its own right. Rhetoric shows how it is the rationality of the internal morality of law that makes it an end.

### Those Who Don't Engage in Actions that Are Their Own End Are Doomed to Have Pleasure as Their End

Appetite is for pleasure . . . the object of wish is the good; pleasure and the good are different. (*EE* VII.2.1235b21–23)

Appetite concerns pleasure and pain, decision (*prohairesis*) neither pain nor pleasure. (*NE* III.4.1111b15–18)

Pleasure misleads the mass of mankind; for it seems to them to be a good, though it is not, so they choose what is pleasant as good and shun pain as evil. (*NE* III.5.1113a33–b2)

Vicious people aim at pleasure because they can't aim at anything good in itself. Thinking that external goods are the only goods, one becomes a pleasure maximizer by default. Ignorance of the noble has the pursuit of pleasure as a consequence, since all goods that are not goods of activity and agency are pursued as pleasures.[33] If I aim at wealth, fame, or political power, they are good because they please me. But when I desire something because I think it good, rather than think it good because I want it, I want to *do* something about it. To think something good I have to care about how I get it, and in particular want it to be a function of my actions and decisions instead of luck or of the favor of another (*NE* I.9.1099b20–25; see *Top.* III.3.118b8–10, *Pol.* VII.1.1323b23–33, VII.13.1332a28–36).[34]

I have to fight for my country because my country's defeat would have undesirable consequences. I might be killed and my family sold into slavery. Why should I care whether my side wins through courage, tricks, or lucky weather? If, though, I think I am fighting on the side of the right, I want not only victory but vindication. I will feel cheated if my side wins through something other than our efforts. Risk and sacrifice are indices of my commitment to achieving the good. Winning through a break in the weather won't feel like a secure win. The losers will see themselves defeated by luck, not by me. I want not only to win but to deserve to win. I want the connection between is and ought that I found in the art of rhetoric. Here that desire is the love for the noble.

The vicious person believes that because something is good he should have it. The virtuous person thinks that because something is good he should *do* it. Therefore, too, the vicious can only want apparent goods, not real goods, since true goods are the goods of activity. Even if they imitate the virtues without ulterior motive (*NE* II.7.1108a28, IV.6.1127a7–8, IV.7. 1127a28), like the miser I will consider in chapter 4, they will not perform an action that is its own end. The vicious want the ends without the effort.

And therefore the ends they want are only the surface of active goods. They want honor instead of doing something honorable. They therefore choose life and not the good life. Ignorance of the goods of activity is ignorance of self as an agent.

The unjust man thinks there is a direct or demonstrative connection between what is good and what he should want. The beginning of ethical virtue and practical wisdom—and the beginning of a separation of ethical from artistic deliberation—consists in recognizing the difference between what is good and what is good for me, the gap between knowing what is good and deciding what I should do. Because something is good, it does not follow that I should have it. What Aristotle says about injustice is a particular application of a more general truth:

> Since the unjust person is greedy, he will be concerned with goods—not with all goods, but only with those involved in good and bad fortune, goods which are, [considered] unconditionally, always good, but for this or that person not always good. Though human beings pray for these and pursue them, they are wrong; the right thing is to pray that what is good unconditionally will also be good for us, but to choose [only] what is good for us. (NE V.1.1129b1–6; see V.9.1137a26–30)

He generalizes the point himself in the *Eudemian Ethics:*

> The absolutely good is absolutely desirable but what is good for oneself is desirable for oneself; and the two ought to come into agreement. This is effected by virtue; and the purpose of politics is to bring it about in cases where it does not yet exist. And one who is a human being is well adapted to things and on the way to it (for by nature things that are absolutely good are good to him) . . . but the road is through pleasure—it is necessary that noble things should be pleasant. When there is discord between them, a man is not yet perfectly good; for it is possible for unrestraint to be engendered in him, as unrestraint is caused by discord between the good and the pleasant in the emotions. (EE VII.2. 1236b39–1237a3)[35]

While death is the most frightening thing (NE III.6.1115a26), it does not follow that life is the greatest good. Instead, the better we are, the more what is good *haplōs* is good for us. "It is shameful not to be able to use good things" (*Pol.* VII.15.1334a36–37). The better we are, the more life is good for us, and the more we are willing to risk it in a good cause. The better we are, the less we are going to be corrupted by wealth, so that the money which everyone desires and thinks good *haplōs* is in fact good for us, but it is good for the liberal man because he knows how to use it, not keep it. The vicious confuse the good *haplōs* with what is good for the individual.[36]

Many people have learned the unhappy news that a man or woman who might rate best in all the relevant properties of a potential spouse is not best for them. When I was a student, I thought the way to get the best possible education was to seek out the best teachers and learn as much as I could from them. It took many painful years for me to learn that the best teacher might not be the best teacher for me. Richard McKeon was the best teacher I ever saw—erudite, well-organized, offering profound insights, devoting great energy to his teaching and his students, making connections between apparently remote ideas, capable of quick and insightful improvisation in discussion. He made books into living arguments, not inert texts to be mined to find some "official position." After each class I felt that I knew far more about whatever we were studying than I had before. So I committed myself to learning as much as I could from him.

But eventually I realized that continuing to learn from him would have made me into a permanent acolyte. His intellectual powers were so much greater than mine that my powers developed through contact with him, but that same superiority meant that continuing with him doomed me to continuing discipleship. Maybe a better student could have profitably studied with McKeon without being condemned to a self-imposed immaturity by the evident distance between his powers and mine. But it would be wrong for me to act on that counterfactual possibility. I could wish that the best teacher would be best for me, but my decisions should be oriented toward what is best for me, not what is best in an abstract sense.

I don't think my mistaken choice of a teacher was vicious, although it certainly was an ethical and not purely a logical mistake. But it shares at least one important feature with vice. My choice of a teacher went wrong because it was not connected to self-knowledge but was instead based on knowledge of external goods. My picture of learning followed the *Symposium*, where Agathon wants to sit next to Socrates hoping that wisdom will flow in his direction, as wine from one jar to another (175d–e). I regarded myself as simply a member of a type, students, and regarded the choice of a teacher as one that could be discerned without engaging my own character. If he's the best teacher, he's best for you and for me. Learning was something that would happen if I came into contact with the best teacher; learning wasn't something that I had to *do*.

### Ethical Internal Ends and Decision: Knowing the Individual

We call people intelligent (*phronimous*) about some [restricted area] whenever they calculate well to promote some excellent end, in an area where there
is no *technē*. (*NE* VI.5.1140a28–30)

Virtue is *more rational* than rhetoric or any *technē*. It is more rational
because virtue extends the scope of rationality beyond what any art can
achieve. It goes where *technē* cannot. Virtue is more rational than art because it is more practical.

Technical deliberations are incomplete at both ends. They begin by postulating, not knowing, some subordinate good, health, political security,
military victory. Because the ethically virtuous man knows the highest good,
happiness as *energeia kat'aretēn,* he can also know lower ends and the individual thing to be done. Conversely, only because the virtuous person knows
what it is good to do can he know that happiness is *energeia kat'aretēn.* Because ethics reaches all the way to the highest human good, it also reaches all
the way to the ultimate individual thing to be done. Aristotle denies that the
art of rhetoric, or any art, reaches the concrete individual:

> No art examines the particular—for example the art of medicine does not
> specify what is healthful for Socrates or for Callias but for persons of a certain
> sort (this is artistic, while particulars are limitless and not knowable)—neither
> does rhetoric theorize about each opinion—what may seem so to Socrates or
> Hippias—but about what seems true to people or a certain sort, as is also true
> with dialectic. (*Rh.* I.2.1356b29–34)

> When our general account is so inexact, the account of particular cases is all
> the more inexact. For these fall under no craft or profession, and the agents
> themselves must consider in each case what the opportune action is, as doctors
> and navigators do. (*NE* II.2.1104a5–10; see I.3.1094b19–27, I.7. 1097a11–
> 14, *An. Post.* I.31, *Met* I.1.981a12–24, VII.15.1039b27–1040a7, XIII.10.
> 1086b32–33)

While the practice of rhetoric is directed at individuals, its art is not. There
is a gap between rule and application, between knowledge and judgment.
Aristotle's ethics has no such gap, and so modern attempts, as for example
in Arendt's appropriation of Kant, to locate the moral life in the gaps between the universal and the particular, through judgment or imagination,
are alien to Aristotle's way of thinking. An art can only take the practitioner
so far; after that, he needs not art but deliberation and judgment.[37]

Because no art concerns individual cases, the universals known by an art can be stated apart from experience. The know-how of the good artisan is therefore not fully captured by the universals of his craft and so cannot be taught. For the same reason, technical knowledge is not automatically motivating as virtuous knowledge is. Teachability and detachment are often taken as marks of the rational, but, in comparison with practical knowledge, Aristotle shows that they are instead signs of the incompleteness of *technē*.

The experienced rhetorician will have a feel for when an audience deviates from his expectations, and the virtuous person a feel for what her friend needs. But that feel on the part of the rhetorician is no part of his art, while the feel of the virtuous person is part of her virtue. The confrontation of the virtues with the ultimate individual is built into the virtue itself (*NE* VI.7.1141b14–16, VI.8.1142a11–15, 1142a23–25, VI. 11. 1143a32–35). The clever person will give money to some individual as a member of a class, such as the class likely to look good on his résumé, the worthy poor, just as I tried to get the best education by finding the best teacher. The person acting from the virtue of liberality, instead, can give money to an individual. Any piece of chicken and any coat might do in the practical syllogism that combines premises such as "I need a covering; a coat is a covering," but the object of liberality is an individual. "Having the right feelings at the right times, about the right things, toward the right people, for the right end, and in the right way, is the mean and best condition, and this is proper to virtue" (*NE* II.6.1106b21–23; see IV.5. 1125b33–1126a1).

Practical science, then, can do what theoretical science cannot, namely know the individual.[38] I think this is the point Aristotle is making when he identifies ethical perception with practical *nous* (*NE* VI.11.1143a35–b1; cf. VI.8.1142a23–30). Friendship above all shows that in praxis what is individual is not necessarily accidental. Therefore, only the virtuous are capable of true friendship, in which the object of friendship is an individual, not a person who fits some description as giving pleasure or serving some use. Regardless of the outcome of continuing debate about whether Greek literature was concerned with individual characters, for Aristotelian friendship an individual is not a bundle of idiosyncrasies but someone whose good one can wish for its own sake.[39] "Those who love for utility or pleasure are fond of a friend because of what is good or pleasant for themselves, not insofar as the beloved is who he is, but insofar as he is useful or pleasant" (*NE* VIII.3.1156a15–16).

Because the arts deal with kinds, not concrete individuals, intentional error can be jstifiable. "In *technē* voluntary error (*ho hekōn hamartia*) is not so bad as involuntary, whereas in the sphere of *phronēsis* it is worse, as it is in the sphere of the virtues" (*NE* VI.5.1140b22–24; see *EE* VIII.1. 1246a37–b8, *Met.* V.29.1025a6–13, *Poet.* 24.1460a18–19, 25.1461b9–12). My physician can judge that I would be better treated in violation of medical rules. She can decide that the external end would be better achieved through bypassing the internal end. The virtuous person has no such option. Practical internal ends have an authority that technical internal ends do not. The internal ends of an art cannot have such final authority because the purpose of art is to make something that has value apart from the activities that bring it about.

The closest ethical parallel to my doctor overruling medical precepts is equity correcting justice. But equity is not a violation of justice but rather the correction of voluntary and involuntary errors legislators make in the pursuit of justice:

> All law is universal, but in some areas no universal rule can be correct; and so where a universal rule has to be made, but cannot be correct, the law chooses the universal rule that holds for the most part, well aware of the error that has been made. And the law is no less correct on this account. For the source of the error is not in the law or the legislator but in the nature of the object itself, since that is what the matter of actions is bound to be like. (*NE* V.9.1137b13–19)

The doctor who violates the rules of the art of medicine might still aiming at healing, but the virtuous person cannot step outside the principles of virtue in the name of virtue. As I will show in the next chapter, decision (*prohairesis*) thus is external to art but internal to virtue. This too makes the virtues more rational than the arts.

# CHAPTER 2

# Decision, Rational Powers, and Irrational Powers

Man, as a principle of action, is a union of desire and intellect. (*NE* VI.2.1139b4–5)

It is our decisions to do what is good or bad, not our beliefs, that make the characters we have. (*NE* III.1112a1–3)

Decision seems to be most characteristic of virtue and to discriminate characters better than actions. (*NE* III.2.1111b4–6; see *NE* VI.12.1144a13–20, *EE* II.11.1228a2–7, *Poet.* 6.1450b8–10, 15.1454a17–19)

## The Need for Psychology: Good Actions and Good Souls

The politician must in some way know about the soul, just as someone setting out to heal the eyes must know about the whole body as well. . . . But the politician must study it for his specific purpose, far enough for his inquiry [into virtue]; for a more exact treatment would presumably take more effort than his purpose requires. (*NE* I.13.1102a18–26)

The first chapter showed how virtuous activities emerge out of ends and actions initially desired and chosen for all sorts of reasons. I used the *Rhetoric* to demystify the idea of an action being its own end. In rhetoric, and in virtuous action, there are two ends, internal and external, and Aristotle's ethics has the complexity it has because both have to be good. External goods such as wealth, the security of one's city, one's own life — these remain good even as we discover that they are not as good as the goods of virtuous activity. Those latter goods are the measure of how much of an external good is good for us, and they make external goods good for us.

But the example of rhetoric should also be ominous. If internal ends are everywhere, activity as its own end could become a purely formal idea, without power to delineate the good life. People, especially those in Aristotle's audience with the aggressive *thumos* of ambitious young men, will search for activities that are not simply the satisfaction of needs, activities that are their own end, without necessarily living virtuously: "Men do not become tyrants to get out of the cold" (*Pol.* II.7.1267a14–16).

To counter the possibility of activity as its own end becoming a purely formal idea, this chapter takes a psychological turn. Without looking at the soul we cannot differentiate virtue from art or even from unlimited acquisition or from unlimited ambition and contest for honor, which also look like they can be chosen as their own ends. Only by reaching down to the soul can the virtues reach up to happiness. Modern virtue ethics, as we will see later, ignores both the relations between virtue and soul and between virtue and happiness that constitute the *dynamis/energeia* dimension. Looking at the relation between the soul, the virtues, and virtuous action will give a different picture of virtuous activity than we got from seeing such activity as the internalization of given ends.

The *De Anima*'s use of the potency/act distinction can guide us. Aristotle defined the soul as the first actuality of an organic body.[1] An organic body is matter and potentiality for life. Its soul is a first actuality. Psychic activities—sensing, desiring, knowing—are the second actuality. Psychic activities do not realize the potentialities of the body but of the soul: this is the difference between my skin turning red from the sun and my seeing red. Similarly, the desiring, persuadable soul is the material perfected and realized in the first actuality of the virtues, which in turn is the *dynamis* realized in virtuous actions. We will discover vices which directly realize the natural potentialities of the desiring soul instead of the first *energeiai* of virtuous habits.[2]

Although the *De Anima*'s distinction between first and second *energeiai* is crucial, practical knowledge needs its own psychology. We can study voluntary action in biology, but decision (*prohairesis*) is visible only in practical science. Nothing in the *Ethics* contradicts the *De Anima,* but it needs to know things on which the *De Anima* is silent. No "metaphysical biology" or anything else imported from some more secure and theoretical science will help us get at practical rationality.[3] Aristotle makes little use of his scientific psychology in the *Ethics*. Instead, two of the most crucial claims that structure the *Ethics* come from "the exoteric logoi," and not scientific psychology: the division of soul into rational and irrational (*NE* I.13. 1102b13–1103a15, *EE* II.1.1219b28–31, 1220a8–11), and the distinction between making and doing (VI.4). In what would be scandalous for a theoretical science, the *Ethics* contains many different lists of parts of the soul, in addition to the rational/irrational division, with no attempt to bring them into relation to each other. Here is a partial list:

- The three things that make someone good and excellent are nature, habit, and reason (*Pol.* VII.13.1332a39–40, 15.1334b7–8, 1134b14–17, *NE* X.9.1179b20, *EE* I.1.1214a11–19).
- Passion, faculty, and habit are called "the three things in the soul" in *NE* II.5 (1105b19–20; see *EE* II.2.1220b11ff).
- There are three kinds of desire, *epithumia, thumos* and *boulēsis* (*NE* III.2.1111b10–12; see *EE* II.7.1223a26–27, II.10.1225b24–26, *Mag. Mor.* I.12.1187b37, *De An.* II.3.414b2, III.9.432b5–6, III.10.433a22–26, *Rh.* I.10.1369a1–4, *Pol.* VII.15.1334b17–25).
- Perception, understanding (*nous*), and desire are "the things that control action and truth" (*NE* VI.2.1139a18).[4]

The *Ethics* needs a peculiar sort of psychology in which we learn more about souls from looking at virtue than the other way around. We can understand *technē* without looking at the soul but we cannot understand praxis without psychology. The basic psychological question is this: are there are specific constraints on the kind of *dynamis* that can give rise to *energeiai* that are worth doing for their own sakes? What can we infer about virtuous habit, a first *energeia* and second nature, from the fact that virtuous activity is its own end?

### The Problem: Rational and Irrational Powers as an Exhaustive Distinction

> Every rational *dynamis* is capable of causing both contraries, but every irrational potency can cause only one; for example, heat can cause only heating, but doctoring can cause sickness as well as health. (*Met.* IX.2.1046b4–7; see VII.7.1032b2–6, *Int.* 13a1, *EE* II.8.1224b25–28)

A natural place to begin understanding the relation between human souls, the ethical virtues, and their *energeiai* in happiness and ethically virtuous activity is by asking whether the virtues as first *energeiai* are rational or irrational *dynameis*. The virtues are *rational* first *energeiai* of the irrational part of the soul (*NE* I.13.1102b31–1103a1). Aristotle calls them rational (*meta logou*) at the end of the at *NE* VI.13.1144b21–30 (see *EE* II.1. 1219b30, II.8.1224a39–b2), and calling them *kata logon* at I.7.1098a7 seems too obvious for argument.

But the virtues lack three usual marks of the rational. First, the rationality inherent in the virtues is not teachable. Next, unlike other rational powers, the virtues are not powers to do opposites. The artful rhetorician can argue both sides of any issue, but no virtue is a power for opposites. I can either drink this bottle of wine or not, but the temperate person will reliably not drink when she should not.

Third, when the arts and sciences are our model for rationality, then reason and emotion are enemies. Rational powers, such as the art of rhetoric, couldn't be powers for opposites unless their rationality was one thing, their desire and decision another. "So in the case of rational potencies there must be something else which decides, and by this I mean desire or decision (*prohairesis*)" (*Met.* IX.5.1048a10–11, see *Pr. Anal.* I.13.32b5–23). Ethical virtues, by contrast, incorporate decision into themselves, integrating rationality and goodness. They are habits of deciding, *hexeis prohairetikē* (*NE* II.6.1106a36–1107a2). Since the virtues are already governed by deliberative desire and desiring reason (*NE* VI.2.1139a23–35, 1139b5–6), they don't need an external desire or decision. The virtues do not lead to virtuous actions either by contact like an irrational *dynamis* or because of a "desire or decision" outside themselves. Because the virtues incorporate decision into themselves, they are modes of practical rationality that are not teachable, are not powers for opposites, and do not exclude emotion.[5]

Hardie seems to be right, and to put the matter more politely than he might, when he says that "the ethical virtues, as defined by Aristotle, do not fit in any simple way into the classification of powers in the *Metaphysics,* as rational or irrational."[6] But there is power in Aristotle's approach. A coherent sense in which the virtues are rational but not capacities for opposites will let Aristotle avoid familiar metaphysical debates about free will and necessity that come from thinking that the distinction between rational and irrational *dynameis* is an ethically exhaustive one. "They also make a bad mistake who reduce 'habit' to the 'power' that follows habit" (*Top.* IV.5. 125b15; see *NE* I.12.1101b10–12, *EE* II.1.1220b16–20).

Before going on, I need quickly to dispose of an obvious objection. Aristotle has a simple answer to the question of whether the virtues are rational or irrational *dynameis*. They aren't *dynameis* at all. They are *hexeis* as opposed to *dynameis,* dispositions, not powers. This objection shouldn't bother us. When Aristotle distinguishes *dynamis* from *hexis* in *NE* II.5, he appeals to a meaning of *dynamis*—"those things by which we are said to be liable to feel the passions" (1105b23–24)—much narrower than the metaphysical account as "a principle of change in another thing or in the thing itself as another," (*Met.* IX.1. 1046a12–13; cf. V.12.1019a15–19), a principle of acting or being acted upon (IX.1.1046a16–17). In fact, one of the kinds of *dynameis* offered in that first chapter of *Metaphysics* IX is a *hexis!* "Another [kind of *dynamis*] is a habit of not being acted upon (*hexis apatheias*) for the worse or to destruction by a principle of change in another thing or in the thing itself *qua* other" (1046a13–15). And in the lexicon in *Metaphysics* V, the entry for *dynamis* says that one variety of *dynamis* is "something through which one accomplishes something well or according to decision (*prohairesis*)" (V.12.1019a23–24). Thus he can say at *EE* II.1.1219a31: "Things in the soul are either *hexis* or *energeia*."[7]

## Decision and the Transition from Potency to Act: Ethical Necessity

> Sophistry is not a matter of ability (*dynamis*) but of decision (*prohairesis*).
> (*Rh.* I.1.1355b20)

Like irrational *dynameis* the ethical virtues they need nothing beyond themselves to account for becoming actual. But if the virtues were as automatic as the irrational *dynameis,* they wouldn't be praiseworthy.

The right kind of *dynamis* will let us articulate the right kind of ethical necessity, which will be parsed by terms like reliability and dependability rather than mere predictability (*bebalōs kai ametakinōtikōs, NE* II.4. 1105a33, see I.10.1100b12–14, VIII.3.1156b6–12), terms which sidestep contemporary debates about free will. Someone who acted virtuously and says that she had no "choice" expresses the sort of inevitability signified by this ethical necessity. Psychology has to develop an idea of the psychic powers for such necessity:[8]

> Suppose someone says that pleasant and good objects are compulsive, since they exercise force upon us and are external to us. . . . It is absurd to blame external objects rather than oneself for being too easily caught by such attractions, and to take the credit for one's good behavior but blame pleasant objects for one's bad behavior. (*NE* III.1.1110b9–15)

Only a totally insensible (*anaistheton*) person would not know that each type of activity is the source of the corresponding state; hence if someone does what he knows will make him unjust, he is willingly unjust. (*NE* III.5.1114a9–13)

It is no flaw in the *Metaphysics* that it presents rational and irrational *dynameis* as an exhaustive distinction. The transition from potency to act requires no further explanation because it *is* an explanation, perfectly adequate to theoretical science. A flame burns the flammable, and calling the one a flame and the other flammable shows that their presence is a sufficient explanation for the actuality, burning. That the transition is automatic and necessary shows that the scientist has correctly identified the potency and thus found a sufficient explanation.

A painter painting or a doctor healing needs a further explanation, and so Aristotle says that in addition to being able to act they must want to do something. To quote a little more of the passage I already cited:

> Rational potencies produce contrary effects, so that if they produced their effects necessarily [as irrational *dynameis* do] they would produce contrary effects at the same time; but this is impossible. There must be, then, something else that decides (*anagkē ara heteron ti einai to kurion*); I mean by this, desire or decision (*orexin hē prohairesin*). (*Met.* IX.5.1048a8–11)

A rational ability, plus a desire, completely explains actualities like painting and healing. To ask for more explanation would deny that the potency *is* the actuality *in potentia*. But what counts as a sufficient theoretical explanation will not do for ethics. In ethics, the actuality to be explained is not virtuous action but acting virtuously. If all Aristotle needed to account for were individual acts of virtue, the other candidates for the genus of virtue in II.5, passion and *dynamis,* might suffice—we can explain any act of courage by pointing to a motive, confidence for example, or to a faculty, such as relative insensitivity to fear. The virtues are powers to perform virtuous actions *as* the virtuous person does them. If acting as the virtuous person would act is right specification of the *energeia,* the correlative will not be a rational or an irrational *dynamis* but a *hexis prohairetikē.*

Virtue differs from *technē,* the paradigm for rational *dynameis,* because only the virtues allow a difference between performing a virtuous act and acting as the virtuous man would act. All the goodness of an art resides in the result, while in the virtues there is goodness both in the result and in the character of the agent who does the action. "What comes into being by the crafts has its 'well' in itself; it is enough that the things come to have a certain quality" (*NE* II.4.1105a27–28). In the arts, there is no problem connecting being good and doing well since being good is fully defined by doing well. The art of rhetoric has internal standards, but those standards are ultimately answerable to the external end of persuading an audience. Arts are judged by their results, while the virtues have to answer to two criteria of excellence.

Late in the discussion of justice comes Aristotle's most explicit recognition that he finds in virtue a *dynamis* correlative to *energeiai*, to actions chosen for their own sake:

> Men think that it is in their power to act unjustly, and therefore that it is easy to be just. But this is not so. It is easy to lie with one's neighbor's wife or strike a bystander or slip some money into a man's hand, and it is in one's power to do these things or not; but to do them as a result of a certain disposition of mind is not easy, and is not in one's power. . . . *How* an action must be performed, *how* a distribution must be made to be a just action or a just distribution—to know this is a harder task than to know what medical treatment will produce health. . . . Men think that the just man may act unjustly no less than justly, because the just man is not less but rather more able to any particular unjust thing. . . . But to be a coward and to be guilty or injustice consists not in doing these things (except accidentally), but in doing them in a certain manner. (*NE* V.9.1137a10–23)

If justice were a rational *dynamis* like *technē* then "the just man could act unjustly no less than justly" as the artful rhetorician can argue on both sides of an issue. But ethics has to find a *dynamis* not for particular acts but for "in a certain manner," as the virtuous man would do them. Aristotle finds such a *dynamis* in the first four chapters of Book II as he disvcovers *hexis* as the genus of ethical virtue.

### The Argument of *NE* II.1–4

> Our moral dispositions are formed as a result of the corresponding activities (*ek tōn homiōn energeiōn hai hexeis ginontai*). (*NE* II.1.1103b21–22)

As he uses the potency/act distinction to find the definition of virtue, the only thing Aristotle can say about virtue to begin his path toward defining virtue is that the good condition of the soul, is the product of repeated individual actions or *energeiai*. Acquiring virtue is a process, a *kinēsis,* called habituation, that transforms an indeterminate *dynamis* into a determinate one, a first *energeia:*

> The virtues are engendered in us neither by nature nor yet in violation of nature; nature gives us the capacity to receive them, and this capacity is perfected (*teleioumenois*) by habit. . . . The virtues we acquire by first having actually practiced them (*energēsantes*). (*NE* II.1.1103a23–25, 31)

Because the subject of Aristotle's inquiry is not good action but good action as a function of character, how virtue is acquired is not an accident but part of its definition. Habituation creates potencies that are neither by nor contrary to nature. Stones never learn to stay up, and while art takes repetition and exercise, habituation is not part of the definition of art. As habituation creates these virtuous potencies that are neither by nor contrary to nature, it creates potencies that are neither rational nor irrational in the sense elaborated in the *Metaphysics*.

Thus *NE* II.1 starts by distinguishing ethical from intellectual virtue: intellectual virtue is "for the most part both produced and increased by instruction, and therefore requires experience and time, while ethical virtue is the product of habit" (1103a14–18; but see VI.8.1142a11–18).[9] In spite of needing time and experience, instruction is not a species of habituation. "Reasoning and intelligence naturally arise as they develop" (*Pol.* VII.15.1334b24–25, see too *Met.* IX.5.1047b32–33). The arts and sciences are not acquired through habituation, and how they are acquired is not part of their definition, so they do not teach about the human soul.

The claim that we become virtuous by performing virtuous actions is a very strong psychological thesis. It narrows which good habits and actions will count as virtuous. Heroic actions, for example, are not the sort of thing we become habituated to, since they are by definition exceptional.While virtuous action is accurately described as acting as the virtuous man would act, and while imitation is a source of learning (*Poet.* 4.1449b12–17), we don't become virtuous by imitating the good person or thinking about what he would do—the aspirant to virtue does not wear a bracelet reminding him to ask What Would Pericles Do? The punishments, rewards, and emotional attachments of the family teach us how to act. We learn through looking at and contemplating the actions of others, especially friends (*NE* IX.9.1169b33–1170a4). But none of these is part of the definition of virtue. Natural virtue, the natural emotions of shame, fear and desire for the noble, emulation and imitation are all important factors in moral development, but they are all external means. None can replace habituation without producing something other than Aristotelian virtue.

Where *NE* II.1 showed that virtue is produced by actions, II.2 shows that virtue is a capacity for performing the *same* sort of actions that produced it. "The activities of the virtues will be found in these same actions" (*hai energeiai en tois autois esontai*) (II.2.1104a29). The demand that the virtues be acquired by performing the same actions—the specific *dynamis/energeia* relation in question—makes the virtues into *kinds*. When, as in II.1, virtuous actions lead to the possession of virtue, habituation is a motion, a *kinēsis*, which takes place over time. When a virtuous habit then leads to actions, the transition from *dynamis* to *energeia* is instantaneous. It is by no means a trivial result to find that such actualization results in the same kind of act that produced the habit in the first place. We become courageous by doing courageous deeds, become liberal through acting liberally, etc. (*NE* II.1.1103a34–b2, II.2.1104a33–b3). Habituation in liberality does not prepare someone to act well with regard to anger. Virtuous actions come in kinds.

We acquire the arts and sciences by practice, but not by performing the *same* actions as they then make possible. We learn to play the piano by playing scales and to paint by learning to draw, but there is nothing equivalent to finger exercises and sketching for courage, temperance, or justice. There is not only a large ethical distance between the arts and the virtues; there is an equally large psychological difference. There are no harmless and risk-free exercises for developing one's moral powers. Gambling for match sticks is no preparation for the risks of playing for money one cannot afford to lose, and courage under fire from blanks does not fully prepare one for facing live ammunition. There is no "practice" for practice, not if practice engages the emotions, pleasure and pain, as well as reason.

Aristotle's distinction between ethical action and *technē*, consequently, legislates against a long history of attempts to provide the moral equivalents of musical exercises, from the laws on drinking that open Plato's *Laws*, which were designed to be training in self-control over pleasures and pains, to Pol Pot's training children for cruelty to their neighbors by exercises in cruelty to mice, chickens, and other small animals, or to the varieties of aesthetic and sentimental education that are supposed to train the emotions and thereby make people good. "If you are going to make your first attempt at educating, you ought to watch out in case the risk is being run, not by a guinea-pig, but by on your own sons and the children of your friends, and you should keep from doing just what the proverb says not to do—to begin pottery on a wine jar" (Plato, *Laches* 187b).

*NE* II.3 continues the process of carving out a subject for practical inquiry by tying the metaphysical and psychological discussion of potency and act to moral experience. Pleasure connects potency to act, act to potency: pleasure and pain accompany the process of acquiring virtues and vices, and they are, further, signs of the instantaneous transition from the virtuous habit to the virtuous deed:

> A sign of our habits (*hexeis*) can be made from the pleasure or pain that ac-companies our deeds. . . . A man is temperate if he abstains from bodily plea-sures and finds this abstinence itself enjoyable, profligate if he feels it irksome. (*NE* II.3.1104b3–8)

> Virtuous action is pleasant, or painless—it certainly cannot be painful. (*NE* IV.1.1120a26–27; see III.9.1117b9–11)[10]

We perform virtuous actions and thereby acquire the virtuous potency—that process is often painful. We act virtuously when we actualize that ac-quired potency—that transition from potency to act is pleasant.[11] That vir-tuous actions are pleasant is an experiential way of saying that they are dependable but not automatic or irrational, the kind of necessity appropri-ate to practical rationality.

Having said that pleasure and pain mark the difference between virtuous acts and the same acts done virtuously, Aristotle begins *NE* II.4 by asking whether there is a vicious circle in the relation of potency and act for the virtues:

> Someone might be puzzled about what we mean by saying that we become just by doing just actions and become temperate by doing temperate actions. For [one might suppose that] if we do grammatical or musical actions, we are gram-marians or musicians, and, similarly, if we do just or temperate actions, we are thereby just or temperate. But surely actions are not enough, even in the case of the crafts. . . . To be grammarians, then, we must both produce a grammat-ical result and produce it grammatically—that is to say, produce it in accord with the grammatical knowledge in us. (*NE* II.4.1105a17–26; see too *Met.* IX.8.1049b29–31)

For the last three chapters he has been acting as though the fact that ac-tions preceded and led to the capacities for those actions was common-place, exemplified both in rational powers like the arts and in irrational powers like strength and health. Now, suddenly, he asks about whether there isn't a vicious circle. Only in the ethical case is the question of a vi-cious circle worth raising, because only there is habituation part of the defi-nition of the final state. This is the first, but far from the last, time we see propositions that are trivial outside the realm of praxis becoming central, substantive theses for ethics. We will see it soon (in the last section of this chapter, "Aristotelian Virtue and Modern Freedom") for the idea of the mean. There is no reason to think that the exercise of the arts is pleasant in the way virtuous activity is.

### Practical Knowledge and Inference Patterns: *NE* II.4

> Decision (*prohairesis*) is most closely bound up with virtue, and it discriminates character (*ēthos*) better than action (*praxis*) does. (*NE* III.2. 1111b4–6)

Talking about *ēthos* we do not say that a person is wise or of good understanding, but that he is gentle-tempered or temperate (*NE* I.1103a7–8):

> A person is not said to be of a certain *ēthos* because he is fond of sweet or bitter things. (*EE* II.10.1227b8–10)

The distinctive direction of inference establishes the virtues as a distinct, practical, form of rationality and solves the problem posed by the threat of the vicious circle in *NE* II.4. Missing from *technē* are just those features of virtue which allow it to be the *dynamis* not only of particular good actions but of the good life as well, continuing the dimension of *energeia* that links soul to virtue and then to virtuous action and finally to happiness:

> What is true of crafts is not true of virtues. The products of a craft determine by their own character whether they have been produced well; and so it suffices that they are in the right state when they have been produced. But for actions expressing virtue to be done temperately or justly, it does not suffice that they themselves are in the right state. Rather, the agent must also be in the right state when he does them. First, he must know; second, he must choose them (*prohairesis*), and choose them for themselves (*di' auta*); and third, he must also do them from a firm and unchanging state. (*NE* II.4.1105a26–33; see VI.5.1140b22–24, VI.12.1144a17–20)[12]

There is no problem of circularity for coming to possess the arts or physical qualities such as strength. One gradually grows able to play more difficult pieces on the piano or lift heavier weights. The same power is at work at the start and the end of the process. It just becomes quantitatively more powerful. But acting virtuously, from a stable virtuous character, choosing an act for its own sake, is different in kind from merely doing what is virtuous. In becoming virtuous, we acquire new powers, new *hexeis,* first *energeiai.* We do not simply strengthen or shape naturally existing ones. These new powers include the ability to act virtuously, reliably, effortlessly, pleasurably, and at once.

In the arts, barring chance, the inference from product to artist is secure: looking at a painting tells us if it was skillfully produced, while a courageous or just act does not always indicate the presence of a virtuous agent (*NE* II.4.1105a26–33, V.8.1135a15–1136a10). The quality of your poem tells me that you know what you're doing. I can also tell from the quality of your liberal gift that you know what you're doing, not that you are a liberal person. There is a difference between a virtuous act and that act done as the virtuous man would do it, but no such distinction for the arts. It would be a strange complaint if I said that the construction of this house is just fine, but I would prefer that it were done as the good architect would do it.

Technical production doesn't allow a dependable inference from artist to product, only from product to artist. Given all the right circumstances, an artist cannot be counted on to produce his product. The artist must also want to do it. "Knowing what is healthy or fit . . . makes us no readier to act appropriately if we are already healthy; for having the science of medicine or gymnastics makes us no readier to act appropriately" (*NE* VI.12.1143b24–26). That direction of inference, from product to agent but not conversely, is characteristic of rational *dynameis,* since they can produce opposites.

But neither the direction of inference between process and product that is permitted in the arts, nor the one that is barred, makes sense for virtue. We can't infer from action to agent because of the difference between a virtuous action and acting as the virtuous man would act. But we can count on the virtuous man acting virtuously; the good person, unlike the artist, cannot say, "I could have acted virtuously but I didn't want to."[13] Even more strongly, we can count on the virtuous man acting virtuously in circumstances of deliberative uncertainty, where no one can spell out in advance what the right action would be. The direction of inference for the virtues creates a new form of rationality, with a new form of necessity, unique to praxis. This rationality is not exhibited in teaching and learning, but in a virtuous person's actions and in the pleasures taken in those actions.

The difference between rational *dynameis* and virtue as structures of inference appears most explicitly at the beginning of the discussion of justice:

> What is true of sciences and *dynameis* is not true of *hexeis.* For while one and the
> same capacity or science seems to have contrary activities, a *hexis* that is a contrary

has no contrary activities. Health, e.g., only makes us do healthy actions, not their contraries; for we say we are walking in a healthy way if we are walking in the way a healthy person would. (*NE* V.1.1129a11–17; see VI.13.1144b10–12, 1144b30–1145a6, VIII.5.1157b6–10, *EE* II.10.1227a23–28, VIII.1. 1246a37–b8, *De An.* I.5.411a3–7, III.6.430b21–24)

We impute virtuous actions to the good person as a human being, artistic productions to the artist as an artist. Hence virtuous actions can, while artistic actions cannot, be integrated into a *eudaimōn* life. To be a bad surgeon is not to be a bad person, while being a miser is. "They call someone a bad doctor or a bad actor, though they would never call him simply bad, since each of these conditions is not a vice" (*NE* VII.5.1148b6–9; see *Soph. El.* 20.177b13). Calling someone virtuous says something about his or her soul, while calling someone skilled does not. There is a life of virtue, but no life of *technē*. *Eudaimōnia* is *energeia kat'aretēn*, not *energeia kat'aretēn kai technēn*.[14]

Aristotle maintains that one cannot infer from proficiency in any craft to an assessment of a person's soul and character. While the denigration of *technē* and the limitation of good character to Aristotle's short list of virtues seems alien and offensive to modern ears, we do retain something of his intuition. Many of my students think being an inept writer is nothing to be ashamed of; they distance the skill from their selves. Some, though, take any criticism of their writing as a personal attack. They see writing as a personal and ethical act, and therefore not purely a skill. People might divide over which inferences from a particular ability to character are licit but agree that some abilities are separable from character and others are not. This is Aristotle's distinction between arts and virtues.

Friendship offers a place to see the kind of necessity appropriate to the ethical direction of inference. Friendship, a *hexis* (*NE* VIII.5.1157b29–31), is distinct from the *pathos* of feeling affectionate (*philēsis*) (1157b28–29), and from *eunoia*, the *dynamis* for being well-disposed toward people (*NE* IX.6.1166b30–1167a21, *Rh.* II.1.1378a9–14). The natural love a mother feels for her offspring is friendship as the realization of an irrational *dynamis*. The friendships of utility and pleasure, like rational *dynameis*, always need some desire or decision outside themselves and therefore are unstable and transitory. These friendships have internal ends in the same way that the arts do, as objects of knowledge rather than decision, and only to that limited extent they can wish their friend's good for his own sake (*NE* VIII.3.1156a10–19). Utility and pleasure friends will argue concerning the right amount in a given exchange because there is no inference from the friendship to friendly action.

Friendship between good people is permanent and solid, since the two friends love and care about each other (*NE* VIII.3.1156b9–10; see VIII. 1.1155b31, IX.8.1168b3). True friendship, while less calculating, is *more rational* than the lesser forms. Mutuality guarantees stability, letting true friendship exhibit the practical necessity and direction of inference of reliability rather than predictability. This is ethical necessity.

Rational *dynameis* lead to imperfect actions—actions that aim at a good that is good because it is desired—because such actions are caused by the conjunction of two things, a rational *dynamis* plus decision or desire. *Hexeis,* in contrast, lead to activities that are their own end because the *hexeis* themselves are, considered as *dynameis,* complete. *Complete activities can only be the realization of such complete potencies.* Only because virtuous *habits* are their own good, desirable in themselves, are virtuous *actions* their own good. *Actions that are their own end can only be the realization of such good potencies.* I will complain in chapter 6 that, when in *Metaphysics* IX he discusses the varieties of kinds of *dynameis* and *energeiai,* Aristotle says nothing about whether different kinds of activities require different kinds of powers. In particular, he says nothing about what constraints there are, if any, on the powers that could be realized in perfect *energeiai.* Unlike the *Metaphysics,* the *Ethics* draws a correlation between the kind of power and the kind of activity. Complete activities can only be the realization of complete potencies. Only the virtues are complete powers. Only virtuous actions as their own end are complete activities.

### *NE* II.5: Habit, the Genus of Virtue

> Of things in the soul, some are *hexeis* and *dynameis;* others are *energeiai* and processes. (*EE* II.1.1218b35–36; see *NE* I.8.1098b31–1099a3)

Aristotle begins *NE* II.5 by listing "three things in the soul" (*ta en tē psuchē*) (1105b19–20). We are now in a position to provide a rationale for the list. Two of the three things in the soul, habit and *dynamis,* are correlatives to *energeia.* The third thing in the soul, passion, is not a correlative of *energeia* but a contrary, a contrary of *praxis* (see *EE* II.2.1220b6–30). Praxis is synonymous with *energeia* for ethical purposes, although I will try to firm up that identity in chapter 4.

While these three terms are metaphysically freighted with the potency/ act distinction, Aristotle gives the passions a specifically ethical meaning, and then defines *dynameis* and *hexeis* in terms of passion.[15] Passions are things in the soul accompanied by pleasure and pain. "By passions, I mean appetite, anger, fear, confidence, envy, joy, love, hate, longing, jealousy, pity, in general whatever is accompanied by pleasure or pain" (*NE* II.5. 1105b21–23; see *Rh.* II.1.1378a20–23). The passions are ways in which the appetitive or persuadable soul is acted upon.

"By capacities (*dynameis*) I mean what we have when we are said to be capable of these passions—capable of, e.g., being angry or afraid or feeling pity" (1105b23–25). *Hexeis*, finally, are ways in which we stand well or badly with respect to the passions (*pros ta pathē echomen eu ē kakos*, b26). Standing well means both being affected by them appropriately, at the right time with the right person, etc., and also rightly taking up the passions into a decision and hence an action. If passions are both modes of being acted upon and incipient desires, *hexeis* must stand well in both respects.

These three things in the soul are powers to act rooted in being acted upon, in passion. Practical rationality is the rationality of responsive and receptive beings, not a rationality opposed to emotion. The different relations between being acted upon and acting let us start solving the primary problem of this chapter—how a potency could be rational as embodying and rationalizing decision rather than requiring a further decision for actualization as the rational *dynameis* of *Metaphysics* IX do. We have now posed that problem as how the rational necessity of virtue could run along a line of necessary inference from agent to act.

The rational *dynameis* of the arts and sciences, unlike *dynameis* for feeling passions, are *dynameis* for initiating actions without themselves being moved. "What acts is incapable of being acted upon, when it does not have its form in its matter. . . . It does not have the same matter as what it acts upon" (*Gen. Corr.* I.7.324a5–11, 324b34, 328a20ff.). Rational *dynameis* do not have the same matter as what they act upon and they therefore do not display the rationality specific to responsive and receptive beings. Since the matter of a rational power differs in kind from that of the thing it is acting upon, we need decision or desire to bring the two powers together into an *energeia*.

But in the practical sciences, the alignment of rational with "form separate from matter" and irrational with "enmattered" does not hold. Hexeis are enmattered rational powers, since they are about both actions and passions (*NE* II.3.1104b14, II.6.1107a4–9). The principles of health exist in different matters, in the doctor's mind and the patient's body, and therefore a decision must be added to the doctor's skill to bring it to bear on healing the patient. But the principles of good action are hexeis, the first *energeiai* of the passions, their development and realization, and therefore they are not a form different in kind from their matter, which makes them unteachable.

I started this chapter by noting three obvious objections to thinking of the ethical virtues as rational: they can't be taught, they aren't powers for opposites, and they aren't rational as opposed to emotional. The fact that virtue cannot be taught, far from making it irrational, actually makes it more rational than the arts. "The unproved assertions and opinions of experienced and elderly people, or of *phronimoi,* are as much deserving of attention as those which they support by demonstrations (*ton apodeixeon*)" (*NE* VI.11.1143b11–13). Their virtuous actions are proof of their *phronēsis.* If we pay attention to their reasoning, we will reach better decisions, but we won't become virtuous in the process. The ethical virtues are more rational than the crafts because the crafts need something outside their own productive ability, namely the distinct ability to teach, to mark them as rational. Like the power to cause opposites, the ability to teach is a rational deficiency. Virtues are more rational than the arts.

There are exactly three things in the soul because habits complete the other two things in the soul, passions and the capacities for feeling them. *Hexeis* develop both the capacity for feeling certain passions *and* those passions themselves. "Justice is that *hexis* which renders men apt to do just things and which causes them to act justly and to wish what is just" (*NE* V.1.1129a6–9). In spite of its lack of fit with the other psychological classifications I mentioned at the beginning of the chapter, his blithe declaration that there are three things in the soul has a justification after all.

The virtues bring the soul into good condition and in that way they are complete in themselves. Because the relation of soul to virtue is perfect—the soul is fully realized, fully active, in being virtuous—so too is the relation of virtuous habit to virtuous act perfect. The transition from virtuous habit to virtuous action has a completeness other realizations lack. Virtuous habits, unlike other moral states, are simply and completely actualized in corresponding actions. That is why pleasure does not attach to the vices as it does to the virtues in Book X. The virtues are *the* realizations of the passions.

### Practical Inference and the Ergon Argument

Decision is the principle (*archē*) of praxis. (*NE* VI.2.1139b4–5)

The virtue of a human being will be that state that makes a human being good and makes him perform his function well. (*NE* II.6.1106a22–24)

In section above titled "Practical Knowledge and Inference Patterns: *NE* II.4" I showed that the virtues were different from the arts because of their difference in the direction of inference. Theoretical reason and *technē* draw inferences from effect to cause. Playing the flute proves that I play the flute. Practical reason runs the opposite way. If someone is witty, she will say witty things in the right circumstances. Only the practical pattern of inference allows further inference to the soul, and, I will later show, to happiness. This change in the direction of inference for practical science and for ethical deliberation is in a way the key to the entire *Ethics*. The claim that "all virtue has a twofold effect on the thing to which it belongs: it not only renders the thing itself good, but it also causes it to perform its function well" (*pasa aretē, ou an hē aretē, auto te eu echon apotelei kai to ergon autou eu*) (*NE* II.6.1106a15–17) is nontrivial and substantive for praxis, while it can be a purely formal proposition for other goods and powers.[16]

To see a little more of what is at stake in the double claim in *NE* II.6, consider what it would mean for the nutritive soul. Its *energeiai* are growth, stability and reproduction in kind. There are vices and virtues of the nutritive soul; indeed there are virtues and vices of the body. "It is not only vices of the soul that are voluntary; vices of the body are also voluntary for some people, and we actually censure them. For we never censure someone if nature causes his ugliness; but if his lack of training or attention causes it, we do censure him" (*NE* III.5.1114a21–25).[17] But the two criteria of II.6 collapse into each other in these cases. For the nutritive soul to be in good condition is simply for it to do its work well. Its work is not done for its own sake but for the sake of the states—growth, stability and reproduction—it leads to. "The nutritive soul has no virtue contributing to the proper function of man, since it has no power to act or not to act" (*NE* VI.12.1144a9–11; see *Mag. Mor.* I.2.1185a26–27).

On the other side, the double thesis of II.6 can be interpreted as false rather than trivial for the arts. An art might fully perfect and develop my faculties but do no good in the world. Dermatology and cosmetology are no less arts because they don't cure cancer, but a putative courage that only operated when the outcome didn't matter—Scott again comes to mind—would not be a virtue.

Not only are virtuous acts praised, but the virtuous man is himself praised, while the praise we give the artist is simply derivative from the value of his products, and the same holds for the nutritive soul. The novelist whose insightful and moving depictions of life were motivated by a need for a steady income is no less an accomplished novelist because of that motivation, while if we discover that someone's acts of generosity were motivated by a desire for reputation, we don't think of him as truly generous. We are not praised or blamed for passions or faculties but for *hexeis* (*NE* II.5.1105b28–1106a3; see too 1101b10–12, III.5.1113b26–33).[18] As I will develop the point in chapter 6, only human beings regularly fail to realize their essence. Only for people is realizing one's essence and ergon an achievement, and so worth praise. Only the ethical virtues make the identity of the two effects of virtue into an achievement:

> Every activity (*energeia*) aims at actions expressing its state of character (*hexis*), and to the brave person bravery is noble; hence the end it aims at is also noble, since each thing is defined by its end. The brave person, then, aims at what is noble when he expresses bravery in his standing firm and acting. (*NE* III.8. 1115b20–22)

At just the moments when Aristotle argues for his most critical points, he repeatedly moves from a statement with a purely formal general meaning to that same statement carrying a demanding substantive sense within a restricted area. This typical argument pattern makes it easy to convict him of committing the most elementary fallacies. We have already seen that the virtues both do well and bring the doer into good condition is trivial for all the virtues other than the ethical virtues. I now want to show, similarly, that the ergon argument of I.7 also is trivial and formal outside praxis, substantive for it. Then I will look at the way it is the virtues are not only about the mean, but are themselves means, another manifestation of the same pattern of thought. In each case, what is otherwise trivial and formal becomes a weighty thesis because the direction of inference has been reversed.

All the ergon argument claims is that people, like particular crafts or organs, have functions, and that something's function "is the same in kind as the function of an excellent individual of the kind" (1098a8–9), and consequently "each function is completed well by being completed in accord with the virtue proper to that kind of thing" (a15). Not much seems at stake here, and Aristotle acts as though he is not asserting anything controversial. But he makes substantive claims by extending both sides of that argument.[19]

On the one side, functioning well means having good effects. In a household dominated by small children, the virtue of a knife, that it can cut well, might have bad consequences. But ethical virtue always has good effects. Aristotle extends the other side too. Having a virtue means some matter or power being in good shape. The world-class athlete who has the virtue of running fast, but who does so through a regimen of drugs, has not put his body in good condition. Excelling at the arts of music could develop a soul unsuitable for citizenship (*Pol.* VIII.6.1341a5–14; see Plato, *Laws* VIII.846d–e). Neither of these virtuous extensions, to good effects or good condition, then, holds for the arts or for the excellence of the nutritive soul. The conditions under which Aristotle is entitled to extend the ergon argument in both directions will be the subject of chapter 3. But that he does make these extensions, and make them without comment, is central to his argument. Only the extended sense of II.6 connects virtue to happiness.

The virtues, unlike the rational potencies of *technē*, have the direction of inference that makes the locus of value the person's character rather than the products of those potencies. Therefore the substantive interpretation of the ergon argument and of the twofold effect of virtue applies only when the second and third criteria from II.4 apply, when acts are chosen for their own sakes and are a function of character (*NE* II.4.1105a28–33). Because we can infer from the presence of virtuous habits to the reliability of virtuous deeds, we can draw the further inference that because someone acts virtuously—not just performs virtuous acts—he or she is a good person, while no such inference is allowed from being a good physician, rhetorician, or accountant. Dickens's ability to write about the poor says nothing about his own moral character. The direction of inference creates is unity among the virtues, not the arts. Only the virtues connect good actions to the soul and to happiness along the *dynamis/energeia* dimension.

Because the direction of inference runs from character to action, the unity of the virtues becomes plausible. Explicit attention to the unity of the virtues occupies very little of Aristotle's time in the *Ethics*, just a few lines at the end of Book VI (VI.13.1144b30–45a2). The claim that someone must possess all the virtues in order fully to possess any of them of course makes ethical virtue even more rare and difficult to achieve than it would be if one could possess the virtues separately. It puts very high standards on the virtues. I find the unity of the virtues both attractive and repellent. There is good reason to want the unity of the virtues to be true. It is more than disappointing to find that Rousseau's passion and eloquence are not matched by his attitude toward women and children in his personal life, that Dickens exhibited greater moral sensitivity in his writings than in his life, or that the brilliant music making of Bill Evans or Stan Getz was compatible with self-destructive heroin addiction. The advantage and disadvantage of insisting on the unity of the virtues, as the contrast to the crafts shows, is that the virtues become very deeply a matter of the person's character, and not simply of actions.

The substantive meanings of the ergon argument of *NE* I.7 and of the claim of II.6 about the double effect of the virtues are both valid only for the ethical virtues. There is a third place in Aristotle's argument which moves from formal to substantive meaning. Later in II.6, still on the way to the definition of virtue, he infers that since virtue aims at a mean, it is itself a mean. "Virtue is a mean in so far as it aims at what is intermediate" (1106b27–28; see II.9.1109a22–23, *EE* II.2.1220b33). This crucial inference from being about a mean to being a mean is invalid except for the virtues, although Aristotle once again does not indicate the restriction.

The idea of hitting the mean seems omnipresent in human activity, but the mean will be part of the definition of the ethical virtues alone. *NE* VI.1 begins by saying that the virtues are means, with a level of generality that applies to the arts and sciences too:

> In all departments that have been reduced to a science, it is true to say that effort ought to be exerted and relaxed neither too much nor too little, but to the medium amount and as the right principle decides (*ta mesa kai ho orthos logos*). Yet a person knowing this truth will be no wiser than before; for example, he will not know what medicines to take merely from being told to take everything that medical science or a medical expert would prescribe. (*NE* VI.1.1138b26–32)

While the arts like the virtues aim at hitting a mean, the arts are not themselves means. The doctor aims at the intermediate, bleeding the patient neither too much nor too little. The persuasive speech leaves something to the decision of the hearers. Too much and the audience will be unsure what they are asked to conclude. Too little, and the hearers will feel their role usurped, and will rebel. But it does not follow that the arts of medicine or rhetoric are themselves means. As we will see, because of the intimate relation of practical reason and passion, the virtues will be means between vicious extremes by being *about* means of actions and passions. Only in the virtues, and not in the arts, is there a difference between doing a virtuous act and acting virtuously, and therefore only there is there an inference from being about the mean to being a mean. Only the virtues are means; only the virtues perfect and reveal the human soul.[20]

These three argumentative moves of Aristotle, then, have something in common. All of them are crucial inferences without which the overall argument falls flat. In none of them does he indicate that they apply especially, or with different force, to the ethical virtues. Indeed, he develops each point through comparison to the arts or to physical powers such as strength and health. Yet each of them must be so restricted.

## Aristotelian Virtue and Modern Freedom

> External things, like any instrument, have a limit: everything useful belongs among those things an excess of which must necessarily be either harmful or

not beneficial to those who have them. In the case of the good things connected with the soul, however, the more it is in excess, the more useful it must
necessarily be. (*Pol.* VII.1.1323b7–11)

The virtuous person will reliably act according to her character. If she
always does what is right, could she do otherwise? If she is not compelled
by an external good, is she instead compelled by her internal desire for the
noble? If she always makes the right decision, how is it a decision? What is
the concrete, practical meaning of the virtuous direction of inference?

We ran into a variant of this problem in chapter 1. There is no rule that
the rhetorician should always limit himself to argument and never resort
to other methods of winning, and we wondered if there was a parallel for
the ethical virtues. I now can give a deeper answer, using the practical
direction of inference and the unique rationality of the ethical virtues. The
difference between the freedom found in the voluntary and the freedom
the virtuous person exercises in decision, the difference between the rationality of rational *dynameis* and the rationality of virtuous *hexeis*, parallels
the difference between thinking and knowing. I can think whatever I like.[21]
I can think contradictions. But I can only know things that are true. More
can be thought than known. Consequently it looks like the thinker, relying
on a rational *dynamis,* acts more freely and has a wider field of possibilities
than the knower. Being disciplined by the truth restricts freedom.

On the other hand, the knower has thoughts that no mere thinker can
have. What the thinker thinks might be true, but he does not know it, but
only thinks it. The ignorant person can believe that the world is flat or
round, but she cannot know that it is round. Similarly, the virtuous person
can decide to do something that the person simply acting from a rational
*dynamis* cannot do, namely act virtuously for its own sake. It is, as Aristotle
said in the lines I quoted from *NE* V.9, "easy to lie with one's neighbor's
wife or strike a bystander or slip some money into a man's hand, and it is in
one's power to do these things or not; but to do them as a result of a certain
disposition of mind is not easy, and is not in one's power" (1137a6–9).
The liberal man cannot decide to waste his money, but only he can decide
to act liberally. While there are things that can be thought but not known,
the advantage is not all on that side.

To return to the analogy to rhetoric. The Aristotelian rhetorician was
limited to argument, while the sophist does anything to win. The sophist,
without an internal end, looks freer than the Aristotelian and has available a
wider range of means of persuasion. But there is one thing the sophist cannot do: reason with someone. He can *use* reasoning, but using reasoning
to manipulate is not reasoning. The freedom of the sophist has a price.

Anyone can decide to do a virtuous act, just as the sophist can use reasoning, but deciding to act virtuously is not open to all.[22]

The voluntary nature of rational *dynameis* is captured by the remark in the *Politics* that the democracy consists in doing as one likes (Pol. VI.2. 1317b12–13). Similarly: "To be under constraint, and unable to do everything one might resolve to do is advantageous. The license to do whatever one wishes cannot defend against the low element in every human being" (Pol. VI.4.1318b38–1319a1). By contrast, practical reasoning and virtuous action correspond instead to these words from the *Metaphysics*, which is at the greatest possible distance from the libertarian conception of freedom as indifference:

> In a household the free people are least at liberty to act at random, but have everything or most things ordered, whereas slaves and beasts have only a little ordered to the common end [of the household], and mostly [are at liberty to act] at random; for that is the sort of originating principle that the nature of each of them is. (*Met.* XII.10.1075a18–23; see I.2.982b25–26)

> One should not think it slavery to live in harmony with the constitution, but safety. (*Pol.* V.9.1310a34–36)

Who, then, is more free, the person acting from voluntary abilities to do or not do all kinds of things, or the person who chooses to achieve internal goods? The virtuous person is not free to act viciously and the purely voluntary agent is not free to engage in actions that are their own good. The promiscuous person is free to have sex with anyone he can catch, but not free to love, while the lover is committed to an individual, and so restrained from other sexual objects. The purely voluntary agent, like the sophist in the first chapter, is condemned to being judged by results, since results are all he can point to. The virtuous person can be judged by intention and character as well as results.

## CHAPTER 3

# The Varieties of Moral Failure

The *Ethics*, like the *Rhetoric*, focuses on how things go right. Central ethical phenomena for contemporary concern, such as moral dilemmas, moral luck, moral partisanship, tragedy, are at best peripheral for Aristotle, in spite of the ingenuity of philosophers who find precedent in Aristotle for their own concerns. Even *akrasia*, which Aristotle does talk about, occupies a different place in his moral universe than in ours.[1]

I have two simple questions. If Aristotle does not care primarily about moral dilemmas, moral luck, tragedy, the failure to be morally motivated, and the rest, why doesn't he? If the Greeks were as aware of the place of conflict in life as we are, why are these things peripheral phenomena for Aristotle? And, second, what does he worry about instead? Where we locate the most significant dangers of moral failure reveals a lot about our sense of the moral landscape. I want to look at the conditions under which Aristotle's concentration on success makes sense.

First, then, why doesn't Aristotle focus, as so many moderns do, on moral failures and dangers, such as tragedy and moral luck? Moral failures and dangers are mostly invisible in Aristotle's own exposition for three reasons. First, the *Ethics* follows Aristotle's procedure in other sciences by looking at things working out smoothly. His physical works focus primarily on nature, not chance. Metaphysics is a science of substance, not accident. Second, the background assumption of the naturalness of the polis—an assumption whose content I will spell out here and in chapter 5—makes it plausible to expect such smoothness:

If we were on the moon, we should ask neither whether nor why [an eclipse] was taking place; the answers to both questions would be simultaneously obvious, because from the act of perception we should be able to apprehend the universal. (*An. Post.* II.2.90a24–29)

Living in the polis gives us a privileged epistemic position. Aristotle's *phronimos* and his political philosopher are in the position with regard to political truth that someone on the moon would be toward eclipses: once they saw the phenomenon, the cause would be obvious. "The principle (*archē*) is the fact (*to hoti*). And if it appears accurately, then there will be no need to ask for the why (*dioti*)" (*NE* I.2.1095b6–7).[2] We are not in that position today, and so need to take a more critical stance. As I will argue at the end of this chapter, no longer being ethically on the moon will transform the nature of *phronēsis* and with it the nature of virtue.

There is a final reason why Aristotle's attention is not on the phenomena of conflict, tragedy, and luck which attract us today. These phenomena are individual failings. The moral failures I focus on in this chapter are more structural features of praxis.[3] Starting from the first sentence of the *Ethics,* Aristotle looks at practices, not at individual agents, at carpentry and not at Hermocrates the carpenter, and at courage rather than Achilles. The goods of practices, intermediate between the ends of particular actions and the final end of happiness, allow Aristotle to construct a practical science, with rational and causal connections centering around virtue as the middle term connecting the human soul and particular actions with happiness. Here too, in making virtuous practices the focus of attention, he follows the same procedure as in the theoretical sciences, where, for example, we look at nature by studying things that have a nature, neither nature in general nor individual bodies. The central phenomena are species rather than being as such or individuals.[4]

The varieties of moral failure draw attention to the conditions under which Aristotle's project makes sense, the conditions under which praxis is rational and rationality can be practical. The conditions under which praxis can be rational are the conditions under which one can undertake *energeiai* rather than *kinēseis.*

Those are reasons why Aristotle doesn't worry about the kinds of moral failure that preoccupy us. What, though, are the varieties of moral failure that he should worry about? "Every craft (*technē*) and every method (*methodos*), and likewise every action (*praxis*) and decision (*prohairesis*), seems to aim at some good" (*NE* I.1.1094a1–3). Craft or art, method, action, and decision are middle terms that connect a good with a desire that aims at it. The varieties of moral failure are generated by the ways in which goods and desires can fail to be properly connected. I want here to lay out the four kinds of moral failure, saving examples for when I look at each in detail.

First, some aspect of human need and desire might not be subject to a practice at all. There may be no internal good corresponding to some given external good. "In all pursuits *directed by a science,* we must labor and be idle neither too much nor too little, but the intermediate amount prescribed by right reasoning" (*NE* VI.1.1138b26–29). But not all aspects of life have such scientific treatment. There is no guarantee that the objects of our desires can be secured through our deliberate efforts.

The other three places for the emergence of failure can be arrayed alongside a sentence from MacIntyre: "No quality is to be accounted a virtue except in respect of its being such as to enable the achievement of three distinct kinds of good: those internal to practices, those which are the goods of an individual life, and those which are the goods of community." [5] Practices must have their own internal, guiding standards of excellence. But, second, what if there is an internal end for either art or virtue, but achieving that end does not lead to achieving the given end that motivated the practice in the first place? An internal end not aligned with its own external end will be my second kind of moral failure. They fail, that is, to meet the standard of MacIntyre's idea of goods internal to practices.

Third, some practice might achieve its good. Yet there is no guarantee that the goods internal to practices are the goods of a happy life. Aristotle's arts, for example, have goods internal to practices but not to the good life.[6] For a virtue to fail to be connected to the good condition of the soul is the third kind of moral failure. They are not MacIntyre's "goods of an individual life." Fourth, a virtue might contribute to human flourishing, yet in a way that makes its happy practitioner at odds with the community in which he or she lives. The anti-Aristotelian separation of ethics from politics will be the final kind of moral failure.

### Failures Degree Zero

For the noble man the same things are both advantageous and noble; but for the multitude these things do not coincide, for things absolutely good are not also good for them, whereas they are good for the good man; and to the noble man they are also noble, for he performs many noble actions because of them. But he who thinks that one ought to possess the virtues

for the sake of external goods does noble things only by accident. (*EE*
VIII.3.1249a7–16)

> One should not train in virtue as the city of the Lacedaemonians does. For it is
> not in this way that they differ from others, by not considering the greatest of
> good these things to be the same things others do, but by considering that
> these things are got through some sort of virtue. But since they consider these
> good things and the gratification deriving from them to be greater than that
> deriving from the virtues, the sort of virtue in which they are trained is only
> that useful and necessary for the acquisition of good things. That the sort of
> virtue is rather to be cultivated that governs the use of these good things, that
> is preeminently the sort of virtue that is cultivated in leisure, and that it is to be
> cultivated on its own account, is evident. (*Pol.* VII.15. 1334a40–b3; see too
> *EE* VII.15.1248b37ff., VII.14.1333b5ff.)

Before considering the four varieties of moral failure, I need to make explicit
a deep presupposition of Aristotelian practical rationality and of the first sentence of the *Ethics*. There are goods we aim at. The external goods that we
think are good really are good. They have value beyond being the occasions
for virtue.[7] Aristotle situates his vision of the good life between those, call
them Platonists, who insist that only internal goods are truly good, and
those, such as the Spartans in my quotations and the ambitious young men
who are the audience of the *Ethics*, for whom external goods are the only final ends. The *Ethics* is the complex and rewarding work it is because Aristotle insists that both kinds of goods really are good. The *Rhetoric* showed
that even instrumental activities have internal goods. The *Ethics*, and my first
chapter, showed that even virtuous activities aim at external goods.

Aristotle's enterprise would be impossible in a world in which poverty
was better than wealth, or being scourged better than being honored, or a
world in which wealth and honor made no difference to the quality of one's
life. Classifying natural goods as indifferents or rejecting them as goods of
the flesh would make replace Aristotle's project by a different kind of moral
inquiry.[8] Aristotelian deliberation and practical reasoning could never get
started without presupposing external goods. People rightly think that natural goods are good but wrongly infer that they should therefore desire and
choose such goods. The difference between what is good and what I
should do sets the task for deliberation, because natural goods aren't always
good for the individual).

It is hard, emotionally and practically, to accept the fact that something is
truly good but not good for me: in the first chapter (at VI.4) I used the example of the best teacher not being the best teacher for me. Recognizing the

difference between what is good and what is good for me, what I should wish
for and what I should choose, is the beginning of Aristotelian practical wisdom. The better we are, the more natural goods are good for us. That is,
natural goods are good for people for whom they aren't the greatest goods.
External goods guarantee against the circularity of the virtues being the
measure of virtue and the moral narcissism that regards the lack of attention
to consequences as a mark of virtue. Ethical virtues have value in a practical
universe that is already value-laden. Practical goods are better than natural
goods and determine when natural goods are good for us:

> The things men fight about and think the greatest, honor and wealth and
> bodily excellences and pieces of good fortune and powers, are good by nature
> but may possibly be harmful to some men owing to their characters. (*EE* VIII.
> 3.1248b27–31; see *NE* V.1.1129b1–6, *Pol.* I.2.1253a33–37)

> The excellent person is one of a sort for whom on account of his virtue the
> things that are good unqualifiedly are good. (*Pol.* VII.13.1332a22–23)

There is a further aspect of failure degree zero, another background assumption that must be true for Aristotle's project even to begin. The *Ethics*
doesn't presuppose much metaphysics, but arts and virtues require a human world of regularities, not chance. "It does not appear that nature is
episodic, like a bad tragedy" (*Met.* XIV.3.1090b19–20). It must be a world
in which our actions and interventions can make a difference, rather than a
world that is fully fated or determined. If one lives in a world without room
for *technē* and praxis, then one may as well live a life of present pleasures.
Thus Croesus thinks Solon a fool for claiming that "no man is happy until
one sees the end." Solon lives in a political world of *technē* and praxis, and
Croesus does not. So Croesus "sent [Solon] away, making no further account of him, thinking him assuredly a stupid man who would let by present goods and bid him look to the end of every matter."[9] Aristotle consequently puts the Asiatic vision of chance, determinism, and fate aside in
order to discuss happiness as *energeia kat'aretēn:*

> If it is *better* to be happy as a result of one's own exertions than by the gift of
> fortune, it is reasonable to suppose that this is how happiness is won; inasmuch
> as in the world of nature things have a natural tendency to be ordered in the *best*
> possible way, and the same is true of the products of art, and of causation of any
> kind, and especially the highest. (*NE* I.9.1099b20–25)[10]

Just as I asked in chapter 1 what "best" meant in the claim that deliberators
"assume the end and consider how and by what means it is to be attained;

and if it seems to be produced by several means they consider by which it is most easily and best (*kallista*) produced" (*NE* III.3.1112b16–17), so here I ask what "better" can mean in the assertion that it is "*better* to be happy as a result of one's own exertions than by the gift of fortune."

### First Failure: No Art or Virtue Possible

The most artful of these works are those which involve chance the least. (*Pol.* I.11.1258b36–37; see *Top.* III.3.118b8–10)

There is no knowledge by demonstration of chance conjunctions. (*An. Post.* I.30.87b19)

There are arts, aren't there? (Plato, *Gorgias* 450c)

"Every craft and every method, and likewise every action and choice, seems to aim at some good" (*NE* I.1.1094a1–3). What if there are goods for which there are no practices, no internal goods? (I am going to limit practices here to arts and virtues; nothing turns on not explicitly considering "method and decision" or trying to differentiate them from art and virtue, respectively. "Method" rarely appears in the rest of the *Ethics,* and I have already shown the relation between action and decision in chapter 2.) There is, I believe, nothing substantive under the title of such useful qualities as "teaching," "leadership," or "being a good parent" in spite of all the self-help books that sell so well.[11] These are not *kinds* of actions, valuable and desirable as they might be. They are all good qualities, but no one knows how to do them intelligently. We only apply those names retrospectively because of success. Schools of Education make claims about teaching as an art, but there is as little reason to take those claims seriously as there is for charm schools. Actions such as leading, charming, parenting, and teaching fail to be "practices" in this most minimal way. There is an indefinite set of things we might do that could succeed as leading, parenting, and teaching. Apart from success, there are no recognized standards of what doing well at these activities consist in.[12]

The *Rhetoric* opens with apparently very open criteria for an art:

All people, in some way, share in both rhetoric and dialectic. . . . Some do these things randomly and others through an ability acquired by habit, but since both these ways are possible, it is clear that it would also be possible to do the same by following a path; for it is possible to observe (*theorein*) the cause of why some succeed by habit and others accidentally, and all would at once agree that such observation is the activity of an art (*technē*). (I.1.1354a1–10)

There is a large problem with that argument. Observing causes of success doesn't give someone a rational capacity for making something, as Aristotle defines *technē* in *NE* VI.4.1140a20–21. I can have a historian's knowledge of the origins of wars without being able to prevent them. The *Ethics* itself may discover the reasons some people do virtuous acts by habit or by luck, but the *Ethics* is not thereby a *technē* for virtue.

Even within the *Rhetoric* there are things people do for which there is no art. There is no art of convincing someone that one has certain emotions, no art, in that sense, of sincerity. Success rather requires, as Aristotle states in the *Poetics,* either a "sympathetic nature" or madness:

> If their natural powers are equal, those who are actually in the emotions are the most convincing; he who is agitated blusters and the angry man rages with the maximum of conviction. And that is why poetry needs either a sympathetic nature or a madman, the former being impressionable and the latter inspired. (*Poet.* 17.1455a30–36)

There is no claim that studying how these stylistic effects are created will be of any practical use. Actors and politicians may give pleasure, but no matter how successful they are, they do not achieve their good by art. Therefore, there are ends for which there is no art or virtue. The art of rhetoric may be able to explain these things, but not produce them.[13] Without internal or guiding ends, these are not really practices at all.

Writing clear prose is unfortunately such an activity for me. I can identify causes of success in others' writing, but there is little carryover from that ability to a productive power. There is no internal object I aim at as a way of intelligently approaching the external end. I do not deliberate about how to express myself effectively. I just try to remember the tricks I have learned.

The *Gorgias* offers an ethically important example of the failure of the opening inference of the *Rhetoric.* Polus maintains that the art of rhetoric can defend us against those who want to do injustice to us but sees no need for an art to protect us from committing injustice. Socrates has the opposite concerns. He thinks that it takes a lot of intelligence to avoid committing injustice, while it isn't worth giving much attention or energy to the threat of being injured by another. Some people by habit or chance have ways of avoiding being injured—some make themselves inconspicuous or create an appearance of having nothing that anyone would want, and others make themselves look terrifying—and others have ways of avoiding harming others—they have a lower threshold of guilt or fewer ambitions than others—but whether there could be arts of avoiding being injuring or of injuring others seems a very different proposition.

## Second Failure: Art and Virtue Exist, But Do Not Work Well Enough

Virtue is not acquired and preserved by means of external goods, but the other way around. (*Pol.* VII.1.1323a40–41)

Good men must be useful. (Plato, *Meno* 96e)

It is shameful to be unable to make use of good things. (*Pol.* VII.15. 1334a36–37)

Homer has above all taught the rest how to speak falsehoods as a poet ought. (*Poet.* 24.1460a18–19)

Sometimes there are goods we would like to acquire or achieve, and we can intelligently aim at them. We have passed the first hurdle and can rationally deliberate and aim at our good. While both the *Rhetoric* and the *Ethics* insist that success at the internal end does not guarantee success at the external end, there must be some correlation between internal and external end, although the kind of connection will vary and will be different for the arts and the virtues. Socrates and Thrasymachus fight over whether virtue pays and whether it ought to pay. Aristotle's cooler way of framing the same problem is to ask about the relation between internal and external ends. Since internal and external ends are distinct, there is always the possibility that, for a variety of reasons, the internal end will not lead adequately to the external one.[14]

### Virtue or Art Ineffective

It is quite possible for brave people not to be the best soldiers. Perhaps the best will be those who are less brave, but possess no other good; for they are ready to face dangers, and they sell their lives for small gains. (*NE* III.9. 1117b17–20; see *EE* III.1.1229a21–32)

The liberal man is an easy person to deal with in money matters; he can be cheated, because he does not value money, and is more distressed if he has paid less than he ought than he is annoyed if he has paid more. (*NE* IV.1. 1121a4–7; see V.9.1136b20–21, *EE* VII.2.1237b30, *Rep.* 343d)

People blame fortune because the most deserving men are the least wealthy. But this is really perfectly natural: you cannot have money, any more than anything else, without taking pains to have it. (*NE* IV.1.1120b17–20; see I.8.1099a5–7)

The existence of internal ends generates a further complexity. We might do our best, and follow the dictates of some art or virtue, and still fail. A man's very bravery could contribute to the army's defeat in battle. If integrity frequently created dangers that were avoided by people without moral scruples, the kind of value such a virtue represented would be severed from the external goods it was supposed to secure. (The classic example is the person whose honesty compels him to reveal the location of a Jew to a Nazi.) Morality could then start to wear its worldly failure as a badge of pride. Some forms of virtue, such as some Christian accounts and some interpretations of Socrates, can flourish without being rewarded. The *irrationality* of the world means that good deeds are often punished, and that there is consequently the need for a justice beyond this world and perhaps beyond reason, in which these irrationalities are straightened out.[15] When the fact that virtue is its own reward becomes a reason to be careless about external success, Aristotle's ties between virtue and honor no longer make sense. Neither does Aristotle's idea of proper pleasures supervening on virtuous activities make sense, since that pleasure comes in part from seeing our good efforts realized in the world. When such moral failure becomes the rule rather than the exception, we have left Aristotle's world.[16]

The general correlation between Aristotelian virtue and external success has contemporary counterparts. Thus Charles L. Black argues that most cases in which law does not produce justice are corrigible failures of lawyers and judges, not failures of the law itself. Legal justice, that is, is the internal end through which we generally achieve the external end of justice. Bad results, he says,

have almost always been traceable to some kind of obtuseness with regard to technical possibility. The techniques of our law were sharpened for attaining the sensible, the just result. They are not always adequate to justice, or to the correcting of injustice. There are some musical compositions that you couldn't play on the piano. But I repeat, it is overwhelmingly true that if you seek ye shall find, in the technical weaponry, the means needful for a fair outcome.[17]

In the second variety of moral failure, there is an internal end, but it is not connected strongly enough to the external end. The general correlation between internal and external success Black asserts is no necessary truth, but a contingent one:

> Largely because of the slavery issue, individual legal arguments and judicial decisions in the antebellum period are often marked by conflict between the pursuit of the internal goods of the tradition (logical argument, textual fidelity, and so on) and the external goods of maintaining the Union and the institutional power and prestige of the courts.[18]

Slavery then created not only a moral crisis in which argument failed and only force could settle the issue, but it produced an epistemological crisis of practical reasoning because internal goods were no longer means to securing external ends.

Health is an external end, and there is a medical art which rationally tries to accomplish it, so we are past the first sort of failure. But there still can be failure. Medicine might be able to treat only unimportant ailments. Dermatologists confidently clear up acne, but psychiatrists are helpless in front of severe depression. My methods of self-control work only when it doesn't matter much whether I'm in control or not. An art or a virtue of justice allows me to adjudicate about most contracts, torts, and even crimes, but when it comes to constitutional law and fundamental questions of justice, courts rely on prejudices that seem to lie beyond argument.

In these cases, an internal end exists, but it is not strongly enough connected to the initial given end. While, for example, Aristotle says that "virtue, once it obtains equipment, is in a certain manner particularly able to apply force, and the dominant element is always preeminent in something that is good, so that it is held that there is no force without virtue" (*Pol.* I.6.1255a13–16; see VII.1324b22–1325a14), he also says that nature unfortunately does not work things out so that despotic, free, and slavish souls are easy to identify: "Nature wishes to make the bodies of free persons and slaves different. . . . Yet the opposite often results: some having the bodies of free persons; while others, the souls" (*Pol.* I.5.1254b27–34). Should nature fail like that in more central cases than slavery is for Aristotle, Aristotelian practical reasoning and virtue would have to be replaced by a different kind of practical reasoning that would either ignore consequences in favor of intentions, or consider consequences as morally relevant in a way different than Aristotle does. As Jeremy Waldron puts it, "The curse of injustice . . . deprives us of any guarantee that our own good intentions will bear good fruit."[19] Aristotle's good person does not live in a world cursed by injustice.

## Virtue Outdone by Something Else

With a view to action experience seems in no respect inferior to art. (*Met.* I.1.981a31)

Not only are there no guarantees that the guiding end will regularly achieve the given end. Experience, luck, or something else might do better. The internal end of a virtue or art may not be connected strongly enough to the external end because of a comparative disadvantage.

Machiavelli, for example, proposes to teach an art of ruling. But his art, rational and teachable as it is, is inferior to whatever moved Moses, Theseus, Romulus, and Darius, who had no Machiavelli to teach them. People who don't know what they're doing succeed anyway, through luck, divine favor, or fate. It is a cosmic failure that rationality should lose out to other means of securing the external end. The connection of internal to external good is too weak to be reliable because fortune can enable someone else to get the external good. Aristotle appears open to this possibility: "*phronēsis* is not the only thing which acting in accordance with goodness (*kat'aretēn*) causes happiness; we also speak of the fortunate as faring well" (*EE* VIII. 2.1246b36–1247a2). Yet the thrust of the *Ethics* is in the other direction: "if it is better to be happy as a result of one's own exertions than by the gift of fortune, it is reasonable to suppose that this is how happiness is won" (*NE* I.9.1099b20–21). Other circumstances may not be so reasonable. What if it was better to be lucky than good?

The weaker the connections between internal and external end, the more vulnerable art or virtue is to competitors who ignore the internal end altogether. It's one thing for a lawyer occasionally to lose cases by sticking to argument, or even for her occasionally to aim at the external end when it looks as though argument will fail. But it would be quite another thing if argument consistently lost out to either nonargumentative direct evidence or to appeals to the judges' prejudices. In any given case, it could be right for the artful rhetorician to deploy something that lies outside her art, but if she regularly resorted to the inartistic, then too the value of art would be transformed.

## Virtues Become Vices as They Aim at External Success

Those of the Greeks who are at present held to be the best governed and the legislators who established these regimes evidently did not organize the things pertaining to the regime with a view to the best end, or the laws and education with a view to all the virtues, but inclined in a crude fashion toward those which are held to be useful and of a more aggrandizing sort. (*Pol.* VII.13.1333b5–10)

Both the arts and the virtues can become corrupted by being directed to an external end; what was an internal end becomes a collection of means for achieving the given end. The sophist deploys the same arts as the rhetorician and dialectician, but directs them by a purpose and choice outside the faculty itself. He lives by the external end alone:

> In the case of rhetoric, however, there is the difference that one person will be [called] *rhētōr* on the basis of his knowledge (*kata ten epistemen*) and another on the basis of his deliberative choice (*kata ten prohairesein*), while in dialectic "sophist" refers to decision [of specious arguments], "dialectician" not to decision (*ou kata ten prohairesin*), but to ability (*kata ten dynamin*) [at argument generally]. (*Rh.* I.1.1355b18–21)[20]

While the sophist is governed by an ulterior purpose, it does not follow that the rhetorician and dialectician don't care about winning and ignore all external ends. The rhetorician and dialectician aim at the external end via the internal end. This is the difference between arguing and using argument, the difference between *phronēsis* and cleverness (see *NE* VI.12, VII.9.1152a10–14, *Top.* VIII.11.161b19).

In the *Politics,* Aristotle makes a similar criticism of Spartan education, here criticizing a virtue, not a craft, for being subordinated to an external end:

> The Spartans, so long as they persevered in their love of exertion, had preeminence over others, while at present they fall short of others in both gymnastic and military contests. For it was not by exercising the young in this manner that they stood out, but merely by the fact of their training against others who did not train. The element of nobility, not what is beastlike (*to kalon all' ou to thēriōdes*), should play the leading role. For it is not the wolf or any of the other beasts that would join the contest in any noble danger, but rather a good man. (*Pol.* VIII.3.1338b24–32; see II.9.1271a21–b3, VII. 15.1334a30–b3)

When the fit between external and internal end becomes unreliable, Aristotelian virtue cannot develop. If the courageous man wisely flees to fight another day, he will be acting as the courageous man would act, but not act courageously—this has no parallel in the arts. Still, the circumstances in which it is right for the courageous man to retreat cannot be usual. If the habit of acting appropriately in battle led equally to fighting and fleeing, there would be no identifiable virtue.[21] Moreover, practices of praise and blame make sense only in a world in which good and bad actions are constantly visible. Machiavelli thinks that virtue and vice are opaque because people deceive themselves and judge only by what they can see and what is in their own interest: the line between reasoning and rationalizing, between cleverness and *phronēsis,* disappears.[22]

Ethical internal ends have a different kind of authority than artistic internal ends do, so that overriding a virtuous internal end in the name of a good external end is more problematic than overriding a technical end. To poison the enemy's food rather than act courageously in battle is a more serious worry than winning over a jury with personal charm rather than argument. Moral failures have a different place in the world from artistic failures. Because of the greater authority of the internal ends of the virtues, *phronēsis,* unlike *technē,* is about the individual. No art is about the particular, and so the practitioner always has to decide, on the basis of something other than art, whether to aim at the internal or external end in a particular case. The physician can recognize that the art of medicine would fail a particular patient and aim at externally defined health instead. She can step outside the art of medicine and aim at the external end. Because virtue is about the highest good, there is no such stepping outside.

### Third Failure: Individual Practices in Conflict with a Happy Life

To seek everywhere the element of utility is least of all fitting for those who are magnanimous and free. (*Pol.* VIII.3.1338b2–4)

There is not the same kind of correctness in poetry as in politics, or indeed any other art. (*Poet.* 25.1460b13–15)

The modern age was as intent on excluding political man, that is, man who acts and speaks, from its public realm as antiquity was on excluding *homo faber.* (Hannah Arendt, *The Human Condition*)[23]

Virtue and skill would become competitors if the virtues were to demand so much knowledge that the other two criteria of *NE* II.4, choice and character, became minimized. What if, on the one hand, it took a lot of knowledge to act virtuously, if knowing the right amount of a given passion or action required specialized study? What if, to be a competent politician or judge, you had to learn economics, or psychology beyond the minimal amount Aristotle thinks necessary? What if, on the other, the study needed to perfect one's skills destroyed the desires necessary for virtue? The professional estate planner might be more effective than the person possessing the virtue of liberality at giving the right amount of money to the right people, and psychologists might give better advice than parents or religious authorities, to the extent that practical success came to depend on emotional detachment instead of emotional engagement. The more I understand economics, the more I will let the poor die of hunger because I know that generosity only creates welfare dependence, and the more will I see selfishness not as a vice but as a natural passion with desirable outcomes. What was a virtue now looks like sentimental weaknesses.

For a final example, what if rhetoric were the route to *phronēsis?* Adepts at finding the available means of persuasion could easily succumb to what Veblen called a "trained incapacity" and neglect the development of their own virtues by relying on craft instead. The preliminary stratagem of finding arguments on both sides of a question could become the whole of practical reason, making any consequent decision arbitrary. Thus modern lawyers increasingly find that the demands of technique eliminate any sense of justice not derivative from their craft, much like Aristotle's professional musicians.[24]

A moral psychology which makes the emotions a constitutive part of good action and the good life becomes obsolete when the internal goods of virtue are surpassed by the internal ends of art, for which the emotions are only an encumbrance. If logos unencumbered by feeling were superior to the interrelation of thought and character that I showed in the last chapter to be unique to virtue, it would be silly to deliberate when we can calculate instead. Machiavelli recommends that the aspiring prince act as a "prudent archer" does, "who when the place they wish to hit is too far off, knowing how far their bow will carry, aim at a spot much higher than the one they wish to hit, not in order to reach this height with their arrow, but by help of this high aim to hit the spot they wish to" (*The Prince,* c. 6). Such self-deception became obsolete once Galileo shows how to calculate the correct initial angle for the arrow.

The basic problem in this new set of failures is one that Aristotle expresses in that crucial claim that the virtues both "render the thing itself good, and also cause it to perform its function well" (*NE* II.6.1106a15–17). The virtues satisfy two distinct conditions of excellence, while the arts need satisfy only the second. A new set of moral failures, specific to ethics, comes about when the two conditions are not jointly satisfied. I can have an art which fully perfects my artistic skills while doing nothing for, or even harming, my development as a moral being. Like the professional musician I will look at next, I can become good at causing effects in the world at the cost of stunting the growth of my soul.

In the second variety of moral failure, Machiavelli recognized that the lucky man might do better than someone who had learned Machiavellian lessons. But *The Prince* itself poses the threat—Machiavelli's hope—that an *art* of ruling might be more powerful and effective than the traditional *virtues*. Socrates suggests the superiority of *technē* to virtue at the beginning of the *Republic* when he points out to Polemarchus that when it is question of using money, the economist is more useful than the just person, and the just person seems useful only when the money is useless, preserved rather than used (333d–e).

It is not only the worthless man, or the lucky one, who might be a better fighter than the courageous one. The professional soldier might be better too. The courageous Polish cavalry was as helpless against the technology of German tanks as an innocent and just layperson would be against the craft of an accomplished litigator. Gorgias is better than his physician brother at getting patients to take their medicine and is therefore better at healing. Rhetorical skill is more powerful than medical skill. But what if Gorgias possessed a skill, such as an art of foreseeing unintended consequences, that also made him better at achieving *moral* results than the virtuous person?

For example, a growing number of academic departments have discovered—or have been told—that the traditional practice of taking turns in ruling and being ruled is obsolete, that rotating the office of department chair is no longer functional given the special skills needed in the contemporary university. The world in which we could rule and be ruled in turn is a better world than that dominated by expert leaders, but that by itself does not tell us how to respond to changing circumstances. Political life might be obsolete in the face of the modern administrative state. For better or worse, traditional academic self-governance has as much chance of persisting as the Polish cavalry.

When an art does a job better than virtue itself can, people have several options. Men engaged in the noble occupation of hunting were threatened when the womanly and methodical cultivation of the fields generated more utility with less risk than did their mode of life. They could respond by making the uselessness of hunting further evidence of its nobility, or by taking over farming for themselves, thereby conferring their own nobility on the activity. We can reserve some competitions for amateurs alone, as the modern Olympic Games tried to do, or prevent working-class professionals from learning some skill, for example by making it too expensive, like playing polo or mastering Greek composition. Virtue wins the competition against art by changing the rules, and then the distinction between virtue and art becomes a division by social class. In the 1960s, college basketball outlawed dunking. Blacks were much better at it than whites, and so dunking denigrated the skills that the people making the rules associated with good basketball. Their sons couldn't successfully compete. Virtue's superiority over art seems an aristocratic defense of privilege engaged in a futile struggle against the evidence. Lack of utility is proof of nobility.[25]

Often the victory of art over virtue presents itself as the danger of specialization, as in the treatment of music in *Politics* VIII. Becoming too good a musician is vulgar. "It is evident that the learning [of music] should neither be an impediment with a view to later activities, nor make the body vulgar and useless with a view to military and political training" (*Pol.* VIII.6.1341a6–7).

Aristotle's response to specialization is more philosophically interesting and more morally threatening than changing the rules to maintain aristocratic privilege. Specialization, he thinks, can only have an extrinsic motive. It cannot be the development of the artful power itself. Music would be a fit part of civic education if musicians "did not exert themselves to learn either what contributes to contests involving expertise in the art or those works that are difficult and extraordinary (which have now come into the contests, and from the contests into education)" (1341a8–14). The professional musician, according to Aristotle, not only deploys a talent disconnected from the internal goods of the individual's soul—the third kind of failure—but *consequently* does not appeal to internal standards of the practice either, but aims at pleasing the audience and so commits the second kind of failure as well by aiming merely at the external end, just as vices aim at pleasure as a surrogate for the good. I would like to dismiss this criticism of artistic excellence as being only an expression of aristocratic prejudice, like the ban on dunking, but think it is much more integrally tied up with the central motifs of Aristotle's thought.

Professional musicians supposedly lose the internal end of music by aiming at providing pleasure for their listeners. When arts aim at external ends, they stop being arts worthy of a citizen. When a virtue aims at an external end, it is then a virtue no longer either:

> We reject the education involving expertise in the art [of music] both in instruments and performance—we regard as involving expertise in the art that with a view to contests, for one who is active in this does not undertake it for the sake of his own virtue but for the sake of pleasure; hence we judge the performance as not belonging to free persons but being more characteristic of the laborer; and indeed the result is that they become vulgar, for the aim with a view to which they create the end for themselves is a base one; the spectator,

being crude himself, customarily alters the music, so that he makes the artisans engaging in it with a view to him of a certain quality themselves and with respect to their bodies. (*Pol.* VIII.6.1341b8–18; see III.4.1277b3–7, VII.16. 1335b5–11)

This third source of moral failure, that virtues give way to skills that better achieve the same end, seems something that is especially important to worry about today. My example of the courageous Polish cavalry being beaten by the skills of building and using tanks is a topos that been used ever since the invention of the phalanx, if not before. Where in better times virtue ruled, now we calculate instead. For example, after quoting from the *Iliad* (14.96–102), the Athenian Stranger says:

> Homer too realized that it is bad tactics to have triremes lined up at sea in support of infantry in the field. This is the sort of habituation that will soon make even lions run away from deer. And that's not all. When a state which owes its power to its navy wins a victory, the bravest soldiers never get the credit for it, because the battle is won thanks to the skill of the steersman, boatswain, and rower and the efforts of a motley crowd of ragamuffins, which means that it is impossible to honor each individual in the way he deserves. Rob a state of its power to do that, and you condemn it to failure. (Plato, *Laws* IV.707a–b)

Countervailing stories tell of the triumph of virtue over skill, Gandhi's self-restraint and nonviolence against all the arts and powers of the British. However encouraging such stories are, though, the overall picture is one of worry about the power and appeal of art beating out virtue. Aristotle can maintain the primacy of praxis when arts are practiced only by noncitizens and slaves and are not effective in attaining important ends. Things are different when medicine really works, or when scientific agriculture vanquishes traditional practices. We can now choose to make a living at a craft. Indeed, the very expression, "making a living," is so unintelligible to Aristotle that our ease in understanding it shows our distance from Aristotle's world. It is one thing for ethics to neglect *technē*; it is another for ethics to be confronted with a regime of *technē* in competition with it. Even the enthusiasts of technological progress rarely look forward to an increased role for academic bureaucrats. While Aristotle seems to us blind to the possibilities of highly ethical virtues being developed and expressed through the practice of a craft, he was very alert to the possibility that the more people's lives are organized around *technai,* the more ethics becomes a matter for one's private, nonpolitical life.

As I mentioned in the last chapter, the practical direction of inference (so that regarding virtue one cannot infer from act to agent) means that the ethical virtues are unified while the arts are not. When virtues compete against each other, they are no longer the best condition of the soul, and so are no longer Aristotelian virtues. This moral failure is expressed eloquently by Learned Hand:

> You may take Martin Luther or Erasmus for your model, but you cannot play both roles at once; you may not carry a sword beneath a scholar's gown, lead flaming causes from a cloister, Luther cannot be domesticated in a university. You cannot raise a standard against oppression, or leap into the breach to relieve injustice, and still keep an open mind to every disconcerting fact, or an open ear to the cold voice of doubt. I am satisfied that a scholar who tries to combine these parts sells his birthright for a mess of pottage; that when the final count is made, it will be found that the impairment of his powers far outweighs any possible contribution to the causes he has espoused. If he is fit to serve his calling at all, it is only because he has learned not to serve in any other, for his singleness of mind quickly evaporates in the fires of passions, however holy.[26]

Hand seems to celebrate the incompatibility of the virtues as he presents examples of admirable moral qualities, but if he's right, Aristotle's own project falls apart.

## Arts, Virtues, and Moral Development

> Being the recipient of unjust treatment is less bad [than committing injustice], and yet there is no reason why it should not incidentally be a greater evil. But this sort of thing is of no concern to science, which declares pleurisy a worse thing to suffer from than a stumble; nevertheless on occasion the latter might incidentally turn out to be worse—if someone stumbled, and because of his fall happened to be captured or killed by the enemy. (*NE* V.11. 1138a35–b5)

Since I argue in chapter 1 that instrumental actions are perfected into actions done for their own sakes, one might also expect that instrumental faculties, i.e., rational powers, are perfected into virtues, habits of choosing for their own sakes. But this is not the case. There is no pathway from art to virtue. Acting instrumentally can be perfected into praxis, but arts are never perfected into virtues. Some goods are aimed at by the arts, others by the virtues. The arts are, in Aristotle's eyes, psychic and ethical dead ends.[27]

The denigration of *technē* is one of those features of Aristotle's thought I mentioned at the beginning as both attractive and repellent. It is attractive because it follows from his strict separation of praxis from *poiesis,* doing from making, a separation essential to carving out a special place for ethical virtue and for the idea of doing something for the sake of the noble. Equally, it is repellent because it blinds Aristotle to the important human capacity to find challenge and satisfaction in a diversity of (nonpolitical) activities. The contempt Aristotle expresses for *technē* and for artisans is not a bubbling up of nonphilosophical class prejudices against trade or money. It is central to his developing the autonomy of praxis.

At different times, different sorts of crafts have been held up as pathways to virtue. Thus science makes people honest, makes them respect the external world and not give in to their own hopeful fantasies. Or skill at writing and speaking makes people aware of audiences and so less self-absorbed. None of these initiatives is without counterargument, though: scientists neglect the moral dimensions and human consequences of their activities, and the skilled rhetorician panders to his audience. Later I will discuss Constant's account of how commerce is supposed to promote virtue, but here it is worth insisting on Aristotle's own asymmetry. There are artistic practices which make men's souls vulgar, but none—especially not rhetoric—that equip people for citizenship. Aristotle's radical separation of virtue from the arts has its appeal: it protects the autonomy of ethics, but it has its cost too in the absence of pathways from art to virtue.

Facility in a craft can make the practice of a virtue more difficult. The magnificent man "will spend gladly and lavishly, since *nice calculation is shabby;* and he will think how he can carry out his project most nobly and splendidly, rather than how much it will cost and how it can be done most cheaply" (*NE* IV.2.1122b7–10). If I am adept at "nice calculation," it may be harder for me to act virtuously. If I can calculate with precision how long I will live, how much money I need for my retirement, how much to take care of my family, what need have I for the virtue of liberality? I can simply donate to charity everything left over from what I need for myself and my family. In the *Rhetoric* Aristotle points out that a speech that contains nothing but a logical demonstration will be unpersuasive because it has no *ēthos* (*Rh.* III.17.1418a9–21; see *Poet.* 6. 1450b8–10). "Talking about *ēthos* we do not say that a person is wise or of good understanding, but that he is gentle-tempered or temperate" (*NE* I.13. 1103a7–8). When pure rationality and *technē* seem to do virtue's job better than virtue can, such rationality is an obstacle to the development and exercise of virtue. It is easier to deliberate about living than about living well, and so tempting to aim at living just because we can approach it rationally.

Virtuous rationality can degenerate into the greater certainties of art, but technical rationality does not develop into the ethical rationality of virtue. Courage does not perfect some *technē* of resistance in battle, as the experienced fighter seems to think:

> In fighting nonprofessionals, the professional soldiers are like armed troops fighting unarmed, or like trained athletes fighting ordinary people. . . . However, professional soldiers turn out to be cowards when the danger overstrains them and they are inferior in numbers and equipment. For they are the first to run. (*NE* III.8.1116b13–17)

But what if that last remark were false? What if professionals achieved the external end more reliably and efficiently than those acting from virtues of character? If virtues go undeveloped because of this technological substitution, we have moral failure and lack of virtue, and indeed unhappiness. The arts have internal goods which give the stability of a rational capacity for making, while the virtues have internal goods that have the kind of reliability and dependability found in character. Powerful arts offer the prospect that we can act successfully without knowing ourselves. As the arts become more successful, the place of the virtues in the good life becomes more precarious.

Why should technology triumph over virtue? An easy answer is that the crafts progress and develop but virtue doesn't. Where the "art of war" used to be no art at all, but only some useful rules of thumb that supplemented the primary cause of martial success, courage, people discovered principles and so that the art of war became a true art that was able to do without virtue and successfully compete against it. We used to listen to our mothers telling us how to eat, but now we have dieticians who know what they're talking about. But we might tell the story differently. Aristotle's optimism that rhetoric doesn't threaten politics suggests that we don't need to worry about *technē* as long as virtue itself is strong. We might regard the bureaucratization of contemporary university life not as a discovery of new professional skills but a failure of academic virtues.

Because of this difference between the internal ends of the arts and the virtues, *phronēsis* perfects the virtues differently from the way it perfects arts. *Phronēsis* makes possible a unity of the virtues but no unity of the crafts. The crafts are unified only to the extent that they are all subject to external regulation by *phronēsis* in its political form. One can be a good shoemaker without being a good sculptor, but—here Aristotle is in opposition to the quotation from Learned Hand a few pages ago—one cannot be courageous without also being temperate, just, and witty.

The perfect realization of the arts does not transform them into perfect *energeiai*. It simply puts good products to good uses. The perfect realization of the ethical virtues is different, for the activities they direct are themselves perfected into virtuous activities. Because not all activities can be perfected in this latter way, the ethical virtues do not exhaust human activity. No matter how virtuous we are, we still need methods and arts. It is not always better to act virtuously instead of through art. Therefore this type of moral failure, like the others, is a permanent possibility.

### Fourth Failure: Virtues in Conflict with the Goods of Community

If virtue is the capacity of conferring benefits, then the greatest virtues must be those which are the most useful to others, and, for this reason, justice and courage are the most honored; for the latter is useful to others in war, and the former in both war and peace. (*Rh.* I.6.1366b3–6)

Bold acceptance of danger for our own, our country's, or our friends' rights is sublime. The crusades and ancient knighthood were adventurous; duels, a wretched remnant of the latter arising from a perverted concept of chivalry, are grotesque. Melancholy separation from the bustle of the world due to a legitimate weariness is noble. Solitary devotion by the ancient hermits was adventurous. Monasteries and such tombs, to confine the living saints, are grotesque. Subduing one's passions through principles is sublime. Castigation, vows, and other such monks' virtues are grotesque. (Immanuel Kant)[28]

Intolerance, by placing violence on the side of faith, placed courage on the side of doubt. The fury of the believers has excited the vanity of those who could not believe, and in this way man has made a virtue of a system which he ought naturally to have considered as a misfortune. Persecution provokes resistance. Authority, by threatening any opinion whatsoever, provokes any courageous spirit to take up that very opinion. There is in man a principle of revolt against every form of intellectual constraint. This principle can be carried to the point of fury. It can cause many crimes; yet it issues from all that is most noble in our soul. (Benjamin Constant)[29]

In the fourth kind of moral failure, a virtuous practice has no place in a community. When ethics and politics become distinct, there is moral failure because the human function cannot be fully actualized. Man stops being a political animal.

In this kind of moral failure, the kind of community we live in prevents an internal practical good from being connected to human flourishing. These are communities where Aristotle's happy declaration of harmony will not apply: "When everyone competes to achieve what is fine and strains to do the noblest actions, everything that is right will be done for the common good, and each person individually will receive the greatest of goods, since that is the character of virtue" (*NE* IX.8.1169a6–12). Not only does virtue pay, it pays for others. There is no guarantee that a multitude of flourishing individuals will constitute a flourishing community. Once again, when virtue and happiness are only externally related, so too are individual happiness and the goods of the community.[30]

Without a connection between the goods of practices and human flourishing, Aristotelian nobility and practical reason disappear. For him, the methods of personal ethical deliberation are the same as the methods of rhetorical deliberation and persuasion. "On any important decision, we deliberate together, because we do not trust ourselves" (*NE* III.3. 1112b10–11). "Humans have a natural disposition for the true and to a large extent hit on the truth" (*Rh.* I.1.1355a15–16). Aristotle does not need an independent theory of human nature because he can rely on people's practical judgment, in the right circumstances, to hit the truth. Losing such confidence creates the need for an ethical theory founded in human nature.[31]

One sign of the difference between the ethical values of Aristotle's polis and the modern state is the modern denigration of rhetoric. The comparison to rhetoric with which I began this book would never occur to most contemporary moral thinkers. The modern citizen as subject must be on guard against manipulations and frauds that are the civilized substitute for force and coercion. To stay free, we have to resist rhetoric. Aristotle's citizen would think of rhetoric first as an agent, not part of the audience. Instead of effective rhetoric increasing the ways in which one can be dominated, effective Aristotelian rhetoric increased the opportunities for domination, and for reciprocity. If the modern has to resist rhetoric to stay free, the ancient had to practice rhetoric to stay free.

The fourth kind of failure comes from a discrepancy between the goods internal to the good functioning and flourishing of the individual, on the one hand, and the goods internal to a self-sustaining and excellence-promoting community, on the other. The virtues of the good man and the good citizen then conflict, and justice cannot be both a good condition of the soul and be directed at another's good.[32]

Thus Benjamin Constant in "The Liberty of the Ancients Compared with that of the Moderns" (1819) argues that in the Greek polis, courage avoided all four of my dangers of moral failure. Courage was a practice with an internal end. It made its possessor into a better person and so was a mode of activity central to human happiness. It contributed to the goods of community not only by preserving the polis but by being a paradigm for the virtues in general. It made someone a good citizen by developing the qualities of discipline, self-control, and self-sacrifice. The courageous man learned to value the good life, whether in himself or in his entire polis, over life itself. Therefore courage not only was part of flourishing for the individual but was central to his identity as a citizen.

But Constant argues that courage is no longer functional: "An age must come in which commerce replaces war. We have reached this age."[33] The polis has been replaced by the state, and so courage must be replaced by the virtues of commerce, a long distance from Aristotle's claims that the mechanical and mercantile lives are inimical to virtue (*Pol.* VII.8.1328b39–41), or the remark in the *Laws* (705a) that commerce "fills the land with wholesaling and retailing, breeds shifty and deceitful habits in a man's soul and makes the citizens distrustful and hostile." The marketplace replaces the battlefield as the school for citizenship. There we acquire the virtues of probity, of satisfying others, of discipline, self-control, and self-sacrifice in entirely new forms. The virtues of commerce are not only part of flourishing for the individual, but are central to his identity as a member of the new state, as a producer and a consumer. "Commerce inspires in men," Constant writes, "a vivid love of individual independence. Commerce supplies their needs, satisfies their desires, without the intervention of the authorities."[34]

The good ancient politician manifested a generalized form of courage in all his actions. The good modern citizen acts as a wise and decent producer and consumer in all of his, pursuing self-interest and tempering it to accommodate the interests of others. "The aim of the ancients was the sharing of social power among the citizens of the same fatherland: this is what they called liberty. The aim of the moderns is the enjoyment of security in private pleasures; and they call liberty the guarantees accorded by institutions to these pleasures."[35] The modern virtue of commerce, like Aristotle's ethical virtues, brings together the traditionally opposed cooperative and competitive virtues, but in a new form in which nobility becomes obsolete. The modern virtue of commerce is then, for Aristotle, a moral failure. We are all liberals now.[36]

## The Moral Significance of Moral Failure

Although [the Spartan legislators] rightly think that the good things that people compete for are won by virtue rather than by vice, they also suppose (not rightly) that these goods are better than virtue itself. (*Pol.* II.9. 1271b7–10)

Any set of social relationships which embodies the tradition of the virtues is bound to be vulnerable and fragile. For the pursuit of those institutional goods without which the social framework within which the virtues are practices cannot be sustained—such goods as those of power and money—is always at best in tension with the asceticism in respect of such goods required by the Aristotelian virtues of temperateness and justice. Being virtuous may on occasion be the cause of being socially and political defeated, an insight whose classical statement is by Machiavélli. (Alasdair MacIntyre, "After Virtue and Marxism")[37]

The moral failures I have detailed are not vices or mistakes. They are alternative ways of living, maybe even the best way to live in certain circumstances. To finish this examination of the varieties of moral failure, I want to show how the varieties of moral failure, by heightening the contrast between Aristotle's world and ours, can help us orient ourselves toward our own moral circumstances.

We who live in political circumstances that would be in his eyes unnatural need to attend to moral failure, both to understand Aristotle better and to understand ourselves better. Unless we are on the moon, moral truths, because of their dependence on habituation and good laws, are not open to Aristotelian practical knowledge. But there are other kinds of moral knowledge not imagined by Aristotle, and not so rooted in social facts, to which we can aspire. This taxonomy of the varieties of moral failure can help us discover such knowledge.

*Phronēsis* has to be very different in contemporary circumstances, because it cannot be simply the *orthos logos* of the ethical virtues. It has jobs to do unimagined by Aristotle, because of the relation between virtue and *technē* and the increased role of *technē* in our lives. It is common to distinguish a slave society from a society with slaves. Similarly one can distinguish a technical or technological society from a society that contains *technai*. Aristotle's conceptions of ethical virtue, *phronēsis,* and the good life make sense only within a nontechnological society, a society in which man's political nature is central. Living well requires a different kind of practical rationality when one must negotiate a world dominated by *technē*.

Earlier I noted how *phronēsis* stands in a different relation to the virtues it perfects and to the arts it perfects. *Phronēsis* simply puts good products to good uses; it stands in an external relation to those products. Contemporary *phronēsis* would need to emphasize this function of *phronēsis*, which Aristotle could afford to regard as subordinate. A new dimension of *phronēsis* is needed to coordinate the arts and their ends.

"In *technē* voluntary error is not so bad as involuntary, whereas in the sphere of *phronēsis* it is worse, as it is in the sphere of the virtues" (*NE* VI.5.1140b21–24). The more attenuated relations between internal and external ends I have pointed to suggest that the *phronimos* must today consider something approaching what Aristotle means by voluntary error, this time "in the sphere of *phronēsis*." Achieving the internal end can point one way and accomplishing the external another. *Poetics* 25 is devoted to voluntary technical errors, cases in which there is a conflict between an external end such as pleasing the audience and the internal end of making a good drama. "Correctness in the art of poetry is not the same as correctness in the art of politics" (1460b13–15). The better the polis, the more aligned are internal and external ends, of both the arts and the virtues. We have to worry when, for example, justice according to law is at odds with what we think to be just on other standards, as was the case, in an earlier example, when the injustice of slavery was authorized by law.

*Phronēsis* today cannot simply presuppose and ratify existing practices and *ēthē*. While Aristotle does not unreflectively take as the virtues those practices currently praised in Athenian society—I will reject that common accusation in chapter 5—he does see those common practices and opinions as the material on which *phronēsis* reflects. Recurrent divergences between internal and external ends require new habits of critical reflection. And most often, such discrepancies occur because of the conflict between virtue and craft. It is as true today as in ancient Athens that more citizens believe in astrology than in evolution, but that fact about popular beliefs has a different political meaning today. Given the role of expert knowledge in our lives, common beliefs must be more subject to criticism today. Because *phronēsis* can have a greater distance from common practices and *ēthē* today, there is room for ethical relations to all people and not only our own community. Here is a final new dimension for *phronēsis* today. In the Introduction I listed among the features of the *Ethics* I found both attractive and unavailable the lack of a function for *phronēsis* apart from the ethical virtues. Here we see why such an understanding of *phronēsis* makes no sense for us.

This chapter has asked what has to be true for Aristotle's project to work. I tried to answer the question by looking at the ways things can go wrong. Knowing what must be true for Aristotle's project to make sense is far from seeing why it should be true. He affirms the very strong conclusion that the exercise of the best condition of the soul and the best consequences go together, and that the best quality a citizen can have is virtue. Aristotle has to prove that the *energeia* of the human *dynamis* is identical with the *energeia* of human kinetic actions that aim at goods. That is the subject of chapter 4. Then he has to prove that the exercise of the soul's good condition is identical with the best political actions. That will be the subject of chapter 5.

## Passion and the Two Sides of Virtue

### The Ethical Virtues and the Good Life

The same standard of excellence does not apply to an achievement as to a possession (*ou hē autē ktēmatos kai ergou*). (*NE* IV.2.1122b14–15)

The function argument, and the conceptual connection between function and virtue, make it necessary to answer this question: how can the concept of being in a good condition for rational activity be used to set a standard for the appropriateness of response? What contributions can the appetitive part of the soul make to rational activity, and what state of this part of the soul counts as a good condition for rational activity? (Christine M. Korsgaard, "Aristotle on Function and Virtue")[1]

As I argued in the Introduction, Aristotle has to prove that the power of doing good actions for their own sake is the best condition of the soul and, as well, the route to happiness. The last chapter explored ways in which the two sides of *energeia* could fail to intersect, which shows what is at stake in asserting that virtues considered as the perfection of actions aiming at external goods are the good condition of the soul. This chapter shows what entitles Aristotle to assert such an identity.

Ethical virtue and the ethical virtues have a strange career in the *Ethics,* a strangeness that is easy to miss because it seems natural to us to associate a work called ethics with praiseworthy things like virtues. My analogies to the *Rhetoric* have tried to make that association less automatic. Virtue, both as singular and plural, carries at least the following meanings in the *Ethics:*

1. Ethically virtuous actions are acts worth choosing and doing for their own sake. They are *energeiai* in the sense that they are their own end, and so are complete in themselves. This was the meaning of the virtues in my chapter 1.
2. The ethical virtues are, collectively, the *energeiai* of the irrational but persuadable part of the soul (*NE* I.7.1098a4–5). This was the meaning of virtues in chapter 2.

In addition to the subjects of my first two chapters, though, virtue has three more meanings:

3. Virtue (*aretē*) has the purely neutral sense of the excellence of anything. For example, wealth and health are virtues (*Rh.* I.6.1362b12–18; see *Pol.* III.13. 1283a37), and coats, houses, and ships have virtues which are simply their best state (*EE* II.1.1218b36–1219a5; see I.12.1101b14–18, II.6.1106a15–26, *Ph.* VII.3.246b6–10). There is nothing specifically moral about this sense of *aretē.* Just as the *Metaphysics* teaches us that anything that is is in some sense an *energeia,* the excellence of anything can be called a virtue. We therefore have to ask if morality or ethics can be set off from virtue in this neutral sense. Is there an Aristotelian equivalent of a delimited set of actions or problems called "the moral"?
4. The ethical virtues are, distributively, kinds of traditionally praised activity.
5. Virtue functions as the differentia for saying what sort of *energeia* or activity happiness is. The genus of happiness (*eudaimonia*) is *energeia,* and its differentia is virtue, since happiness is *energeia kat'aretēn* (*NE* I.7.1098a16, I.8. 1099a29–31, I.13.1102a5–6, *Pol.* VII.1.1332a8–11, b23, VII.8.1328a37–38). Virtue, the differentia, then, designates the *dynamis* made active and actual in the *energeia* of happiness.

Aristotle can be defended from fatal accusations of ambiguity and special pleading only if we can draw reasonable connections among those senses of virtue and the different roles virtue plays in the *Ethics.*

We could easily rescue Aristotle by singling out one of those meanings of virtue and making it fundamental. Privileging the *dynamis/energeia* relation, defining virtue as what brings the soul into its best condition (#2) would be a kind of naturalism that relied on an antecedent definition of human nature. We could privilege the *dynamis/energeia* relation in the opposite direction by first knowing what happiness is and then defining virtue through its connection to happiness (#5). Making the *kinēsis/energeia* relation basic, we could define the virtues as the activities that are praised and desired within the community, a sort of conventionalism (#4). We could start with the plural virtues and try by induction to find out what virtue itself is, discovering, say, that they were generally useful character traits (#3).[2] Last, we could privilege the *kinēsis/energeia* relation in the other direction by stopping at the end of my first chapter and regarding it as self-sufficient. The good life is doing for its own sake whatever actions our station and its duties have assigned us (#1).

Any of those reductions would present us with a coherent ethical theory, and several of the possible variants are familiar versions of ethical theory. None has the richness of Aristotle's. None faces the crucial issue: *Why should all and only acts that realize the soul be chosen for their own sakes?*

Distinguishing the two dimensions of *energeia* shows that although the virtues are good both for the individual who exercises them and for the community, it is good *for* each in a different way. It is good for the individual as the *energeia* of the *dynameis* of his or her soul. Virtue puts the soul in its best condition. It is good for the community as the *energeia* of beneficial *kinēseis*. Virtuous activity has laudable and desirable results. Activity that is its own end connects virtue as psychically satisfying—the *dynamis/energeia* dimension—and virtue as socially beneficial and conventional—the *kinēsis/energeia* dimension. Harmony between the two sides of *energeia* prevents the virtues from being either instrumental—praised and justified by their results—or self-indulgent, valued for their effect on the soul, not the world.[3] Aristotle holds that someone who does not aim at the noble, and so have his soul in the best condition, will not do well in the world either.

This chapter looks at how the two dimensions of *energeia* intersect for the ethical virtues. We can see more clearly what is at stake by noting that *phronēsis* faces the same problem. *Phronēsis* has two roles and meanings. It is, first, the *orthos logos* of the ethical virtues, the principle or right rule that defines the mean. But *phronēsis* is also the best condition of the part of the thinking soul concerned with variable things. Why should Aristotle think that the activity of the best condition of the thinking soul is prescribing the right rule for the virtues? In this chapter I will explore the equivalent problem for the ethical virtues.

This chapter will clarify the connections between the first two aspects of the ethical virtues mentioned above—(#1) ethically virtuous actions are activities worth pursuing for their own sake; (#2) the ethical virtues are *energeiai* of the irrational but persuadable part of the soul, the subjects of my first two chapters. The relation between "moral" and "nonmoral" meanings of *aretē* (#3) will turn out to be a corollary of that demonstration, as we clarify the relation between moral and nonmoral goods, the goods of activity, and the external goods of fortune. Virtue as the locus of praise (#4) needs separate consideration in the next chapter. There I will ask why should the excellence of the irrational but persuadable part of the soul be located in actions chosen for their own sakes that are in turn identified with the traditional ethical virtues. The final chapter will connect virtue to happiness (#5) through consideration of *theōria*, where the intersection of the two sides of *energeia* reappears in a different form.

## Why Can't We Accumulate Money, or Cheat, or Boast, For Its Own Sake?

> Virtue when it is equipped with resources, is in a way particularly adept in the use of force; and anything that conquers always does so because it is outstanding in some good quality. This makes it seem that force is not without virtue. (*Pol.* I.6.1255a13–16)

Writing to Morris Cohen, Oliver Wendell Holmes challenged Aristotelian virtue:

> Man is like a strawberry plant, the shoots that he throws out become independent centres. And one illustration of the tendency is the transformation of means into ends. A man begins a pursuit as a means of keeping alive—he ends by following it at the cost of life. A miser is an example—but so is the man who makes righteousness his end. Morality is simply another means of living but the saints make it an end in itself. Until just now it never occurred to me to think that the same is true of philosophy or art. Philosophy as a fellow once said to me is only thinking. Thinking is an instrument of adjustment to the conditions of life—but it becomes an end in itself. So that we can see how man is inevitably an idealist of some sort, but whatever his ideal and however ultimate to himself, all that he can say to anyone else is—*Je suis comme ça*. But he can admit that a person who lives in a certain emotional sphere should be indifferent to intellectual justifications although he reserves to himself his advantage of believing that he can explain the other and that this other can't explain him.[4]

As I showed in the first chapter, acts that are their own ends emerge out of acts originally done instrumentally. Both the miser and the good man make some means into the grand end of their lives. Holmes therefore infers that there is no difference between them. There is nothing the good man can say to the miser except, "*Je suis comme ça*." Anything that is is an *energeia*. Anything that a person does is a practical *energeia*. Anything that a person does for its own sake is a perfect *energeia*. Doing something for its own sake is a purely formal idea. Any normative content would have to be smuggled in from outside. When Camus imagines Sisyphus as happy, he agrees with Holmes in thinking that anything can be done for its own sake. No acts are *worth* choosing for their own sakes. Some just are so chosen.

Can Aristotle respond to Holmes? Are *good* actions the only kind entitled to the title of actions that are their own end? Why can't the boaster who has no ulterior motive of money or honor (*NE* II.7.1108a28, IV.7. 1127a28, see IV.6.1127a7–8) choose an action that is its own end? "One who pursues excessive pleasures, or pursues things to excess and from decision (*dia prohairesin*), for their own sakes and not for the sake of some ulterior consequence, is a profligate" (*NE* VII.7.1150a19–22). How, then, is such a profligate different from the virtuous person who decides and acts on things for their own sake? Why are *praxeis* the only practical *energeiai*?[5]

I want to tell my own variation on Holmes's story. I was very bored in high school. My energy and talents were not being developed or put to any use. I found an outlet for my abilities in cheating. I gave my answers on tests to friends. If my friends didn't know the answers, that was because the teachers were, we thought, incompetent. Thus my cheating was a just response. The teachers got what they deserved. There was risk in what I did, and so courage, I thought. While figuring out the answers to the tests took no effort, I needed a lot of ingenuity and cleverness to succeed at cheating.

Assume that cheating was, as I then thought, the fullest development of my faculties possible in the situation. It was a means toward helping friends. I also observed some norms—I would never steal the teacher's set of answers rather than figure the test out for myself—and I chose cheating for its own sake. I got pleasure and the pride in succeeding in accomplishing something challenging. I was a virtuoso.

But cheating is not a practice with an internal end. Even in the circumstances as I described them, it is not a virtue. Cheating has the wrong sort of connection between psychic development—the application of intelligence, the voluntary undertaking of risks, the discovery of elegant solutions to practical problems—and the actions I chose. It isn't enough for an action both to achieve external ends and to bring the soul into good shape. Cheating might have done both. But it cannot be the good development of the soul because it does not do for its own sake something *worth* doing in the first place. Proving that conclusion, instead of deferring to conventional moral judgments against the miser and the cheat, is not trivial.[6]

Consider a less morally dubious example. I want to act generously. I decide that the best way of helping people is through anonymous donations. If I give without revealing my identity, the beneficiaries are less likely to feel humbled or to consider themselves under obligations to me. Hiding my identity is good for me too. If I give anonymously, it is more likely that I will do it with the right motives, not for self-display or for the sake of reputation, but out of a sincere desire to help others. I fulfill the Aristotelian demand that the virtuous do good and do well. But my generosity is very far from Aristotelian liberality. It might be a new virtue, suited to new circumstances, but it falls short of his virtue because the connection between how it puts my soul into good condition and how it benefits others is contingent. It lacks the required practically transparent relation between the two sides of *energeia*, since I can only act nobly by making that motive invisible. As we will see, cheaters and misers also fail the test of making the two sides of *energeia* work together.[7]

### Virtues as Good Condition of the Soul vs. Virtues as Acts Chosen for Their Own Sakes

The principle of an action—the source of motion, not the goal—is decision; the principle of decision is desire and goal-directed reason. That is why decision requires understanding and thought, and also a state of character; for acting well or badly requires both thought and character (*praxeōs men oun archē prohairesis hothen hē kinēsis all' oux hou heneka, proaireseōs de orexis kai logo ho heneka tinos*). (*NE* VI.2.1139a31–35)

Every activity aims at the end that corresponds to the habit of which it is the manifestation (*telos de pasēs energeias esti to kata tēn hexin*). So it is with the activity of the courageous man: his courage is noble; therefore its end is nobility, for a thing is defined by its end. (*NE* III.7.1115b20–22)

The efficient cause of an action is a decision (*prohairesis*). The final cause of an action is conformity to the corresponding *dynamis*. Efficient causes operate along the *kinēsis/energeia* dimension, formal and final causes along the *dynamis/energeia* line. Stripped of that technical language, when we find means to our end, by that fact we feel the right amount of passion. The virtues are habits of deciding rightly. A good decision is that by which we achieve our end. What is the connection between choosing well and effectively and standing well with respect to the passions (*NE* II.5.1105b26), the two dimensions of virtue? I will show that the virtuous person *feels* the right amount of passion by *deciding* on the right thing to do. Why should anyone think such a thing is true?

An analogy might help. I used to wonder how an autofocus camera could know when a given image is in focus. There is no homunculus inside the camera body who sees that the image is sharp. It turns out that when the image is in focus, the amount of light that gets through the lens is maximal. When less light gets through, the image is blurred. Being in focus is a mean: the camera quickly tests different openings of the lens until it finds one that is neither too narrow nor too open. The virtues put the actions and passions for which they are means in focus. The virtues see more accurately than vices or other states along the continuum. So, while everyone perceives the moral world according to his or her own character, only the virtuous person sees things as they truly are. Thus, as I argued in chapter 1, only virtuous deliberation extends all the way down to individuals.

When the autofocus camera lets in maximal light, it takes the sharpest pictures. There is a necessary—a mechanical—connection between being in good condition and doing its work well. This is a trivial connection, virtue with meaning #3. What about the ethical virtues? Will they deliberate well toward their end if and only if the virtues hit a mean with regard to actions and passions? Will they lie in a mean concerning actions and passions only if they deliberate well? The connection between the two dimensions of deliberation and decision looks far from trivial. Isn't it more likely that there are really two sets of virtues, one concerned with feeling the right amount of passion and therefore having one's soul in good shape, and the other concerned with choosing the best action?[8]

My thesis, then, connects three of the senses of virtue listed at the beginning, and will thus allow Aristotle to rebut Holmes. Virtue belongs in the definition of happiness as *energeia kat'aretēn* (#5) only if there is a necessary connection between virtue as the best condition of the desiring soul (#2) and a set of actions worth choosing and doing for their own sake (#1). Aristotle can then rebut Holmes without invoking any exiguous theories of human nature. Holmes's "man who makes righteousness his end" chooses not only acts that are their own end but acts that are the fullest realization of his nature. Not so for the miser, nor for me in my cheating life. Only actions worth doing for their own sakes can truly be done for their own sakes. Decision is that necessary connection between the two sides of virtue and of *energeia*. Since decision combines the efficient, formal, and final causes, virtuous actions are self-contained, self-justifying, their own end, in a way that sets them apart from other actions, just as natural substances are set off from other things in the *Physics* because, for any natural substance, the efficient, formal, and final causes are identical (*Ph.* II.7.198a25–27, *Part. An.* I.1.641a25–28, *Gen. An.* I.1.715a4, *Met.* XII.10.1075b8–10, *De An.* II.4.415b12–21).

In neither physics nor ethics do the formal, final, and efficient causes just happen to coincide, which is what was wrong with my anonymous donor. In nature, the three causes coincide because of the unique relation that form or substance has to matter in natural substances. Something analogous is at work in praxis. Decision combines the three causes because of its relation to the passions, the material cause of virtuous actions—the relation of form to matter, act to potency. I want to turn back to the text of the *Ethics* to show how Aristotle uses ethical decision to integrate the purpose, motive, and form of virtuous action.

## Passions and the Definitions of the Virtues

The Understanding is by the flame of the Passions never enlightened, but dazzled. (Hobbes, *Leviathan*)[9]

In *NE* II.5, where he defines the genus of virtue as *hexis* as opposed to passion and faculty, Aristotle tells us that virtuous habits consist in "standing well" with respect to the passions. The Greek is no less ambiguous about the relation of passion to habit: *hexeis de kath' has pros ta pathē echomen eu ē kakos* (1105b25–26). Virtue is a habit of choosing the mean. I want to show that the virtuous man feels the mean amount of passion by choosing the right means to an end. That will show that deliberation about what to do, leading to an *energeia* relative to a given end and a *kinēsis,* will also lead to an *energeia* of the *dynamis* of the desiring soul.

If decision is the final, efficient, and formal cause of action, the passions are its material cause. While passions aim at pleasure, we decide to pursue the good. "Passions are those feelings that so change men as to affect their judgments, and that are also attended by pain or pleasure (*esti de ta pathē, di hosa metaballontes diapheousi pros tas kriseis*)" (*Rh.* II.1. 1378a20). "Appetite is for pleasure . . . , the object of wish is the good; pleasure and the good are different" (*EE* VII.2.1235b21–23). "Appetite concerns pleasure and pain, decision neither pain nor pleasure" (*NE* III.2. 1111b16–18; see III.4. 1113a33–b2). When the virtues put the irrational soul into good condition, pleasure and desire will be to the good as matter to form.

Virtue neither accepts the given passions nor rejects them, as the vices do. It transforms and actualizes them into desires for actions that are their own end; *dynameis* are realized in *energeiai*. "Neither by nature nor contrary to nature do the virtues arise in us" (*NE* II.1.1103a23–24). "The end is the cause of the matter. Matter is not the cause of the end" (*Ph.* II.9.200a33–34). The importance of the passions as matter for the ethical virtues comes both from what they are—potential desires—and from what they lack, namely determination. Since the passions are the part of the irrational part of the soul that follows reason, they are apprehensions of an object. At *Rhetoric* I.11.1370a19 Aristotle distinguishes among the desires those desires "which are due to our being convinced; for there are many things which we desire to see or acquire when we have heard them spoken of and are convinced that they are pleasant." The passions relevant to the virtues are apprehensions of objects that require a practical response to become complete.[10]

Since the passions are responses to an object accompanied by pleasure or pain, they are intimations of ends. While themselves nonmoral—in the language of *NE* II.5, they are not a subject of praise and blame—they can be the source of morality. Pleasure is an intimation of, as well as a substitute for, the good:

> To feel pleasure or pain is to act with the sensitive mean towards what is good or bad as such. Both avoidance and appetite when actual are identical with this: the faculty of appetite and avoidance are not different, either from one another or from the faculty of sense-perception; but their being is different. (*De An.* III.7.431a5–16)

Deliberation, starting from the emotions, aims, in Dewey's words, not only at "emotional comfort but intelligent control."[11] Developing the ethical life out of the passions converts the perception of an object accompanied by pleasure or pain into an action chosen for its own sake. Understanding this transition will let us distinguish the good person from the miser, the cheater, the anonymous donor, as well as from the dermatologist and the Machiavellian we met in the last chapter. However, this hypothesis runs into a series of difficulties when we turn to the functions of the passions in the particular virtues.

We need to address at least the following problems or aporias and use them to see how virtuous decision works:

1. Although the delimitation of the ethical virtues in *NE* I.13 makes the passions coextensive with the irrational but persuadable part of the soul, we are later told that only courage and temperance are virtues of that part (*ton alogon meron*) (*NE* III.10.1117b24). Therefore two questions. Why should

only these two virtues be called the virtues of the irrational part of the soul?
How can all the ethical virtues, and not just courage and temperance, be the
realization of the passions?

2. The definition of *hexis* in *NE* II.5 as that in the soul through which we stand
   well or badly toward the passions implies that virtues are about the passions,
   and the particular virtues are differentiated from their genus by specifying
   the passions that each is about. But some of the virtues do not seem to be
   differentiated by passions (*NE* IV.1.1119b21–26, IV.2.1122a18–21,
   IV.3.1123b1–4, IV.4.1125b1–4). Justice and magnificence are the most
   obvious cases. Does that mean that some virtues, namely courage and
   temperance, are about passions, while the rest are about actions? How could
   that be squared with the definition of *hexis* as standing well toward the
   passions?

3. Aristotle also tells us that the virtues are about both passions and actions
   (*praxeis kai pathē*) (*NE* II.2.1104b13–14). His phrasing leaves it quite open
   whether some virtues are about passions and some about actions or all virtues
   are about both. Which is it?

4. The passions corresponding to the ethical virtues are very narrowly defined.
   Courage is not about fear and confidence in general, but fear and confidence
   with regard to a noble death in battle. Taken together, such virtues cannot exhaust the desiring soul. Why is the good condition of these specific passions
   the good condition of the entire desiring soul? Aristotle presents no virtues
   corresponding to several of the emotions highlighted in *Rhetoric* II. Many
   good and praiseworthy actions are not the manifestation of any particular
   virtue. Do they have no place in the good life? If Aristotle's ethical virtues
   are useful throughout life, and not only in extreme situations, why should
   they be defined so narrowly? Is this Aristotle's way of demarcating the moral?

5. Why are the virtues the only *energeiai* of the passions? Why aren't vicious
   habits and impulsive actions *energeiai* too, only bad *energeiai*? Why are
   the virtues the only realizations of those passions which count as part
   of a good life? This last is the question posed by Holmes's challenge to
   Aristotle.

## All the Virtues Are About Both Actions and Passions

Virtues are concerned with actions and feelings. (*NE* II.2.1104b14)

Bravery and temperance seem to be the virtues of the nonrational parts.
(*NE* III.10.1117b24)

Why does Aristotle single out courage and temperance as the virtues of the irrational soul (aporia #1)? On the other hand, why does he say that all the virtues are both about passions and about actions (*praxeis kai pathē*) (aporia #3)?

All the ethical virtues are active through being affected. If decision is deliberate desire (*NE* VI.2.1139b5, see III.3.1113a10–12), both desire and practical reason have their active and receptive sides. Practical reason accurately determines how things are and decides what is best to do. The presentation of the particular virtues moves from courage and temperance, the two virtues of the irrational part of the soul where the passions are passive in a standard, prephilosophical sense, to justice, which seems to have no passionate material at all. As the *Ethics* advances from courage and temperance through the more social virtues, the virtuous person is increasingly active and attentive in looking for situations for exercising his or her virtue. The argument of *NE* III.6–V moves from virtues that are more hypothetically praiseworthy, and more dictated by circumstances, to virtues that are more self-sufficient.

This order of presentation is ethical progress. As the ratio between receptivity and spontaneity changes, the shifting meaning of passion transforms the meaning of the proposition that the virtues are about actions and passions. In courage and temperance passion makes demands on us. We find ourselves needing to act courageously. We are human animals with the uniquely human possibility of going wrong about animal desires. If we don't act temperately, we will be vicious by default. The other virtues confront situations that are ethically richer, more complex and challenging (e.g., *NE* IV.3. 1124b6–9, 24–26). If courage and temperance never came up, our ethical lives would not thereby be impoverished, but someone never challenged to act liberally, wittily, or justly would lead an ethically incomplete life.

The passions as inchoate desires can be developed and satisfied in different ways, and so Aristotle puts them on continua to indicate that these different ways can be arranged in terms of the more and the less. When we care just how they are completed, their perception is accompanied by pleasure or pain, and we deliberate about things that can be otherwise through our intervention. "The courageous man feels and acts as is appropriate and as reason guides him" (*NE* III.7.1115b20). We feel as reason tells us; reason speaks to us through deliberation. Virtues such as magnificence and justice are means about passions, even though not about independently identifiable passions, because our deliberations about how to act magnificently or justly put the desiring soul into good condition.[12]

## Why Are the Virtues So Narrowly Defined?

By choosing good things or bad things we are people of a certain kind.
(*NE* III.2.1112a1–2)

If Aristotle's moral passions are broader than we would expect in one sense, their scope is also narrower than expected: the passions that are correlative to the virtues are given surprisingly limited domains (aporia #4). Although supposedly more deferential to ordinary beliefs than Plato, Aristotle explicitly denies the more general and standard meanings of courage and temperance. Far from ratifying standard practice, Aristotle carefully limits the situations that call for courage as fear of death in battle (*NE* III.6. 1115a30). He excludes other frightening or dangerous situations, which permit something that can only metaphorically be called courage (*NE* III. 6.1115a15), and similarly for the other virtues. The virtue of temperance is not concerned with common appetites, but limited to pleasures of food, drink, and sex.[13]

Aristotle needs the virtues to be narrow because only then can there be strict correlations between potency and act. We met this strictness in chapter 2 when we saw that virtuous habits are produced by activities of the same kind, eliminating all kinds of candidates for virtue not produced by habituation, such as heroic actions, and all kinds of moral education that did not start from things done for their own sake, such as seductions and punishments. Only in the narrowly defined virtues is there the requisite necessary connection between potency and act.

Other median states of deciding, with regard to other passions, might also be the good condition of souls and could also lead to good actions. But the requirements for virtue are more strict. There must be a passion, a habit of deciding that lies in a mean toward it, and a characteristic kind of action that expresses that habit. Maybe there are other passions, e.g., pity, without an identifiable set of actions that they lead to. Maybe there are other actions, helpfulness, say, without an associated set of passions. The vagueness of pity and helpfulness, compared to courage and temperance, show that such things have a different function in our moral lives from Aristotelian virtues.[14] There are no virtues apart from characteristic virtuous acts, and no virtuous acts that do not spring from corresponding habits. Aristotle's domain for "the moral" is very restricted because the demands of the intersections of the two dimensions of virtue are so rigorous.

This restriction and rigor have practical consequences. As I will argue in the next chapter, fewer people can be good and happy the more the virtues have to meet this pair of demands. It may be tempting to see such elitist consequences as motivating Aristotle's picture of virtue as he designs a philosophical articulation of the good life designed to show that only a few wealthy, politically powerful, adult Greek males can be happy. I think, though, that that's too easy. I see Aristotle presenting a compelling and challenging picture of the good life. It has the unfortunate implication—which of course doesn't bother him at all—that the good life is so restricted, another feature of the *Ethics* that I find simultaneously attractive and repellent.

Only those conditions of the soul which issue in acts worth choosing for their own sake count as virtuous *energeiai* of the soul. Only those acts that are their own end which also realize the good condition of the soul count as virtuous *energeiai*. The two continua of passions and habits symbolize the two sides of virtue. Hence the importance of the fact I mentioned in chapter 2 that only the ethical virtues are not only about means but are themselves means.

Many good and praiseworthy actions do not manifest any particular virtue. Courage toward fears in all but the noblest situations is courage by metaphor (*NE* III.6.1115a15) and similarity (*homoiotēta*) (1115a19). These are more than verbal extensions, but ways we can live the best lives we can even in situations that do not call for full virtue. Someone who is courageous in the strict sense will also be able to be courageous in more extended ways (*NE* III.6.1115a35–b2), and the same holds for the other virtues. "A lover of the truth who is truthful even when nothing is at stake will be keener to tell the truth when something is at stake (*en hois diapherei*), since he will avoid falsehood as shameful (*aischron*) [when something is at stake] having already avoided it in itself [when nothing was at stake]" (*NE* IV.7.1127b3–7).[15] Only if these *a fortiori* arguments, that courage about battle and telling the truth when something is at stake are somehow focal, appear plausible, can the narrowness of virtue succeed. Then the narrowly defined virtues can be central to the moral life.

### Virtues and Vices as *Energeiai*

Great men are always themselves, no matter what happens to them. Their luck may change, and one moment they may be lifted up to the heights, the next crushed, but they themselves do not change, but always remain determined and seem so comfortable with their own style of behavior that everyone can easily see fortune has no power over them. Weak men behave very differently. For they become conceited and overexcited when they have good fortune, presuming that everything good that happens to them is a reward for *virtù* they do not, in fact, have. The result is they become intolerable and hateful to all those who have to deal with them. And this causes their luck to change quickly, and, as soon as they stare ill fortune in the face, they quickly develop the opposite vices, become inadequate and unselfconfident. (Machiavelli, *Discourses,* III.31)

Why are the virtues the only realizations of those passions which count as part of a good life (aporia #5)? What's wrong with the life of cheating, or the endless accumulation of Holmes's miser, or the lives of force and fraud that Machiavelli celebrates?

From the beginning I've been interested in those movements of thought in the *Ethics* in which a neutral term becomes normative: like the available means of persuasion in rhetoric, function, virtue, the mean, and activity all do double duty as a neutral term without normative, let alone ethical, connotations, and then do the work of discriminating something proper from something external. In the *Rhetoric* the available means of persuasion are contrasted to any old expedients (*ek pantos tropou*). Here in the *Ethics* people have functions in ways that knives and hands do not, functions that are not relative to some further use or further whole. Knives and hands can have virtues, too, but on the other hand there is no virtue of the nutritive soul. The mean is a formal, even mathematical, idea, and yet the virtuous person aims at the mean relative to us, a rational and ethical notion. Similarly here. The vices are *hexeis,* and so first *energeiai* of the desiring soul. And yet in another sense the virtues are, and the vices are not, *energeiai* of the passions.

Only the virtues count as *energeiai* of the passions because only in them is the transition from potency to act nonarbitrary, hence smooth, hence pleasant. The vices, by contrast, realize either too much or too little of the passions. The wrong amounts of a passion are wrong because they are amounts that cannot be fully realized in an action, and so while virtuous habits determine the actions they lead to, vicious *hexeis* are indeterminate. The virtues are actual causes of actions, while vices are inevitably only potential causes (*Ph.* II.3.195b18; see *An. Post.* II.12.95a10–22).

Because vicious habits need further determination, they do not lead smoothly to vicious actions, and so not pleasantly, even if some of them have pleasure as their end. Since the relation of passion to a vicious *hexis* isn't smooth, neither is the subsequent relation of *hexis* to act, and hence the acts that come from any nonvirtuous *hexis* are to some extent arbitrary: "Error is multiform . . . , whereas success is possible in one way only" (*NE* II.6.1106b29). Vices direct attention and action to the wrong people, at the wrong time, the wrong place, etc.

Opposite vices tend to result in the same action, and a single vice often leads to opposite actions. Cowardice and rashness both lead to running away (*NE* III.7.1116a7–9). This feature of vice results from the indeterminate nature of vice as never fully causing their actions as virtues do. At the extreme, vices become actions which, far from complete in themselves, destroy themselves:

> Evil destroys itself, and when fully present becomes unbearable. (*NE* IV.5. 1126a12–13)

> Good men are in concord with themselves and with each other, since they are practically of the same mind, for their wishes are stable. . . . Base people, however, cannot be in concord, except to a slight degree, just as they can be friends only to a slight degree. (*NE* IX.8.1167b4–10)

> Vicious people are at odds with themselves and do not love themselves. (*NE* IX 4.1166b7–8; see I.8.1099a11–13, IX.6.1167b5–15, *EE* VII.6. 1240b12–15)

As in the *Physics,* such regularity that the virtuous person has comes from the identity of formal, efficient, and final causes. "For teeth and all other natural things either invariably or normally come about in a given way; but of not one of the results of chance or spontaneity is this true" (*Ph.* 198b23; see also 196b29, 197b14.) Nature is regular, while chance, spontaneity, and violence are not. Virtuous habits are consistent and reliable. In chapter 2 I suggested that ethical necessity should be parsed by terms like reliability and dependability rather than mere predictability, but it is necessity nonetheless. "No human achievement has the stability of activities in accord with virtue: they appear to be more lasting even than our knowledge of sciences" (*NE* I.10. 1100b11–14; see 1100b30–33, VIII.3.1156b6– 12, VIII.8.1159b7–9, *EE* II.6.1222b16–20).[16]

Someone might object here: some vicious habits seem quite predictable and in that sense determinate. (In the last chapter, we also confronted the durability in the love of the mother for the child whom she gives away to have a better life.) The coward always runs away, and the miser never spends his money, so these vices have regular modes of behavior connected to them. Since the courageous man will not always stand and fight but knows when to retreat, vice can be *more* predictable than virtue. Where then is the difference between the determinate quality of virtue and vice?

A vicious habit, no matter how obsessive or predictable, does not actualize the particular passion that provoked it, but some more general passion: the coward fears not death in noble circumstances but death, or perhaps even danger as such.[17] The ambitious man wants honor and does not care about the source (*NE* IV.4.1125b8), while the unambitious do not want honor, regardless of the source. To see why only the virtues, and not the vices, are the *energeiai* of the passions and of this part of the soul, recall my analogy between vice and sophistic. There is no art of so-phistic. The sophist either uses no art at all, or pretends to use or is in other ways parasitic on the art of rhetoric. There is no art of poisoning, simply acts of poisoning that are parasitic on the art of medicine. So too vice is not a kind of character in the strong way virtue is. Cheating is not a practice. Nor is the endless accumulation of the miser.

In the final section of this chapter I will argue the capacities for self-love, for loving another person, and for doing things that are their own end stand and fall together. Holmes's miser does not love himself. In my cheat-ing example, I thought I had friends, but if I did, they were at best friends of utility and pleasure, not shared activity. The shared risks of getting caught were not shared activities. Consequently, this difference between virtue and vice is the difference between treating others as friends and merely flattering them; flatterers are "apparent admirers and apparent friends" (*Rh.* I.11.1371a22–23; see *NE* VIII.8.1159a15–16, *Pol.* V.11. 1314a1–4). Just as sophistic often imitates success since it has no internal end of its own, many vices, such as rashness, profligacy, and boasting, imi-tate the internal ends of virtues because they cannot have internal ends of their own. Prodigal men, while giving away a lot of money, are "not really liberal; their gifts are not noble, nor given for the nobility of giving, nor in the right way; on the contrary, sometimes they make men rich who ought to be poor, and will not give anything to the worthy, while heaping bene-fits on flatterers and others who minister to their pleasures" (*NE* IV.1. 1121b4–7). Those with the goods of fortune alone "try to imitate the great-souled man without being really like him, and only copy him in what they can, reproducing his contempt for others but not his virtuous con-duct" (*NE* IV.3.1124b2–5; see III.7.1115b29–32, IV.7.1127a20–22).

Where sophistic makes the external end, winning, its principle and so is ignorant of the internal end of rhetoric, the vices take the external end as their end by making a passion into the principle of action. To make one's passions into a principle is a form of ignorance and error. The passions are indeterminate principles that prevent us from knowing the concrete individual. Thus having the virtue regarding anger means "not being led by emotion but only becoming angry in such a manner, for such causes and for such a length of time as reason may ordain" (*NE* IV. 5.1125b33–1126a1). The liberal person knows his beneficiaries as he tries to help them for their own sakes. The spendthrift regards his benefi-ciaries as an audience to impress in more general terms. As the analogy to sophistic shows, external ends are not knowable, but internal ones are.

The pursuit of external ends can prevent us from developing internal goods.

My fifth aporia is solved. Aristotle locates the best development and use of the desiring soul without an extra-ethical appeal to a human nature founded in a transcendent metaphysical biology, and without resorting to a conventionalism in which liberality is stipulated as good and miserliness as bad. He has ethical criteria for distinguishing Holmes's "man who makes righteousness his end" from the miser. He has found something like the maximum of light in my analogy to the autofocus camera in virtuous actions as fully satisfying realization of the passions.

### Energeia and the Mean

> It is rather the part of virtue to act well than to be acted upon well. (NE
> IV.1.1120a11–12)

We can now, finally, say how the virtuous habit determines how much of a passion is the right amount without using an external measure.[18] The right amount of fear and confidence is that amount that permits someone to act courageously. The right action is not the one that feels good, although it will be pleasant to the good man. The person of practical wisdom determines the mean amount of the passions by deliberating about how to achieve a given end. The mean is that *hexis,* that method of organizing passions into a deliberate desire (NE III.3.1113a10–12), which is fully determinative of action. With too little fear, or too much, the eventual act must depend on further factors. The right amount is that amount which transforms the passion into a decision without other intervening factors. Only thus can moral goodness be understood as simply the complete and right development of the passions, and not as one factor among many to be weighed in a decision. People who are not virtuous can do virtuous actions, but they do them nonvirtuously because virtue is not the only determinant of their actions. It is right to call the virtues, as *hexeis* and actions, the *energeiai* of the passions in a way vices and other habits and acts are not, because a virtue is nothing but the *energeia* of some passion.

We act virtuously when virtue is not one consideration among others.[19]

The ethical virtues are not composed of pairs of dispositions, one for feeling the mean amount of a passion and the other for finding the means to a given end (aporia #3). Each virtue is a single habit of deciding.[20] Feeling the right amount of passions means feeling that amount which leads to a noble action, and a noble action is that act which fully develops the passion into an action done for its own sake. Feeling the right amount and acting well are two sides of the same *hexis,* and not two stages in a process, or two separate dispositions both required for virtue. "Every activity (*energeia*) aims at actions expressing its state of character (*hexis*), and to the brave person bravery is noble; hence the end it aims at is also noble" (*NE* III.7.1115b20–22). The virtuous man does not first feel the right amount of passion and then act well: feeling the right amount of passion is, *in potentia,* acting nobly and appropriately.[21] There is a necessary connection between the two sides of *energeia,* virtues as *energeiai* of the soul and ethically virtuous actions as *energeiai,* acts worth choosing for their own sake. One cannot know how to locate the mean amount of passions, or know why a certain habit is the right mean between vicious extremes except through knowing what to do.[22]

## The Rationality of Virtue

> *Akrasia* and vice are entirely different, for vice is unconscious (*lanthanei*) whereas the akratic man is aware of his infirmity. (*NE* VII.8.1150b35–6)

In chapter 2 I looked at the rationality of virtue by seeing how virtue could be rational without being taught or being a power for opposites. Here I want to reconsider a further feature of rationality. Typically, to be rational is to be unemotional, but that mark cannot be right for the virtues either. The virtuous relation of reason and emotion will lead, in the final section of this chapter, to the hidden psychology of the *Ethics.*

When practical knowledge includes perception, judgment, and decision, then neither pleasure (or pain), nor the passions, nor the body, is evil, as they must be with more detached conceptions of reason. Vice turns out to be much less interesting than it is on other conceptions of virtue. Virtue is a mode of knowing and of right thinking. The vices are culpable kinds of error (*NE* III.1110b28–1111a1, III.5.1114a3–7, IV.2.1122a13–16, VII.2.1145b36–1146a5, VII.4.1148a2–4). Some vices are more voluntary kinds of ignorance than others:

> Profligacy seems to be more voluntary than cowardice. (*NE* III.12.1119a21)

> It is fair not to regard *hamartēmata* and *atykhēmata* as of equal seriousness with unjust actions. Mistakes (*atykhēmata*) are unexpected actions (*paraloga*) and do not result from wickedness (*ponērias*). Offenses (*hamartēmata*) [or, as Kennedy translates them "personal failings"] are not unexpected but do not

result from wickedness. Unjust actions are not unexpected and do result from wickedness. (*Rh.* I.13.1374b4–9; see *NE* V.9.1135b11–27, *Pol.* III.11. 1281b26–28)

As I mentioned in the first chapter, practical rationality involves self-knowledge, knowledge of oneself as a practical agent. Vice, by contrast, is ignorance of self. Hence my epigraph: "Akrasia and vice are entirely different, for vice is unconscious whereas the akratic man is aware of his infirmity." Therefore one can say something for the virtues and vices similar to what Aristotle says in defining *technē* and its opposite: "Art is a rational quality concerned with making that reasons truly. Its opposite, lack of art (*atechnia*), is a rational quality, concerned with making that reasons falsely" (*NE* VI.4.1140a20–23).[23] Like *technē*, virtue is a rational quality, this time concerned with doing. Vice is a rational quality that reasons falsely. Like *atechnia*, vice is not a mere privation but takes effort, effort wrongly directed at the wrong end.

Therefore, there is no such thing as radical evil. Vices are habitual ways of making errors, doing things at the wrong times, with the wrong objects, the wrong ends, etc. Aristotelian vices carry no connotations of sin. They are ways of going wrong. They are rational failures. "No one of virtue is foolish or senseless (*ēlithoios oud' anoētos*) (*NE* IV.3.1123b3–4). Ignorance of particulars excuses, but wrong opinions make for vice, as we give to the wrong person, for the wrong reasons, at the wrong times.

Some errors are more culpable than others, some less corrigible, and some do more harm. Some merit the name of vices, while others do not. There is nothing more to the vices than that. Thus the extremes associated with *megalopsychia* "are not thought to be actually vicious, since they do no harm, but rather mistaken" (*NE* IV.3.1125a18–19), a judgment Aristotle qualifies by saying that the small-souled man is not foolish but rather too retiring or timid, "for men's ambitions show what they are worth, and if they hold aloof from noble enterprises and pursuits, and forgo the good things of life, presumably they think they are not worth of them" (*NE* IV.3.1125a24–27). Here is a form of error that is both rational and emotional. Consider too his assessment of the extreme of prodigality, and why it should not be called a vice:

> Correct [the prodigal] by training, or otherwise reform him, and he will be liberal, for he will now give his money to the right objects, while he will not get it from the wrong sources. That is why he is thought to be not really bad in character; for to exceed in giving without getting is foolish (*ēlithiou*) rather than evil or ignoble (*mochthērou oud' agennous*). The prodigal of this type therefore

seems to be much superior to the mean man, both for the reasons stated, and because the former benefits many people, but the latter benefits nobody, not even himself. (*NE* IV.1.1121a23–30)

Virtue and vice are practical forms of knowledge and error. Since practical knowledge involves emotion, the vices fail emotionally as well as rationally. The vices simultaneously (1) choose the wrong circumstantial variables, (2) fail to engage in an action that is its own end, and (3) feel excessively or deficiently. The example of prodigality shows how the three kinds of failure come together. "The prodigal errs (*diamartanei*), since he feels neither pleasure nor pain at the right things or in the right way" (1121a8–9). He is "indifferent to nobility of conduct," and thus "careless how they get his money. . . . Hence even his giving is not really liberal: his gifts are not noble, nor given for the nobility of giving, nor in the right way; on the contrary, sometimes he makes men rich who ought to be poor" (1121b1–7).

Whether an error is blameworthy or not depends on its distance from the mean. The metaphor of distance includes the difficulty of acting well, the difficulty of correcting the habit, its naturalness, and the amount of harm done. The vices are extremes, and since there is only a matter of degree between a vice and other forms of error, Aristotle has no need to draw definite lines between vices and other kinds of mistake. Thus, for example, the discussion of "shabbiness," the vice of deficiency connected to magnificence, is said to be "a vice, but it does not bring serious discredit, since it is not injurious to others, nor excessively unseemly (*aschēmones*)" (*NE* II.2. 1123a31–33). So too with the vice of inirascibility: "People who are not angered by the right things, or in the right way, or at the right times, or toward the right people, all seem to be foolish" (*NE* IV.5.1126a6–8). Yet in this case foolishness is blameworthy. It is the foolishness of the man who doesn't feel appropriate anger when he or his family are insulted. Not to be aware of insults is slavish and so blameworthy.[24]

Three properties of virtue correspond to the three dimensions of the vices I listed, corresponding respectively to formal, efficient, and final causes: (1) virtues lie in a mean with regard to emotions, while the vices result from too much or too little emotion; (2) virtues choose what is appropriate; and (3) virtuous action is its own end, while vicious acts always are for the sake of something else. The discussion of justice begins with questions tying these three dimensions together: "The questions we must examine about justice and injustice are these: What sorts of actions are they concerned with? What sort of mean is justice? What are the extremes between which justice is intermediate?" (*NE* V.1.1129a1–5).

Whoever divided the *Ethics* into books arranged the virtues according to which of these three each discussion emphasizes. The discussion of courage and temperance focuses on how these virtues are means with regard first to fear and confidence and then to the pleasures of taste and touch. Book IV shows how the virtues do what is appropriate, while the vices go wrong by giving to the wrong person, getting angry at the wrong time, giving pleasure in conversation in the wrong way. Justice, finally, requires extensive discussion of how just acts are done for their own sake and consequently are done from a just character. "Justice is a mean, but not in the same way as the other virtues, but in the sense that it is related to a mean, while injustice relates to the extremes. Justice is that quality through which a man is said to be disposed to do by deliberate decision that which is just" (*NE* V.5. 1133b32–1134a2). The argument begins from virtues best understood as a mean state with regard to the *emotions*, goes through virtues which we know through their characteristic *actions*, and ends with justice, which is manifested in action that is its own end and is characteristic of the just *person*. This development is an ethical progress from more passive to more active virtues.

The challenge Thrasymachus issues in *Republic* I makes sense for justice, because only justice is measured by an independent standard. What I can have is shaped not only by what is good for me or what I deserve, but also by what you own. The more justice concentrates on what is psychically satisfying along the *dynamis/energeia* dimension, the more it seems that it couldn't be bothered with such external accidents as who owns what. I should choose what is best for me. On the other hand, if justice is connected to property, then it is hard to see how it could be the good condition of a soul. Because it is not evident whether there are any particular passions or desires that justice realizes, Book V begins with an explicit discussion of the potency/act relation:

> What is true of sciences and *dynameis* is not true of *hexeis*. For while one and the same capacity or science seems to have contrary activities, a *hexis* that is a contrary has no contrary activities. Health, e.g., only makes us do healthy actions, not their contraries; for we say we are walking in a healthy way if we are walking in the way a healthy person would.
>
> Hence sometimes the nature of one or two opposite *hexeis* is inferred from the other, sometimes dispositions are known from the things in which they are found. For instance, if we know what good bodily condition is, we know from this what bad condition is as well, but we also know what good condition is from bodies in good condition, and know what bodies are in

good condition from knowing what good condition is. (*NE* V.1.1129a13–21; see *EE* II.10. 1227a23–28, VIII.1.1246a37–b8)

Those remarks apply to all the virtues, but they occur at the start of the discussion of justice. Other virtues start with a continuum of actions and passions in the soul and find which logos is its mean and *energeia*. But the discussion of justice begins with the logos and the mean, lawful actions and fair distributions, and finds the corresponding power. Justice is a more active virtue than the other ethical virtues.

### The Hidden Psychological Presupposition of the *Ethics*

Logoi stimulate and encourage liberal youths. Given innate *ēthos* and true love of the noble (*philokalon*), they can be influenced by virtue. (*NE* X.9. 1179b7–10)

I ended chapter 3 with some speculations that go beyond the *Ethics* itself, thinking there about what *phronēsis* would have to look like in our quite different circumstances. I want to end this chapter too by going beyond the text. The *Ethics* ends with a transition to the study of politics, and that transition can put the project of the *Ethics* in a broader context. Aristotle asks in the final chapter whether nature, habit, or reason is the source of virtue. The *Ethics* itself is concerned with the development of rational goodness, which presupposes nature and habit. To complete this look at the psychological dimensions of Aristotelian virtue, I want to ask these questions, which the *Ethics* presupposes but does not address:

- What is the soil of nature and habit in which ethical language and reasoning can be effectively planted? What natures and habits, that is, form the background for this development of rational goodness?
- And more specifically, what is the source of the power to engage in acts that are their own good?

Young men with innate *hos* and love of the noble (*philokalon*) can be influenced by virtue (X.9.1179b7–10), and I want to end this chapter by exploring that innate *hos* and love of the noble. Love of the noble, we learn later in X.9, is the product of specific political conditions, which begin in the family, and come from good laws (1179b31–1180a1). Behind that love stands a natural base, innate *hos*, which I want to identify with what he elsewhere calls *thumos*. *Thumos* is the source of ambition, aggression, love, and, to use a term that Aristotle does not, personal identity. People must be both intelligent (*dianoetikous*) and spirited (*thumoeideis*) if they are to be led easily toward virtue by a legislator (*Pol.* VII.7.1327b36–38; see 13.1332b8–10, 15.1334b7–8):

> *Thumos* is the faculty of our souls which issues in love and friendship. An indi-
> cation of this is that *thumos* is more aroused against intimates and friends than
> against unknown persons when it considers itself slighted. . . . Both the element
> of ruling and the element of freedom stem from this capacity for everyone.
> (*Pol.* VII.6.1327b40–1328a7; see Plato, *Rep.* 374–76)[25]

What is *thumos* and how does it lead to such things? I leave *thumos* untranslated because spirit, ambition, anger, and assertiveness all seem partially right, but more importantly because I need to leave open its status, possibly as simply a posit. Maybe we refer affectionateness, the power to command, and the love of freedom to *thumos* because we can't explain them.[26]

*Thumos* seems to be a mysterious answer to the mysterious question, Why should people generate internal ends and love the noble for its own sake? Deliberation as a search for the "easiest and best" means to a given end does not obviously lead to the constitution of internal ends, any more than facility at satisfying natural needs leads to a pursuit of the good life. Getting better at instrumental reasoning simply makes people better at instrumental reasoning. It gives no access to the kind of reasoning involved in choosing acts for their own sakes. In chapter 3 I said that art is a dead end, not a pathway to virtue. As we've seen, internal ends do not offer a completely satisfying method for best securing given ends; there are too many other ways of doing that. A being made up of reason and desire alone would never discover goods internal to practices.

In the *Ethics,* Aristotle simply dismisses people who live without desiring the noble (*NE* I.5.1095b19–20). Today we reasonably assume that the chief enemy of morality is selfishness.[27] Aristotle assumes instead that his audience are ambitious and active young men who need to figure out how to live an active life. Starting from self-interest, we would find acquisition, pleasure, and selfishness the primary threats to and alternatives to virtue. Aristotle, taking *thumos* as given, sees the desire to rule despotically and live tyrannically as the threat.

Therefore Holmes's miser is a more interesting ethical phenomenon than the person who simply wants to become rich as a means to being happy. Thus in *Politics* I, when talking about people who aim at unlimited acquisition, Aristotle says: "The cause of this disposition is preoccupation with life but not with the good life; so, desire for the former being unlimited, they also desire productive things without limit" (*Pol.* I.9.1257b40–1258a2). The task of the *Politics* is to show how nature and habit can produce citizens who care about the good life. The task of the *Ethics* is to show how our rational powers and our *thumos* can be fulfilled through virtuous activity. Like Holmes's miser, people are ingenious at finding ends in themselves, not all of them part of virtue, living well, or happiness. "It has happened to human beings that they make play an end" (*Pol.* VIII.5.1339b31–32). Such development of ends in themselves is evidenced in the pride of accomplishment found in the crafts. It is shown in impractical, useless competitions such as Scott and Amundsen's race to the South Pole. Wars of conquest and battles for political supremacy are further manifestations of the desire for the goods of activity. The way those activities are considered signs of nobility shows that they are valued in themselves. The miser is proud of his useless hoard, as I was of my skills in cheating. The ability to engage in pointlessly collecting money, in cheating, or in conquering city after city for their own sake creates the perverse accomplishments of the boaster who exaggerates his own accomplishments not to win a higher position, but without ulterior motive (*NE* II.7.1108a28, IV.6.1127a7–8, IV.7.1127a28).

While these examples show how a love of honor propels people into activities that are their own end instead of activities directed at given ends, they are not the good development of the *thumos* or of the human soul in general. Aristotle must show how the *thumos* is fulfilled in—and that ambitious young men listening to the lectures on ethics will be fulfilled in—doing virtuous actions for their own sake, not through *thēoria* alone as Socrates argues, and not, as many of his audience must have thought, through political ambition for domination. The *Ethics* is that demonstration.

Aristotle introduced *thumos* in the *Politics* to explain why Asians make natural slaves:

> The nations in cold locations, particularly in Europe, are filled with *thumos,* but relatively lacking in thought and art; hence they remain freer, but lack [political] governance and are incapable of ruling their neighbors. Those in Asia, on the other hand, have souls endowed with thought and art, but are lacking in *thumos;* hence they remain ruled and enslaved. But the stock of Greeks shares in both, just as it holds the middle in terms of location. For it is both spirited and endowed with thought, and hence both remains free and governs itself in the best manner and at the same time is capable of ruling all, should it ob-

tain a single regime. (*Pol.* VII.7.1327b23–32; for more on slaves lacking *thu-mos* see *Pol.* I.13. 1260b12–14, *Hist. An.* IX.1.608a33–42, *Part. An.* III.1. 661b33–34)

The existence of natural slaves, some of whom can be quite proficient at *technē*, shows that thought by itself is a dead end. Even if we doubt the existence of Medes and Persians who possess logos without *thumos,* we can rescue Aristotle's point that technical proficiency does not lead to moral goodness and happiness. Only spirit, *thumos,* ambition can push people from life into the good life. Without ambition, people would not have the ethical problems that the *Ethics,* and ethical virtue, are designed to over-come. *Thumos* as a character trait of some animals gives no help. Nor can *thumos*—rightly translated as "anger" in III.2, where Aristotle rejects it as a candidate for the genus of decision, *prohairesis*—be a source of friendship or love for the noble. Such *thumos* has nothing normative or rational about it. *Thumos* both sets the problem and creates the solution.[28]

The moral geography of *Politics* VII, populated by Asians with logos and no *thumos,* wild Europeans with *thumos* and no logos, and finally the Greeks who have both, may seem bizarre and repugnant; the description of the ages of man and natural development in *Rhetoric* II.12–14 comes closer to home. The young, who are *thumetikoi,* are characterized by the love of the noble, as opposed to the attention to utility that increases with age:

> The young love honor, but love victory more; for youth longs for superiority, and victory is a kind of superiority. They have both of these characteristics more than a love of money, and they are least lovers of money because they have not yet experienced want. . . . They choose to do noble things rather than things advantageous to themselves; for their live more by natural character than by cal-culation, and calculation concerns the advantageous, virtue the honorable. (*Rh.* II.12.1389a13–34; see *NE* VIII.3.1156a24–b6)

Given their love of the noble and concomitant contempt for considerations of utility, ardent young men do not automatically develop into virtuous people. Similarly, the vices are not a regression to a common animal na-ture but a perversion of the human power to decide on and do things for their own sake. Love for the noble, if not oriented to virtuous action, eventually dissipates to be replaced by a cynical concentration on utility: "They live for what is advantageous to themselves, not for what is noble, more than is right, through being fond of themselves. (The advantageous is good for the individual, the noble absolutely)" (*Rh.* II.13.1389b36–1390a1).

The moral psychology, with its trajectory that starts from a love for the noble and eventually, unless redirected to virtue, deteriorates into a concern for utility, is exemplified in the *Ethics'* discussion of liberality:

> [The profligate] is easily cured, both by growing older and by poverty, and is capable of reaching the intermediate condition. For he has the features proper to the liberal person, since he gives and does not take, though he does neither rightly nor well. If, then, he is changed, by habituation or some other means, so that he does them rightly and well, he will be liberal, for then he will give to the right people and will not take from the wrong sources. (IV.1.1121a20–25)

Good action, and the good life, depend on a desire not just that there be good results but that I do good. The desire for acting cannot be explained by a desire for the benefits of those actions. Doing good certainly looks far more expensive than simply the existence of good results—recall the artful rhetorician who had to limit itself to argument, and so might lose a case against someone without such scruples, and similarly the liberal person who decides whom to benefit rather than hiring an expert to make the particular decisions for him—so we need to show why anyone would want to do good rather than just see it that good be done. Virtuous action is not an obviously effective strategy for satisfying preexistent needs. If you want pleasure or wealth, Aristotle says, you must concentrate on getting pleasure or wealth, and not dream that, if you act virtuously, pleasure and wealth will follow in its train (*NE* IV.1.1120b17–20).

*Thumos*, then, both allows us to love and to engage in actions that are their own end. That is why I call *thumos* the capacity for personal identity, and why for Aristotle to take things morally is to take them personally.[29] To look forward to Kantian language, we cannot treat good actions as their own ends without treating some people as their own ends too. In a more Aristotelian idiom, we cannot do actions for their own sake without doing things for our friends' own sakes. While we might impute the competitive and commanding side of *thumos* to animals and uncivilized people, the capacity for friendship is much more narrowly distributed. Just as *thumos* is both natural to some animals and limited to only some humans, so too for friendship.

The ability to perform actions that are their own end is mysterious if we think the psyche is populated only of reason and bodily desires. Exactly the same mystery appears in understanding friendship. Friendship consists in loving and being loved (see *Rh.* II.4.1381a1–2), but more in loving (*NE* VIII.8.1159a33–34). One side of friendship isn't mysterious at all. The desire to be loved needs no explanation. Being loved is an effective means of satisfying other desires:

> Because the many love honor, they seem to prefer being loved to loving. . . . The many enjoy being honored by powerful people because they expect to get whatever they need from them, and so enjoy the honor as a sign of this good treatment. Those who want honor from decent people with knowledge are seeking to confirm their own view of themselves. (*NE* VIII.8.1159a12–24)

Loving, though, is less easily explained, and less common, than wanting to be loved. It is riskier, the benefits are not obvious, and so only it merits praise (*EE* VII.8.1241a35–37). Explaining why people should want to do things for their own sake is equivalent to explaining why good people should love and not just want to be loved. "All people, or the majority of them, wish noble things but choose beneficial ones; and treating someone well, *not* in order to be repaid, is noble, but being the recipient of a good service is beneficial" (*NE* VIII.13.1162b34–1163a1; see *Rh.* II.23. 1399a28–32).

The centrality of activity in Aristotle's thought comes into play here:

> It is rather the part of virtue to act well than to be acted upon well. (*NE* IV.1. 1120a11–12)

> It is a law of nature (*physikon*). Activity is a more desirable thing, and there is the same relation between effect and activity as between [the beloved and the lover]: the person benefited is as it were the product of the benefactor. (*EE* VII.8.1240a40–b3)

Rooting friendship in *thumos* has advantages over modern discussions of altruism. We today take selfishness as a given and then try to explain altruistic behavior. For Aristotle, all friendship (*philia*) is rooted in self-love (*philautia*). Self-love is not a datum like selfishness.[30] The right kind of self-love is an achievement, love for what is best in us. On the other side, unlike altruism, Aristotelian friendship is normative, available only to the good. "Good people wish goods in the same way to each other insofar as they are good" (*NE* VIII.3.1156a9–10). People who are not good cannot wish goods to each other.

Friendship and the desire for the noble, then, are the good development of the *thumos*. Both are possible, though, only within a polis. Outside a polis, the emotions rooted in *thumos*, assertiveness and competition, are destructive and bellicose. Hence Aristotle's moral psychology is a description of the souls of citizens and not a more general account of human nature. Therefore while moderns might agree with Aristotle in seeing pity, the pain one feels toward undeserved misfortune, as characteristic of a good character, we would part company with him in his parallel praise for indignation (*nemesis*), the pain felt at undeserved good fortune, since its goodness depends on the identification of taking things morally with taking things personally.[31] In Aristotle's eyes, substituting acquisitiveness for *thumos* makes for good slaves, people who do not want to rule but want to be left alone to consume. Where moderns worry about apathy and "bowling alone," Greeks worried about *stasis*.

Love for the noble is incoherent in the wrong conditions. Slaves would be silly to develop a taste for actions that are their own end. After all, their lives are so precarious that slavish pleasures are the only goods worth pursuing. Outside the right community, the virtues of commerce and the pleasures of private life swamp the more demanding life of virtue that Aristotle presents as the happy life. It is therefore the genius of modern politics and morals to dampen the *thumos* through the development of acquisitive appetites instead.[32]

On the other hand, a citizen who lives in a community in which virtue is praised and vice punished, a community in which natural ambitions can be satisfied in activities which allow him to stand out within the community, can reasonably choose to engage in activity for its own sake. It may not make you rich, and it may even result in your being less honored than those who run after honors, but it will satisfy the ambitions of the love for the noble. The descriptions of the virtues show how the love for the noble can be realized, in the right circumstances, into the decision to engage in actions that are their own end:

> Complaints and recriminations occur solely or chiefly in friendships of utility. . . . In a friendship based on virtue each party is eager to benefit the other, for this is characteristic of virtue and friendship; and as they vie with each other in giving and not in getting benefit, no complaints nor quarrels can arise, since nobody is angry with one who loves him and benefits him. (*NE* VIII.13.1162b5–10)

Virtuous action is both an activity of living well and an activity of sustaining a community in which such good living is a coherent and admirable activity. Even in the right community, the love for the noble does not develop automatically into virtue. Hence the corruptions of the vices, and the uniquely human possibility of perversely doing for their own sake things like the unlimited acquisition of Holmes's miser. Hence as well the rather disheartening narrative Aristotle presented in *Rhetoric* II.12–14 in which the initial love for the noble, if people are left to take their natural course, atrophies and is replaced by a narrow concentration on utility and a lowering of expectations from the good life to life itself (see *NE* VIII.1. 1155a11–16). Even in the right conditions, the virtue will always be an achievement worthy of praise. Specifying those right conditions will be part of the political task of virtue outlined in the next two chapters.

## Aristotle's Ethical Virtues Are Political Virtues

The practical virtues are exercised in politics or in warfare (*tōn men oun pratikōn aretōn en tois politikois hē en tois polemikois hē energeia*). (*NE* X.7. 1177b6–7)

One reason for the revival of Aristotle's *Ethics* is a dissatisfaction with moral theories based on duty or obligation. The revival was stimulated for many by Elizabeth Anscombe's "Modern Moral Philosophy," which claimed that an ethics of obligation was incoherent without a background of divine command.[1] Since Aristotle was a pagan, we who live after the death of God can appropriate his ethics as virtue ethics without worrying about theology. Modern moral theories might be incoherent when truncated from divine commands, but Aristotle's virtue ethics had no theology to start with.

That strategy has two obvious problems. First, the *Ethics* is not a "virtue ethics." Its subject is *eudaimonia*, happiness, and it discusses virtue because happiness is virtuous activity. Contemporary virtue ethics locates ultimate value in good agents without the ties to happiness, the soul, and external goods that I have been stressing.[2] But, in addition, Aristotle's ethics is precisely as incoherent without the polis as an ethics of duty without divine command. That relation between Aristotle's ethics and the polis is the subject of this chapter.

My last chapter brought together the first two of the five meanings of virtue I listed there—the ethical virtues as sets of actions worth choosing and doing for their own sake, and as the best development of the irrational

124

but persuadable part of the soul. I exhibited Aristotle's strong conclusion that virtuous activities can be actions chosen for their own sakes if and only if virtuous habits are the best development of the moral part of the soul. Virtuous *actions* are praised because of their results; *being virtuous* means choosing those actions for their own sake. These were the two dimensions of *energeia* and virtue.

I listed three more meanings of virtue. One of them, virtue as the differentia for saying what sort of activity happiness is in the definition of happiness as *energeia kat'areten,* will have to wait until the final chapter, when we look at happiness and the philosophical life. Here I need to bring together the other two senses of virtue, which look the least philosophically interesting. First, in addition to the central sense of habits and acts that are worth praising and choosing for their own sakes, virtue also has the general and nonmoral sense of the excellence of anything. Therefore we have to ask the critical ethical question: does Aristotle have criteria for setting off the moral from the rest of human activity? Chapter 3 looked in some detail at Aristotle's distinction between the realms of virtue and *techne,* and here we will see that the field of the ethical virtues is even narrower than the contrast with *techne* itself requires. *The polis, the Greek city-state that Aristotle sees as the unique locus for political life, provides an answer to the demarcation of the virtues.* While the polis, he says, comes into existence for the sake of life, it exists for the good life. We will find that the political as the locus of the good life enables Aristotle to mark off the ethical.

The final meaning of virtue referred to kinds of traditionally praised activity. That meaning raises questions about whether Aristotle is not simply ratifying conventional opinions and mores. How can the ethical virtues be political virtues without that identity implying a moral conservatism? Doesn't deference to existing conventions for virtue destroy the rationality of virtue? I want to approach these questions through a comparison between Aristotle and some contemporary topoi and opinions about ethics.

### Ancient and Modern Morality: The Terms of Contrast

Citizenship fills only a small place in modern life, and does not come near the daily habits or inmost sentiments. ( John Stuart Mill, *The Subjection of Women*)[3]

We read Aristotle to know ourselves. We inevitably read him through contrasts between his thought and modern morality. When modernity first characterized the ancient morality it was rebelling against, it didn't highlight the contrast between virtue ethics and an ethics of obligation, as philosophers often do today, but instead relied on three other contrasts: (1) Today, the scope of morality is limited, while Aristotle's virtues, since they concern the good life as such, were unrestricted. (2) In Aristotle, only citizens, that is, male, adult, property-holding, native born members of a city-state can be good, while today everyone can be moral. (3) The universal duties of contemporary morality make categorical demands on us, while Aristotle's virtues are more flexible.

The first topos claims that where the subject-matter of ancient ethical theory was broad, modern moral theory has a narrow scope. Ancient ethics had as its subject the good life and the human good, while the "peculiar institution" of modern morality concerns duties and most centrally duties toward others. Most of what makes for a modern good life is independent of morality. As Harry Frankfurt puts it, ethics orders "our relations with *other people*," not with "*what to care about* [and] what to do with *ourselves.*"[4] Not only is the right prior to the good, but the good is prior to morality. Moral goods, that is, are only one kind of ultimate value. Moral and prudential considerations are opposed in modern morality but not in ancient ethics.[5]

The narrower the scope of morality, the usual comparison continues, the higher the standards; morality becomes categorical. Those parts of modern life to which we give the title of morality must be met with a rigor and precision far above what Aristotle thinks appropriate to action. A third change accompanies these two, a broadening of who gets to be a moral agent. In opposition to aristocratic privilege, modern moral demands are limited to those acts which everyone can perform. David L. Norton puts this commonplace succinctly: "Modern morality . . . makes minimal demands upon the intelligence and developed moral character of moral agents, requiring little or nothing of them in the way of wisdom, courage, or integrity."[6] Modern morality applies to everyone, and its objects are as universal as its subjects. Thus Bernard Williams says:

> It is often thought that no concern is truly moral unless it is marked by . . . universality. For morality, the ethical constituency is always the same: the universal constituency. An allegiance to a smaller group, the loyalties to family or country, would have to be justified from the outside inward, by an argument that explained how it was a good thing that people should have allegiances that were less than universal.[7]

My three commonplaces can all be explained, and corrected, by noting a further, neglected but more fundamental contrast: Aristotle's ethical virtues are political virtues, while modern morality defines itself in opposition to the political. Modern morality applies to, and is appropriate for, citizens in the modern sense of subjects, *but not rulers,* of the modern state. Honesty, respect for the sanctity of contract, avoidance of harm to others, are the virtues of strangers and of citizens en masse, as the critics of modern morality, such as Rousseau and Nietzsche, remind us. (Small wonder then that we today think of rhetoric as something citizens need to defend ourselves against, rather than something that citizens need to practice.) The demands of modern morality notoriously do not apply to rulers, who have to have dirtier hands than the rest of us. Citizens as rulers need an ethics of good agents. Citizens as the ruled need a morality of right actions.[8] As Benjamin Constant puts it:

> The advantage that liberty, as the ancients conceived it, brought people, was actually to belong to the ranks of the rulers; this was a real advantage, a pleasure at the same time flattering and solid. The advantage that liberty brings people amongst the moderns is that of being represented, and of contributing to that representation by one's choice. It is undoubtedly an advantage because it is a safeguard; but the immediate pleasure is less vivid; it does not include any of the enjoyments of power; it is a pleasure of reflection, while that of the ancients was one of action. It is clear that the former is less attractive; one could not exact from men as many sacrifices to win and maintain it.[9]

While modern morality defines itself in opposition to the political, Aristotle sees questions of the best human life as the subject of the science of politics (*NE* I.2.1094b27–28, 1095a2–11, *EE* 1216b35–39, 1218a33–35, 1234b22–24). Political wisdom and *phronēsis* are the same quality of mind, although their essence is different (*NE* VI.8.1141b23–24). Achieving the good for the state is "a nobler and more divine" (*kallion kai theioteron*) achievement than achieving the good for the individual (*NE* I.2.1094b7–10; see *Pol.* VII.15.1334a11–15). The *Ethics* is a political inquiry, directed primarily at statesmen.[10]

We moderns have reversed the relation between ethics and politics. The *Ethics* presents a single good practical life, while the *Politics* offers a diversity of possible ways communities can organize themselves to live well. Today, we assume a plurality of ways of living well, with politics coordinating these differences by a *modus vivendi,* overlapping consensus, or public reason. In Aristotle different opinions about justice produce different states with different conceptions of the good life. Today different opinions about living well produce different moralities that have to be coordinated.[11]

In the last chapter I identified as morally radical and improbable Aristotle's thesis that all and only acts that realize the soul can be chosen for their own sakes. Here, to complete the picture, we have another radical and unlikely thesis: *All and only those activities are part of the human good which are activities of good citizens in the good polis.* These are actions commanded by law. If the activities of the human function were not limited to political activities, then the polis could not satisfy the development of the human good. Man would not be a political animal if political activities realized only part of human nature. The polis would then not exist for the sake of the good life but only for a part of the good life. The ethical virtues can be integrated into happiness only if they are integrated in a unified domain of ethical activity of the polis.

Only within the polis are the two dimensions of virtue—*energeiai* as the perfection of *kineseis* and *energeia* as the realization of a psychic *dynamis*—connected. Citizens' souls are fulfilled in political activity. Politics sets the ends for ethical activity and provides the resources for achieving those ends. Contemporary virtue ethics truncates Aristotelian ethics by neglecting the relation of virtue to law, as well as the relations of virtue to the soul and to happiness. Substituting "tradition" for law might create communitarianism, but not Aristotelian ethics. Unless the ethical virtues are political virtues, justice could not be all the virtues, relative to another person (*NE* V.1.1130a10–13); justice as virtue in general could not be "closely related" (*NE* V.1.1129a26–31) to particular justice. Virtue, and therefore happiness, "is found among those who have law in their relations" (*NE* V. 6.1134a30):

> Just as there is no ethical excellence or deficiency for beasts, so not for gods either: the one is above the virtues, and the deficiency of the other is not the same thing as ethical deficiency. (*NE* VII.1.1145a25–27)

> The law instructs us to do the actions of a brave person—not to leave the battle-line, e.g., or to flee, or to throw away our weapons; of a temperate person—not to commit adultery or wanton aggression; of a mild person—not to strike or revile another; and similarly requires actions that express the other virtues, and prohibits those that express the vices. (*NE* V.1.1129b19–25)

The law commands virtuous actions. Conversely, *the virtues enable us to do for their own sake what the law commands.* The thesis that Aristotle's ethical virtues are political virtues will then be no accidental consequence of the limitations of his imagination to conventional objects of praise. The domains of justice and of virtue are co-extensive; the question is how deep that coincidence goes. I claim that it goes very deep indeed: acting virtuously, we do for their own sake things that the law commands us to do. Thus:

> Actions that spring from virtue in general are in the main identical with actions that are according to law, since the law enjoins conduct displaying the various particular virtues and forbids conduct displaying the various particular vices. Also the regulations laid down for the education that fits a man for civic life (*pros to koinon*) are the rules productive of virtue in general. (*NE* V.2.1130b22–26; see too V.7.1138a4–7)

> Legislators make the citizens good by forming habits in them, and this is the wish of every legislator. (*NE* II.1.1103b5–6; see *Pol.* VIII.1.1337a14–21)

> It is the special business (*ergon idion*) of the legislator to create in men the disposition to use private property in common. (*Pol.* II.5.1263a39–40)

Our distance from Aristotle becomes clear. We hold that law is coercive and that good actions should be freely chosen: you can't legislate morals. Aristotle's law prescribes virtue. What the law cannot prescribe is not the realm of freedom but of the particular, of the choice of who, what, where, etc.[12] The law orders us to be liberal but is incompetent to say to whom you should give money, since it prescribes general types of action (*Rh.* I.2. 1356b29–34, *NE* I.7.1097a11–14). Failing to do what the law prescribes is blameworthy, but virtuous action does not go above and beyond the law. It does for its own sake what the law tells us to do.

This relation of virtue to law makes Aristotle's ethics very different from contemporary virtue ethics. Our virtues exist in a realm of freedom left indeterminate by the rights that structure our relations to each other. Beyond the law is the realm of privacy. To act generously, I must think about what I should give someone over and above what they can rightfully claim from me or from the state. I have a right to do as I like with my property, and generosity falls within the scope of doing as I like. The virtues lie in the realm of the permissible as opposed to the required and the prohibited. Aristotle's law requires virtue.

In chapter 2 I contrasted the modern conception of freedom, which resembles Aristotle's rational power to do opposites, with Aristotelian virtue, which is rational but oriented to good ends. MacIntyre says that "it is characteristically, even if not only, in *how* they play out their roles that individuals exhibit their individual character."[13] Substitute in that sentence "doing what the law commands" for "playing out one's roles" and this is exactly Aristotle's meaning (as well as the difference between MacIntyre and Aristotle). *It is in how people do what the law commands that they exhibit their character.* Vicious people express their character either by failing to do what the law commands, or by doing it in the wrong way, misinterpreting, for example, the command to be liberal as requiring one to be a spendthrift. The virtuous person sees doing for its own sake what the law commands as the most fulfilling thing he can do.

## Parallel Developments of Political and Ethical Autonomy

> In one sense the same persons rule and are ruled, but in another sense different persons. So education too must necessarily be the same in a sense and in another sense different. For, so it is asserted, one who is going to rule nobly should first have been ruled. (*Pol.* VII.14.1332b41–1333a3)

The ethical virtues are civic virtues because self-rule—knowing oneself as an agent and choosing acts that are their own end—develops through being ruled politically. The *Ethics* tells us that we become virtuous by performing virtuous acts. In the *Politics* we learn that people become political rulers through being ruled: "The ruler learns by being ruled. . . . The good citizen should know and have the capacity both to be ruled and to rule" (III.4.1277b9–16). Good souls contain a specifically political relation between ruling and being ruled. "The soul rules the body with the sway of a master; the intelligence rules the appetites with constitutional or royal rule" (I.2.1254b6–7), and that constitutional rule is defined as persuasion and obedience:

> The nonrational part [of the soul] apparently has two parts. For while the plant-like part shares in reason not at all, the part with appetites and in general desires shares in reason in a way, in so far as it both listens to reason and obeys it (*kathkoon kai peitharchikon*). . . . The nonrational part also is persuaded (*akoustikon*) in some way by reason. (*NE* I.13.1102b28–1103a3)

For reason to rule politically, we must to listen to our own reason, and we learn to do that by listening to and obeying the reason of others, and most of all the reason of the laws, which is, as the *Politics* says, reason without desire (III.16.1287a32, see *NE* V.6.1134a35–b1). Practical rationality can develop through reflection on virtuous habits only if the process of habituation, and its origin in the law, are themselves rational to begin with. Only in the political context does acting virtuously lead to becoming virtuous. Outside the polis, there is nothing to do for its own sake. Once the connection, via the political process of habituation, between external ends and choosing something for its own sake is severed, the connections between *energeia* and *dynamis* are severed too, and virtue has nothing to do with either souls or happiness.

Chapter 2 developed the idea of virtue as the good condition of the soul. Here we can take that a step further and see the virtues as the virtues of the souls of *citizens*. Aristotle's moral psychology is an account of the souls of citizens, not all humans but humans living in the conditions under which people can flourish. Since the virtues are the good conditions of the souls of citizens, there is no depth psychology in the *Ethics*. Prying beneath the surface of civic souls would uncover not true human nature but the barbarian privation of the conditions under which human nature can flourish. Aristotle bars exits from the polis to such a "natural" world to allow exits in the other direction, to *theōria*. If there were an exit from politics to common human nature, one could avoid politics and get directly to metaphysics, living as a citizen of the world, of a kingdom of ends, or a heavenly city. Instead, as I will lay out in the final chapter, the *Ethics* shows that the only route to *theōria* is through the political life.

In what follows I will show how my thesis about the political nature of the virtues sheds light first on the particular virtues (the next section). I will then turn to an obvious rejoinder to my thesis, that Aristotle's distinction between true courage and merely political courage in *Ethics* III.8, along with his distinction between the good man and the good citizen in *Politics* III.4, both suggest that political virtues fall short of true ethical virtues (the following sections, "The Good Man and the Good Citizen" and "How Is *Phronēsis* Acquired?"). It turns out that one source of the difference between ancient and modern virtue is that for Aristotle the natural and the political are not opposed, as they are for us (the section "The Natural and the Political"). In the final section, "Aristotle's Ethics and Ours, Again," I return to the initial topoi of ancient and modern and discuss how high Aristotle's noncategorical standards are, how broad the moral life is, and who can be good and happy.

## The Political Nature of the Ethical Virtues

Given the commonplace that Aristotle's ethics is broader than modern moral theory, the first thing to note about each of the virtues is its restricted scope. The last chapter gave one reason for the narrowness of the particular virtues: Aristotle focuses on habits and activities that are strictly speaking correlative: courageous action is nothing but the *energeia* of the virtuous habit of courage, while not only in the vices but in all sorts of otherwise desirable behavior, there is no such one-to-one relation between *dynamis* and *energeia*. But Aristotle does not always make evident the political nature of these restrictions on the particular virtues. I want to run through the particular virtues to illustrate this *dynamis/energeia* alignment of (1) political souls, (2) first *energeiai* of the virtues, and (3) second *energeiai* of virtuous political activities.

## Courage

> Those who are not capable of facing danger courageously are slaves of those who go against them. (*Pol.* VII.5.1334a21–22)

Aristotelian courage is not self-sacrifice.[14] Modern moral theory is based on a mistaken opposition between self and others, but Aristotle would regard that opposition as not merely an intellectual mistake but an error exemplified in *vicious* selves. If personal identity derives from citizenship, then courage is instead a conquering and despising of those fears that separate one's self from civic identity and so falsely lead one to feel courage as self-sacrifice.

When personal identity is civic identity, an entirely different moral psychology comes into play, one which makes courage on the battlefield noble and chosen for its own sake while courage in the face of the fear of poverty is not. If we today regard taking things personally and taking them morally as distinct, even at odds, I showed in the final section of the last chapter that Aristotle's virtuous man has a personal orientation to the world of value, an orientation ultimately rooted in the *thumos,* and so in competitive emotions that do not sit easily with contemporary associations of morality with equality or beneficence. Ethical value cannot be reduced to the impersonal values encountered by theoretical knowledge:

> If one were to abstract and posit absolute knowledge (*to ginōskein auto kath' auto*) and its negation . . . , there would be no difference between absolute knowledge and another person's knowing instead of oneself; but that is like another person's living instead of oneself, whereas perceiving and knowing oneself is reasonably more desirable. (*EE* VII.12.1244b29–34; see *NE* VIII.9. 1160a20–23, Plato, *Laws* V.732a, 739c)

No one can be good without taking things personally: Aristotle blames the inirascible man for failing "to defend himself; such willingness to accept insults to oneself and to overlook insults to one's family is slavish" (*NE* IV. 5.1126a3–8). "Men of great-souled nature are not fierce except toward wrongdoers, and their anger is still fiercer against their companions if they think that these are wronging them" (*Pol.* VII.6.1328a9–10). "A city is maintained by proportionate reciprocity. People seek to return either evil for evil, since otherwise [their condition] seems to be slavery, or good for good, since otherwise there is no exchange" (*NE* V.5. 1132b31–1133a2).[15]

When the personal is the political, the civic self includes the desire to be truly worthy of praise and honor and the desire to avoid shame and blame, where moderns might place these external to the self. The *megalopsychos* "is concerned with honor, because it is honor most of all that he claims as what he deserves" (*NE* IV.3.1123b22–24). Like the inirascible man who doesn't defend himself, the pusillanimous man does not try to get what he deserves (*NE* 1125a19–27). Where today impartiality is a mark of the moral, Aristotle's good man will favor family and friends (*NE* 1126b27, IX.9.1169b12, IX.11.1171a21–b28), and has moral relations in the full sense only with fellow citizens (*NE* V.6.1134b8–18).[16]

Aristotle announces without argument that only military courage counts as true virtue. Reading his account politically makes the limitation more defensible and more interesting. He takes as given that courage is a mean concerning fear and confidence, and asserts that although we fear "all evil things, for example, disgrace, poverty, disease, lack of friends, death, it is not thought that courage is related to all these things" (*NE* III.6.1115a10–12). Courage cannot cover all evils, "because there are some evils which it is right and noble to fear and base not to fear, for instance, disgrace" (a14). But that reason for exclusion from courage does not apply to many evils that people fear: "It is no doubt right not to fear poverty, or disease, or in general any evil not caused by vice and not due to ourselves. But one who is fearless in regard to these things is not courageous either (although the term is applied to him, too, by metaphor)" (a17–19).

There is an important reason buried here: courage concerns those fears connected with situations we are responsible for creating. Unless there is a hidden political premise, that criterion would not eliminate poverty or disease. But Aristotle would not regard it as courageous to fear the poverty one risks by gambling. Or consider some examples that highlight the difference between Aristotle's ethical world and ours. Am I courageous if I quit a degrading job and try to earn a living by oneself? Am I courageous not to fear the health risks that come with my playing football after knee surgery? Recently I heard someone claim that Elvis Presley was courageous because he dared to wear pink suits in Nashville. Is the value of his life internally connected to the ends he risked it for? If it is, is wearing pink in Tennessee a noble identity?[17]

Aristotle thinks that only in military courage is the value of one's life internally connected to the reasons for risking it. Contrast the internal connection between the value of one's life and the reasons for risking it with the man who "has nothing of value besides life to lose . . . who will barter his life for trifling gains" (*NE* III.9.1117b17–20). What he does is neither difficult nor pleasant. Courage affirms that one's personal identity is civic identity, as it directs one's thumos toward noble ends rather than toward the destructive bravado it would manifest itself in without the discipline of courage. One risks one's life fighting against someone else who is also risking his life. This element of competition is, I think, the unstated reason why Aristotle identifies courage with combat in battle, not with naval engagements, or with struggles against storms or poverty.[18] One risks one's life for a good that is one's own in the deepest sense; this is both difficult and something that one does gladly and through choice, not in the spirit of sacrifice but with an awareness of the seriousness of possible loss.

## Temperance

> Man is the most unrestrained and most savage of animals when he lacks virtue, as well as the worst where food and sex are concerned. (*Pol.* I.2. 1253a35–37)

While elsewhere in the Greek world it may be the virtue of women (*Rh*. I.5. 1361a6–7), in Aristotle's hands temperance is the noble distancing of oneself from the genus animal in the definition of man as political animal (*Pol*. I.2.1253a7–11). The temperate person knows that his animal nature is realized in the differentia, citizenship.[19]

The genus animal is the material basis for the form, political animal. Generic pleasures are the material basis for the political pleasures of activities that are their own good. Where he limits the scope of courage to political objects, temperance concerns the most nonpolitical of objects, the pleasures humans share with other animals (*NE* II.2.1104b35; see Plato, *Rep*. VIII.558d–559c, *Laws* 782d–783a). Temperance is not about food, drink, and sex, since those are functions of the nutritive soul, which has no virtue (*NE* VI.12.1144a9–11). It is about the specifically human desires and pleasures for food, drink, and sex. I once knew someone who used to run ultra-marathons because he really loved drinking beer, and the only way he could drink as much as he liked was by running off the calories. Because his intake and output were in balance, he was healthy. His nutritive soul was in good shape. But such health would not qualify him as temperate. There is nothing noble in running ultra-marathons in order to drink a lot of beer. He compensated for his sensual weakness in one direction by strength of will in another, much as in the *Phaedo*'s caricature of virtue as intelligently exchanging pleasures and pains (69a).

Temperance is that habit of choosing which affirms membership in the human species, political animal, rather than its genus, animal. Its political function reveals itself in the remark that, as the law can make political cowardice illegal but cannot legislate against cowardice in the face of disgrace and poverty, so war and the threat of war "compel men to be just and to behave with temperance" (*Pol.* VII.15.1334a25–27; see *Rh.* I.9. 1366b13–14). To be nonpolitical is a vice. The insensitive and the self-indulgent are vicious because they are nonpolitical. The wrong relations between soul and bodily pleasures can make someone apolitical and thus less than fully human.[20]

While intemperance is clearly blameworthy, why should someone deserve praise for resisting the temptations of the flesh? There is nothing noble in resisting desires and pleasures we share with animals.[21] But refraining from self-indulgence differentiates citizens from children (*NE* III.12. 1119a33–b3) and slaves (*NE* III.10.1118a23–25, b21). Not gratifying shameful desires is one way we show ourselves to be civic rulers rather despots like Sardanapalus (*NE* I.5.1095b19–22, *EE* I.5.1216a16–19), and citizens rather than slaves.[22]

Only on this political interpretation can temperance be a virtue and not simply a necessary condition for good action. A slave "needs only a small amount of virtue, just enough to prevent him from failing in its tasks owing to intemperance and cowardice" (*Pol.* I.5.1260a34–36), so temperance is a necessary condition for slaves, and nothing praiseworthy. Such slavish virtue is the minimal morality of modern ethics. People need self-control in order to accomplish anything worthwhile, but no one can for that reason practice self-control for its own sake.

The pleasures of activity, we will discover in *Ethics* X, are defined by the activities they complete. The common pleasures of the body are the greatest possible distance from such pleasures, and so it might seem sensible to remove them as much as possible from the good life. Instead, these pleasures are useful reminders that living well does not overcome or denigrate life itself, that the soul is the first actuality of the body and not something inserted into a body as a prisoner. The temperate enjoyment of the common pleasures reflects an understanding of the relation of life to the good life, body to soul and self to community. Such enjoyment is therefore part of a picture of practical reason that is itself embodied, a good condition of the appetitive soul. Virtuous self-sufficiency does not rise above animal nature. It specifies it by perfecting it. In the temperate person "the appetitive element must be in harmony with reason" (*to epithumētikon kata ton logon*) (*NE* III.12.1119b15–18).[23]

Courage and temperance are the virtues of the irrational soul (*NE* III.10.1117b24). They make the irrational soul as such virtuous because they are the only aspects of the irrational soul relevant to one's civic identity and one's virtue as a citizen. That does not mean that every appetite is somehow realized in hitting means about fear and confidence and carnal pleasures, but that someone who has a courageous and temperate soul is a person who sees the true worth of *all* of his desires. It is for this reason that *NE* III.12, which is an extended comparison of courage and temperance, ignores the limitations of the virtues to proper spheres and compares courage as the virtue concerned with pains to temperance, the virtue concerned with pleasures. This is a nice example of the ways in which Aristotle's virtues are both restricted—there are many desires and passions that are not the material for virtue—and complete: these two virtues are enough to make the entire irrational soul in good condition.

Therefore, unless even the nonruling citizen has temperance and courage, "he will not perform any of the duties of his position" (*Pol.* I.13. 1260a2–3). In people in the prime of life and the prime of political activity, "their temperance is combined with courage, and their courage with temperance, whereas in the young and old these qualities are found separately; for the young are courageous without self-control, the old are temperate but cowardly" (*Rh.* II.14.1390b3–6). Immediately after declaring that man is a political animal in *Politics* I.2, Aristotle notes that "as man is the best of animals when perfected, so he is the worst of all when sundered from law and justice. . . . When devoid of virtue man is the most unscrupulous and savage (*anosiotaton kai agriotaton*) of animals, and the worst in regard to sexual indulgence and gluttony (*aphrodisia kai edoden cheiriston*)" (1253a29–39). The vices of rashness and intemperance characterize the man without law or virtue. Intemperance slides into general baseness (*NE* III.10.1118b1–3).

## Liberality, and the Other Virtues of *Ethics* IV

Wit is cultured insolence (*hubris*). (*Rh.* II.12.1389b11–12)

It is not noble (*kalon*) for a woman who has any sense to grow angry. (Sophocles, *Trachiniae* 552)

Courage and temperance fit into almost all lists of the virtues, although they are usually broader than in Aristotle's hands. They are easy to see as virtues because they do good for others or put us in a position to do good for others, and because we seem to give something up in each. What is good about, and what is difficult about, the virtues of *NE* IV must follow a different model. Besides, that these—generosity, magnificence, magnanimity, the nameless virtue concerned with small honors, mildness, friendliness, truthfulness, and wit—should exhaust something, even in the complicated way that courage and temperance exhaust the virtues of the irrational soul, seems very unlikely. And yet to act virtuously must be to act according to some particular virtue.

The virtues of *NE* IV help us to see virtue as responding to situations that challenge the reciprocity essential to citizenship. Courage and temperance might lend themselves to conceiving a conflict between first and third person points of view. My exercising them is good for you, and so praised, while costly and noble for me. It is good for the community that all citizens are courageous and temperate. Such a picture of virtue does not fit Book IV at all. Instead of a conflict between first and third person points of view, *megalopsychia* and *megaloprepia* are virtues that cannot be universalized. What if everybody did it? is not even intelligible when addressed to the *megalopsychos* or the *megaloprepēs*. "The magnificent person is like a scientific expert (*epistēmoni*), since he is able to observe (*theōrēsai*) what will be the fitting amount (*to prepon*), and to spend large amounts in an appropriate way" (*NE* IV.2.1122a34–35, see II.6.1106b9–12). Expertise is exceptional. The virtues of Book IV call for more knowledge than courage and temperance do, and so are not as widely distributed. The challenge is to excel without exempting onself from the community. Competitive virtues cannot be universal.[24]

The friendliness of *NE* IV.6 is a mean between those who are ingratiating, and so slavish, and the quarrelsome who don't mind causing pain to others, and so are despotic in character. To be friendly is to have the habits of neither slaves nor despots, and so to be capable of ruling and being ruled politically. The magnificent man equips triremes and choruses and so does for its own sake what the law commands. Therefore the vices associated with *megaloprepia*, being banausic (*NE* IV.2.1122a31, see II.7.1107b19) and niggardly, are ways of making oneself an exception to the community. Similarly, the *megalopsychos* represents the community's judgment of nobility and honor, and so is "moderately pleased . . . when he receives great honors from excellent people" (*NE* IV.3.1124a6–7), but has contempt for being honored by small people or for small things. (Contrast Coriolanus, who cannot find anyone noble enough properly to honor him.) One sign of the political nature of his virtue is that since he does not think that even honor is the greatest good, he will not derive excessive pleasure or pain from good and bad fortune (1124a15–16). Rather than be a member of the community through universalizing his maxims, he

> is the sort of person who does good but is ashamed when he receives it; for doing good is proper to the superior person, and receiving it to the inferior. He returns more good than he has received; for in this way the original giver will be repaid, and will also have incurred a new debt to him and will be the beneficiary. Magnanimous people seem to remember the good they do, but not what they receive. . . . It is proper to the magnanimous person to ask for nothing, or hardly anything, but to help eagerly. . . . When he meets people with good fortune or a reputation for worth, he displays his greatness, *since superiority over them is difficult and impressive.* (*NE* 1124b9–21; see Plato, *Laws* V.729b1)

We can see the political nature of magnanimity through the contrasting extremes, which Aristotle, agreeing with common opinion, calls errors, not vices. The magnanimous man knows the place of his virtue and his virtuous actions in the community in circumstances where such knowledge is difficult to achieve. The person who, as Churchill said of Clement Atlee, is modest because he has a great deal to be modest about faces no great challenge about his membership in the community and so his citizenship, but the person of great achievements does.

"This sort of excellence is found in the sorts of expenses called honorable . . . and in expenses that provoke a good competition for honor, to the benefit of the community" (*NE* 1122b19–23). The asymmetrical giving relationship in liberality is a manifestation, and a preservation, of inequality. So is the virtuous competition for honors. So too the *megalopsychos* aims at showing his superiority, but before an audience of fellow-citizens. Even truth-telling, which seems to be more reciprocal than those virtues, features practicing self-deprecating irony and concealment in one's dealings with inferior people. But liberality still requires the equality of citizenship as opposed to more patronizing forms of charity that can exist outside political relationships, and in this way liberality is a model for the rest of the virtues of Book IV. Modern successors to liberality might be motivated by feelings oriented toward a basic moral equality of all humans, which is very far from the equality of citizens. "What we count as self-sufficient is not what suffices for a solitary person by himself, living an isolated life, but what suffices also for parents, children, wife, and, in general, for friends and fellow citizens, since man is naturally a political animal" (*NE* I.7.1097b8–11). "It is nobler to benefit friends than strangers" (*NE* IX.9.1169b12;

see IX.11.1171a21–b28). The ways Aristotle's political virtues embody specifically political equality and inequality again reflect the basic difference in orientation between his and modern, apolitical, morality exemplified in the difference between liberality and contemporary generosity, which should help those most in need, not one's friends.

In similar ways, hitting the mean toward anger makes one fit for civic life, while the inirascible man foolishly and slavishly fails to perceive when he or his family is insulted (*NE* IV.5.1126a3–8). The person who gets angry too easily or at the wrong things is like the man who insists on standing on his rights (*NE* V.10.1137b34–1138a3). Neither can participate in the reciprocity of civility.

Aristotle's delineation of the virtues in Book IV depends on its particular political context. This context makes coherent Aristotle's separating the virtues for small and large honors and expenditures. Different roles in the political community require distinct abilities to choose appropriate occasions and objects. In other circumstances, the self-deprecating irony which Aristotle sees as a virtue of social intercourse might suggest a parallel anonymity or disguise for civic performances requiring great wealth, as with contemporary anonymous donors. Aristotle has a single virtue, liberality, concerned with getting and spending. But virtuous getting in his polis is pretty much limited to using only one's own property and not another's (*NE* IV.1.1119b25–26, 1120a34–b2), so that acquiring wrongly is the vice of injustice and not a vice contrary to liberality itself. Communities with more complicated economic systems might need distinct virtues for getting and for spending. Those extreme habits which Aristotle says are foolish rather than vicious might become true vices.

The virtues of Book IV make sense only under social inequality combined with civic equality. The corresponding vices make people unsuitable for citizenship either through being so slavish or so despotic that they cannot participate in political ruling and being ruled. If the virtues of courage and temperance are the virtues of the irrational soul and of *epithumia*, the virtues of Books IV and the justice of Book V are the virtues of the *thumos*. The combination of equality and inequality occurs even in the word for one of the virtues, *megaloprepia*, combining greatness and appropriateness or measuredness. We want to do better than our equals, and yet be recognized and honored by those same equals (*NE* IV.4.1125b16–17). If we have a hard time today stomaching Aristotle's picture of the magnificent or the magnanimous man, or his remarks about self-deprecating irony and the contempt the virtuous man shows toward others (*NE* IV.3.1124b5–6), our reactions are based on a different background assumption about equality.

Numerical equality is central to contemporary morality, and the burden of proof is on those who would exempt some areas from such equality and, for example, make reward proportional to merit. We justify such exceptions by removing an area from the domain of morality, separating, for example, a realm of expertise, in which people's opinions are valued in proportion to their knowledge, and a realm of morality, in which everyone's opinions are weighted equally. The friendly person treats everyone alike, and at the same time does "what is suitable (*hōs harmozei*) for each" (*NE* IV.6. 1126b26–27). The virtues of Book IV are difficult because they demand both equal treatment to all, with no special favorites, and actions that take into account the peculiarities of individual situations.

## Justice

> All just behavior is relative to a friend. (*EE* VIII.10.1242a20–21; cf. Plato, *Statesman* 311c)

The discussion of justice confirms the civic interrelations of equality and inequality, especially in contrast to the modern presupposition of universal moral equality. Justice here is an ethical virtue, not a description of impersonal political arrangements. Distributive justice concerns just forms of inequality, while modern justice as a political arrangement without friendship must be much more committed to numerical equality. Aristotelian justice cannot be blind. Like temperance, justice is the triumph of second nature over first, and so civic identity over a more natural and isolated kind of identity.[25]

The unjust man conceives the moral life as a conflict between selfish desires and duties toward others, as the coward conceives of courage as self-sacrifice and the intemperate man sees temperance as bondage. Justice is complete virtue toward another person (*NE* V.1.1129b27). That is, the lawfully just person is not simply someone who obeys laws, which in modern morality sets the floor against which virtuous behavior is measured. The lawfully just person finds it possible to do for its own sake what the law commands, and goes beyond the obedient person by deliberating about what the law's commands require in any particular situation. The courageous person will respond to the necessity of risking his life by doing so for the sake of the noble, not simply because the law orders him to fight or through fear of the consequences of military defeat. The lawfully just person does something even more difficult: he sees the fact that something is lawful as sufficient reason to do it for its own sake. Justice differs from the earlier virtues because it has no specific emotion it must measure, as courage consists in the right amount of fear and confidence. Without such a passion, it is even harder, and more praiseworthy, to choose the lawful for its own sake.

The good relations within a family only resemble justice (*NE* V.6. 1134b8–17). Ethical friendship derives from just civic relations, not from intimate, prepolitical relations, since it is *thumos,* not *eros,* "that creates affectionateness" (*Pol.* VII.7.1327b40–41). Indeed, one of the major differences between Plato and Aristotle is the way Aristotle severs the relation between *thumos* and *eros* and creates this new and specifically political relation between *thumos* and *philia.*[26]

When the ethical virtues are political virtues they depend on a political community of friendship and *homonoia.* Our democratic morality of rights and rules is codifiable and so can be categorical. Rules make morality more democratic. The companion charge to Aristotle's ethics being aristocratic is that modern morality is legalistic. Open communities and their corresponding moralities must be legalistic. Only closed communities with tacit knowledge—virtue is acting as the *phronimos* would act—can be communities of virtue. Even the virtue of corrective justice, which concerns not the relations of rulers to ruled but the relations between particular private citizens, is a political virtue that preserves and restores civic relations.[27]

The second feature of Aristotle's thought I mentioned in the Introduction as both attractive and repellent was the tie between ethics and the lawful. That tie is expressed in the idea that "justice is complete virtue toward another person" (*NE* V.1.1129b27), combined with the idea that "everything that is lawful is in a way just" (V.1.1129b12; see V.6.1134a29–b1). As I will show in the next section, there is never a conflict between the demands on the good man and those on the good citizen. Aristotle therefore cannot conceive of ethical obligations to disobey the state. There is no right of rebellion or revolution. What are for us important exemplars of morally praiseworthy action are, for Aristotle, unintelligible.[28]

This section has shown how our understanding of the particular virtues has to be transformed by seeing the connection between virtue and law. But if virtue is doing for its own sake what the law commands, law must be transformed as well. Law must be connected to the good life. Purely positive law might command obedience, but you cannot drive on the right side of the road for its own sake, or have any emotional attachment to rules of that sort. Aristotle's state may not have been limited, in the sense that there was no zone of privacy into which the polis could not intrude, but it must be limited in another sense: law is limited to commanding things which, done for their own sake, are virtuous. The administrative regulations that occupy so much of our law have nothing to do with ruling and being ruled in turn.

### The Good Man and the Good Citizen:
### The Virtues and Political Souls

> The true politician seems to have put more effort into virtue than into anything else, since he wants to make the citizens good and law-abiding. (*NE* I.13.1102a7–10)

> The principal care of politics is to produce a certain character in the citizens, namely to make them virtuous, and capable of performing noble actions. (*NE* I.9.1099b29–32)

> To promote friendship is thought to be the special task of the art of government. (*EE* VII.1.1234b23–24)[29]

There is an obvious problem with my thesis that the ethical virtues are political virtues. Both the *Ethics* and the *Politics* deny that identity. In *Ethics* III.8 Aristotle presents five states of character which produce courageous behavior but which themselves fall short of courageous character.[30] The first "trope," political courage, is most like true courage, "because it results from a virtue; for it is caused by shame and by desire for something noble, namely honor, and by aversion from reproach, which is shameful" (1116a27–29). If true courage differs from political courage, then doing something from the "desire for something noble" (*dia kalou orexin*) must differ from doing something for the sake of the noble (*tou kalou heneka*). What is the difference?

The person of political or civic courage does what the law, or a superior officer, commands, motivated by shame or hopes of being honored. But he does not choose for its own sake what the law commands. Following orders, he does not exercise *phronēsis* and so he does not act for the sake of the noble, or do anything for its own sake.

The conscripts in the second trope "are worse to the extent that they act because of fear, not because of shame, and to avoid pain, not disgrace" (1116a31–32). People who are forced to be brave (1116a33–34) are less courageous since "the brave person must be moved by the noble, not by compulsion" (1116b2–3). Being repeatedly motivated by compulsion and punishment does not eventually lead to autonomous action.

The difference between these tropes of courage recalls the distinction between being moved by desire for the noble and being moved by shame and fear, which I used at the end of the last chapter to show the need for *thumos* as well as reason in the good life, and Aristotle returns to that distinction in the last chapter of the *Ethics,* the transition to politics:

> It is the nature of the many to be amenable to fear but not to a sense of shame, and to abstain from evil not because of its baseness but because of the penalties it entails. (*NE* X.9.1179b7–10)

> The many yield to compulsion more than to argument and to sanctions more than to the noble. (*NE* X.9.1180a4–5)

People conscripted into courage are followed in the series of tropes by those who act courageously through experience, through emotions, and, finally, through ignorance. The professional soldier appears brave and is

> most capable (*malista dynantai*) in attack and defense. . . . In fighting nonprofessionals they are like armed troops fighting unarmed, or like trained athletes fighting ordinary people; for in these contexts also the best fighters are the strongest and physically fittest, not the bravest. [But professional soldiers turn out to be cowards when the danger overstrains them. . . . In contrast to the courageous] they are more afraid of being killed than of doing something shameful. (*NE* III.8.1116b9–23)

Habituation in professional courage cannot lead to true courage—we learned in chapter 3 that no art can be perfected into a virtue. Not just any repetition leads to virtue, only habituation rooted in law and the desire for the noble. If the citizen soldier acts often enough and successfully enough by aiming at honor and avoiding shame, he can become habituated to virtue and so fully virtuous. Only potentially rational actions can lead through habituation to fully rational actions. Law is reason without desire (*Pol.* III.16.1287a32). To become virtuous, the young must be commanded by law (*NE* X.9.1180a1–4): "People become hostile to an individual human being who opposes their impulses . . . whereas a law's prescription of what is decent is not burdensome" (*NE* X.9.1180a23–24; see *Pol.* VI.4. 1318b38–1319a1).

The citizen soldier moved by shame is potentially rational. Both the things to which we can become habituated and the habituation itself must be rational from the start for the outcome to be virtuous and rational. Only ethical habituation, and not repetition of the lower tropes, leads to an understanding of why something is the right thing to do and why courage is noble. The citizen soldier acts according to reason, even though not his own, while the others are not acting according to reason at all. "Virtue is not merely a state in accord with correct reason (*kata ton orthon logon*), but the state involving the correct reason (*meta tou orthou logou*)" (*NE* VI.13. 1144b26–28). The citizen soldier, motivated by shame and the desire for the noble, can come to do these things for their own sake. Political courage is inferior to true courage but is the route to it.

### How Is *Phronēsis* Acquired?

> *Phronēsis* is the only virtue peculiar to the ruler. The other virtues, it would seem, must necessarily be common to both rulers and ruled, but prudence is not a virtue of one ruled, but rather true opinion (*doxa alēthēs*) [is]. (*Pol.* III.4.1277b25–29)

How I can square my claim that the moral virtues are political virtues with the distinction between the good man and the good citizen (*Pol.* III.4. 1276b13–33, III.8.1288a38–b2, IV.7.1293b5–7, VII.14.1333a11– 12, *NE* V.2.1130b25–29)? The *Ethics* tells us that one cannot have ethical virtue without *phronēsis* or *phronēsis* without ethical virtue (*NE* VI.13. 1144b30–32), while the *Politics* restricts *phronēsis* to rulers. Even in the best state, he says there, it is "only the statesman, the man who controls or is competent to control (*ho politicos kai kurios hē dynamenos einai kurios*), either by himself or with others, who is essentially also a good man" (*Pol.* III.5.1278b4–5). I want to affirm the challenging implication of Aristotle's argument: *only rulers can exercise full virtue.*[31]

Where the ruler has *phronēsis,* the nonruler has true opinion (1277b28– 29). Modern ears might assume that true opinion means unjustified true belief, and so *phronēsis* consists in true opinion plus the appropriate justifications. Instead, true opinion is what the man of political courage had in *Ethics* III.8. For the citizens to be virtuous without exercising *phronēsis,* true opinion must be more than slaves' "participation in reason only to the extent of perceiving it" (*Pol.* I.5.1254b23–24).

Two features of the claim that "*phronēsis* is the only virtue peculiar to the ruler" need detailed consideration. First, in lines I quoted before, "the ruler learns it by being ruled. . . . The good citizen should know and be able (*epistasthai kai dynasthai*) both to be ruled and to rule" (*Pol.* III.4. 1277b9–16; see IV.11.1295b5–25). We acquire *phronēsis* through acting virtuously with true opinion, much as the citizen-soldier can become truly courageous. Second, *phronēsis*, this intellectual virtue peculiar to rulers, is about the means, while ethical virtue is about ends (*NE* VI.12.1144a7–9). How *phronēsis* is about means will tell us still more about the rationality of virtue, as we learn about our rational relations to both means and ends.

### *Phronēsis* Unique to the Rulers

Power (*dynamis*) belongs by nature to the young, and *phronēsis* to those who are older. (*Pol.* VII.9.1329a15)

There can be no education specific to the ruler, not if he learns to rule by being ruled. There is no Aristotelian equivalent of the curriculum of *Republic* VI and VII. And since "the education and the habits that make a man virtuous are the same as those that make him a political or kingly ruler" (*Pol.* III.18.1288a35–b1), one becomes a *phronimos* by acquiring the ethical virtues. One becomes courageous by performing virtuous actions, but one does not become practically wise by performing practically wise actions but by acting with moral virtue.

"Virtue is of two sorts, virtue of thought and virtue of character. Virtue of thought arises and grows mostly from teaching, and hence needs experience and time. Virtue of character results from habit" (*NE* II.1. 1103a14–16). Neither teaching nor habituation can account for acquiring *phronēsis*. Like *sophia*, *phronēsis* is not a *dynamis*. Unlike the ethical virtues, neither *sophia* nor *phronēsis* is the *energeia* of some more primitive *dynamis* with specifiable properties of its own. They are the good condition of the thinking soul, but that soul does not have the same kind of natural basis as the desiring soul. There is no organ of thought that stands to thinking as the eye stands to seeing (*De An.* II.4.429a18–b6, *Gen. An.* 736b28–29). (Aristotle thought that the brain had nothing to do with thinking; it was an air conditioner that cooled the blood.) Because one becomes a *phronimos* by becoming ethically virtuous, there can be no independent etiology of *phronēsis*. For the same reason, as I will show in the final chapter, there is no education for philosophers either. We have *phronēsis* through two things, being ethically virtuous and being in a position to rule.[32]

The citizens of *Politics* III have ethical virtue without *phronēsis*, a possibility which *Ethics* VI denies. Possessing *phronēsis* isn't the issue: the ruled citizens of *Politics* III have ethical virtue without *exercising phronēsis*. The potency/act distinction does not apply to *phronēsis*. Thus Aristotle says that *phronēsis is* the *orthos logos*, not that it possesses the *orthos logos* or that it is knowledge of the *orthos logos* (*NE* VI.13.1144b27–28).[33] Of course *phronimoi* sleep, and engage in leisure activities, so in that sense the potency/act distinction applies, but *phronēsis* is neither the perfection of a corresponding kind of *kinēsis*, as the ethical virtues are, nor the good condition of some power of the soul we can specify independently. Without exercising *phronēsis*, one is not a *phronimos*, while one can be virtuous without acting virtuously.

### *Phronēsis* Is to Means as Ethical Virtue Is to Ends

*Phronēsis* is about means, ethical virtue about ends. (*NE* VI.12.1144a7–9, 1144a20, VI.13.1145a4–6, X.8.1178a16)

We become *phronimoi* by acquiring and exercising the ethical virtues. Nonruling citizens possess the virtues imperfectly, as they are governed by right opinion. Such people do not lack, therefore, a full appreciation of moral ends. Rather, the imperfectly virtuous lack the intellectual virtue concerning means. Recall that in the first chapter I noted that both in the art of rhetoric and in ethical virtue we discover internal ends through limitations on the available means for achieving a given, external end. The artful rhetorician does not differ from the sophist by having the right moral ends but by practicing an art which limits the choice of means. Similarly, while the rulers and ruled share ends, rulers alone exercise *phronēsis*, a virtue concerned with means. Rulers deliberate about and supply the means that allow all citizens to achieve those ends. Rulers, for example, set the framework that regulates public discourse, and the rest of the citizens, in talking about themselves and each other in the right ways, act virtuously within that framework. Legislators decide which aspects of the education of children are a public function and which should occur primarily within the household, and virtuous citizens then see that their children are educated in accordance with such provisions. *Phronēsis* is knowledge of means, and the ruler supplies the means so that the citizens can act virtuously. For citizens to act justly, liberally, with wit, etc., depends on the provision of means, which is the job of the state not the individual (*Pol.* VII.12. 1332a28–33; see also VII.11.1331b18–21). "The absolutely good is absolutely desirable but what is good for oneself is desirable for oneself; and the two ought to come into agreement. This is effected by virtue; and *the purpose of politics is to bring it about* in cases where it does not yet exist" (*EE* VII.2.1236b38–1237a1).

The person with right opinion accepts the provision of whatever means are given, while the phronimos *knows* which means to supply. It is for that reason that after distinguishing *phronēsis* from economics, legislation, and political science (*NE* VI.8.1141b24–34), Aristotle brings them back together by saying that "a man cannot pursue his own welfare without economics and politics" (VI.8.1142a9–10). The many virtuous people who "can practice virtue in their own concerns, but [who are] unable to do so in their relations with another" (V.1.1129b33–1130a1), live by right opinion and not *phronēsis*. The wealthy man will choose how to spend his money to outfit a chorus or a trireme; the ruler with *phronēsis* will choose how property should be distributed so that some men have enough wealth to do such things.[34]

Not only do nonruling citizens possess right opinion more thoroughly than slaves possess the ability to understand and follow orders, but the relation of means to ends differs in ruler/citizen relation and the master/slave relation. In slavery, masters provide the ends and slaves the means. But the virtue of political rulers is concerned with means. Citizens do not do things for the sake of the ruler, as would be the case if rulers apprehended the ends and other citizens performed the means. Slaves, without purposes of their own, are instruments of their owners' ends. But a polis contains no such despotic hierarchy of means and ends.

The alignment of the ruler with means and with *phronēsis* is of a piece with the concentration on means I derived from the *Rhetoric* in the first chapter. The *Rhetoric* is committed to reason as the preferred means to persuasion. Similarly, ethical progress and moral development come from intelligent attention to providing the means that enable people to be virtuous. This sort of concentration on the means that the rulers exercise is not the bureaucratic, and in Aristotle's eyes, slavish execution of policies decided on by others. Aristotle's rulers are not administrators.

In the *Ethics,* identifying cases where one kind of action is subordinate to another is unproblematic (I.1.1094a9–16). Bridle-making is subordinate to horsemanship, and military strategy architectonic over horsemanship. My dean has responsibility for the allocation of far more money than I do. Since she gives me orders and I give none to her. It would, on the face of it, seem that her actions and life are more authoritative and better than mine. However, the nature of my dean's job prevents her from distinguishing between the truly important and the merely urgent, and therefore her life is more slavish than mine. Am I subordinate to my dean or she to me?

That my dean also earns far more money than I do only serves to further cloud the issue. On the one hand, it is no surprise that a less noble activity can earn more money than a better one. Aristotle knew wealthy artisans and merchants who could never become citizens. But on the other, without a practically effective sense of the noble, activities *will* be ranked by money, collapsing the practical into the economic. William Ian Miller coins the wonderfully paradoxical term "moral menials" to cover people who might be well-paid but are "necessary evils." When we cannot easily figure out who is subordinate to whom, we lose the intelligibility of praxis Aristotle relies on. Aristotle's distinction between ruler and ruled does not apply to the modern administrative state.[35]

*Politics* III never says that nonruling citizens are defective because they lack *phronēsis*. There is nothing wrong with being ruled, and nothing wrong with acting on right opinion, except in circumstances that call for more. Only a tyrant, not a citizen, wants always to rule and never to be ruled. The life of the citizen is a life spent alternately at ruling and being ruled. His virtuous action is governed sometimes by *phronēsis*, sometimes by right opinion.

Every virtuous citizen must be capable of *phronēsis* when called for. Otherwise he could not be a potential ruler. The true opinion he possesses does not lack rationality, as in a conception of true opinion as unjustified true belief. It only lacks in deliberative scope. The ruled citizen exercises ethical virtue in situations that do not call for *phronēsis*. His ability to do things for their own sake is to that extent limited. If this is the difference between ruling and ruled citizens, then there can be no separate account of acquiring *phronēsis* apart from the process of learning to rule by being ruled. We learn to rule by being ruled. When we are put in a position of ruling, we can exercise *phronēsis*. Only the ruler need exercise, and therefore need possess, *phronēsis*, but the ruler acquires what he needs to exercise *phronēsis* through being a citizen, through being ruled.[36]

### The Natural and the Political

> Regard for *human* nature as the source of legitimate political arrangements is comparatively late in European history; . . . when it arose it marked an almost revolutionary departure from previous theories about the basis of political rule and citizenship and subjection—so much so that the fundamental difference between even ancient republican and modern democratic governments has its source in the substitution of human nature for cosmic nature as the foundation of politics. (John Dewey, *Freedom and Culture*)[37]

For Aristotle, limiting the virtues to their political dimension is not special pleading, because—and here is the underlying assumption that runs counter to very deep modern beliefs—politicizing the virtues is not in opposition to naturalizing them. Aristotle would find unintelligible Rawls's contrast between the political and the metaphysical. MacIntyre gets it just right: "Aristotle sets himself the task of giving an account of the good which is at once local and particular—located in and partially defined by the characteristics of the polis—and yet also cosmic and universal." [38]

Modern pictures of nature make the local and the universal into contraries: nature is what all humans share, as opposed to local conventions. For Aristotle, only the best people live naturally. Those different conceptions of nature are tied to different pictures of human nature, one that fits comfortably to the ruled and the other to rulers. [39] By looking to a different relation between nature and the political, modernity transforms the *thumos* that I placed at the root of both personal identity and the moral feelings. [40]

Contemporary moral psychology suits a world in which moral conflicts, disagreements, and dilemmas are prominent. In that world it is a virtue to be able to step back from one's commitments, have second-order emotions, values, and reasons analogous to the formal political structure of liberal democracies that mediate among interpersonal disputes. [41] We need to be able to see both sides of any issue. We have to be able to question received wisdom, and so question and justify the validity of any given law. While many later writers, especially Cicero and his Renaissance followers, associated practical wisdom with the rhetorical ability to argue both sides of a case, Aristotle can have nothing to do with that idea. [42]

Aristotle's political psychology starts with citizens who identify wholeheartedly with the polis, its constitution and laws. In chapter 2 I highlighted the difference between Aristotle's conception of choice and the libertarian conception of freedom of choice, the liberty of indifference. Aristotle's virtue is not freedom as opposed to coercion but freedom as opposed to servility, whether political or psychological. The moral theory appropriate to contemporary problems tracks Aristotle's conceptions of the voluntary and of rational *dynameis,* while his own ethics concerns choice and choosing the lawful for its own sake.

A moral psychology of citizens has no room for the deliberation about ends. The virtue of doing for its own sake what the law commands not interstitial freedom to do as one likes and so realize oneself where the law is silent. It is the self-realization that comes from deliberating about, choosing, and doing for their own sake acts already recognized as virtuous.

This relation between the lawful and the virtuous is the practical equivalent of the relation between the what and the why, the *hoti* and the *dioti,* with which Aristotle begins the *Ethics.* The person who acts lawfully is in a position to act virtuously. "The *archē* is the *to hoti.* And if it appears accurately, then there will be no need to ask for the *dioti*" (*NE* I.2.1095b6–7). On the other hand, there is a difference between lawful and virtuous actions. "The political man should also not regard as irrelevant the inquiry that makes clear not only the that, but also the why. For that way of proceeding is the philosopher's way in every discipline" (*EE* I.6.1216b35–37). This is the difference between *phronēsis* and right opinion. The relation between the what and the why reinforces his thesis that there is no deliberation about ends. "Nor should we make the same demand for an explanation (*aitia*) in all cases. On the contrary, in some cases it is enough to prove rightly the fact (*to hoti*) that they are so. This is the case with principles, where the fact is the primary thing—it is a principle" (*NE* I.7. 1098a34–b3). When the lawful is given, we don't look for justifications or explanations; we deliberate about what to do.

### Aristotle's Ethics and Ours, Again

> The wise person, the just person, and other virtuous people all need the good things necessary for life. Still, when these are adequately supplied, the just person needs other people as partners and recipients of his just actions; and the same is true of the moderate person and the brave person and each of the others. (*NE* X.7.1177a28–32)

> A man's acts can no longer can be noble if he does not excel as greatly as a man excels a woman or a father his children or a master his slaves. (*Pol.* VII.3. 1325b3–5)

> The life of money-making is undertaken under compulsion. (*NE* I.5. 1096a5–6)

Morality, starting from the modern postulate of freedom, must be categorical. If something is good, it is always good. If it is good, it is good for me. If it is always good, I should always pursue it. Failing to pursue something good would be an infringement on freedom, either external coercion or internal irrationality. If something is intrinsically valuable—worth choosing for its own sake—then it must be desirable all the time, for everyone, in all circumstances. Aristotle would find such an attitude characteristic of *pleonexia*, not virtue, since *pleonexia* consists precisely in the idea that because something is good, it must be good for me, and therefore I should have it. In the first chapter I cited my own practice as an example of such a vice when I decided that since someone was the best teacher, he must be the best teacher for me. And if something is good, the more of it I possess, the better. If it is good to study with the best teacher, then the more I had to do with him, the better. Economics may be a field for maximizers, but to think about all of life economically is slavish (*Pol.* I.9.1257b40–1258a2). There is a difference, invisible to economic rationality, between urgency and importance, between necessity and true value. Someone for whom the good life consists in acquiring as many goods as possible could not understand those ethical distinctions.

Just because something is worth doing for its own sake does not mean that it is always worth doing, or that I should do it. I shouldn't always do what is most worth doing. Although it is more noble to think about Aristotle than to shovel snow off my sidewalk, it doesn't follow that I should choose to do the former. There is a difference, invisible to economic rationality, between urgency and importance, between necessity and true value. There is a difference between being worth choosing for its own sake and worth choosing regardless of circumstances; the first is Aristotle's idea and the second the modern idea of absolute value. Someone for whom the good life consists in acquiring as many goods as possible could not understand those ethical distinctions. Hobbes, for example, organizes all obligation and right around the fear of violent death. Such fear may well be the most urgent of desires, but it is not the most important. Something can be best without being best for me. I can know what is best without knowing what to do. The practical instead is the domain of things that are intrinsically good, yet only good in circumstances. Aristotle's goods worth choosing for their own sakes are the goods of activity, while the intrinsic goods of modern morality need not be.

Such a domain is intelligible only politically. The city has more unity than an alliance, because it is made up of things with *less* unity than the alliance (*Pol.* II.2.1261a24–29), and so its unity is an immense practical achievement. We shouldn't be misled by the apparent stability of praise and blame and forget the extent to which the polis was a locus of competition as well as harmony. Aristotle saw the polis as the only possible location of things that can be chosen for their own sakes. Today we search hopefully for other ways of escaping a life of categorical morality which makes the idea of the noble unintelligible.[43]

Ethically virtuous actions are worth doing for their own sakes. But they have such intrinsic worth only given the presence of circumstances that are not themselves desirable. Virtuous acts are only good in particular circumstances, yet are still intrinsically good. Without poverty, liberality would be unintelligible. Courage is only good in a world in which poleis have to fight other poleis, but that does not mean that courageous action is not worth engaging in for its own sake, or that courage does not bring the irrational soul into its best condition. I can regret the fact that my country is at war, but I will act courageously without regret.

Virtuous actions are both necessary and noble. Necessity does not always disqualify an act from being noble.[44] "Friendship is not only necessary (*anagkaion*), it is also noble (*kalon*)" (*NE* VIII.1.1155a29). "Ruling and being ruled are not only necessary, they are also beneficial" (*Pol.* I.5. 1254a21–22). For people who are free in the modern sense, doing anything from necessity is ignoble, because coerced.[45]

From a god's point of view, all practical goods are only conditionally good because of a situation in which the agent finds himself, a situation that is not itself absolutely desirable. It would be an ethical mistake, though, to infer from the fact that in a better world we wouldn't have to risk our lives defending our country that therefore we should not see courageous action as having intrinsic value. The ethical agent pursues all such goods unreservedly because they are goods for him, and therefore are the proper objects of decision. In the final chapter I will have to show why Aristotle does not himself make this ethical mistake when he says that the ethical virtues appear "trivial and unworthy of the gods" (*NE* X.8.1178b17–18).

A polis in which no one had to act courageously, or one in which corrective justice was unnecessary, might be a better polis; otherwise, we would have to welcome war, poverty, and crime as opportunities for displaying our virtues. But "no one chooses to make war for the sake of being at war, nor aims at provoking such a war; a man would seem absolutely murderous if he were to make enemies of his friends in order to bring about battles and slaughter" (*NE* X.7.1177b9–10). Since the polis requires civic participation in war, courage is, for the individual citizen, not conditionally but categorically a good thing.[46] The crucial ethical demarcation comes from political and nonpolitical givens and necessities. If the given ends to which the virtues respond were simply facts of nature—poverty is caused by bad weather, nature has endowed humans with evil passions—then we should work, through *technē,* to counter those natural powers. Under the assumption that poverty and disease are natural, not political, events, it is not courageous to face them confidently . The givens to which the virtuous agent is receptive are for Aristotle political givens. Honor and shame, praise and blame, mediate between the noble and the necessary, between personal advantage and the external compulsion of the law.

Justice is about the goods of good and bad *fortune* (*NE* V.1.1129b3), which indicates the hypothetically good nature of praxis:

> Some goods must be present, while others must be supplied by the legislator. Hence we pray for the city to be constituted on the basis of what one would pray for in those matters over which fortune has authority (we regard it as having authority over the external things we regard as desirable) but the city's being excellent is no longer the work of fortune, but of knowledge and intentional choice. (*Pol.* VII.12.1332a28–32; see also VII.11.1331b18–21)

The statesman provides for the goods of fortune. These goods are within his control, but are simply given to the ethical agent. The virtues are good ways of acting not toward all given ends but toward politically given ends. The terminus of my *kinēsis/energeia* dimension of virtue is political. To Aristotle—and here his thinking obviously diverges far from modern thinking—there are no tragic virtues in which the individual acts nobly with regard to nonpolitical givens. At the beginning of chapter 3, I noted that nothing in Aristotle corresponds to the contemporary concern with tragic choices and tragic virtues. His vision of the polis as the sole locus for living well prevents him from being attentive to these possibilities. Courage concerns responses to the humanly produced given of war, not to naturally, divinely, or fortuitously produced givens such as disease. We act courageously against human opponents. Hence Aristotle's seemingly arbitrary restriction of courage to military valor. If we today view poverty as more a human product and less natural or inevitable, that could change the scope of courage.

Similarly, I mentioned the fact that liberality does not include a virtue of rightly getting money; the best one can do is avoid injustice (*NE* IV.1. 1120a34–b2). Because getting money is merely necessary, while spending is noble, liberality is more concerned with spending than getting. Aristotle says that acquiring wealth is merely necessary, but the inference is that because there is no noble way of becoming wealthy, the good man possesses and uses, not acquires, wealth well. As we have already seen, restrictions on who can be virtuous follow from this stress on activity. Here I want to observe that this restriction follows too from the subordination of individual ethics to politics. All the other virtues follow the same pattern of being responses to things that are given to the individual agent, but which are determined politically. Politics is more self-sufficient and more noble than ethics because what are given to the individual are matters for political deliberation.

The practical life lies between the life of money-making and the contemplative life, between pure necessity and pure purpose, between pure receptivity and pure spontaneity. As I will show in the final chapter, one of the practical functions of *theōria* is to keep the political life from degenerating into the economic, while the necessities serve to remind us that we cannot live as gods. Since the virtues are good in the first place because they lead to external goods, it is easy to think that that is what they are for. The contemplative life will help us to avoid that thought. Knowing that the political life is happy in only a secondary way (*NE* X.8.1178a9) will help us keep the ties between intrinsic goods and their external counterparts.[47]

Some acts could never become part of the life of virtue or of the good polis: the most obvious examples are *energeiai* of the nutritive soul and correspondingly slavish activities that can be done well but cannot be done freely:

> The virtue of the nutritive soul is apparently shared, and not specifically human. For this part and this capacity more than others seem to be active in sleep, and here the good and the bad person are least distinct. . . . This lack of distinction is not surprising, since sleep is inactivity of the soul insofar as it is called excellent or base. (*NE* I.13.1102b1–8)

> There is no element of virtue in any of the occupations in which the multitude of artisans and market-people and the wage-earning class take part. (*Pol.* VI.2. 1319a26–28)

The body, the nutritive soul, and slavish occupations have virtues in the way sharp knives have virtue—meaning #3 of virtue at the beginning of chapter 4—but such virtue is not political: we cannot do these things justly. Much of what we would regard as central to a good moral life Aristotle would consign to the realm of necessity. At the opposite extreme are acts that are necessarily *energeiai* and are always engaged in for their own sakes. *Theōria*'s goodness regardless of circumstances makes it nonpolitical. In modern morality, such absolute goodness makes something a categorical moral good, but Aristotle throws such values out of the realm of the practical and the ethical altogether.

Only the polis with active civic participation allows us to distinguish intrinsic value from absolute value. Without it, we couldn't articulate a sense of goodness that applies to things which are good only because of circumstances, but which, in those circumstances, really are noble and choiceworthy. Without that essentially political sense of the goods of activity, we cannot distinguish moral actions from mixed actions. Outside a polis the relation between the contemplative life and the political life could be one of conflict, as could the relation of the good man and the good citizen. The virtues are one, and the soul is one, because of the unity of the polis.

The political nature of ethics and the good life comes at a high price, which modern liberalism finally refused to pay. To oversimplify, the Aristotelian good life depends on political participation. Political participation depends on leisure. Leisure depends on household slaves. Modern liberalism constructed a good life which did not depend on political participation and consequently made slavery politically, although not economically, unnecessary. There followed an empirical debate about whether slavery was economically beneficial or not. As long as the good life was a political life, such a debate could not be possible.[48]

The move away from the political ancient ethics to modern antipolitical morality cuts more deeply still. The family and the polis are no longer self-sufficient and are therefore under threat from economic life. Here is an example of the phenomenon I mentioned at the beginning of the Introduction, that the central features of Aristotle's ethical thought, in this case the political nature of the good life, is both attractive and repellent.

## The Political Standards of Ethical Virtue

> Aristotle does not admit a clear distinction between the rules of morality and the rules of prudence. . . . [He] did not distinguish sharply, as Kant tried to distinguish, the rationality of the moral law and the rationality of "enlightened self-interest," or, to use Aristotle's word, "self-love." (W. F. R. Hardie, *Aristotle's Ethical Theory*)[49]

Now that we know that Aristotelian ethical virtues are political *energeiai* of specifically political souls, we should look again at my three initial commonplaces: (1) Morality is for us one source of value among others for us, while ancient ethics, including Aristotle's, was all-encompassing. (2) Aristotle allows fewer people to be virtuous and happy than in the universal scope of modern moral theory. (3) Aristotle's noncategorical moral standards stand in contrast to the categorical, yet minimal, morality of today. It is a mistake, first, to find in Aristotle a laudable breadth of the scope of ethics in contrast to the narrower range for morality today. Nothing could be broader than happiness, but virtue excludes many other possibilities for goodness. Many. I've already given examples of good acts that may be their own ends that do not qualify as virtues or part of the human *ergon,* such as courage in the face of poverty, and heroic and supererogatory actions. Activities done through *technē* do not as such count. *Enkratia* does not count. None of these good actions is tied to happiness as the ethical virtues are. The subject of the *Ethics* is the human good as such, and not a restricted domain such as our relations to others. But our knowledge of the human good comes from political knowledge of the virtues.

I want to revisit the commonplace that modern morality consists of categorical demands, compared to an Aristotelian flexibility and openness to the demands of virtue. For three reasons, Aristotelian ethics can make no categorical demands. First, the judgment of the *phronimos* is the final ethical standard, and so Aristotle repeatedly tells us not to look for inappropriate forms of precision (e.g., *NE* II.2.1104a7–10, II.6.1107a28, X.10.1137b27–37, *Pol.* 1282b3). While the virtues, like the arts, are only valuable because they lead to actions that are already considered good, the user is the ultimate judge for the arts, but the doer, the *phronimos,* is the final judge for action. The advantage of a categorical morality is that it tells us that there are many things we don't need to take into account in a moral decision. There are no such principled exclusions for a virtue that relies on perception.

Second, categorical demands make no sense for Aristotelian virtue because there are no competitors for the good to override. There is nothing outside ethics against which the good can be categorical. Categorical duty makes sense only if there are competitors, such as happiness, egoism, or evil. The judgment of *phronēsis* is final because it is comprehensive. Categorical duty is ultimate, by contrast, because it is decisive. In the first chapter I pointed to the American strategy of bombing Serbia, which avoided risks to American soldiers and consequently avoided acting courageously. It is always possible to decide to aim directly at the external end instead of the internal end. Chapter 3, in its discussion of the second type of moral failure, outlined some of the circumstances in which that change of aim was attractive. There is no rule that one should act courageously whenever possible, only the obvious rule that one never act as a coward would. There are no categorical demands associated with the virtues.[50]

Third, there is a distance, overcome only by deliberation, between knowing the good and knowing what to do. Aristotle does not need categorical standards that accompany modern moralities of obligation. Morality is categorical when the highest good is also, as Mill says, "the criterion for right and wrong."[51] For Aristotle, knowing the good never tells us directly what to do, nor can it be the criterion for right and wrong, because deciding what to do takes deliberation, not just knowledge of the good. Aristotle would see categorical morality as a demand for inappropriate and excessive precision, a mark of bad character, which is why the just man will take less than his legal share (*NE* V.10.1137b34–1138a3).[52]

The political nature of Aristotle's ethical virtues adds depth to the contrast between ancient and modern morality. The modern state starts from the idea that each of us has basic rights to freedom, and therefore the coercive power of the state can be exercised only with a justification that overcomes the presumption that the individual is free to act as he or she likes. Within such a state, moral standards are either what exceeds the coercive demands of a minimal morality or the values of acting in a realm of freedom where the law is silent. Aristotle's laws are no less coercive than those of the modern nation-state, but there is no background of individual freedom and rights. He instead starts with law, and with people acting virtuously because the law commands them and habituates them to act well, and then finds not a realm of freedom but of choosing for its own sake what the law commands.

If morality is not categorical but defers instead to the judgment of the *phronimos,* how can it be determinate at all? Aristotelian ethics offers no decision procedure. The law determines the standard for virtue and vice. The generalities of law and the decisions of the *phronimos* are the only ways of determining virtue and vice. The *Ethics,* then, would oppose conceptions of virtue that include all habits necessary for living and succeeding in a variety of purposes—a common modern way of conceiving the virtues nonpolitically—and that thereby set a standard suitable for blaming those who fail to meet it but no reason to praise those who do meet it. Equally, it would oppose a picture of virtue limited to habits exercised in the best life alone that would allow blame for those who weren't up to it. We praise the hero but don't blame people for failing to be heroic. As Jonathan Shay puts it, "I cannot hold soldiers to an ethical standard that requires martyrdom in order simply to be blameless."[53]

The virtues are narrowly delimited because not every situation will be one in which virtue and vice are the only alternatives. The proper standard for virtuous actions is that level of performance at which both praise and blame come into play. Locating virtue and vice at places where both praise and blame apply is Aristotle's alternative to the categorical demands of modern morality:[54]

> Courage decides and stands firm because that is noble or because anything else is shameful. Dying to avoid poverty or erotic passion or something painful is proper to a coward, not to a brave person. For shirking burdens is softness, and such a person stands firm to avoid an evil, not because standing firm is noble (*NE* III.7.1116a12–16)

That criterion determines the scope of the virtues. When virtue and vice are the only possibilities, avoiding vice means doing a virtuous act.

## Who Can Be Good?

> Christian morality (so called) has all the characters of a reaction; it is, in great part, a protest against paganism. Its ideal is negative rather than positive; passive rather than active; innocence rather than nobleness; abstinence from evil rather than energetic pursuit of good; in its precepts (as has been well said) "thou shalt not" predominates over "thou shalt." In its horror of sensuality, it made an idol of asceticism which has gradually compromised away into one of legality. It holds out the hope of heaven and the threat of hell as the appointed and appropriate motives to a virtuous life: in this falling far below the best of the ancients, and doing what lies in it to give the human mo-

rality an essentially selfish character, by disconnecting each man's feelings of
duty from the interests of his fellow creatures, except so far as a self-interested
inducement is offered to him for consulting them. (John Stuart Mill, *On
Liberty*)[55]

The final contrast between Aristotle's ethics and ours is the commonplace
that today morality is for everyone while Aristotle's is limited to a few good
men. That contrast between ancients and moderns, too, has more complexity than was at first apparent. There are times when Aristotle says that
the virtues and happiness are available to everyone. The virtues do not take
special external equipment, nor natural psychic gifts. Happiness "will be
widely shared; for anyone who is not deformed for virtue will be able to
achieve happiness through some sort of learning and attention" (*NE* I.9.
1099b18–20). In another sense virtue and happiness are evidently rare,
and most men lead lives ruled by pleasure and not thought (*NE* I.5.
1095b19–30, *Pol.* I.2.1252b2–7, VI.4.1319b30–32).

In chapter 3 I showed that to be good and act well one must grow up
in a polis in which one's own psychic requirements are in harmony with the
external system of praise and blame, and in which the external system of
praise and blame accurately represents what is truly praiseworthy and
blameworthy. At the end of chapter 3 I noted that once we can no longer
presuppose such happy harmony, *phronēsis* must have new roles that go beyond presupposing and ratifying existing practices and *ēthē*. Here we can
see that such *phronēsis* will make ethics and politics far more distinct from
each other than they are in Aristotle's thought. In the next chapter I will
reconcile Aristotle's claims that happiness is widely available and that virtue
is rare by showing that possessing the first *energeia* of virtue is rare, while
it is easy for those with virtuous habits to act virtuously and so be happy.
Human nature has to make its own environment—internal and external,
virtues and constitutions, desires and appropriate objects of desire—in
which humans can flourish. Aristotelian moral education is the acquisition
of a first *energeia,* after which everything is fairly smooth and easy. Modern
morality stipulates the equal and universal possession of the equivalent of
Aristotle's first *energeia:* everyone has full and equal moral status, whether
rooted in easily accessible moral knowledge, moral sentiments, or something else. You don't have to *do* anything to be a moral subject. All the
important modern moral problems are located in the equivalent of the transition from this shared first *energeia* to the second *energeia,* while for Aristotle the possession of virtue leads easily to its actualization.[56]

The claim that most people are not in a position to be truly good is difficult for moderns to accept. We do, though, believe that people with at

least a fair amount of power can *do* both greater amounts of good and of evil than the rest of us. Because of their position and opportunities, political leaders have a greater capacity for doing both good and bad than I do. Aristotle takes that one step further and thinks that you have to have power to *be* good. Not for him the Christian, or Machiavellian, separation of doing well from being good. What one is, one's ethical being or character, is a function of what one has chosen or done (*NE* III.5.1113b6–14, 1114b21–25) One's soul can only be in the best possible condition if one has chosen and done the best actions, actions that require wealth and political power. Therefore his claim about magnanimity that sounds repugnant to modern ears is a simple application of that thesis about functions and the relation between doing good and being good:

> The great-souled man thinks he is worthy of great things, and is worthy of them, especially of the greatest things. He has one concern above all. Worth is said to make one worthy of external goods; and we would suppose that the greatest of these is the one we award to the gods, the one above all that is the aim of people with a reputation for worth, the prize for the finest achievements. All this is true of honor, since it is the greatest of external goods. Hence the great-souled man has the right concern with honors and dishonors. (*NE* IV.3. 1123b15–23)

Under a reasonably stable idea of what sorts of power are needed to do great good and harm, only a few people—citizens and rulers of states—can do good and therefore be good. We can accept without too much trouble the idea that political leaders can do more good and more harm in the world than other people. Aristotle infers further that such politicians can be both better and worse than the rest of us.

Aristotelian ethics is less universal than modern morality because Aristotle's virtuous person can have full ethical relations with fewer people. Fellow citizens and friends, and not family members or strangers, are the central cases of people toward whom he acts virtuously. "It is not proper to have the same care for intimates and for strangers" (*NE* IV.6.1126b27). While modern generosity is directed at the most needy, liberality is most directed at our friends, and to the good. Virtue acts best toward the best objects (*NE* I.2.1094b9–10, X.4.1174b21–23, *Pol.* VII.4.1325b41–1326a5). I am happier and more fulfilled when I help a good friend than when I help someone needy. I need objects of appropriate scope for my decisions. It is better to be honored by someone in a high position. Helpless, needy people provide no scope for the virtues of anger, wit, and friendliness. The political circumstances of Aristotle's virtue are very demanding conditions for the intersection of the two sides of virtue, in which the most fulfilling actions, the ones that connect virtue to soul and to happiness, are also the most productive of goodness. In other political circumstances, such as ours, his virtues no longer look attractive.

The modern ideas of interiority and personality become possible by severing the connection between being good and doing good. The more we separate doing good from being good, the more we acknowledge diversity in the modes of power that can help us to do good, and so modern pluralism develops from this greater sense of interiority. Without a strong distinction between appearance and reality, it is easier for Aristotle than for us to deny the separation of doing good from doing well. But equally, there is a modern kind of exteriority missing from Aristotle. Aristotle's external goods don't have the kind of stable, independent existence that rights do today, or that money has. Honor is the greatest of external goods, not money, and it is given by others, and has that much objectivity and no more. It is a purely political objectivity. There is no verdict of history to give an extrahuman objectivity.

Others, especially Charles Taylor in *Sources of the Self,* have traced the changes made by the development of interiority from the ancient world to the present. But the lack of exteriority is equally important. Having no goods that are fully interior or exterior in the contemporary sense is a condition for the rationality of ethical life. Recall that in the first chapter I noted two ways in which the art of rhetoric was rational. The first, which it shared with all other arts, was that it is a rational power of making. It calculates how to achieve its object, instead of living by guesswork, prayer, luck, or pure determination. The second, unique to dialectic and rhetoric, was that persuasion is a matter of argument, *logos:* rhetoric establishes rational connections between speaker and hearer. Now we are finally in a position to see the ethical analogue of this second sense of rationality exhibited by rhetoric. The public practices of honor and praise create an internal and rational connection from the activities of the virtuous person to the civic audience who judge those performances. The relation between internal and external ends must be ethically knowable, transparent, not opaque.

The rationality of the ethical life depends on the rationality of the polis. The polis must embody a system of praise and blame that gives the right kind of feedback so that the virtues can both develop and be exercised. The polis must also embody a system of success and failure. For true Aristotelian virtues to develop and flourish, good actions must succeed, for the most part, and bad actions fail. It is the job of the polis to make that happen. The rationality of the polis would be exhibited when the best men rule, and when they find ruling an expression of virtue and not a burden.

Unfortunately, the rational nature of the ethical life at the same time restricts the good life to the few men who can virtuously rule a polis. Aristotle sees no imperative to universalize morals. From the point of view of modern morality, Aristotelian ethics exhibits a scandalous indifference to the large number of people it excludes from the good life. His virtuous person has no obligation to evangelize and make as many people as possible virtuous. Aristotle certainly could know that people beyond citizens can become virtuous. He notes that slaves and masters can be friends, although not as masters and slaves. The love that mothers exhibit toward their children is a paradigm for a certain kind of friendship. We can see each of those observations as demonstrating that noncitizens are capable of exhibiting virtue, at least the virtues that do not depend on owning lots of private property or aiming at high civic honors. But Aristotle sees no such significance in such facts.

Increasing the number of people capable of virtue is no minor adjustment and improvement to Aristotle's vision. To take seriously such apparent counterexamples to his limitation of moral goodness to citizens would threaten the connection between virtue and happiness, which is why I listed that intimate connection as one of the features of the *Ethics* I find both attractive and repellent. If women, slaves, and other noncitizens could be virtuous but not happy, then happiness couldn't be *energeia kat'aretēn*. And then the ethical life would be less rational, since this crucial connection would be severed.

Recall that the Aristotelian counterpart to the categorical nature of modern morality is a flexibility that comes from the fact that virtuous actions are intrinsically but not absolutely good. Demarcating the realm in which both virtue and vice apply is a job for the statesman in deciding which necessities can also be noble. As fortunate circumstances permit citizenship to be narrowed to certain classes of people, activities such as war become necessary rather than noble, and so the virtues become fewer:

> Although it is possible for one man or a few to be outstanding in virtue (*diapherein kat'aretēn*), but where more are concerned it is difficult for them to be proficient with a view to virtue as a whole, but some level of proficiency is possible particularly regarding military virtue, as this arises in a multitude; hence in this regime the warrior element is the most authoritative. (*Pol.* III.5. 1279a39–b3)

This is a major and incommensurable difference between Aristotle's ethics and ours. That everyone can act morally is as deep a presupposition of modern morality as there is, and Aristotle's idea that the better the state, the more limited the number of men who can be good and happy is as directly opposed to that presupposition as possible.

The passage I just quoted asserts that the greater the numbers, the lower the standard for virtue. Modern morality has developed by extending the moral franchise and lowering the demands of virtue, confirming Aristotle's claim that as expanded opportunities for participation in the polis accompany a concomitant dilution of excellence. But must such a covariation be true? Can't we develop a world in which more people are more virtuous? To explore that possibility, I want to end this chapter with an analogy between the polis and a modern, nonpolitical phenomenon, American higher education.

Picture a small, traditional, pastoral liberal arts college. It offers a superb education to a small number of students. It does so by excluding large numbers of people who could profit from such an education. Is it under an obligation to expand? There would be clear gains for many people if such a college did expand. There must be compelling reasons if it is to justify resisting such a change.

When schools admit a larger and more diverse student body, the ends of education change, just as Aristotle says in the passage from the *Politics* I just quoted. The larger the institution the harder it is for all the citizens, in Aristotle's words, to care about each other's virtue. Larger institutions must be more bureaucratic than smaller ones. But there would likely be changes other than size. Activities at the college which were ancillary become part of the college itself. Now the college must prepare students who worry about jobs after college, and so adds degree programs in business. It must accept students who can profit from its education but who are not as prepared as the students it is used to, and so has to add courses in freshman composition and even remedial writing.

A greater number of students now receive an excellent education from this liberal arts college. The education of more traditional students is enhanced by a more diverse student body. The faculty gains too. The tenure of someone in the philosophy department becomes more secure because of the larger student body, which assures the financial health of the college. Since some of the new faculty could be making more money in nonacademic settings, there is the chance that paying them more will trickle down to paying philosophers more too.

But there are losses alongside the gains. My citizenship is not debased when the franchise is extended to eighteen year olds. Even people who opposed the extension of voting rights to poor men and to women did not feel lowered by those proposals. They opposed them on other grounds. But I am lowered when remedial writing teachers and career counselors become members of the faculty, because teaching and education are then redefined in ways that compromise my own work. My own teaching is less effective and less what it ought to be when my students also take classes where performance is measured by all sorts of criteria alien to my conception of academic excellence. I can personally testify that teaching philosophy at an institution with degree programs in business, communications, nursing, social work, and nutrition is more tainted with compromises than teaching philosophy at a college without such programs.

Teaching philosophy at a more "comprehensive" institution differs from what it is at my imagined liberal arts college. Being a student at such a place is different too. But must it be worse? The issue, partly prudential and empirical and partly not, is whether I should extend the franchise of a good liberal arts college, and similarly whether Aristotle's citizen should extend the franchise to other people who could become virtuous. That issue should be settled by deciding whether that new class can participate in living well and virtuously, as living well and virtuously is defined by that polis. When the franchise broadens, are the ethical standards of justice and virtue lowered, or merely transformed? Aristotle assumes that they are lowered, and a refutation of Aristotle would require showing that the new ethical standards are different, not worse.

My analogy shows that one of the less attractive features of the *Ethics* cannot be easily dismissed. I claimed in the Introduction that the same features of the *Ethics* I found most attractive were also those that are most repellent. Here is an instance in which Aristotle's mode of thinking lets us assess modern assumptions that are normally held too closely to allow scrutiny. In deciding how widely to extend citizenship, we decide about the meaning of the good life and the connection between virtue and happiness, the subject of my final two chapters.

# The Ethical Dimensions of Aristotle's Metaphysics

### The Metaphysics of Misery

The definition of "man" must be true of every man. (*Top.* VI.1.139a25–27)

People think that good people come from good people in just the way that human comes from human, and beast from beast. But while nature wishes to do this, it is often unable to. (*Pol.* I.6.1255b1–4)

The soul spends rather a lot of time in error. (*De An.* III.3.427b1–2)

People achieve their end less often than other substances. For people, and for people alone, it seems, nature is merely an ideal. Although nature does nothing in vain, human nature seems ill-designed to reach its end. "Most men . . . identify the good, or happiness, with pleasure. . . . The mass of mankind are evidently quite slavish in their tastes, preferring a life suitable to beasts" (*NE* I.5.1095b19–20; cf. *Pol.* I.2.1252b2–7, VI.4.1319b30– 32).[1] Only good people aim at the true good (*NE* III.4.1113a25, VI.12. 1144a34–36). Reason, the distinctively human power which is our natural end (*Pol.* VII.15. 1334b15), causes corruption as well as perfection: people evade responsibility by using argument to excuse base acts: "the many . . . take refuge in arguments, thinking that they are doing philosophy, and that this is the way to become excellent people" (*NE* II.4.1105b12–14). Not only do most men live by pleasure rather than reason, but although man is a political animal, few live in poleis, and of those who do, few are citizens.

164

Human exceptionalism should be very troublesome. It is bad enough for *any* substance regularly to fail to reach its end and be what it truly is. It is all the worse for human beings, the most substantial and real of substances, who have the most being and who are closest to the divine. This should be the last place for nature to fail. Why are the highest human ends not regularly realized?[2]

Such regular failure is less surprising when we recall how, as I argued in chapter 2, the ethical virtues fit neither category in *Metaphysics* IX.2; they can be neither rational and irrational *dynameis* (1046b5–7). These peculiarly moral powers seem simply to occupy a different part of the world than that covered by metaphysics, perhaps a noumenal realm of freedom distinct from the phenomenal world of the *Metaphysics*.

The trouble with that explanation is that human practical activities are central examples within the *Metaphysics* itself.[3] Of his examples of perfect *energeiai* in *Met.* IX.6 — seeing, understanding, thinking, living well, and being happy (1048b23–25) — only the first might extend to nondivine beings other than humans, and living well and being happy probably don't apply to the gods. Understanding (*phronēsis*), happiness, and living well are not only specifically human but specifically *practical*.[4] Far from having no place in the Aristotelian cosmos, humans are central to it. Yet Aristotle does not note this crucial fact that people are the only substances, apart from the gods, capable of his own examples of perfect *energeiai*.

Aristotle never offers metaphysics as a guide to morals. He seems untroubled by the paradox with which I began, that humans, of all substances, do not regularly realize their nature. He never asks how knowing man's place in the universe helps us know how to live, or how metaphysics contributes to *phronēsis*. Ultimately and surprisingly, I believe that we need *phronēsis* for metaphysics because we need the practical knowledge of how people realize their nature in order fully to understand substance, activity, and even god. It takes *phronēsis* to know that "man is not the best thing in the universe" (*NE* VI.7.1141a20-21). The *phronimos* needs that knowledge to put a proper value on praxis, as I will show in the final chapter when I talk about the place of *theōria* in the best life. Human praxis is the paradigm of substance and activity, and so morals is a guide to metaphysics.[5]

Before showing how metaphysics depends on ethics, I need to respond to an objection to this whole line of argument. One could claim that people in fact achieve their end no less regularly than other substances or other animals. It is individual substances that have natures, not "nature" overall. Only a small percentage of acorns become trees (see *Ph.* II.8.199b18–26), so it is no surprise that humans are not regularly virtuous or happy. Without an expectation of an overall purpose or economy of nature, it is no failure of nature that potential beings do not reach full development. Without a designing and creating God, there is no theodicy, no point in asking why things are the way they are.[6]

But if it is inappropriate to ask Aristotle why so few people are happy or virtuous, so much the worse for Aristotle. Most acorns and fish eggs fail to achieve their nature because of external conditions. Although such conditions also limit the capacity of people to realize their natures—when citizens of a polis are enslaved, for example—people also fail because of their own actions. People in a position to become virtuous do not. Such failure is blameworthy in a way the failure of fish eggs is not. Either there is something uniquely imperfect about human nature, or we have to think again about the use of metaphysics in praxis and the place of praxis in the universe.

For example, according to Aristotle the eastern races who are "natural" slaves can possess both excellent rational and irrational *dynameis*. They are capable of *technē*, and have the irrational *dynameis* of strong bodies (*Pol.* I.2.1252a32–34). But lacking *thumos*, as I argued in chapter 4, they cannot decide and so lack practical rationality. They are ethically incomplete, incomplete as human beings, and so belong to another and are a part of another (I.6.1255b6–12). People need more than rational and irrational *dynameis* for their *energeiai* to be complete. Without the virtues as habits of deciding, humans are incomplete substances and cannot realize their nature.[7] Needing to have powers beyond the possibilities offered in the *Metaphysics* makes human beings metaphysically troublesome.

People look like a metaphysical embarrassment because they don't regularly realize their nature, and because the ethical virtues are neither rational nor irrational *dynameis*. Here is the explanation for both. The more a first *energeia*, such as ethical virtue, has to internalize its conditions of success, the more difficult it is to achieve that first *energeia*. Once achieved, though, the easier it will be for that first *energeia* to realize the second *energeia*, since all the conditions for its success are built in. This is the reliability I distinguished from predictability as following the practical direction of inference in chapter 2. If all this sounds "metaphysical" in the sense of abstract and dependent on the peculiarities of Aristotelian ontology, Aristotle himself makes the point in concrete terms:

No human achievement has the stability of activities in accord with virtue. . . . Indeed the most honorable among the virtues themselves are more enduring than the other virtues, because blessed people devote their lives to them more fully and more continually than to anything else. (*NE* I.10.1100b11–16; cf. *EE* II.6.1222b16–20)

If it is better to be happy as a result of one's own exertions than by the gift of fortune, it is reasonable to suppose that this is how happiness is won; inasmuch as in the world of nature things have a natural tendency to be ordered in the best possible way. . . . To be left to fortune would be too contrary to the fitness of things. (*NE* I.9.1099b20–25; cf. *EE* I.3.1215a13–19)

To each man there falls just so large a measure of happiness as he achieves of virtue and *phronēsis* and of virtuous and prudent action. (*Pol.* VII.1. 1323b21–23)

Therefore, it is no design flaw for fewer men to be happy than animals are healthy. While most people are not virtuous, virtuous people are happy far more often than acorns grow into oaks or chicks survive long enough to become mature birds. Creating its own conditions for success is a mark of practical *energeiai* and so of happiness.[8] A craft will succeed if its materials are right, but it is no part of the craft to create its own enabling conditions. The crafts are consequently imperfect, and so, while *technē* is one of the "states in which the soul grasps the truth in its affirmations and denials" (*NE* VI.3.1139b15–16), it is not part of a good life. The arts aim at ends outside themselves, and their actualization depends on something outside themselves.

But happiness is a perfect *energeia;* it is the final end toward which all other activities, perfect and imperfect, are directed. For the final human goods to leave the existence of the conditions for their success to something else would make them less perfect. Certain factors are irrelevant to a medical decision, but nothing is ruled out as irrelevant to the virtuous man. Just as in chapter 2 I showed that the difference between practical and technical rationality was that practical reason has decision built into it, so practical reason does not take the conditions for its operation as given but as part of its own business. The virtues are responsible for their own conditions of realization.[9]

It is harder to be virtuous than to be healthy or than to have some particular skill, because virtue must create its own conditions for success. Possessing the virtues is not only more difficult than possessing irrational or rational *dynameis,* it alone is praiseworthy. It is harder to be in a position to do something through internal means alone, but easier to succeed once one is in that position. Thus Aristotle can say that happiness "will admit of being widely diffused, since it can be attained through some process of study or effort by all persons whose capacity for virtues has not been stunted or maimed" (*NE* I.9.1099b18–20; *EE* I.5.1216b35–39, *Rh.* I.1. 1355a14–16), while also noting that acting virtuously is difficult (*NE* II.6. 1106b31–33, II.9.1109a24, V.9.1137a9–14).

Aristotle's distinction between first and second *energeiai* replaces the Platonic distinction between becoming and being. The conditions which together create the first act are externally related to each other and to the first act they produce, and so this is a realm of accidents and chance. The first actuality of virtuous habit is a product of actions done for external reasons, of pleasures and pain as external guides to action, of praise and blame as another set of external guides. The second actuality corresponds to Plato's realm of being: once the first act is achieved, all is smooth sailing from there. The virtuous man is will be happy if nothing more intervenes. There is nothing more anyone can do to be happy than act virtuously. The relation between virtue and happiness is not like the Kantian relation in which the good man merits happiness, because there happiness is awarded by another—nature or God. Aristotelian happiness is something that one does, and which makes its own enabling conditions.[10]

Because no craft creates its own conditions of success, while practical goods are responsible for their own conditions of realization, two further properties of the virtues follow: they must internalize the judgments of appropriateness that dictate when one should activate one's powers, and they must say what counts as success. This is another respect that makes practical reason more rational than technical reason. The user, not the artisan, judges the value of the products of art (*Pol.* III.1.1282a17–23), but the virtuous man is the final authority concerning what he does. As I argued in chapter 2, practical decision is external to the rationality embodied in the crafts, but that decision is internalized in the rationality of the virtues. Here I want to develop the consequence that because decision is internalized, and because the ends of action are internalized in virtuous as opposed to instrumental action, so the virtues must create the conditions of their own actualization.

Because Aristotle does not himself explicitly interrelate ethics and metaphysics, I need to approach the problem provoked by my paradox indirectly. I will first ask about the relation between some of the distinctions Aristotle makes in *Metaphysics* IX—between passive and active *dynameis* in IX.1, between rational and irrational powers in IX.2, between innate (*tōn syngenōn*) and acquired (*tōn ethei*) powers in IX.5, and between perfect and imperfect *energeiai* in IX.6—with an eye to wondering about the place of people, and human flourishing, in these distinctions and so in nature. My next section, then, is an ethical commentary on *Metaphysics* IX. Far from making the *Ethics* depend on the technicalities of the *Metaphysics*, I want to show how the *Metaphysics* makes sense only by considering the central case of virtuous activity. After that I will ask what all those distinctions have to do with Aristotle's conception of virtue and the relation of virtue to happiness, so that I can finally see why the best of animals and the most divine of mortal substances so rarely reaches its end.

## The Varieties of Power and Actuality

> Greek metaphysics is not a good guide to the structure of Greek ethics.
> (Nicholas White, *Individual and Conflict in Greek Ethics*)[11]

*Metaphysics* IX lists a series of contrary pairs of powers and actualities, *dynameis*, and *energeiai*. There are three pairs of kinds of potentialities. *Met.* IX.1 begins by telling us that *dynameis* are either active or passive. *Met.* IX.2 distinguishes rational from irrational powers. *Met.* IX.5 introduces a third distinction, that between innate and acquired powers. Finally, *Met.* IX.6 tells us that *energeiai* are either perfect or imperfect. This treatment cries out for a moral interpretation because by itself it is incoherent in at least four ways:

1. Aristotle draws no connections among the distinctions I just listed. He simply explores one and then the next.
2. We hear nothing here about the further, apparently apposite, distinction, between first and second *energeiai*. We get no clues about the relation between this distinction and any of the four in *Met.* IX.
3. Despite the considerations of natural substances in prior books of the *Metaphysics*, we see nothing here about nature as an internal principle of motion, although it would be useful to know about the connection between nature and each of the distinctions of the *Metaphysics*.
4. Human, practical examples seem included indiscriminately alongside other illustrations.

### *Met.* IX.1: Active and Passive *Dynameis*

> "Potency" means (1) a source of movement or change, which is in another thing than the thing moved . . . and also (2) the source of a thing's being moved. (*Met.* V.12.1019a15–20)

*Dynameis* are either active, "an originative source of change in another thing," or passive, "a potency of being acted on . . . of being passively changed by another thing" (*Met.* IX.1.1046a10–17; see V.12.1019a32–b2). Active and passive *dynameis* come together to make a single *energeia* in the thing acted upon (*Ph.* III.2.202a12–22, III.3.202b5–7, V.1.224b4–8,

25–26, VII.1.242a6–8, *De An*. III.2.425b26–426a13, *Gen. An*. 742a30–32, *Met*. IX.8.1050a30–32, *NE* IX.7.1168a3–8). He limits the discussion in *Met*. IX.1 to "potency in the strictest sense, which is, however, not the most *useful* for our present purposes" (1046b36–1047a1; see IX.3. 1047a30–32). Where potencies in the strictest sense are potencies for motion, actualities in the strictest sense are not motions. But Aristotle does not focus on this difference in this chapter. Whether perfect *energeiai* can be the realizations of both active and passive *dynameis* is at this point at open question.[12]

A world made up only of inanimate substances could not display the active/passive distinction among *dynameis*. What is hot can burn, and what is oily can be burnt, to use his examples, but why should we call fire active and gasoline passive? Fire is acted upon by the oil as much as oil is by fire. "What acts also gets acted upon by what is being acted upon" (*Gen. An*. 768b16), so that both substances change and they act on each other.

Once rational powers are introduced in the next chapter, the difference between an active and a passive power is clear: the art of building, his other example of an active *dynamis* in *Met*. IX.1, acts on bricks, and rational powers can act without themselves moving or undergoing change. Only active rational powers can embody a single logos in multiple matters, while in nature each soul is uniquely tied to its body.[13] Therefore Aristotle's argument requires the advance from passive and active powers to rational and irrational ones. More important, so does Aristotle's universe. The apparently incoherent series of pairs of *dynameis* is in fact a progressive deepening of the idea of a rational power.

### Met. IX.2: Rational and Irrational *Dynameis*

> Since some of these principles are inherent in inanimate things, and others in animate things and in the soul and in the rational part of the soul, it is clear that some of the potencies also will be irrational and some rational. (*Met*. IX. 1.1046a36–b2; cf. IX.5.1048a8, *Int*. 13.22b36, *NE* V.1.1129a13)

*Met*. IX.2 distinguishes rational from irrational powers. All rational powers belong to living things, although not all the powers of living things are rational (1048a5). Why is there no intermediate stage in *Met*. IX in which Aristotle distinguishes animate from inanimate powers? Animate powers are in the *De Anima* first *energeiai*, powers that are at the same time but in another respect actualities. But in the *Metaphysics* he quickly skips over animate powers to get to rational ones.[14] Neither these rational nor irrational powers are first actualities. He operates with a more austere ontology here.

Rational powers are powers for opposites, while irrational powers lead to only one effect. A doctor can increase or decrease a patient's bloody supply, but a leech can only remove blood, not add it. A doctor can increase or decrease a patient's temperature, but an ice bath can only do one of those. Rational powers need something further to determine which of the opposites they will do.[15] Although Aristotle will tell us in *Met.* IX.5 that rational powers can have determinate *energeiai* through a further "desire and decision," he does not say so here. We do not know, not here, and maybe not even in IX.5, whether the further determinant is itself rational or irrational. Here is the first place where ethics needs greater precision and depth than apparently is enough for the *Metaphysics.*

If a further irrational power determined which way a rational power should be actualized, the highest good would be irrational. If the virtues grasp an end through desire and so, it seems, irrationally, while *phronēsis* determines means to that end rationally, then a rational power, *phronēsis,* is in the service of an irrational one, the ethical virtues. Many moralists differ from Aristotle and accept such a metaphysics, confining rationality to the calculation of means to ends that are themselves beyond reason. If, on the other hand, a rational power is determined by a further rational power, that further power needs further determination, since it too is a power for opposites. It is hard to see how that regress could end except in an irrational power. There is good reason why the virtues can be, by the standards of *Met.* IX, neither rational nor irrational.[16]

This puzzle about whether there is room in the *Metaphysics* and so in the universe for the ethical virtues arises because Aristotle says nothing about whether these paired properties of *dynameis* also characterize the *energeiai* they lead to. The crucial ethical question is whether the *energeiai* of active *dynameis* are themselves active, those of irrational *dynameis* irrational, etc.

At first it looks as though they must be, and seeing why not will also show why Aristotle does not present animate *dynameis* as an intermediate stage: none of these *dynameis* is a first *energeia*. An *energeia* is in actuality what the *dynamis* is potentially, and so the properties of potentialities should carry over to their realization. The transmission of properties seems plausible for the distinction between active and passive powers. It makes sense to say that the activity of fire heating something is active while the realization of being burned is passive. But it is not clear that "rational" and "irrational" apply to *energeiai.* (And we will see in the next section that the transmission of properties from *dynamis* to *energeia* is even more questionable when we distinguish between natural and innate *dynameis*.) If a rational *dynamis* is a capacity for opposites, how are its *energeiai*, which are determinate, rational?

Ethics clearly needs a deeper analysis of rational powers than the *Metaphysics* provides. To provide it, I want to return to the contrast I drew in chapter 1 between what the rhetorician and what the virtuous person knows, because they are rational powers in different ways. Rhetoric is a rational *dynamis*, but its *energeiai* are not themselves rational. Rhetoric and dialectic, because they are universal faculties, make no one wiser (*Rh.* I.2. 1356a32–34; see *Met.* III.1.995b18–25, IV.2.1004b25, XI.4. 1061b7–10, *Rh.* I.4.1359b2–17, *Soph. El.* 11.171b5–7). To see how the ethical virtues can be rational without being powers for opposites, we must turn from these universal faculties to the sciences. The sciences know something and so are not indifferent to truth and falsity. I can think that the world is flat, but I can't know it. While the knower can choose whether or not to exercise his knowledge, he doesn't have it in his power to know opposites.[17]

In the universal arts, reasoning is a formal capacity for drawing inferences, accusing and defending, supporting and refuting. The principles of a rhetorical or dialectical argument are always principles *pros ti*, principles because they are the starting points of inferences rather than because of anything in their own nature. These principles are separate from the arts of argument and are therefore irrational. In the sciences, *logos* is no longer formal. It does not just reason. It knows. The principles of the sciences are true principles, objects of knowledge even if not of proof. The universal faculties for opposites are perfected into "qualities through which the soul achieves truth in affirmations and denials" (*NE* VI.3.1139b15–16), not by adding "desire or decision" but by hitting on a principle of knowledge (*Rh.* I.2.1358a1–28, I.4.1359b12–17).

But in another sense the sciences too are powers for opposites, since their uses are not determined by the sciences themselves. That the sciences don't determine their own uses does not mean that the science of medicine is equally about health and disease. Still, while medicine can be used equally to kill or cure, it is still about health.[18]

The virtues part company with the sciences on just this point. They don't have uses determined by something outside themselves. The virtuous person doesn't choose whether or not to act virtuously in the way the person who knows who to speak Russian chooses whether to speak Russian. Unlike the arts, the virtues are rational in their activity, and not only in their power to become something.[19]

## *Met.* IX.5: Innate and Acquired *Dynameis*

> As all potencies are either innate, like the senses, or come by practice, like the
> power of playing the flute, or by learning, like artistic power, those which
> come by practice or by rational formula we must acquire by previous exercise.
> But this is not necessary with those which are not of this nature and which
> imply passivity (*epi tou paschein*). (*Met.* IX.5.1047b31–34)

Maybe the *energeiai* of active powers are active, the realizations of passive powers passive. It took some doing to find rationality in the activity of rational *dynameis*. But the transmission of properties from *dynamis* to *energeia* seems to make no sense at all for the third distinction, between innate and acquired *dynameis*, introduced in *Met.* IX.5 and exemplified, respectively, by the senses and knowledge. While powers can be acquired or innate, what sense could it make to characterize their *energeiai* that way? In fact, we will see that it is through turning to this third distinction that Aristotle can make connections between properties of *dynameis* and properties of *energeiai*, which he fails to make for active vs. passive or rational vs. irrational *dynameis*. Those connections between the properties of *dynameis* and *energeiai* will make sense of the nature of happiness and thus of my initial paradox about the rarity of human flourishing.

I have been complaining that Aristotle simply presents one distinction after another, rather than showing how one develops out of the prior ones. In this case, it seems that Aristotle equates the irrational/rational distinction with the innate/acquired one, and even with the passive/active one, as in the passage in the epigraph to this section. The three pairs of kinds of powers then collapse into a single contrast. Powers are either passive, innate, and irrational or they are active, acquired, and rational. The only qualification is the hedge that some active, acquired, and rational potencies are rational in some further sense too, not rational as powers for opposites but rational as acquired through learning. If the passivity Aristotle mentions here is the same as that of *Met.* IX.1, then all irrational and nonacquired powers will be passive. As I suggested in talking about *Met.* IX.1, the nonhuman world, or at least the inanimate world, contains no active powers.[20]

After introducing this distinction of innate and acquired powers Aristotle finally notes that because rational powers are powers for opposites, the conjunction of a rational power with its matching power does not necessarily produce a definite effect, and so "therefore there must be some other deciding factor (*to kurion*), by which I mean desire or decision" (1048a10). When we met rational powers in chapter 2, we were not told that their realization took desire or decision. The new distinction between innate and acquired powers seems to require this elaboration. It is hard to see why.

If the *Metaphysics* were about natural substances alone, the distinction between natural and acquired powers would have no place. Perception develops gradually (*NE* VIII.12.1161b24–26), but it is not an acquired power. "We do or undergo many of our natural [actions and processes], e.g. growing old and dying, in knowledge; but none of them is voluntary" (*NE* V.8.1135a34–b1). There is no reason for the argument of *Met.* IX to proceed as it does except to include human praxis. Dividing powers into acquired and natural is metaphysically important because with acquired powers we get a new kind of internal principle that goes beyond the definition of nature as an internal principle of motion. After all, the genus of virtue, *hexis,* is chosen from three things that "grow" in the soul, passions, *dynameis,* and habits (*ta en te psyche ginomena, NE* II.5.1105b19–20). *Hexeis* are acquired *dynameis,* but they are acquired in the narrower, ethical sense that requires decision and not the broader sense in which most human behavior is learned.

Habituation allows something to *become* an internal principle. Nothing counts as acquiring a power without the power becoming more voluntary and subject to desire and decision. In such cases, the act is prior to the power. We are on the road to my claim that human practical *energeiai* have to create the conditions for their own success. They create their own enabling conditions by creating themselves as powers and principles.

We, and other animals, acquire many powers, but not all of them count as acquired as opposed to natural powers. Both health and strength are produced and preserved by mean amounts, just like the virtues (*NE* II.2.1104a11–18). But health is a natural, not an acquired, *dynamis.* Better, it is the *energeia* of a natural *dynamis.* Health and strength are not acquired *dynameis* and the distinction of first and second act does not apply to them. When we are healthy and strong, we do not acquire a new internal principle of motion; we are better able to use our natural internal principles. It is *because health and strength are not rational dynameis that they are not acquired dynameis either.* Physical virtues like health are simply a proportion of opposites, while ethical virtues, although produced by such means, involve decision. Only they are means about means.

But what about *technē?* Art seems to be as much a rational and an acquired power as virtue is. But only the virtues, and not *technē* or health and strength, allow a distinction between doing a virtuous deed and doing it virtuously. Someone who performs virtuous acts reliably and predictably but without *prohairesis* does not have an acquired *dynamis.* Virtue is a cause and principle in a stronger sense than is art, and so is more rational than art, since once chance is eliminated, the product is sufficient evidence that art is the cause, while the virtuous act is not sufficient evidence of virtuous agency. This makes the virtues into principles of action in a way *technai* are not.

Therefore, we have the important ethical and metaphysical result that voluntary powers are coextensive with powers acquired by performing the acts first. Acquired powers can be exercised voluntarily, and so they are all rational. Conversely, all rational powers are acquired as we come to exercise them voluntarily. If the transition from potency to act for a given power is voluntary, then it follows that that power itself has been acquired and is not innate. Here is our first connection between the properties of a potentiality and those of an *energeia*. While the *Metaphysics* draws no connections between the properties of *dynameis* and *energeiai*, the *Ethics* already has. *Ethics* II searched for the definition of virtue by seeing how it is acquired. By performing good actions, we acquire the ability to do them. The good acts we perform without possessing the virtues are good because of the results they lead to, while the good actions that realize their allied *dynameis* are their own end. Fully rational powers must be acquired.

## *Met.* IX.6. Perfect and Imperfect *Energeiai*

> Of these, we must call the one set movements (*kineis*) and the other actualities (*energeiai*). For every movement is incomplete—making thin, learning, walking, building; these are movements, and incomplete at that. For it is not true that at the same time a thing is walking and has walked, or is building and has built, or is coming to be and has come to be, or is being moved and has been moved. . . . But it is the same thing that at the same time has seen and is seeing, or is thinking and has thought. The latter sort of process, then, I call an actuality, and the former a movement. (*Met.* IX.6. 1048b28–34)

The first five chapters of *Met.* IX gave three contrasts among *dynameis:* active and passive, rational and irrational, acquired and innate, progressively deepening the idea of rationality. *Met.* IX.6 announces a different distinction: "Since we have now dealt with the kind of potency which is related to motion, let us now discuss actuality" (1048a25–26), and Aristotle will go on to distinguish perfect from imperfect actualities.

Aristotle himself says nothing to correlate perfect and imperfect *energeia* to his pairs of *dynameis*. He never explains whether the properties of *dynameis*—active vs. passive, rational vs. irrational, innate vs. acquired— carry over into their *energeiai*. He never says that some *dynameis* are *dyna-*

*meis* of *kinēseis* and others of *energeiai,* or that his reason for elaborating these different kinds of *dynameis* relative to motion was to build to an understanding of perfect *energeiai.*

While Aristotle never offers a correlation between kinds of *dynameis* and kinds of *energeiai* in the *Metaphysics,* he does in the *Ethics* and *Politics,* as practical issues about transitivity of properties between potency and act become critical. "The activity of imperfect things is imperfect" (*EE* II.1. 1219a37–38), and "nothing incomplete is happy because it is not a whole" (b7–8). Aristotle organizes the *Ethics* and the *Politics* around the question he fails to raise in the *Metaphysics.* The crucial question is this: since happiness is an *energeia* of a certain sort, possessing the qualities that *energeiai* have of completeness and desirability, what kind of *dynamis* must it have?

The *Ethics* turns in Book I from happiness to virtue in order to approach just that question. The good life is a perfect *energeia* of an active, rational, and acquired first *energeia* that is itself perfect. The virtuous habits are perfect first *energeiai* that lead to perfect second *energeiai* of virtuous activities, and happiness comprises those activities in a complete life. Because it internalizes its conditions of success, happiness will be rarer than health. Irrational powers have to be moved, by something else, into contact with another power before they can be realized. Rational powers can move themselves, but they need something outside themselves, desire or decision, to be actual. Neither an irrational nor a rational power, then, can internalize its conditions of success.

The first step toward such internalization is to be an acquired capacity. The more a first *energeia,* such as a virtue, has to internalize its conditions of success, the harder it is to achieve. Once achieved, though, that first *energeia* will easily realize its second *energeia,* since all the conditions for its success are built in. We engage in virtuous action more continuously than in any other kind of practice. This configuration reaches its extreme formulation for *theōria* when Aristotle says that it is best because it is most continuous, "for we more capable of continuous study more than any continuous action (*prattein hotioun*) (*NE* X.7.1177a21–22). It is right for the best substance to realize its (first) nature less frequently than inferior substances, because once it does, it will realize its second, acquired, nature more continuously.

## Aristotle vs. Modern Ethics, Yet Again

The term "virtue" is often used to pick out qualities of two kinds: either particular facets of what is seen as a good life, such as generosity (in the modern sense), or kindness, or liberality; or else properties which have the effect of bringing about, preserving, or maintaining the good life: courage, temperance, constancy, and (on some readings) justice. Let's call these latter "preserving" qualities. It is central to Aristotle's theory that while he picks out a great many preserving virtues, these are also considered to fall into the first class, and to be proper parts of the good life. Being a causal condition of the good does not rule out being constitutive of it. (Charles Taylor, "Justice After Virtue")[21]

The virtues internalize their conditions of success. For that reason Aristotle directs the attention and energy of ethics and politics to acquiring good first *energeiai:* education is the first concern of politics; caring for one another's virtue distinguishes a polis from a mere alliance. Education is not only for the young; establishing both the internal and external conditions for virtue is the continuing task for politics: "It is not enough for people to receive the right nurture and discipline in youth; they must also practice the lessons they have learned, and confirm them by habit, when they are grown up. Accordingly, we shall need laws to regulate the discipline of adults as well" ( *NE* X.9. 1180a1–4). The goal of virtuous action and of politics is to make "good people come from good people," in spite of nature not always cooperating.

Modern moral theory, instead, turns its attention to the movement between the first and second *energeia.* Moderns posit the possession of the power to do right—ought implies can—and then worry about failures to exercise the power. Modern moral theory then needs free will to explain why people so frequently fail to realize their nature.

The demand for moral equality changes the nature of the first *energeia* into a capacity imputed to all. That modern equal capacity must be less demanding than Aristotle's virtuous habits and consequently makes more open and indeterminate the modern equivalent of Aristotle's second *energeia,* so that we see a variety of ways of living well, culminating in MacIntyre's claim that the "good life for man is the life spent in seeking for the good life for man."[22] If everyone is capable of being virtuous, then the connection Aristotle constructs between virtue and happiness must be severed. Aristotelian ethics cannot be universalized, yet another feature of the *Ethics* that is both attractive and impossible for us.[23]

What I earlier called the hidden psychology of the *Ethics* assumes that if I can set my own purposes and so act as a free and rational agent, I will do so. Most men in his view do not reach the antecedent, but those who do pass easily to the consequent. In Kant, by contrast, all rational beings propose ends to themselves, but few make that rationality their end: "Rational nature is distinguished from others in that it proposes an end to itself."[24] And: "The capacity to propose an end to oneself is the characteristic of humanity (as distinguished from animality)."[25] Therefore all Kant's moral problems are in going from first to second *energeiai:* I know what is best but lack the will to move from that knowledge to action. Obligation replaces actualization.

## The Place of Man in Nature

Good people's life together allows the cultivation of virtue. (*NE* IX.9. 1170a12)

To recapitulate briefly: I began with the seeming paradox that people, while the best of all composite substances, do not regularly achieve their own nature. I addressed this paradox by asking what sort of *dynamis, energeia,* and *ergon* such a rare highest human good calls for. The paradox is resolved: the more a first *energeia,* such as a virtue, has to internalize its conditions of success, the more difficult it is to achieve that first *energeia,* but, therefore, the easier it is to achieve the second *energeia.* The life of praxis, then, consists in creating the conditions for its own flourishing. Because the virtues sustain their own conditions for realization, the tense test of *Met.* IX.6 applies to *energeiai* and specifically to praxis—it is at the same time true that the virtuous person is doing something and has done it (see *NE* X.4. 1174a14–16). The virtues are not, like *kinēseis,* fully active only when they are not yet successful.[26]

The argument of *Met.* IX has an implicit ethical structure because the world has an ethical structure. We cannot fully know about being without knowing about the good, and humans can know about the good only through reflection on the human good. Reflection on man's place in the cosmos is the task of *theōria,* the metaphysical task to which the ethical life leads and which satisfies the metaphysical urge, the drive toward *energeia,* that I mentioned in the Introduction.[27] In *Physics* II we learn that art partly imitates nature and partly completes, perfects, it (194a21–22, 199a16–17), but the world does not need art to be complete. It needs praxis.

Being rational and human is the culmination of being an animal, just as animals are substances *par excellence.* Nature is an internal principle of motion and rest, but animals have insides and selves in a stronger sense signaled in the *De Anima* by the distinction of first and second *energeiai.* Animals have desires, which require seeking out an environment in which those desires can be satisfied and actualized, while plants and nonliving substances wait for the conditions of *energeia* to come to them.[28]

People have even more insides than other animals. They not only have to find the appropriate environment for actualization, but that environment must be a specifically human and made environment. Desires and ends are not inherently veridical like the senses. That human nature must erect the conditions for its own success allows Aristotle to say without contradiction that man is by nature a political animal while poleis are human products and consequently not universally available (*Pol.* I.4.1253a30–31). For the same reason he can say that virtue and happiness are both easy (*NE* I.9.1099b18–20) and difficult (II.6.1106b31–33, II.9.1109a24, V.9. 1137a9–14). *Ethics* II.1–2 told us that the virtues are the products of actions. But the appropriate conditions for *realizing,* as well as developing, our acquired human natures are equally products of actions. Those appropriate conditions for realization are political. Hence my stress in chapter 3 on the political conditions for Aristotle's enterprise and in chapter 5 on the way the ethical virtues are political virtues.

Just as only humans can be happy, only people can be vicious rather than merely deformed (*NE* VII.7.1149b26–1150a8). Virtuous action creates the conditions for its own flourishing—temperance "preserves *phronēsis*" (VI.5.1140b11–12) and "virtue preserves the principle, while vice corrupts it; and in actions the end we act for is the principle" (VII.8.1151a15–16) while vice destroys itself:

> Whatever someone [regards as] his being, or the end for which he chooses to be alive, that is the activity he wishes to pursue in his friend's company. Hence some friends drink together, others play dice, while others do gymnastics or go hunting, or do philosophy. They spend their days together on whichever pursuit in life they like most; for since they want to live with their friends, they share the actions in which they find their common life. Hence the friendship of base people turns out to be vicious. For they are unstable, and share base pursuits; and by becoming similar to each other, they grow vicious. But the friendship of decent people is decent, and increases the more often they meet. And they seem to become still better from their activities and their mutual correction. For each molds the other in what they approve of, so that "[you will learn] what is noble from noble people." (*NE* IX.12.1172a1–14)

While all animals have desires, which require seeking out an environment in which those desires can be satisfied and actualized, the practical virtues search more actively. While the virtues, like desires, search for circumstances in which they can be actualized, only the virtues search for circumstances in which they *should* be actualized, and in which their actualization is good. That search is precisely what deliberation is. The crafts do not sustain themselves because they do not search for conditions in which to realize themselves, or try to create such conditions.

There is a character, Mark Tapley, in *Martin Chuzzlewit,* who is always cheerful but who thinks that such cheer is no virtue because he always finds himself in happy circumstances. So he seeks out miserable conditions in which his cheerful disposition will be a virtue. That is not how the virtuous person preserves the conditions for the flourishing of virtue. The courageous man does not look for occasions for war and prefer war to peace, but aims at sustaining a world in which courage is a virtue, in which acting courageously is good for the soul and beneficial for others. The liberal person does not work to sustain conditions of inequality and poverty the better to exercise his or her liberality, but conditions, outlined in chapter 3, "The Varieties of Moral Failure," in which liberality is a virtue.[29]

Human nature has to make its own environment in which people can exercise the human function, be virtuous and happy. People frequently make their own environments, sometimes in obvious ways and sometimes in a more surprising fashion:

> We reach the Karluv Most. I am struck by the extraordinary light, in which blue, blue gray, and gray are offset by a kind of smokiness. I wonder if it might be pollution, but there are few cars in Prague and almost none in the central quarter. "The smokiness," says Swoboda, "is the atmospheric effect of the decomposition of the sandstone that has gone into the construction of the bridge itself, an interesting example of an artistic entity making possible the unique conditions under which it may best be appreciated. . . .
>
> It is the same with mathematics.[30]

It is the same with human flourishing. Human nature has to make its own environment—internal and external, virtues and constitutions, desires and appropriate objects of desire—in which humans can flourish. Only creatures who do not achieve their end naturally—irrationally—need to, and can, make an *energeia,* a *eudaimōn* life, out of particular *energeiai.* The other nondivine beings who more regularly achieve their nature are not called happy.[31] Therefore *Ethics* I.12 asks whether "happiness is one of the things we praise or rather one of those that we honor" and notes that praise and honor are the possibilities since it is already clear "that it is not a *dynamis*" (1101b10–12). Happiness and the happy man belong alongside the gods as objects of honor and absolute value rather than praise, which is always relative (1101b12–14). All other *energeiai,* which are praised rather than honored, are merely relatively good, good of their kind, the *energeia* of a *dynamis,* and/or good because of what they accomplish. Happiness, in contrast, is good absolutely, because it is a perfect *energeia,* itself realizing the properties of *energeia,* and not just relative to the *dynamis* it actualizes. It is the absolute culmination of both dimensions of *energeia*.

*Metaphysics* IX began by telling us that *dynamis* and *energeia* are relative terms. We cannot know that the things we praise are good *energeiai* without knowing what *dynamis* they actualize. I praise my son's athletic achievements because I know his abilities. But we honor, as opposed to praise, happiness because its properties as an *energeia* are not relative to the human *dynamis*. This difference between relative *energeiai*, *energeiai* of some *dynameis*, and *energeia* as such will be the difference between the political and the theoretical life in my final chapter.

We should then not lament the fact that we do not regularly achieve our end. Instead of complaining about moral luck, we should realize that it is only *because* we can perform acts for accidental reasons that we can eventually come to engage in them for their own sake. That is, it is only because the first *energeia* of virtue is so difficult and rare than the second *energeiai* of virtuous activity and happiness can be achieved at all. It is because, like other animals, we naturally possess *dynameis* for motions that we can perform virtuous acts without being virtuous. We *acquire* the capacity for perfect *energeiai*.

The human substance, considered as the achieved substance and second nature of being virtuous, reaches its end with the regularly of a first act realizing its function. It is for this reason that Aristotle says that the good man can

> bear many severe misfortunes with good temper, not because he feels no distress, but because he is noble and magnanimous. . . . A truly good and wise person, we suppose, will bear strokes of fortune suitably, and from his resources at any time will do the finest actions. . . . The happy person could never become miserable, since he will never do hateful and base actions. (*NE* I.10.1100b28–35)

The purpose of any substance is to continue to be itself. Since animals are not immortal, they transform this end into reproduction. But this transformation is not a *faute de mieux* response to mortality as an inferior condition. It is a development of the self-sustaining and self-continuing properties of substance in general into a higher form than their individual substance as such has:

> For any living thing that has reached its normal development . . . the most natural act is the production of another like itself . . . in order that, as far as its nature allows, it may partake in the eternal and divine. That is the goal towards

which all things strive, that for the sake of which they do whatsoever their nature renders possible. (*De An.* II.4.415a28–b3; see *Caelo* I.9.279a17–30, *Gen. Corr.* II.10.336b27–337a7, *Met.* IX.9.1050b28–30)

In general, to be is to be a member of a kind, and so things act to affirm that membership. Thus the end of each substance is not only to persist as itself but to reproduce in appropriate ways (*EE* II.5.1222b15–22). Even non-rational powers have this power to reproduce themselves, as heat heats other bodies. But this reproducing function reaches new heights for praxis, as it not only reproduces itself but creates conditions in which it can develop, for itself and for others, through education, laws, and friendship. If virtue must construct its own environment for flourishing, then part of being virtuous is contributing to the virtues of others. "Every individual should promote the virtue of his children and his friends" (*NE* X.9.1180a31–32). By this reasoning, the second nature of the virtues is more natural, more substantial and real, than the first nature of our innate capacities.[32]

The fact that virtue must create its own enabling conditions allows a reinterpretation of the way that *Politics* says that in good poleis citizens rule and are ruled in turn (III.6.1279a8–16). Alternating rule looks like self-sacrifice, similar to Plato's philosophers reluctantly descending back into the cave. If virtue did not foster its own enabling conditions, then my best life would either be constrained by having to engage in politics or I would forfeit opportunities to engage in the best political activity by having to let others rule too. But if virtue sustains its own enabling conditions, I give nothing up in alternating ruling and being ruled.

Virtue friendship provides an example of the way human *energeiai* are rare because we must create the conditions for our own flourishing. Like happiness, virtue friendship is rare (*NE* VIII.3.1156b24–25). It is easier to have relationships based on accidents, but accidentally based relations are more fickle and mutable. Virtue friendships are the most permanent and the most rare, just as happiness and virtue are both invulnerable and unusual (1156b11–12, 17–18). In virtue friendships, we have to create the conditions for the success of our efforts, building up trust over time (1156b24–32). Thus the discussion of friendship contains the most explicit connection between the metaphysical potency/act distinction and my ethical thesis that only humans are happy, *eudaimōn,* because only they create the conditions of their own realization:

> Being is choiceworthy and lovable for all, and we are insofar as we are actualized, since we are insofar as we live and act. Now the product is, in a way, the producer in his actualization; hence the producer is fond of the product,

because he loves his own being. This is natural, since what he is potentially is what the product indicates in actualization. (*NE* IX.7.1168a5–9)

## Happiness as the Culmination of Being

The three properties of *dynameis* singled out in *Met.* IX.1–5—active, rational, and acquired—assume ethical forms as they are marks of a power that creates its own conditions for realization. The virtues are active, rational, and acquired in ways that go beyond the requirements for activity, rationality, and being acquired demanded by the *Metaphysics*. As I will show, they are more active and more rational than other *dynameis*, which are powers for motions, and are acquired in the more demanding form in which an *energeia* precedes and leads to its *dynamis*. The virtues are active in ways that makes praxis a deeper instance of self-motion than natural motions. Their rationality makes the virtues ways of deciding instead of powers for opposites. The specifically ethical sense in which the virtues are acquired makes them second natures, permanent and self-sustaining.

I've been insisting on the paradox that the properties of a *dynamis*, whether it is active or passive, etc., do not carry over into a corresponding *energeia*, yet an *energeia* is nothing but the realization of a corresponding *dynamis*, so that its properties must be transmitted. Virtue and happiness, the first and second *energeiai* of the good life, do take up properties of their respective *dynameis*, but in an unexpected way.

The pairs of *dynameis* in *Met.* IX.1–5 are powers for motion. Powers for activities do not participate in such contrariety. The mutually exclusive alternatives of *Met.* IX disappear once attention turns to *dynameis* for activities. Therefore, the sense in which the virtues are active does not oppose passivity but includes it. Similarly, the rationality of the virtues includes and perfects an irrational aspect of the virtues, their receptivity. Finally, the acquired aspect of the virtues does not exclude their natural and innate aspect, as some of my acquired skills and personality traits overcome natural deficiencies, but includes and perfects nature. A look at each of these pairs shows how praxis completes the ontology of the *Metaphysics*.

### Active vs. Passive Powers

The virtues are active, but not active as opposed to passive powers. Instead, they lead to activities that depend on receptivity. Virtues are powers that seek out objects by which to be affected. Eyes don't go looking for beauty to maximize their *energeia*. Although some objects are better than others, we see well whatever objects we are presented with. Practical powers are both more open to better objects and more dependent on those objects than natural powers.

Sight is one of Aristotle's examples of a perfect *energeia* in *Met.* IX.6. Since it is passive, irrational, and innate, it is not part of the good life. I might admire and even praise your superior eyesight, but my own failing vision is not blameworthy, not unless years spent reading and writing about Aristotle is blameworthy in the first place. This chapter began with the disappointment that fewer people are happy than animals are healthy, and the expectation that the better the substance, the more regularly it should realize its nature. But the case of vision shows that predictability marks out an inferior sort of activity. Vision does its work well whenever a good eye is presented with a good object. Yet precisely because of that automatic connection, the excellent realizations of sight have no necessary connection to the good life, because they do not involve decision.

"Health is not a praiseworthy thing; for neither is its work (*ergon*). Neither is acting strongly; for neither is strength. Rather, although they are good, they are not praiseworthy" (*EE* VIII.3.124823–25). Sight is like the natural virtues that Aristotle talks about at *NE* VI.13.1144b30–1145a2, and like shame in *NE* IV.9, a power for good that is not rationally constituted. Seeing well might be a necessary condition of my acting virtuously, but it is not part of living well.

It is part of being virtuous to desire to act virtuously and to look for conditions in which virtuous action is appropriate. We are not praised or blamed for our passions but for feeling them at the right time toward the right objects, etc., and that rightness is measured not by the quantity of emotion felt but by the actions it leads to. Aristotle expresses this new sense of activity that depends on receptivity and searches for opportunities by showing how right action is determined by a judgment of the right place on the continuum of passions. We locate that place by deliberating about what to do.[33]

As the *Ethics* advances from the virtues of the irrational part of the soul, courage and temperance, through the more social and active virtues discussed in Book IV, the virtuous person is increasingly active and attentive in looking for situations for exercising one's virtue. The more "passive" virtues, courage and temperance, require less equipment, while the more active virtues depend on the good fortune of having material goods, honor, and living in a good country. As the *Ethics* advances, the meanings of "active" and "passive" become more sophisticated. For example, receiving honors is not something one passively undergoes, because receiving them depends on doing honorable things and on the virtue of greatness of soul, *megalopsychia* (*NE* IV.3), which both leads a person to seek honors and also to assess correctly, without over- or underestimation, the value of the actions being honored. The corrective justice of judges making someone whole after an assault similarly seems responsive, necessary for the preservation of law and order but hardly an activity that is part of the good life, but such judging turns out to be a way of being active as it engages powers of judgment and perception in deciding whom to compensate, by how much, etc. Virtuous actions, recall, are activities that are both necessary and noble, and so are active in being responsive.

The way the virtues seek out opportunities for their own exercise, though, sets political problems. There is no impulse to politicize as much of the human world as possible, either by maximizing the number of citizens in a polis, or by spreading the news of politics among the barbarians. On the contrary, as we saw in chapter 5, the better the life, the smaller the number of citizens and the larger the ratio of noncitizens to citizens.

The reason for these restrictions is now evident. The better the life, the higher the standard of the second *energeia*, the more external conditions have to be in place for the first act to exist (*Pol.* VII.13.1332a29–33).[34] The best life requires the most fortunate external conditions, and in those conditions, whom Aristotle allows to participate in the best life will also be most restricted.

This deeper sense of activity provides an internal criterion for distinguishing virtue from vice. If part of being an activity is to act in ways that sustain the conditions of success for one's actions, then the virtues are active in a way that the vices are not. Vicious people cannot have the practical continuity in their lives in which virtuous action creates the conditions for its own success and virtuous habits create and sustain the conditions in which they can be exercised. Standing well toward the passions is more active than standing badly toward them.

### Rational vs. Irrational Powers

Next, ethically deepening the idea of a rational power lets virtue and *prohairesis* go beyond the rationality of *Met.* IX.2. Rational powers need decision to cause action. In the virtues, the decision that makes the realization of a rational *dynamis* determinate is itself rational in a different and more perfect way. Aristotle thus evades the possibility that our rational powers are ultimately in the service of an irrational final end, in the way Bradley, for example, defined metaphysics as "the finding of bad reasons for what we believe on instinct," a finding which itself no less instinctual.[35]

The rational powers engaged in perfect practical activities are not indifferent to how they are actualized, as the rational powers of the arts are. The doctor can kill or cure by virtue of his medical power. When he is killing, he is not acting medically. But all the courageous man's actions are the actions of a courageous person. The difference between *technē* and virtue, then, tracks the distinction I discussed earlier from *Met.* IV between the universal arts of dialectic and rhetoric, which are indifferent to the uses made of them, and the sciences, which although they know contraries, are about one, such as health, and know the other, disease, only as a privation.

Like irrational powers, virtues activate themselves when confronted with an appropriate object. Unlike the other rational powers, they do not need an additional desire or decision. When at the end of *Ethics* VI Aristotle shows how ethical virtue and *phronēsis* are connected, he does so by setting out two ways in which moral and intellectual virtue can fall apart. Cleverness is a purely rational *dynamis,* and so ethically fails just because it is indifferent to its ends. Natural virtue seems to go wrong not by being directed to the wrong ends, like cleverness, but by not having sufficient direction from *phronēsis,* which is about means. Natural virtue shows how an irrational *dynamis* can go wrong, subject to ethical censure exactly because it is irrational, like a "heavy body which falls heavily because it has no sight" (*NE* VI.13.1144b10–12; see 1144b30–1145a6).

Internalizing desire and the act of decision perfects practical rationality. "Decision is the principle (*archē*) of praxis" (*NE* VI.2.1139b4–5; see *Poet.* 6.1449b38–1450a2). This is the difference between virtue and continence: self-control is a rational power that is less dependable and good than virtue because it needs a further desire to determine in each case whether the self-controlled man will control himself this time or not. The continent man not only is imperfectly good but is imperfectly rational, since his reason does not rule politically but despotically. My reason is not exercised as fully when I rule a slave as when I govern fellow citizens. Similarly, I don't exercise my reason fully when I govern recalcitrant desires as when I deliberate with the cooperation of the emotions. The practical reason of the self-controlled person cannot choose things for their own sake.

Instead of creating conditions for its own exercise, each art has a secondary capacity for teaching. But the virtues' mode of reproduction is not distinct from virtuous action itself, while the arts needing this secondary capacity make them only imperfectly rational. In this way Aristotle can resist Socrates' assumption that to be virtuous one has to be able to explain oneself and teach virtue to others. To act virtuously is to act to sustain the conditions for the exercise of the virtues. Therefore, *phronēsis* and political wisdom are the same faculty (*NE* VI.8.1141b23–24): "Wisdom produces happiness not as an art of medicine produces health but as health produces health" (*NE* VI.12.1144a3–5). The virtues produce virtue as health produces health.[36]

Therefore Aristotle attacks the sophists at precisely the point in his argument when he moves from ethics to politics, from the virtues to creating circumstances in which the virtues can develop and flourish. Virtuous people cannot teach virtue, while the sophists pretend to. But in fact what the sophists do is reproduce themselves. Instead of teaching virtue, they teach others to be sophistic teachers of virtue (*NE* X.9.1181a12–b12). If virtue cannot be taught, either by the virtuous or by professional teachers, the task of reproduction, of virtuously creating the conditions for further virtue, falls to politics.

## Natural and Acquired Powers

Ethical activities deepen our understanding of what it is to be an active and a rational power. Similarly, and finally, they deepen our understanding of acquired powers. It is one thing to say at the beginning of *Ethics* II that the virtues are neither by nor contrary to nature. It is another to say that they perfect our nature. While acquired, the virtues are more natural—because we are realized in them more fully—than the passions and *dynameis* that are natural in the sense of given, in the same way that the polis, more natural than the family, takes intentional effort and innovation (*Pol.* I.4. 1253a30–31). Virtuous second natures come into being through building an insides, a self. Instead of imitation, the relation of art to nature, we have second nature, the relation of an acquired *hexis* to the natural *dynamis* it realizes, neither art nor nature. The virtues become an internal principle, while *technē*, when successful, always remains an external principle.

The ethically deepened idea of an acquired power is no longer the contrary of the innate, just as active and passive powers are interrelated in a new form of activity and rational and irrational powers in a new form of rationality. Virtue is neither by nature nor contrary to nature, but the virtues are not simply painted on top of natural powers. The acquired habits of the virtues are themselves the *energeiai* and perfection of the natural powers. Where we might have thought that natural powers are more internal than acquired ones, the opposite is the case. Aristotle's distinction between innate and acquired *dynameis* shows that habits and other acquired powers are no less real than innate powers. Acquired and rational powers are as much part of the furniture of the cosmos as the natures studied in the *Physics*.

## Happiness as a Perfect *Energeia*

Ethically deepening the three sets of contrary properties of *dynameis*, finally, deepens the idea of a perfect *energeia*. Seeing is a perfect *energeia*, but it only perfects the power of sight. We know nothing about whether the world would be better if everyone's eyes were working all the time, or even, more modestly, if animals are better off for seeing well. The final practical *energeia* perfects not only the human ergon—the virtues both "render the thing itself good, and also cause it to perform its function well" (*NE* II.6.1106a15–17) again—but perfects all the imperfect *energeiai* that humans must engage in. The *Ethics* and *Politics* show in detail how human happiness and the virtues are perfect because they *perfect* existing imperfect activities and structures. The imperfect are perfected by modes of activity that create their own success conditions.

Virtues include their own enabling conditions by ensuring that virtuous actions usually lead to good results. Courageous people usually succeed in battle, and their virtue is usually recognized and praised by others. The regularity of connection between good acts and good results makes agents more rational, while in other conceptions of morality such regularity would compromise the autonomy of the good by turning to extramoral considerations of consequences. The good state provides a rational structure in which people can rationally participate. The polis has to offer a rational structure, in which connections between motives, acts, and consequences are evident, so that to choose the good for its own sake is not to choose good in spite of possibly bad consequences. To deliberate well, one must aim at good consequences. Even though they are only the given end, not the guiding end, of action, without them deliberation could not take place.

The virtues are the best kind of *dynamis* because they are neither rational nor irrational, because they are active in a way that includes receptivity, and because they are acquired in a way that makes them more natural than the natural as given. They are perfect *dynameis* because they exhibit the best possible connection between potency and act. The relation between virtue and virtuous action does not obliterate the potency/act distinction but reconstitutes the distinction in a way appropriate for perfect *energeiai*. That reconstitution can only be done by the change in direction of inference I highlighted in chapter 2 and by the transformations of the kinds of *dynameis* I've been showing here. The virtues as perfect *dynameis* are already an intimation or imitation of divine activity. The gods have no *dynameis*, since they are always active. The closest that material beings can get is to have the *dynameis* represented in the virtues.

## CHAPTER 7

# Living Politically and Living Rationally:
# Choosing Ends and Choosing Lives

The most supreme science is the one which knows that for the sake of which each thing is to be done. (*Met.* I.2.982b4–6)

All things of this sort have room for a free sort of study, but experience in them is a necessity (*panta de ta toiauta tēn theōrian eleutheron echei, tēn d'empeirian anagkaian*). (*Pol.* I.4.1258b9–12)

## We Deliberate about Means, Not Ends

Nothing in the Aristotelian corpus has led acute minds to say silly things as much as the two chapters on *theōria* at the end of the *Ethics*. Some have dismissed *NE* X.7 and 8 by calling them early and adding the insulting epithet of Platonic, and others have explained them away by calling them ironic.[1] When "Platonic" and "ironic" are terms of abuse, or the contrast between the philosophical and the political life is posed in terms of a choice between anachronistic terms like egoism and altruism, something is wrong.

But these two chapters would not have caused trouble if there weren't some real difficulties. I see three serious problems.

First, the *Ethics* gave us no reason to expect the elevation of *theōria*, and the *Ethics* doesn't seem to be the kind of book that should have a surprise ending. If *Ethics* X.7 and 8 were not there, no one would notice that they were missing, in spite of the promise Aristotle makes at *NE* I.5.1096a4–5

189

to consider the contemplative life later. No one would infer from the rest of the *Ethics* that it would not be complete without moving us from the political life to a better life outside politics.[2]

Second, not only does the assertion that the life of *theōria* is the happiest life not seem motivated by the rest of the *Ethics;* even worse, it seems incompatible with the true ending of the *Ethics* in the next and final chapter, with its transition from ethics to politics. *NE* X.9 is a fitting conclusion because practical knowledge is knowledge that leads to action.[3] The most important component of good action is a good upbringing, which is the responsibility of politics, not ethics. The *Ethics* shows us the true values of different human activities. The statesman, as Aristotle notes at the beginning of the *Ethics* (I.2.1094a26–b4), determines who engages in what practices under what conditions in the state. The transition to politics in X.9 is thus compelled by Aristotle's overall argument. If X.7 and 8 show that we should prefer the philosophic to the political life, then that move interrupts an otherwise smooth argument from the articulation of the good life to an inquiry into how to establish its conditions.

Third, not only did it not seem to fit what comes before and what comes after, but it is hard to see how this discussion makes sense as part of a practical inquiry. *Theōria* is introduced as an answer to the question, what is the best and happiest life. This question is naturally understood—and frequently understood by commentators—as a question about *choosing* the best life: should I study more philosophy or try to alleviate world hunger? But the idea of choosing a life, let along choosing between the political and theoretical life, is hard to square with Aristotle's conception of choice as deliberate desire (*bouletikē orexis, NE* III.3.1113a10–12), where we deliberate about things that are in our control and are attainable by action (1112a30–31).[4] To choose between the political and theoretical life would be to deliberate about ends. And Aristotle insists that *we deliberate not about ends but about means* (*NE* III.3.1112b11–12).

We choose actions, but can we choose lives? If I know that the philosophic life is best, how could that knowledge function practically? Would the person who knows that the philosophic life is best have to be compelled to do anything else? If contemplation is the best *activity*, does it follow that the philosophic life is the best *life*?

Can we choose between the philosophic and the political life? Aristotle knows that activities can conflict, and so sometimes we have to choose between alternatives. "People fond of playing the flute are incapable of attending to arguments if they overhear someone playing the flute" (*NE* X. 5.1175b13–17; see VII.14.1154a26–27, *Part. An.* IV.10.686a25–687a2, *Pol.* VIII.4.1339a7–10). But he never presents the comparison of the political and the theoretical lives as a conflict. He never invites me to worry that my time spent understanding Aristotle is time away from eliminating, or fighting, war.

All along I've been arguing that actions done for their own sake do not stop aiming at external goods. In chapter 5 I argued that the distinction between the good man and the good citizen never turns into a conflict. For the same reasons, the question of the best life is never presented as a conflict between lives, as it frequently is by Socrates, for example in the *Apology* where he forces people to choose between the pursuits of wisdom and money, or in the *Gorgias,* Socrates and Callicles divide over a choice of lives, and a choice of the appropriate object of *eros* for people who want to live an active life. But if the two lives are not posed as alternatives for a choice, how can the decision about the best life can be an item for *practical* knowledge? How can knowing that the contemplative life is best while the political life is perfect and happy in a secondary way (*NE* X.8.1178a9) be practical? Throughout I have tried to explain how ends can be rational without being subject to deliberation. We do choose happiness, and choose actions that are their own end, but in those cases there is nothing like choosing between alternatives. Deciding which is the best life is the hardest test of the rationality of ends.

### Man Is Not the Best Thing in the Universe

Virtue has two *energeiai:* virtuous actions are the actualization of virtuous habits, and happiness is *energeia kat'aretēn.* These final chapters of the *Ethics* speak to the relation between those two *energeiai.* The *Ethics* ends with a discussion of *theōria* not to invite individuals to become more contemplative but to help the statesman—Aristotle's audience throughout— understand the relation between happiness and virtue.

I propose to show how the comparison between the two lives can be practical by bringing in a second fixed star for interpreting Aristotle's *Ethics* alongside the dictum that we deliberate about means and not ends. When he distinguishes *phronēsis* from *sophia,* Aristotle told us that *"man is not the best thing in the universe"* (*NE* VI.7.1141a20–21; see also 1141a34– 1141b2, *Part. An.* I.1.641a35–b12, *EE* II.1.1219a35–39, *Pol.* VII.15. 1334a22–33). The political life is not the best life only if man is not the best thing in the universe.[5]

The practical character of the inquiry into the best life invites a question that I think has not been raised before and which reorients the discussion of *theōria* in a more fruitful direction: Who can know that man is not the best thing in the universe?

The student of first philosophy will know what the best things are, and hence know that man is not one of them. She will note that the examples of perfect *energeiai* in *Metaphysics* IX are all human activities, but also see that the gods of *Metaphysics* XII engage in activity even more perfectly (e.g., *Met.* XII.7.1072b24–25, *Caelo* II.12.292a22–28). However, this truth has no obvious bearing on practice. If we were to discover that Mars contains a species far more intelligent, generous, and just than humans, I don't see why that would have any consequences at all for how we should live.

The *Ethics* does not import the proposition, "Man is not the best thing in the universe," from the *Metaphysics*. Only someone with *phronēsis* can know what humans are at our best. Only someone who knows what humans are at our best can know that there is something better, and what it has to do with us. Only someone living the happy political life can know that it is not the best possible human life.

*NE* VI.7 lists Thales and Anaxagoras as people with *sophia* and not *phronēsis* (1141b3–4), but there is no indication that these are exemplars of the philosophic life as opposed to the virtue of wisdom. *NE* X.7 and 8 contain no examples at all.[6] While Thales and Anaxagoras may be wise, I do not believe they led a philosophical *life*. I could pass most of my life being imprisoned and tortured, and my philosophical training could help me contemplate the beauty of the maggots and vermin who are my cellmates (*Part. An.* I.5.645a2–23). But I would not be *eudaimōn*, and so this would not be a philosophical life.

If political activity allows the *phronimos* and good citizen to know how good human nature is, then *theōria* will not be antipolitical, as in the traditional contrast between the *vita contemplativa* and the *vita activa*, nor prepolitical, placed in the household and family or in the individual apart from the polis.[7] Contemplation derived from reading the *Metaphysics* could be antipolitical. Contemplative activity as the culmination of political activity will not be.

The relation between the political life and the contemplative life is a final—in several senses of the word—articulation of the problem which motivates the entire argument of the *Ethics*. If both happiness and ethically virtuous activities are *energeiai* of the virtues, happiness is then a single *energeia* made up of discrete *energeiai* of virtuous activities. Happiness is an activity engaged in for its own sake, made up of activities each of which is engaged in for *its* own sake. The fundamental question is how these particular activities can be part of a single, integrated, and unified good life without losing their own intrinsic value as virtuous actions.[8]

Happiness must be made of acts that themselves have intrinsic value. An action is part of the happy life if and only if the act is its own end. The good actions which comprise happiness are parts of happiness *because* they are chosen for their own sakes. Otherwise they would be means to happiness. On the other side, a *eudaimōn* life cannot be made up of *energeiai* without itself being an *energeia*. Otherwise it would not be a life. The good man would do what is best at every moment without those deeds having coherence or continuity. That would not be a good life. It would not be continuous, self-sufficient, or pleasant, because it would not be not *a* life. Thus my bi-conditional: an action is part of the happy life if and only if the act is its own end.

Until *NE* X.6, we learn about happiness only by learning about virtue. Here Aristotle finally can speak directly about happiness because to talk about it directly is to talk about contemplation. Therefore the discussion of contemplation is the necessary conclusion of the inquiry into the good life just as contemplation itself is the culmination of the good life. To understand the relation of contemplation to the good life is to explicate the problem of happiness that structures the entire *Ethics*.

Happiness is an *energeia* made up of *energeiai*. The good person has to make his life one *energeia* out of many. He has to unify it while still respecting the integrity and value of component *energeiai*. "Nothing incomplete is happy because it is not a whole" (*EE* II.1.1219b7–8). In the *Poetics* Aristotle denies that lives have the unity that actions do, so that one cannot make a good tragedy or epic out of a whole life (1451a16–23). The narrative unity that many moderns substitute for *theōria* denies that dictum of the *Poetics*. But in the *Ethics* Aristotle must deny it in a different way. Happy lives must be unified. "Nature is not likely to be episodic . . . like a bad tragedy" (*Met.* XIV.5.1090b19–20).[9]

### The Happy Man Will Do *and Contemplate* What Is in Accord with Virtue

Political activity points us to the contemplative life. Seen as many *energeiai*, the best life is political; seen as a single *energeia*, the best life is contemplative. *"The happy man will do and contemplate most of all the actions in accord with virtue"* (*NE* I.10.1100b19–20, see also IV.2.1122a35, IX.4. 1166a27, IX.9.1169b33–1170a4, *EE* I.6.1216b37, 1245b6). Since it is better to see one's life as a unity, the contemplative life is best, and the political life happy in a secondary way. And if the political life is happy in a secondary way, and if "happiness extends just as far as *thēoria* extends" (*NE* X. 8.1178b28–29), then it follows from those two premises that *the political life is also theoretical*, although in a secondary way. What that can mean?[10]

While in *NE* X.8 Aristotle says that animals are not happy because they cannot engage in *thēoria* (1178b24–25), he says earlier animals are not happy because they do not engage in *ethical* activity (I.9.1109b32–1100a1; see also III.2.1111b6–10, *EE* I.7.1217a2–29, *De An.* 434a5–10, *Pol.* III.9.1280a32–34, *HA* 1.1.488b24).[11] Those two statements are consistent because to engage in ethical activity is to have all one needs for *thēoria*. "Living must be considered a kind of knowing" (*EE* VII.12. 1244b29).

Human rationality manifests itself primarily in political organization, not in science. The rationality manifested in political organization gives us access to the rationality of the universe, not the other way around. Where others have found in poetic creativity an approach to divine activity, for Aristotle politics is our sole access to the divine.[12]

The philosophical life develops from the political life, but the two lives are not the same. Prior to deciding which is best, we have to know how individuate the two lives:[13]

> The question is raised even on the part of those who agree that the life accompanied by virtue is the most worthy of choice (*hairetōtaton*), whether the life of citizenship and activity (*politikos kai prakitos*) is desirable or rather a life released from all external affairs, for example some sort of contemplative life (*hoion theōrētikos tis*), which is said by some to be the only life that is philosophic. It is manifest that [the political and the contemplative lives] are the two modes of life principally chosen by the men most ambitious of excelling in virtue (*hoi philotimotatoi pros aretēn*). (*Pol.* VII.2.1324a25–32)[14]

One must decide which life is best. But as a coda he notes that some say that a contemplative life is the only philosophic life. At a minimum, then, the identity between the philosophic life and a life made up of contemplative acts is not self-evident. *Theōria* as the organizing principle of a life is not the same as *thēoria* as the content of a life.[15] Failure to ask how to individuate the two lives lies behind the common presupposition that one must either choose between them or somehow try to combine them. Just as earlier I raised the question, which might be thought too obvious to address, of who can recognize that man is not the best thing in the universe, so I also reject the idea that the difference between the political and the philosophical life is obvious. If these chapters of the *Ethics* do not reenact the debate between Socrates and Callicles on the philosophic vs. the political life, what do they do?

### Whether End or Act Is the Controlling Factor in Virtue

Aristotle has two distinct ways of distinguishing between *energeiai* and imperfect, kinetic, instrumental actions. *"It is disputed whether decision (prohairesis) or act (praxis) is the more controlling factor (kuriēteron) in virtue"* (*NE* X.8.1178a34–35; see *Rh.* I.13.1374a9–14, *EE* II.11.1228a12–17). Which of those we take as controlling leads to what I will call the Two End or the Two Act interpretation of the difference between *kinēsis* and *energeia*, which will lead to different relations between the political and the philosophical life. Although Aristotle has already told us that decision is the controlling factor in virtue (e.g., *NE* III.2.1111b4–6, III.3.1112a1–3, *EE* II.10. 1228a2–7), when he finally addresses the question of the best life he poses the issue noncommitally to show what difference it makes to one's understanding of the good life whether one sees virtue ruled by decision or by action.[16]

First the Two Act interpretation. There are differences among actions: some are slavish or instrumental, while others are noble and free. Participating in an assembly trying to figure out the best policy is an activity, an *energeia*. Flattering an audience in order to win political favor is ignoble, slavish, and only of instrumental value. The line between *kinēsis* and *energeia*, on this understanding, is the political line between citizens and slaves (*EE* I.4.1215a35–b14, *Pol.* I.11.1258b36–39, III.4.1277a37–b7, 5.1278a15–21, VII.9.1328b39–41, VIII.2.1337b5–21, 8.1328b2–16). The political and the philosophical life are distinguished by their content, the actions that comprise them.

But acts also are individuated by their purposes and choices:

> Civic friendship (*politikē*) looks at the agreement (*homologia*) and to the thing (*to pragma*), but moral friendship (*ethikē*) at the intention (*prohairesis*); hence the latter is more just—it is friendly justice (*dikaiosynē philikē*). (*EE* VII.10. 1243a32–34; see *Rh.* II.23.1399a28–32)

> With a view to what is noble and what not noble, actions do not differ so much in themselves as in their end and that for the sake of which [they are performed]. (*Pol.* VII.14.1333a9–11)

> One who is active in [competitive musical performances] does not undertake it for the sake of his own virtue but for the sake of the pleasure of his listeners, and

this a crude pleasure; hence we judge the performance as not belonging to free persons but being more characteristic of the laborer. (*Pol.* VIII.6. 1341b8–14)

It makes much difference what object one has in view in a pursuit or study; if one follows it for the sake of oneself or one's friends, or on moral grounds, it is not illiberal, but the man who follows the same pursuit because of other people would often appear to be acting in a menial and servile manner. (*Pol.* VIII.2. 1337b17–21; see also III.4.1277b3–7, VII.16.1335b5–11, *NE* IV.3. 1124b31–1125a1, *Rh.* I.9.1367a-31)

The same act can be done for an external or an internal end. It is noble to despise the risk of death to save one's city; it is obeying the law to do so as a citizen-soldier. The Two End interpretation draws the line between virtuous and merely lawful action, not between the citizen and the slave.

On the Two End interpretation, we distinguish political and philosophic lives according to which *energeia* is in control, individual virtuous acts or happiness. In the political life, the dominant attention and value remains with the individual virtuous actions. The contemplative life places attention and value on the single happy life made up of these parts. When many good actions are fully integrated into one happy life, then one is living theoretically and thereby recognizing that man is not the best thing in the world. When the *energeiai* one performs are only integrated with difficulty and into lesser kinds of unity, then one lives politically.

An example should help. For several years, I have had the good fortune of working with some extraordinary high school teachers through the National Endowment for the Humanities program of Summer Seminars for School Teachers. The program gives them the opportunity for contemplation. We spend a month together reading a difficult book, in my case Machiavelli's *The Prince,* and talking about moral education. On the Two Act interpretation, the summer is more theoretical than the usual life of the high school teacher because we are engaged in the discrete activity of philosophy. On the Two End interpretation, the summer allows their lives to become more theoretical by becoming more chosen for their own sake.

The Two Act interpretation is better known to us: everyone can understand the difference between a courageous and a cowardly act, between the status of a free man and slave. Only good people can know the Two End interpretation. Not everyone can see the difference between doing a courageous deed and acting courageously. Most people can do something courageous; only a few can act with courage. Without the Two Act interpretation, Aristotle's teaching would be purely spiritual or adverbial—an act is virtuous if done with the right motive—while without the Two End reading, his teaching would be too material and would claim that some acts are noble and others should only be performed by more menial types. The Two End interpretation is closer to principles, the Two Act closer to the phenomena.

Do the philosophical and political lives differ by their acts or their purposes? Philosophy and politics name actions, capable of being identified from the outside—the Two Act interpretation. According to the first understanding, a philosophical life is one which contains as many acts of *theōria* as possible. The best way to live is to choose acts that are *energeiai* and avoid those that are *kinēseis*. The statesman will grudgingly perform necessary economic activities and will hire someone else to do them for him if he can (*Pol.* I.7.1255b35–37), although I deny that the philosopher has a corresponding attitude toward the political life.[17]

But philosophy and politics also name ends for which activities are performed, so what is from the outside the same life might be led either theoretically or politically, depending on how the agent understands and chooses—the Two End reading. When Aristotle says that philosophy is better than politics, he *means* by each a life distinguished by its content, the Two Act interpretation. But the *grounds* he offers for this superiority are those of the Two End interpretation, of philosophy as a unified life.[18] Far from an equivocation, Aristotelian science works by moving from what is better known to us to what is better known *haplōs*. And not only Aristotelian science but Aristotelian ethics: it is better to live according to things that are good *haplōs*.

Which interpretation we make dominant is itself an ethical decision of how to live, which life is best. To emphasize matter and particular virtuous actions, I will show, is to live politically. To emphasize integrating form is to live philosophically. Therefore we don't choose between the political and theoretical life by choosing which actions to engage in. When we have to direct our attention to particular resources, exigencies, choices, and actions, it is better to conceive of life as a series of *energeiai*. Those particular virtuous actions are then the primary *energeiai* of my virtuous soul. Sometimes it is better to live as unified a life as possible. The single *energeia* of happiness is then the primary *energeia* of my virtuous soul. But we cannot *choose* to make our lives unified, or decide to lead a philosophic life. We can only, as he says, pray that circumstances permit us to direct attention wisely to the whole rather than the parts, pray that we are not in circumstances where it is better for us to see the principal value of our choices and acts in the particular deeds and results. In section "At the Same Time We Are Happy and Have Been Happy," I will look at the nature of those prayers.

## Happiness Should Be *Energeia Kata Kratistēn,*
### the Virtue of the Best Thing in Us

*Ethics* X.7 begins by arguing that "if happiness is an *energeia kat'aretēn,* an activity in accordance with virtue, it is reasonable that it should be *energeia kata kratistēn,* the highest virtue, which will be the virtue of the best thing in us" (1177a12–13). The happiest life will be the most complete life, and at the same time the actualization of the most complete virtue. But those two criteria do not necessarily coincide—just as little as the two dimensions of the virtues did in chapter 4—unless one is simply defined in terms of the other. The "virtue of the best thing in us" might be so easy to attain that its exercise brings little praise, little benefit, and little pleasure. A great theologian, like a great dermatologist, is not necessarily either happy or admirable.

True, *NE* X.4 had shown that the best *energeia* of a given faculty occurs when that faculty is exercised on the best objects, so that the most pleasant experience of seeing consists in seeing the best objects of sight:

> Every perceptual capacity is active in relation to its perceptible object, and com-
> pletely active when it is in good condition in relation to the best of its objects.
> For this above all seems to be the character of complete activity, whether it is
> ascribed to the faculty or to the subject that has it. (*NE* X.4.1174b14–16; see
> *Part. An.* 645b28–30)

In chapter 5 I showed that such claims have the powerful ethical implication that we should as much as possible spend our time and exercise our virtues toward the best people, not the neediest. That conclusion should have caused discomfort there, and the implications seem even worse here. Because God is a better object than my wife, is worshipping God a "better" activity than loving my wife? Should I choose God over my wife whenever possible? If we find the highest fulfillment in directing our energies toward the highest objects, we might have to neglect all the particular responsibilities toward particular people and events that comprise our practical lives. If philosophy is the best activity, why not do it as much as possible? But what about the possibility that some objects are too good for our faculties? Just as looking at the sun blinds us, couldn't trying to live as philosophically as possible do us harm?

I think the opening inference of *NE* X.7 has to run this way: If the best and most complete *energeia* is the *energeia* of the best and most complete virtue, then the best and most complete virtue will be in turn that virtue which completes and perfects all the virtues, and so completes and perfects our lives. *Theōria* allows us to see the place of our good actions in the world, to understand our lives as a unity, and thus to live better. We engage in *theōria* to the extent that we understand the true value of our activities and see our lives as good. We become divine not by studying theology but by exercising *phronēsis*. As Richard Kraut puts it, "The philosophical life is the life of a good person, that is, someone who has and exercises the ethical virtues." The philosophical life is distinct from the political life, but can only be lived by a good person.[19]

The contemporary scholarly debate between the inclusive and dominant readings of *theōria* dissolves: *Theōria* is the perfection and culmination of *all* the virtues, ethical and intellectual. *Theōria* is by itself the most perfect of activities. Although we will have to discuss this further, *theōria* is divine just because it is the best *energeia*.[20]

### The Virtues Render the Thing Itself Good and Cause it to Perform its Function Well

Living theoretically means living a good life self-consciously and as a single life. Because human rationality comes from man's political nature, living philosophically means living a *practical* life as a self-conscious unity. So far I have made that case without examining the argument of *NE* X.7 and 8 in any detail. I have shown what I think Aristotle must say; now I want to see if he says it.

"If happiness is an *energeia kat'aretēn*, it is reasonable that it should be *energeia kata kratistēn*, the highest virtue, which will be the virtue of the best thing in us." I just showed that this is an argument that we should not simply nod at and assent to. What makes these two inferences plausible? Why, first, if happiness is an activity according to virtue, should it be according to the highest virtue, and why, second, should the highest virtue be the virtue of the best thing in us? Recall, for the last time, my dominant proof-text: the virtues both "render the thing itself good and also cause it to perform its function well" (*NE* II.6.1106a15–17). Aristotle must show how the *energeia* of that best *dynamis* will also be the best *energeia* as such. Is "best" a property that can be transmitted from *dynamis* to *energeia*? Understanding this compact argument will allow us to see how the most perfect life, a life like that led by the gods, perfects the life of ethical virtue.

A little more concretely, the problem Aristotle faces at this stage in the argument is this. All happy lives are complete. And yet the philosophical life completes the other happy life, the political life. Until we get to *theōria* in *NE* X.7 and 8, completeness was a question of time and scope (e.g., *NE* I.9.1100a4–9, I.10.1101a6–13), appropriate for *energeia* as the perfection of a *kinēsis*. Until we get to *theōria*, Aristotle had been speaking of what in the *Metaphysics* he calls "potency in the strictest sense, which is, however, not the most *useful* for our present purposes" (IX.1.1046a1), and of *energeia* in contrast to *dynamis* and *kinēsis*. But when he turns to *theōria*, the good life is no longer the *energeia* of a *dynamis* or of a *kinēsis* but simply *energeia* (see *De An.* III.4.429a21–22, III.8.431b20). "Complete" then no longer means adequate temporal duration but refers to properties like goodness, intensity, and choiceworthiness (*NE* X.7.1177a27–b26), a change signaled by his use here of the pleonastic-looking expression "complete happiness" at 1177a17 and *eudaimonestatos* at 1178a8 (see I.7.1097a25–b6, *Met.* VIII.3.1044a10–11).²¹ *Theōria* shows how we can look at *energeia* without depending on the contrasts to *dynamis* and *kinēsis* that the practical life needed until this point. If we look at *energeia* apart from its contrasts to *kinēsis* and *dynamis*, we will see *theōria*. There is nothing else such an *energeia* could be. Therefore our best happiness will be engaging in the best activity. As Jonathan Lear puts it:

> When Aristotle tries to think through what the gods do, he immediately eliminates all practical activities—all the fulfilling of needs or desires, all busywork. But for gods to be gods they must be active: so Aristotle needs to focus on an activity that isn't itself the practical filling of a need. In other words, if you want to hold onto the bare idea of liveliness and activity but take away from that idea as many marks and features of actual life as lived, you end up with contemplation.²²

In another sense, though, *theōria* is not an exception to my rule that activities that are their own end are the perfection of acts first chosen for an external end. While philosophical *activities* do not perfect some action initially done for an external end, the philosophical *life* perfects the political life. In the last chapter I argued that the world is incomplete without human practical activity because without praxis it would be populated by fewer perfect *energeiai*. As practical activity completes the cosmos, so the philosophical life completes the political life:

> Someone who sees perceives that he sees; one who hears perceives that he hears; and one who walks perceives that he walks. Similarly in the other cases also there is something that perceives that we are active. Hence, if we are perceiving, we perceiving that we are perceiving; and if we are understanding, we perceive that we are understanding. Now perceiving that we are perceiving or understanding is the same as perceiving that we are, since we agreed that being is perceiving or understanding. (*NE* IX.9.1170a29–37; see *De An.* III.2.425b12–25)

Self-perception or self-consciousness accompanies all activity. Activities are by nature self-aware. Animate activity involves separating form from matter, and self-consciousness accompanies any such abstracting activity. Self-perception accompanies activities, not *kinēseis* and not passions. Self-consciousness necessarily accompanies activity, and activities are the only things we are self-conscious of. But although activities are by nature self-aware, it doesn't follow that every time we see, we are reflectively self-conscious of the activity of seeing.

Someone leading a happy political life need not know that there is a better life, called philosophy. But that person already has all that is needed for self-awareness. *Theōria* completes the political life just as self-awareness can complete any *energeia*. Animals are capable of the self-awareness described at *NE* IX.9.1170a29, but only humans can be aware of a life. People can come to understand that our particular choices are not simply responsive but become a coherent whole.

There is no short-cut to *theōria* that avoids the complicated excellences of the political life. If our lives are good enough to be seen and lived as single complete *energeia*, we are living philosophically. And so he says: "The happy man will do *and contemplate* what is in accordance with virtue" (*NE* I.10. 1100b19–20). To lead a life of *theōria*, a divine life, is to lead an excellent specifically human life. The criterion Aristotle uses in Book I in the ergon argument, that the human good must be uniquely human, does not exclude divine activity. Uniqueness was never purely descriptive, as we've seen earlier with boasting, blushing, and being a miser. If we engage in *theōria* and so do the gods, it is still a uniquely human activity:

> No one chooses to become another person even if that other will have every good when he has come into being, for, as it is, the god has the good [but no one chooses to be replaced by a god]. Rather [each of us chooses goods] on condition that he remains whatever he is, and each person would seem to be the understanding part, or that most of all. (*NE* IX.4.1166a20–23)[23]

The first half of *NE* X.7 shows that the life of *theōria* is a realization of *phronēsis*, not of studying theology. Starting with the claim that the greatest happiness will be the best activity and the activity of the best, the argument goes on to show that the properties of *energeia* as such are just what we mean by *theōria*. It is the highest form of *energeia*, the most continuous, most pleasant, most self-sufficient, most loved for its own sake, and most leisured (1177a18–27).

The suggestion that the philosophical life is more than human, and by implication at odds with the practical life, only comes in after that argument. It enters Aristotle's argument in a most ambivalent way, as he first makes *theōria* divine as opposed to human and then turns back to make it human:

> Such a life would be superior to the human level. For someone will live it not insofar as he is a human being, but insofar as he has some divine element in him . . . Hence if understanding (*nous*) is something divine in comparison with a human being, so also will the life that expresses understanding be divine in comparison with human life. (*NE* X.7.1177b26–31; see *Met.* XII.7.1072b24–26)[24]

Isn't it a *nonsequitur* to say that *theōria* is the *energeia* of the best part of us, and therefore a life higher than human (*kreistōn ē kat'anthrōpon*)? Such an inference is coherent only if calling it divine means simply that it has the properties of *energeia* to the fullest degree, not that it is identified as divine by some other source of information about the gods. Hence my formula that *theōria* is *energeia haplōs* and not *energeia* as the *energeia* of a particular *dynamis*.[25] There is no organ of thought, and so here there is no psychic material that is actualized in contemplation. While *theōria* is the activity of the virtue of *sophia*, it is the activity of the whole person, since the good person is identified with his reason (*NE* IX.4.1166a20–23, 1177b26–1178a7, *EE* II.7.1223b26–27, *Pol.* VII.15.1334b15). The activity of the whole person realizes what is divine in us, making *theōria* both human and extrahuman.[26]

If the two lives are both happy, they are both rational. The more rational the political life, the harder it is to tell the two lives apart. The difficulty in making out the relation between them reenacts the trouble we found in chapter 5 in differentiating ethical virtue from *phronēsis*. On the one hand, ethical virtue lacks nothing that it needs *phronēsis* to supply. They are distinct, though, because they actualize distinct parts of the soul. Someone, I argued, can be ethically virtuous without being a *phronimos* if he is not a ruler and so not in a position to exercise *phronēsis*. Only the opportunity is missing. Acting as the ethically virtuous person acts as a ruled citizen is not incomplete in the sense of being deficient. And yet, on the other, ethical virtue can be completed when the person comes to rule as well. Ethically virtuous activity is complete and yet can be further perfected. *Phronēsis*, then, does not complete ethical virtue as a terminus completes a *kinēsis* but by being what it truly is as a rational activity. We reach the end of a *kinēsis* when it is over and the agent is at rest. The end of an *energeia*, though, is different, since an activity is complete at each instant. *Phronēsis* completes moral virtue not by being that to which moral virtue points but by being what moral virtue truly is when it is at its best. *Phronēsis* is simply the rational structure of the moral virtues.

I want to say something analogous about the two lives. The two lives both instantiate the definition of happiness as *energeia kat'aretēn*, but they are virtues of two different parts of the soul. There are only two lives because happiness is rational activity and these are the two rational parts of soul. Activities might be *energeiai* of parts of the soul without being *energeiai* of the person, but lives cannot. *Theōria* is an activity of the whole person, but of the virtue of *sophia*. The political life is an activity of the whole person, but of the virtue of *phronēsis*. There is nothing incomplete about the political life, since it can be happy and therefore perfect, and yet it can still be completed by philosophy. Philosophy completes the political life not as a *kinēsis* is completed by being finished but by being what it truly is as a rational life.

The two lives are hard to differentiate, and to relate to each other, because in a certain sense neither *phronēsis* nor *sophia* has a *dynamis* to actualize. While *phronēsis* is a virtue, the good condition of a part of the soul, we don't possess *phronēsis* when asleep as we do the ethical virtues. We have it in its exercise. As I said in chapter 5, both *sophia* and *phronēsis* are *hexeis* and virtues of the thinking part of the soul, but unlike the ethical virtues they are not the *energeia* of some more primitive *dynamis*. What I said in chapter 5 about *phronēsis* applies even more fully to *theōria*. The virtuous person engaged in political activity might not be in a position to exercise *theōria*. He has nothing missing but the opportunity. *Theōria* and *phronēsis* are consequently not *energeiai* of *dynameis* in the way that political life and ethical virtue are. *Theōria* simply is activity, and the happy life is a philosophical life.

*Phronēsis* and *sophia* are two modes of self-knowledge, and politics and philosophy are two ways of living rationally and reflectively. Self-knowledge has two conditions. The self has to be able to know, and the self has to be something knowable. Neither of these is a condition Aristotle would attribute to all humans. Self-knowledge then is not like a Cartesian power of self-reflection that could be posited to belong to everyone. Only the virtuous person has a self rational enough to be both a self-knower and an object of self-knowledge. "One desires always to live, because one desires always to know, and this is because one desires to be oneself that which is known" (*EE* VII.12.1245a9–11). *Phronēsis* and *theōria* are modes of reflection that work out the rationality already present in virtuous actions. Although the virtuous person may not be able to articulate the principles of virtue or explicate the relation between the goods of activity and the goods of fortune, neither the *phronimos* nor the philosopher knows anything that the virtuous person doesn't already know.[27]

Divine activity consists in the gods thinking about themselves. Two possible implications can be drawn for what the most divine human activity would be. First, we could infer that we too should think as far as possible about the divine, about the same things the gods think about. The gods think about their activity, and therefore we should think about the gods' activity. But we could equally infer that our activity is most divine when we, like the gods, think about our own activity. Like the gods thinking about thinking, the human philosophic life is an act of self-knowledge. We approach divine activity when we, like the gods, know ourselves (*Met.* XII.9. 1074b15–35). Only that second interpretation makes sense of the ending of *NE* X.7, in which the divine in us is something that is ours, not something alien that happens to live inside us as in the *Phaedo*'s picture of the soul as imprisoned in the body.

"There are two things above all which make human beings cherish and feel affection, what is one's own and what is dear" (*kēdesthai kai philein, to te idion kai to agapēton*) (*Pol.* II.4.1262b22–23). These two implications about the most divine human activity come from the fact that what is ours and what is most lovable are not necessarily identical, and therefore there are two possible happy human lives.

However much our contemplative activity may resemble divine activity, there is one insurmountable difference: when we engage in *theōria*, we decide to do so. The gods, who engage in *theōria* continuously (*Met.* XII.7. 1072b14–16, b24), do not choose to do it. Although we do not choose between alternatives, *theōria* still is a practice for humans and therefore an activity that reveals character and involves *prohairesis*. *Sophia* studies things that are not only best but which cannot be otherwise. I cannot *become* one of those things. I can study them, and studying them might be a best way to live, but I will remain distinct from the object of study. There is a difference of kind between variable and invariable beings and so it will always be an effort for me to engage in *theōria*—"being continuously active is not easy" (*NE* IX.9.1170a5–6; see VII.14.1154b20–31, X.4.1175b3– 6)—while god's thinking about itself will be effortless because of the identity of subject and object. Divine self-knowledge is knowledge of self and of the divine as a single thing. "Our well-being is with reference to something other, whereas the divine is its own well-being" (*EE* VII.12. 1245b18). Therefore divine thought can be a pure *energeia*, while nothing I do can be.[28]

The rationality first encountered in practical reasoning gives us access to what is better than humanity. By engaging in *theōria*, we are simultaneously most human and better than human, as Aristotle says: "Such a life would be superior to the human level. . . . For what is proper to each thing's nature is supremely best and pleasantest for it; and hence for a human being the life expressing understanding will be supremely best and pleasantest, if understanding above all is the human being" (*NE* X.7. 1177b26–78a8).

Therefore *nous* is both more than human and what each human truly is. Calling *theōria* divine does not associate it with what we already know to be what gods do, but to argue in the reverse direction: since this is the best possible activity, it follows that it is what the gods do. Reflecting on the nature of happiness as an *energeia* tells us that the most happy life is theoretical. That conclusion leads in turn to the corollary that the gods too contemplate. Aristotle never infers from what the gods do to what we should do.[29]

*NE* X.7 showed that *theōria* is the best activity. But if *theōria* is just *energeia* as *energeia*, pure activity, then it isn't *theōria* as opposed to any other *energeia*, and in particular not *theōria* opposed to political life, that is best. This is the Two End interpretation in which our purposes and decisions make our actions what they are, the interpretation that X.7 must take. Aristotle now has to talk in X.8 about *theōria* as a particular *energeia* and its relation to practical life, what this best activity has to do with the best activity of the human *ergon*. *NE* X.8 returns to the Two Act interpretation, which is better known to us. *NE* X.8 then lets us ask how to tell the two lives apart.

*NE* X.8, unlike X.7, looks like the traditional comparison of the *vita contemplativa* and the *vita activa*. There are two easily identifiable lives, identifiable by what they actualize—intellect alone or composite human nature including the passions—and by what they do—not needing or needing equipment. Yet Aristotle gives a very nuanced and cautious assessment of the relation between such equipment and virtuous action:

> The performance (*praxis*) of virtuous actions requires much outward equipment, and the more so the greater and more noble the actions are. (*NE* X.8. 1178b2–3)

> Even though no one can be blessedly happy without external goods, we must not think that to be happy we will need many large goods. . . . We can do noble actions even if we do not rule earth and sea; for even from moderate resources we can do the actions that accord with virtue. (*NE* X.8.1179a3–6)[30]

Paradoxically, the more autonomous virtues need more equipment but the more autonomous man needs less. Absolute goods are good to the good man, and so he needs less of them.

On the Two End interpretation, *theōria* simply is the *eudaimōn* life. On the Two Act interpretation, *theōria* is a form of life distinct from the political life. Recall my pair of interpretations for the contemplative activity of the participants in my NEH Summer Seminars. Participants lived philosophically either because they were studying philosophy instead of teaching driver's education—the Two Act interpretation—or because they had the leisure, the friendship, and the resources to contemplate the worth of their lives—the Two End interpretation. The series of comparisons between the philosophical and the political life is interrupted by these lines:

> It is disputed whether decision or act is the more controlling factor in virtue, as it is alleged to depend on both; now the perfection of virtue will clearly consist in both; but the performance (*praxis*) of virtuous actions requires much outward equipment, and the more so the greater and more noble the actions are. (*NE* X.8.1178a35–b3)

Aristotle here distinguishes the Two Act from the Two End interpretation of the *kinēsis/energeia* distinction. Virtue depends on both *prohairesis* and *praxis*. As *praxeis*, Aristotle tells us, *theōria* and politics differ significantly concerning the equipment they need, and so in the lives they organize. Mentioning the dispute about "whether decision or act is the more controlling factor in virtue" is a digression unless it is designed to show that, considered as purposes as opposed to praxeis, the contrast between philosophical and political lives dissolves. Distinguished by purpose, what is from the outside the same life can be led either philosophically or politically. The two purposes make for different lives by focusing attention on the one or the many, on substance as form or substance as composite, on *energeia* simply as *energeia* or *energeia* considered as *energeia* of the human *dynamis*, on virtuous activity or on happiness. Therefore I take the quoted passage as Aristotle's reminder, in the midst of turning attention to the Two Act reading of the relation of philosophy and politics, that the fundamental relation between the two lives is their difference in purpose and end.

That happiness and *theōria* are coextensive has different implications, depending on which interpretation one chooses. On the Two Act interpretation, the virtuous but unphilosophical men who are the center of attention in the *Ethics* are less happy than they think they are. They think that their lives are complete, since they choose acts worth doing for their own sakes. But their lives are less desirable and praiseworthy, more constrained and less choiceworthy, than Aristotle has led his readers to believe. If *theōria* and happiness are coextensive, then a life of political activity is not happy. No wonder so many people think that the praise of *theōria* is inconsistent with the rest of the *Ethics*.

Instead of that Two Act reading, my Two End interpretation suggests that people leading politically happy lives are by that fact engaging in *theōria* even though it might not look like it. Instead of *phronomoi* being wrong about their political lives being happy, they are wrong about their lives not being philosophical. *Phronēsis* is a mode of self-knowledge. While their lives are rational and therefore contemplative, it is an inferior form of *theōria* and of happiness just because such people are not aware that they engage in *theōria*. They are not aware of it because their attention lies elsewhere. That is why I could say earlier that if the political life is happy in a secondary way, and if "happiness and *theōria* are co-extensive" (*NE* X.8. 1178b28–29), then it follows that the political life is also theoretical, although in a secondary way. People leading politically happy lives are not wrong about their lives. We were wrong about what *theōria* means.

Unless we see how the political life leads to the philosophical life, we might identify living philosophically with living as Thales and Anaxagoras do. Wisdom has for its object things that are true simply and not just true for people. It therefore isn't good for us as people. "That is why people say that Anaxagoras and Thales or that sort of person is wise, but not prudent, whenever they see that he is ignorant of what benefits himself. And so they say that what he knows is extraordinary, amazing, difficult, and divine, but useless, because it is not human goods that he looks for" (*NE* VI.7.1141b3–9). If that were the model for *theōria*, it could not be a happy life.

While Thales and Anaxagoras can engage in individual acts of *theōria*, only the *phronimos* can know practically that the philosophical life is the best life. Therefore only the *phronimos*, and not people like Thales and Anaxagoras, can live a philosophical life. That Aristotle refuses to identify the philosophical life with traditional philosophical activities is signaled by his hedge when he says that "perfect happiness is some form of contemplative activity" (*theōrētikē tis*) (*NE* X.8.1177a17–18, 1177b19–25, 1178b21–23).

Before turning to a more precise way of understanding the practical relations between the political and the philosophical life, I want to point to a major benefit of my claim that it is through living an active political life and not through studying theology that we know that man is not the best thing in the world. If the route to *theōria* runs through *phronēsis*, then metaphysics doesn't supply premises for ethics. We know everything we need to know about how to live from reflecting on human action. How many unmoved movers there are, what the substance of the pale man is, the relation among the four elements, none of these things has implications for how we should live.[31]

As a consequence, Aristotle has no place for philosopher-kings: philosophy contains no practical knowledge that the *phronimos* does not already know. *Theōria* helps keep politics from collapsing into economics and keeps theory and practice distinct. In that way, there is no room for philosopher-kings because every good person must be a philosopher. What could be a less Platonic configuration of the relation of philosophy and politics than this?

The practical truth that *theōria* is best says little about the content of *theōria*, while it says everything about the place of *theōria* in our lives. Thus the thesis that political science "prescribes which of the sciences ought to be studied in cities" (*NE* I.2.1094b1) is qualified: "*Phronēsis* is not in authority over wisdom or the better part of the soul, just as medical science does not control health. Medical science does not use health, but only aims to bring health into being; hence it prescribes for the sake of health, but does not prescribe to health" (*NE* VI.13.1145a6–9, see *Pol.* VII.14. 1333a37–41). The place of *theōria* in our lives is a political question, while the content of *theōria*, what the person engaging in contemplation might contemplate, is not.[32]

If first philosophy had independent theological conclusions that dictated how we should live, then we should live by imitating divine activity. But that is clearly a fallacy. The gods are immortal and do not need food, but we do not make ourselves better by trying to live as long as possible on as little as possible (*EE* VII.12.1245b13–19, *Mag. Mor.* II.15.1212b35– 1213a7). More to the point, the gods do not exercise practical reason or the ethical virtues. But it does not follow that we can become godlike by ceasing to exercise practical reason, or by exercising theoretical reason to the exclusion of practical reason as much as possible. Divine thinking is not discursive, since that implies unrealized potencies (*Met.* XII.10.1075a5– 10), but it would be silly to try to become divine by neglecting our discursive abilities. We know which aspects of divine activity are best for us by knowing what kinds of activity are best.

### Pleasure Completes the Activity

Pleasure completes the activity. But the way in which pleasure completes the activity is not the way in which the perceptible object and the perceptual capacity complete it when they are both excellent—just as health and the doctor are not the cause of being healthy in the same way. . . . Pleasure completes the activity—not, however, as the state does, by being present [in the activity], but as a sort of consequent end (*epiginomenon ti telos*), like the bloom on youths. (*NE* IX.4.1174b23–33)

To live philosophically is to live a happy life as *an* activity, living happily with the greatest self-knowledge that humans can achieve. Only someone who has lived politically can live philosophically. That political life need not be *finished,* although it has to be *complete,* for someone to live philosophically. To think that one has to stop living politically in order to live philosophically is to think of lives as *kinēseis,* only complete when they are over. Just as Plato has philosopher-kings and Aristotle does not, Plato also has an age for philosophers, while Aristotle does not. While in the *Republic,* philosophers must rule, in the *Ethics* rulers must philosophize.

My thesis that only someone who has lived politically can live philosophically makes the argument of *Ethics* X coherent. The statesman for whom the *Ethics* is written must know that the philosophic life is the best life before moving on the *Politics* to investigate the conditions under which virtue can flourish. That politician need not engage in *theōria,* but he must know that *theōria* is better than politics in order to know the proper value of politics itself and therefore engage in it correctly. Without the distinction between *theōria* and praxis, praxis itself tends to degenerate into a life of conquest and acquisition, led by the *thumos* rather than reason. The only way to engage in practical activities without making them instrumental is by being conscious that man is not the best of all things.

The political life is a necessary condition for *theōria* (*NE* VI.13. 1145a6–9). I now want to parse out several senses of "necessary condition" that relate politics to philosophy. One reason why people have resisted Aristotle's conclusion that *theōria* is the best life is that it seems to follow that the rest of life would be merely a means toward realizing *theōria.* Seeing the full variety of ways in which the rest of life can be "for the sake of" the contemplative life can go a long way toward disarming such resistance.

The discussion of pleasure in *NE* X.1–5 prepares for the treatment of happiness. *NE* X.4 says that pleasure completes the activity, and then carefully outlines different ways one thing can complete something else. Showing the relation between the pleasures of activity and pleasant activities prepares the way for confronting the relation between the activity of contemplation and the activities being contemplated. The powerful analogy between the connection of pleasure to activity and of contemplation to activity lets the discussion of *theōria* presuppose and build on X.1–5. Once we know how pleasure completes activity, we can understand how *theōria* completes our lives.

First and most obviously, the political life is a necessary condition for *theōria* because the leisure necessary for *theōria* can only come in a polis and not in other social forms such as the household.[33] "Most men pursue what is noble only when they have a good margin in hand" (*EE* VII.10.1243b1). *Theōria* requires a context in which politics is sufficiently distant from economics that it generates the surplus that makes it possible for some people to engage in *theōria* as a distinct activity. Consequently Aristotle ends *NE* X.8 by returning to the contrast between the two lives in terms of the differences in resources they need. Living politically, the good man needs significant resources, while to see and live the good life as a single *energeia,* those same resources become distractions. But here, unlike the earlier sections where he highlighted the differences between the two lives (1178a23–b7), he shifts from the Two Act to the Two End interpretation, and says both that the philosopher as a man needs external well-being and that a person living a happy life politically needs only moderate resources:

> We need resources in order to live a good life, although we need fewer of them if we are in a better condition, more if we are in a worse one. (*Politics* VII.13.1332a1–2; see also *NE* X.8.1178b2–3)

This first sense of necessary condition leads to the Two Act interpretation. My High School teachers cannot engage in contemplation without the political decision to give them financial support and honor. Politics provides philosophers with leisure. "The actions of the politician deny us leisure; apart from political activities themselves, those actions seek positions of power and honors, or at least they seek happiness for the politician himself and for his fellow citizens, which is something different from political science (*tēs politikēs*) itself" (*NE* X.7.1177b12–15).[34]

But that sense of necessary condition cannot be the last word. Within a polis, political activity might be a means to philosophical activity, so that the polis should organize itself in the right way for philosophy to take place. But that instrumental relation cannot be true within an individual soul. If engaging in virtuous activity is a means toward philosophical activity, it is a means very poorly suited to its task. Doing well at virtuous activity means performing worthwhile activities for their own sakes. While that experience can prepare someone for the more difficult experience of engaging in philosophy for its own sake, the pleasures of virtuous activity rightly make us want to do more virtuous activity, not something else. If I'm any good at generosity, I want to do more of it. "Whenever we are engaged in two activities at once, the more pleasant activity pushes out the other one, all the more if it is much more pleasant, so that we no longer even engage in the other activity" (*NE* X.5.1175b7–10). If political and philosophical activity are different in kind, then one will drive the other out: either moral virtue will make us unsuited for *theōria* or *theōria* will cause us to see the demands of virtue as a distraction.

Consequently, there must be further ways of conceiving this necessary relation between the political and the philosophical life beyond the right political organization giving us leisure. While *theōria* requires that politics generate the surplus and opportunity for leisure that lets some people engage in *theōria,* that surplus is not only economic but ethical. Understanding the surplus as ethical requires a different sort of necessary condition, and a different understanding of self-sufficiency that is not economic either. The political life has to be far enough from the economic life that someone can choose good actions for their own sakes and not only for their results. Being able to make such choices requires not economic surplus—the idea that noble actions are those that are unnecessary and superfluous—but moral education.

### At the Same Time We Are Happy and Have Been Happy

> At the same time we are seeing and have seen, are understanding and have understood, are thinking and have thought. . . . At the same time we are living well and have lived well, and are happy and have been happy. (*Met.* IX. 6.1048b23–26, see *De An.* III.2.425b11–25)

The different meanings for necessary condition allows us to ask about the relation between the act of contemplation and the activities being contemplated. Is contemplation a separate and distinct act, one of reflection and recollection once the intensity of the moment has passed? Or do we contemplate while we are acting, as seeing that we see accompanies all perception?

Certainly we can sometimes separate the virtuous practical activity from a later contemplation of it, just as we can sometimes deliberate and then act. I act courageously, risking my life in battle, and later can sit back and understand the connection between the experience of fully realizing my emotional and mental capacities and the particular things I was doing and trying to accomplish. And yet I think that that temporal division does not fully capture the nature of contemplation and its relation to what is contemplated. I noted that Aristotle does not join Plato in separating off a period of life as the age for philosophy, following the age for courage and virtuous action. He equally opposes separating *theōria* from the activities it contemplates.

Sometimes the action contemplated and the action of contemplating are distinct. Even to the fully virtuous person, seeing one's life as a coherent whole is difficult, because virtuous activity, while easy and pleasant, takes full attention. Therefore we can theorize better about a friend's acts than our own because we can more easily distance ourselves from the particulars and see the whole, more easily disengage ourselves from the intense concentration on the particular action in order to grasp its significance:

> If being happy consists in living and being active, the activities of the good person are excellent, and hence pleasant in themselves . . . [and if] we are able to observe (*theōrein*) our neighbors more than ourselves, and to observe their actions more than our own, it follows that . . . the supremely happy man (*ho makarios*) will need virtuous friends, given that he decides to observe virtuous actions that are his own, and the actions of a virtuous friend are of this sort. (*NE* X.9.1169b30–1170a4)

Contemplating my friend's actions, I extend and amplify contemplation of my own activities, because the friend is a second self (*NE* IX.3.1166a31, IX.9.1170b6, see *EE* 1245a29–37, *Mag. Mor.* 1213a20–24). I can intensely engage in contemplation because I contemplate a friend's activity. The friend is a second self, but contemplating the friend's actions I contemplate them as my own. The detachment that lets us better contemplate a friend's actions than our own is not disengagement in the sense of not caring how well it is done. We can be more intensely engaged in a friend's actions because we attend to it as an *energeia* and need not be engaged in it as a *kinēsis*, while we sometimes have to think about our actions, even good actions, that way. "The wise person is able, and more able the wiser he is, to study even by himself; and though he presumably does it better with colleagues, but all the same he will be most self-sufficient" (*NE* X.7. 1177a32–b1).[35]

Aristotle's remarks on contemplating a friend's activities soften the contrast between conceiving activity and contemplation as distinct and as united. My friend's activities are in one way distinct from my own—the good man will let his friend perform virtuous deeds instead of doing them himself—and in another sense my own. As the distinction between mind and thine disappears, so does the separation between the two activities. Then *theōria* qualifies as an *energeia* as prescribed in *Met.* IX.6: we engage in understanding and have understood.

I offer an example that I think helps. As the distinction between an activity and its proper pleasures disappears, so does the difference between an activity and the further activity of contemplating it. Although it is not a virtuous activity, I race in bicycle time-trials. A few times each summer, the weather is perfect, everyone is ready to ride, not tired from a previous race or from overtraining. We all ride at or near our best times. When we've finished, we stand around laughing. There is an intense and shared feeling of pleasure at our accomplishments. While we're riding, we think about gear ratios, cadences, and breathing, not about how much we are enjoying what we're doing. So it is tempting to conclude that the pleasure comes after the activity, which itself can be quite painful. Pleasure comes after the activity, and so can the contemplation of the activity, and this activity at least when at its best is thoughtless and unconscious.

I think that interpretation of the time-trial experience is wrong. It is the activity of racing that is truly pleasurable, not the standing around recovering and laughing afterwards. When I anticipate an enjoyable experience, I'm anticipating the riding, not the laughing. It's just that the riding is so enjoyable that the feeling of pleasure continues for a while after I stop riding. While on the bicycle, I enjoy being able to work as hard as I can and having all that work translate efficiently into the smooth movement of the bike. In spite of the breathlessness and exhausting pain, the activity, when it goes well, is intensely pleasant. Instead of being unconscious, I am aware of my body working well, of the connection between body and bicycle. When things aren't going so well, I am not aware of such things but am instead distracted and am attentive instead to fatigue of different kinds, to a lack of smoothness and efficiency. I might be attending to my cadence in both cases, but the nature of the attention is quite different, in the one case constantly checking if I'm going at the right pace and in the other being aware of the rightness of my movements.[36]

If I enjoyed riding and then thought, "I'm really enjoying myself!" I would no longer have the same pleasure. I'd be too aware of how my body is functioning, etc. to enjoy that smooth functioning, and so the pleasure becomes distinct from the activity. That is the relation between activity and pleasure Aristotle corrects when he says that "pleasure completes the activity . . . as a sort of consequent end (*epiginomenon ti telos*), like the bloom on youths" (*NE* IX.4.1174b31–33). I can think so much about having pleasure that I no longer have the pleasure of activity but a different pleasure instead.

I claim that the relation between an activity and its attendant pleasures models the relation between the activity and the further activity of contemplating it. Sometimes setting aside time before or, usually, after an activity can help us to understand the nature and goodness of an activity, as the distinct time for reflection was supposed to help the participants in my NEH Seminars. This is the Two Act interpretation. That distinct time can be a time for learning, a *kinēsis* rather than an *energeia* of reflection and contemplation. The seminar is a *means* to contemplation. On the other hand, their best reflection and contemplation takes place not in the summer but while they are teaching. Contemplation is the awareness of things going as they should. Most of the time, teaching is distracted by having to watch whether this student is falling asleep and that student getting ready to be disruptive, whether there is enough time to get through the material. It's tempting to think that when those things aren't problems, the teaching just happens; there's nothing to think about. The best activity is unconscious.

Once again, I think that that's wrong. When those things aren't problems, one can be intensely and pleasurably aware of the activity, and aware of the activity rather than the *kinēseis* that make it up. I can be aware of my student's successes and failures just because I don't have to be checking whether they're paying attention. The more distracted they are by thinking about when the class will be over, what will be covered on the exam, how to avoid looking silly, the more I am distracted from the activity of teaching into its kinetic, instrumental, aspects. When I don't have to deliberate about extrinsic problems, I can think about the activity. That doesn't mean that there is nothing to think about. There is nothing to deliberate about, but we deliberate about means, and here we are contemplating our ends, the activities that are their own end. The better the activity, the less we can separate it from its pleasures, and the more conscious I can be of it. The better the activity, the less we can separate it from the act of contemplating it.

### Telling the Two Lives Apart

> Any system seems to be most of all its most supreme part. (*NE* IX.8. 1168b31–32)

Aristotle tells us that perception and understanding carry self-awareness with them (*De An.* III.2; see *Met.* IX.9.1074b35), but he fails to say that we can be aware only of *energeiai*. To the extent that my teaching is an *energeia*, I can contemplate it; to the extent that it is a *kinesis*, I cannot. For that reason, any *phronimos*, and no one but a *phronimos*, can reflect on his good actions and thereby engage in *theōria*. The more compelling that argument, the harder it is to tell the philosophical and the political life apart. This quotation from the *Metaphysics* shows that it should be hard:

> We must consider too in which the nature of the whole possess the good and the best—whether as something separate and intrinsic or as its organization. Or is it in both ways just like an army? For the good of an army is in its organization and is also the general. And more so the latter, since he does not exist because of the organization, but it does exist because of him. (*Met.* XII.10.1075a11–15)

The good of the whole can be distinct from the whole and be located in a separate entity, as the general is distinct from the army. Similarly the contemplative nature of happiness can manifest itself in a distinct activity of philosophy. But the good of the whole need not be found in a distinct substance.

The better we understand the two happy lives, the harder they are to tell apart. Still there are crucial senses in which the political life is a necessary condition for *theōria*. Practical life gives us a good life to be unified, as it gives us an activity to contemplate. Practical life gives magnitude and seriousness to *theōria*. Otherwise *theōria* would be a pastime like bicycling.

Politics, then, is a necessary condition for philosophy because it gives us an object to contemplate. Philosophy perfects politics along the *kinēsis/ energeia* dimension. But politics is also a necessary condition because it gives us the right kind of souls to do the contemplating. Only in a good state are there souls that can have *theōria* as their *energeia*. The fully developed soul, as I argued in chapter 5, is the soul of the good man and citizen. Barbarians who don't live in cities do not have fully developed differentiation of functions. They lump slaves and women together, because there is no natural ruling element (*Pol.* I.2.1252b5–9, see also *HA* 608a33–b7; *EE* VII.6. 1240b33–34). They cannot tell the difference between doing and making (*NE* VI.4.1140a7–17, X.4.1174a19–b14, *Pol.* I.4.1254a1–7), or between politics and economics. Only in a polis is the difference between the rule of master over slaves and a king over free men evident. Only there does friendship, "the decision to live together" (*hē gar tou suzēn prohairesis philia*) (*Pol.* III.9.1280b38–39), exist. Theoretical and practical reason are distinct in a polis because only there are ethical and purely instrumental reasoning distinct. Only a good polis can make intelligible the idea of virtuous activity as conditionally intrinsically good, acts that are worth doing for their own sake but only in given circumstances.

## Man Is by Nature a Political Animal

> In the case of human beings, what seems to count as living together is this sharing of conversation and thought (*logos kai dianoia*), not sharing the same pasture, as in the case of grazing animals. (*NE* IX.9.1170b12–14; see IX.9. 1169b18–19, *Pol.* I.2.1253a9–18, 1278b19–20)

This more sophisticated sense of necessary condition leads to a still stronger conclusion. *Man is not the best thing in the universe if and only if man is a political animal.* Those who conceive of philosophy and politics as competing lives can also affirm this bi-conditional, but with a very different interpretation. They think that when someone is no longer a political animal, he or she can *become* the best thing in the universe. That is, the philosophic life is an escape from the world of becoming, as Socrates put it, a preparation for death and immortality.[37] The more faithful Aristotelian interpretation of my bi-conditional is that the full intelligibility of the claim that man is not the best thing in the universe is impossible without knowing the best of man.

Only under this interpretation of the bi-conditional can the statesman legislate about the practices of philosophy without destroying philosophy's autonomy. The Two Act and Two End interpretations come together here because not only can we live a philosophical life by being a *phronimoi*, but we will actually understand divine nature, the nature of pure *energeia*, through being a *phronimos*. Ethical virtue is a necessary condition for *theōria* because only the *phronimos* can know the merely relative value of the best human actions, and only he knows the best human actions as *energeiai*. Other people wrongly believe that their best actions are only means to something better still, pleasures or something else apart from the actions themselves.

Such people therefore cannot know the gods. Since the gods are pure *energeia*, they cannot be known by people who do not understand what an action that is its own good is. Humans understand divine activity only through knowing its similarities and differences from human activity. That is the final sense in which the political life is the necessary condition for *theōria*. The gods do not need ethical virtue in order to engage in *theōria* because their *energeiai* are given by their nature and do not need to be achieved, as human *energeiai* do. But we need ethical virtue to understand divine nature.

Because of these more complex meanings of necessary condition, the philosophic life never transcends politics to become apolitical. The philosopher has learned the lesson of my sixth chapter that human activity completes the universe, that the *Metaphysics* is incomplete without understanding human activity, and the world is incomplete without human activity flourishing within it. The theorist never then has disdain for the merely human on the grounds that man is not the best of all things.

And yet, just as there is more to *phronēsis* than possessing the ethical virtues, there is more to the philosophical life than the political life. The person who lives well politically will be *eudaimōn*, but in a secondary way. The person who lives well politically is not missing something, since his life is perfect and *eudaimōn*. It is only relative to that philosophical life that the political life is compelled. There is nothing deficient about the political life. It is a complete and happy life. It just isn't as good as the philosophical life.

The political life and the philosophical life have different kinds of unity. Things made from heterogeneous parts are more natural, and have more significant unity, than those made from homogeneous parts (*Part. An.* II.1.646a12–24, 646a35–b10, *Pol.* IV.4.1290b25–39). The city has more unity than an alliance, because it is made up of things with *less* unity than the alliance (*Pol.* II.2.1261a24–29): "what is more self-sufficient is more choiceworthy, what is less a unity is more choiceworthy than what is more so" (1261b14–15). A whole made of parts similar in kind is a whole by addition. Its nature comes from the parts. That is the Two Act interpretation of *theōria*. A contemplative life is one in which someone contemplates as much of the time as possible. A whole made of parts different in kind is a whole by integration; its nature comes from the whole, as in the Two End interpretation. In the *Politics,* Aristotle was the first to articulate in theory what the Greeks discovered in a limited way in practice: that true political community is founded on difference, not unity, when they invented the polis and substituted political ties for ties of force and blood.[38] The lack of unity supplied by matter makes possible a higher unity of form in justice and the constitution; the lack of a natural foundation in force or blood makes possible a higher sense of nature which ties nature to end. Similarly here. The good man can lead an integrated life that is made up of a wide diversity of activities (see *NE* I.7.1097a34–b5). The integrated, philosophical life made up of a variety of practical activities is then a better kind of philosophical life than one spent studying theology.

### To Pray That What Is Good Unconditionally Will Also Be Good for Us, But to Choose What Is Good for Us

> The right thing is to pray that what is good unconditionally will also be good for us, but to choose [only] what is good for us. (*NE* V.1.1129b6–7)

We began by wondering how the relation between the two lives could be a practical question, a matter for decision. An accurate understanding of the relation between these two forms of happiness, the political life and *theōria,* solves those problems. The political life is a necessary condition for *theōria.* If we engage in politics for its own sake, how can it improve our lives to know that the contemplative life is the best life? If the political life is happy in a secondary way, it cannot contain envy for the better way or resignation for one's lot. The purpose of my NEH Seminars was not to make participants spend the other nine months of the year yearning to be back in

Collegeville, Minnesota. The political life is perfect, and yet something is missing from it without *theōria*.

I started by asking how the "choice" between the two lives could be a choice and had to take a detour around the questions, Who can know what these lives are, and How to individuate them. Virtue has two *energeiai,* particular virtuous actions and happiness. The two happy lives, politics and philosophy, differently relate particular virtuous actions to happiness. There is one final complication, which will finally let us turn to the question of how all this is practical knowledge. Aristotle rejects the idea that because something is best, it should for that reason be what we decide to do. The space that that rejection opens up for practical reason, for practical knowledge of the circumstantial, has been the theme of my whole inquiry. We don't deliberate about what is best. Against a background knowledge of what is best, supplied by the polis, we deliberate about what to do. Aristotle frames the relation between knowing what is best and knowing what to choose in lines that are familiar from earlier chapters, which will be my final touchstone:

> Since the unjust person is greedy, he will be concerned with goods—not with all goods, but only with those involved in good and bad fortune, goods which are, [considered] unconditionally, always good, but for this or that person not always good. Though human beings pray for these and pursue them, they are wrong; the right thing is to pray that what is good unconditionally will also be good for us, but to choose [only] what is good for us. (*NE* V.1.1129b1–7)

Injustice is not primarily a matter of egoism, any more than the issue of the two happy lives is. Injustice consists in inferring that because something is best, I should do it. But when I know the nature of the best life, it doesn't follow that I should try to live it.[39] Someone who engages in *theōria* in the face of overriding reasons for acting politically and exercising the ethical virtues mistakenly supposes that because something is best, and so the object of prayer, it should therefore be the goal of her deliberations now, and so is analogous to the unjust man of *Ethics* V.

It might be better to be immortal, but it does not follow that we should try to live as long as possible. Trying to live as long as possible is ignoble. "For me to be alive is good, and therefore I should try to stay alive" is a cowardly inference from what is good to what I should do. "Peace is better than war, and therefore I should choose peace over war in those circumstances," is cowardly and imprudent. "In the best states, the best men rule; therefore good men should establish ourselves as rulers" unjustly infers from what is good *haplōs* to what I should do about it. Therefore while my proof-text from *NE* V.1 is about *pleonexia* and injustice, the fallacy in the inference pattern extends more widely:

> Superfluities (*periouisiai*) are better than necessities (*anankaia*), and sometimes more choiceworthy (*hairetōtera*). For living well (*eu zēn*) is better than living; and while living well is a superfluity, living itself is a necessity. Sometimes better things are not more choiceworthy. For example, philosophizing is better than making money, but it is not more choiceworthy for someone who lacks necessities. Superfluity exists when a person already in possession of necessities endeavors to acquire noble things as well. We shall perhaps be not far wrong if we say that what is necessary is more choiceworthy, while what is superfluous is better. (*Top.* III.2.118a7–15)

Calling *theōria* an object of prayer rather than decision doesn't make it impractical. Statesmen can act on the knowledge that the contemplative life is best. We can try to design a life through long-term planning to maximize *theōria*. Therefore the declaration that *theōria* is the best life in *NE* X.7–8 is succeeded by the transition to politics in chapter 9.

It is easier to live philosophically by practicing *theōria* in the ordinary sense of engaging in activities commonly recognized as philosophical. That will be how rightly to take *theōria* into account according to the Two Act interpretation, by organizing a life—one's own for the *phronimos,* that of all citizens for the statesman—to permit as much *theōria* as possible. We best achieve the unity and perfection of the best life by including activities that are *energeiai* by nature, rather than *energeiai* relative to the human *dynamis*. In analogy to my proof-text from *NE* V.1, contemplative activities could be called *energeiai haplōs* while political *energeiai* are only relatively *energeiai*. Just as we should prefer peace to war, so we should prefer philosophy to politics.

The example of my NEH Seminars shows the dangers of the fallacy of thinking that because philosophy is best, I should do it. The teachers who come to my NEH Summer Seminars lead much more virtuous lives than mine. Temporarily setting aside the question of whether their souls are in better condition than mine, they do more good in the world, help more people, and in more challenging circumstances. They are dedicated to teaching and to their students. They put no limits on the time they devote to their students. They teach more classes, with more students in each class; they confront bureaucracies and regulations that exceed those of even the most poorly run college. And they are happy because their work is noble, worth doing for its own sake. They are not in it for status, honor, or money but because of a commitment to educating young people.

In contrast, the life of a college teacher seems as self-indulgent as it does self-determined. I teach pretty much what I choose, and although I do not choose my students, they do choose me. My syllabi are determined by what I think best, not by some test for which I must prepare my students or by some other decision others have made for me. I engage in philosophy in the usual, Two Act sense much more than the high school teachers I meet do.

But the content of my life has less moral value than theirs. If, as these teachers studied more philosophy in my seminar and led more integrated lives, they became increasingly detached from their students and their daily duties, the program would be a failure, with the greater light causing blindness back in the cave. In contrast with the goods, and pleasures, of pure disinterested study, teaching high school could well seem slavish, routine, mechanical. After all, we learn in *NE* X.8.1178b8–18 that the gods don't practice ethical virtues because virtuous actions are, from the gods' point of view, vulgar, trivial, and unworthy of them. I will fail if the participants in my seminars come to regard their lives from the gods' point of view, and so do their job less than whole-heartedly.

But that isn't what happens at all. These teachers become more *eudaimōn* by becoming more theoretical. They become more excited by their daily work because they have ideas by which to make sense out of their daily activities, and so can see what they do more as chosen and less as imposed upon them, more worth doing for its own sake and less instrumental. Because of the experience of study as an activity which is good *haplōs* and an *energeia* as such, they appreciate better the intrinsic values of their more usual activities and therefore live more self-determined lives even though the content of their working lives could be unchanged. The content stays the same, but their purposes and choices change as these same actions come to have intrinsic value.

In that way, *theōria* in the Two Act sense contributes to *theōria* in the Two End sense. Experiencing pure activity helps us to experience more of our lives as *energeiai* and so our lives overall as an activity. I said earlier that practical life needs *theōria* to maintain the distance between the ethical and the economic. The uses of philosophy in the lives of my high school teachers does just that. My teachers more fully understand the great value of their work by knowing that it is not the best possible work.

We didn't need the difficult argument of this chapter to get to the conclusion that it is easier to live philosophically by practicing *theōria* in the ordinary sense. But my example suggests a very different conclusion. Stressing the Two Act interpretation isolates *theōria* from the rest of life. Then the experience of *theōria* in the Summer Seminar might make the teachers resent the routine and frustratingly unleisured nature of their careers. But on the Two End interpretation in which *theōria* completes the political life, knowing that *theōria* is best, like knowing that man is not the best of things, helps us value all things correctly. Philosophy helps people enjoy leisure without becoming insolent (*Pol.* VII.15.1334a22–28). Political *energeiai* really are worth engaging in for their own sakes, because of the human world in which we find ourselves. They are *energeiai*, not *kinēseis*. But they are only conditionally *energeiai*. That is the practical import, according to the Two End interpretation, of the thesis that man is not the best thing in the universe. That is the practical value of *theōria*, how *theōria* perfects the political life.

Leading the political life as a good life requires that we hold simultaneously the dual theses that man is not the best of all substances and that man is a political animal. The happy life is a life simultaneously of commitment and detachment.[40] Without upholding both of these together, we might think that because virtuous *energeiai* are their own end, they are always worth doing, are *energeiai haplōs*. That would be to forget that man is not the best object possible. We could just as well think that, because these virtuous *energeiai* are only worth pursuing because they are the best things to do in particular circumstances and, apart from those circumstances, they would not have value, therefore they are less than fully *energeiai*. We would wrongly infer that because morally good actions are *energeiai pros ti*, they are not *energeiai* at all. Then we would be ignoring the fact that man is a political animal. By upholding both theses, we see that virtuous actions are fully *energeiai*, fully worth doing for their own sake, even though they are not *energeiai haplōs*, the best things that someone can do. Without *theōria*, we cannot know that double lesson.

Therefore we need the Two End interpretation, in which *theōria* is implicated in the entire argument of the *Ethics*.

The advantage and the disadvantage of the Two Act interpretation is that it isolates *theōria* as one specific activity. Taken alone, this interpretation leads to the conclusion that philosophy is a luxury. Ethically virtuous acts correspond to Kant's perfect duties: we must perform these actions whenever they are called for. There is no specific time or circumstance which demands *theōria*, and, like Kant's imperfect duties, it looks as though we should engage in philosophy only when there are not more pressing demands on us.[41]

The trouble is that necessities are never finished. Just as Kant's imperfect duties really are duties and not supererogatory luxuries, so here *theōria* really is a form of praxis and not a relaxation or amusement. Knowing that man is not the best thing in the universe teaches us something practical that the political life itself could not, the difference between urgency and importance, between necessity and true value. Only in the polis is there a difference between urgency and importance, and *theōria* consists in reflection on and understanding of that difference.

The virtues have attractive force. The liberal person not only acts liberally when situations present themselves but actively seeks out opportunities for exercising her virtue. Without that tendency to look for opportunities, the virtues would be purely responsive and so less truly *energeiai* than they are. But that attractive power leads to problems. Searching for situations in which to exercise courage can lead to preferring war to peace; hoping to exercise liberality can make one complacent about unjustly unequal distributions of property, or could lead to someone exerting himself at gathering resources in order to liberally bestow them. "Since magnificence requires extensive property, I had better get rich; since liberality means helping people who need help, I must assure the continuing existence of the poor." So it is in the discussion of *theōria* that Aristotle declares: "No one chooses to make a war for the sake of being at war, nor aims at provoking such a war; a man would seem absolutely murderous if he were to make enemies of his friends in order to bring about battles and slaughter" (*NE* X.7.1177b7–12). Only knowing that *theōria* is best can dampen that attractive force. As David Depew puts it, "only when contemplation is regarded by the citizens as the highest of all activities can the entire range of *other* intrinsically good pursuits, such as political engagement, be clearly distinguished from activities having merely instrumental worth, and so be pursued *as* intrinsic goods."[42] Therefore the need for both detachment and engagement.

The *phronimos* knows that man is not the best thing in the universe. Without knowing that *theōria* is the best activity, he would think that his own activities are the best possible activities. He knows instead that

> the actions of the politician deny us leisure; apart from political activities themselves, those actions seek positions of power and honors, or at least they seek happiness for the politician himself and for his fellow citizens, which is something different from political science itself, and clearly is sought on the assumption that it is different. (*NE* X.2.1177b12–15)

Someone who thinks that political activities are the best human activities neither orients his life to *theōria* nor performs properly the purely practical activities of the *phronimos*. The difference between *phronēsis* and *technē*, recall, is that the artisan produces things without needing to understand their ultimate uses and purposes, while praxis and *phronēsis* need knowledge of the final end.[43] *Phronēsis* needs *theōria* in order to do its own job well. My NEH high school teachers would not lead their lives as nobly as possible without *theōria* because it would then be easier to lose the point and intrinsic value of all the particular actions they perform. Were they concerned only about how their students perform on a standardized test, it would be harder for them to be attentive to teaching and learning for their own sake. That does not mean that they should think about their experience of reading *The Prince* when trying to figure out how to keep order in a classroom—practical deliberation is not a long chain of deductions from a premise about the nature of the best life. It does mean that they will not be mere technicians even when trying to accomplish quite specific external goals.

Throughout this book I have claimed that there are two sources and loci of goodness, the goods of activity and the goods at which practical activity aim. Ultimately, praxis needs *theōria* just because there are these two measures of value. We already know that these two kinds of goodness are interdependent. An action would not be good and praiseworthy if the external end it aimed at were not desirable in the first place, but it is the virtuous person who is the measure of whether, how much, and how external goods are good and desirable. Ultimately, both kinds are put in their cosmic place by *theōria*.

A *phronimos* without *theōria* could counter one virtue with another, as Plato's statesman will weave courage and temperance together (*Statesman* 306a–311b). But, as Plato points out in the *Phaedo,* that form of integration can degenerate into trading virtue for virtue, feeling for feeling (69a). The good man would then grudgingly go to war so that at another time he can lead a more leisurely life. Reason has only an instrumental place in such a life. The virtuous man with *theōria* restrains the magnetizing force of a virtue not in order to distribute it among other virtues but because he recognizes that *theōria* is better than *phronēsis*. Only through *theōria* are all the virtues are seen as virtues, and as neither necessities nor the best things in the world, because it is only through *theōria* that one fully understands the relation between what is best *haplōs* and what is best for me to do. By seeing that practical virtues have both internal and external ends, we neither denigrate the more necessary virtuous actions nor overrate their goodness. The contemplative life perfects politics by placing a true valuation on these things good in themselves.

Now we can fill in more of my earlier claim that politics itself teaches us that there is something better that lies beyond it. The *phronimos* knows that the ethical and political life is a good life because it is made up of actions that are chosen for their own sakes. But knowing this, he knows too that this autonomy is not the most self-sufficient activity possible, precisely because it depends on the passions to inform him what needs to be done and so what it is best to do. The *phronimos* knows that his actions are only chosen for their own sake because of the circumstances in which he finds himself. Therefore he understands what it is to engage in action that is its own end and is worthwhile independent of circumstances. That is *theōria*. Therefore the true *phronimos* must engage in *theōria*. The gods could not be subject to the kind of circumstantial determination we are subject to; therefore they engage in *theōria* too.[44]

But if the *phronimos* has to know that *theōria* is the best activity, why does he not thereby choose always to live philosophically? To think that such an inference from what is best to what should be done is automatic is the definition of injustice in my final proof-text, but what blocks the inference here? As with the relation of *phronēsis* to ethical virtue, the only thing missing here is opportunity. *Theōria* does not require equipment, so that cannot be what prevents the *phronimos* from living philosophically. He lacks neither knowledge or motivation. If the *phronimos* does not live philosophically, it is because it is *right* to be pulled by the attractive force of the ethical virtues. Practical situations make demands on us. Without knowing that man is not the best thing in the universe, we would not even think about resisting those demands. But with that knowledge of what is best, it would still be wrong—be unjust—to resist those demands in the name of *theōria*. *Phronēsis* cannot tell us how to engage in *theōria*, but it does tell us when we should.

## Introduction

1. My hermeneutical point does not at all negate the value I find in so much of the contemporary writing about the *Ethics*. When I wrote about the *Rhetoric*, I found both the quantity and quality of secondary work about it too meager to be of much help. The situation regarding the *Ethics* is the reverse. I feel lucky to live at a time when there are so many acute readings of the *Ethics*. I have learned as much as I can from them, but I have rarely thought of my own interpretation of Aristotle by situating it in relation to other commentators. Therefore I have rarely tried in this book to locate my interpretation relative to others. I want this reading to stand on its own, and am not interested in proving myself right by showing how others are wrong.

2. Terence C. Irwin, *Aristotle's First Principles* (Oxford: Clarendon Press, 1988), 439.

3. Sarah Broadie, *Ethics with Aristotle* (New York and Oxford: Oxford University Press, 1991), 38.

4. Richard Kraut, *Aristotle on the Human Good* (Princeton, N.J.: Princeton University Press, 1989), 327.

5. Kraut, 342.

6. Thanks to Charles Young for extensive discussion on this subject. See too Sarah Broadie, "Introduction" to Aristotle, *Nicomachean Ethics*, trans. Christopher Rowe, philosophical introduction and commentary by Sarah Broadie (Oxford: Oxford University Press, 2002), 45: "There is something important in common between decisions considered as the conclusions of deliberation, and decisions considered as expressions of ethical dispositions. Both are responses to the particularities of a situation, and in both cases the objectives or values that we bring to the situation are relatively abstract by comparison. But facing these with the particularities under which they will be instantiated (if at all) on this occasion makes the commitments determinate."

See, finally, Edward Halper, "The Unity of the Virtues in Aristotle," *Oxford Studies in Ancient Philosophy* 17 (1999): 115–43, at 122: "It is therefore an interesting question whether these two definitions of virtue are really identical, whether, that is, the state that enables a person to function well in such activities [as are praised by "prevailing common opinions"] is the state that can choose the mean of passions and actions."

The following two extracts seem to me to identify the problem and then trivialize it: Jennifer Whiting, "Eudaimōnia, External Results, and Choosing Virtuous Actions for Themselves," *Philosophy and Phenomenological Research* 65 (2002): 280: "On Stoic accounts, what is chosen for itself is ultimately *the aiming* and *not the external result* at which one aims: what the Stoic sage chooses for itself is *aiming*-at-a-certain-sort-of-external-result. But on the teleological (and I submit Aristotelian) account proposed here, choosing a virtuous action for itself *just is* choosing that action simply insofar as it aims at a certain sort of external result. So what is chosen for itself is ultimately the external result at which one aims. Talk of choosing a virtuous *action* for itself is thus elliptical to talk of aiming at a certain sort of *result* for *its*elf—elliptical, that is, for talking of aiming at a certain sort of result simply for the sake of that *result*."

David Bostock, *Aristotle's Ethics* (Oxford: Oxford University Press, 2000), 26. "Aristotle begins [I.7, the ergon argument] by considering the good *for* man, which we may gloss as 'what most benefits a man.' With various qualifications . . . it is not too unreasonable to claim that men aim for what will most benefit them. But the argument about the 'function' of man considers not this notion but the quite different notion of 'the good man,' which Aristotle construes as the one who is *good at* being a man (i.e. one who well exemplifies the specifically human kind of life). But why should one suppose that the good man (good at being a man) can be identified with one who secures the good *for* man (what most benefits a man)? There is evidently no reason at all, or if so then surely the reason must be given. But Aristotle, I think, fails to see that the notions are different. He constantly uses, and I believe thinks in terms of, a single phrase which is ambiguous between the two (*to anthrōpinon agathon* may be translated either as 'human goodness'—i.e. what it is for a human to be good—or as 'human good'—i.e. what is good for humans) so he does not even notice that, in juxtaposing the two parts of his discussion as he does, he is making a disputable assumptions about how the two notions are connected."

7. Kant, *Groundwork of the Metaphysics of Morals,* trans. H. J. Paton (New York: Harper, 1956), 99–100, Riga 71–74/431–33.

8. *NE* X.9.1180b28–1181b12; see too *Rh.* I.2.1356a27–30, *Poet.* 25.1460b13–28.

## Chapter One

1. For the Greek text of the *Nicomachean Ethics,* I have used Bywater's Oxford Classical Text edition (Oxford, 1894). I have consulted a variety of translations to keep the work fresh in my mind. Most of my translations are based primarily on Terence C. Irwin, trans., *Nicomachean Ethics* (Indianapolis, 1985). I have also made use of Aristotle, *Nicomachean Ethics,* trans. H. Rackham (Cambridge, Mass.: Harvard University Press, 1926), Aristotle, *Nicomachean Ethics,* trans. Hippocrates Apostle (Grinnell, Iowa: Peripatetic Press, 1975), Aristotle, *Nicomachean Ethics,* trans. Christopher Rowe, philosophical introduction and commentary by Sarah Broadie (Oxford: Oxford University Press, 2002), Aristotle, *Nicomachean Ethics,* trans. Joe Sachs (Newburyport, Mass.: Focus Publishing, 2002), and *Ethique à Nicomaque,* trans. J. Tricot (Paris: Vrin, 1990). Except when it makes things excessively awkward, I follow Irwin in translating *prohairesis* as "decision" rather than "choice."

For the *Politics,* the Greek text is W. D. Ross, *Aristotelis: Politica* (Oxford: Oxford University Press, 1957). The primary translation I use is Carnes Lord, *Aristotle: The Politics* (Chicago: University of Chicago Press, 1984), but I have also consulted *Aristotle: Politics,* trans. H. Rackham (Cambridge, Mass.: Harvard University Press, 1932), Ernest Barker, *The Politics of Aristotle* (London: Oxford University Press, 1952), *Aristotle's Politics,* trans. Hippocrates Apostle and Lloyd P. Gerson (Grinnell, Iowa: Peripatetic Press, 1986), Simpson's translation (Chapel Hill and London: University of North Carolina Press, 1997), Reeve's translation (Indianapolis: Hackett, 1998), and *Les Politiques,* trans. Pierre Pellegrin (Paris: Flammarion, 1990).

Finally, the text of the *Rhetoric* is R. Kassel, *Aristotelis Ars Rhetorica* (Berlin: de Gruyter, 1971). My translations are based on Aristotle, *On Rhetoric: A Theory of Civic Discourse,* trans. with introduction, notes, and appendixes by George A. Kennedy (New York and Oxford:

Oxford University Press, 1991); I also consulted Médéric Dufour, *Aristote: Rhétorique* (Paris: Budé, 1960), and John Henry Freese, *The "Art" of Rhetoric* (Cambridge, Mass.: Harvard University Press, 1926).

2. I offer this picture of the *Rhetoric* here to begin an interpretation of the *Ethics*. I argue for the picture in *Aristotle's Rhetoric: An Art of Character* (Chicago: University of Chicago Press, 1994). My distinction between internal and external ends is parallel to that between given and guiding ends in Sarah Broadie, *Ethics with Aristotle* (New York and Oxford: Oxford University Press, 1991), esp. 190–98, and to Alasdair MacIntyre's distinction, in *After Virtue*, of goods "internal" to a "practice" from those "externally and contingently attached to it." Alasdair MacIntyre, *After Virtue: A Study in Moral Theory* (Notre Dame, Ind.: University of Notre Dame Press, 1984), 188. In correspondence, Lenn Goodman has suggested the terminology of primary vs. paramount ends: the primary end of the courageous person is victory, while courage itself is his paramount end.

3. Alasdair MacIntyre, *After Virtue*, 188–89: "We call [the goods of practices] internal for two reasons: first . . . because we can only specify them in terms of chess or some other game of that specific kind and by means of examples from such games . . . ; and secondly because they can only be identified and recognized by the experience of participating in the practice in question. Those who lack the relevant experience are incompetent thereby as judges of internal goods."

4. Charles L. Black Jr., *The Humane Imagination* (Woodbridge, Conn.: Ox Bow Press, 1986), 31. Contrast a claim that seems to me to see all such proficiency as constraining: "Legal reasoning is an inherently repressive form of interpretive thought which limits our comprehension of the social world and its possibilities." Peter Gabel, "Reification in Legal Reasoning," in *Critical Legal Studies*, ed. James Boyle (New York: New York University Press, 1992), 17.

5. MacIntyre, *After Virtue*, 193. "What is distinctive in a practice is in part the way in which conceptions of the relevant goods and ends which the technical skills serve—and every practice does require the exercise of technical skills—are transformed and enriched by these extensions of human powers and by that regard for its own internal goods which are partially definitive of each particular practice or type of practice."

6. Lon Fuller, *The Morality of Law*, rev. ed. (New Haven: Yale University Press, 1969), 106.

7. Jeremy Waldron, "Why Law—Efficacy, Freedom, or Fidelity?" *Law and Philosophy* 13 (1994): 275–76: "Of all the institutional forms available for the governance of human society, law brings with it a sense that the form itself attracts our allegiance, quite apart from the ends it is used to pursue. Other forms of governance—such as militarized command or managerial administration—are available and legitimate; and, in certain circumstances, they may be institutionally more appropriate than law. But when they are used, they depend, for loyalty and cooperation of those subject to them, on the subjects' acceptance of and enthusiasm for the ends and purposes they are used to pursue. Fidelity to them as institutions cannot survive widespread disillusionment with those goals (though of course the institutions themselves may survive, as artifacts of power). To that extent, their deployment as modes of government is always politically and ideologically precarious. Fidelity to law, by contract, is predicated on what law is, not just on what it is used for. Legal institutions therefore have an extra layer or dimension of allegiance in society that may be expected to sustain itself, even when people waver or weaken in their enthusiasm for the substantive goals that legal institutions are designed to achieve."

8. The *Poetics* contains a similar limitation to argument and exclusion of spectacle. Thus tragedy can have its proper effect when someone hears the plot apart from a performance (*Poet.* 14.1453b3–7, 6.1450b18–19, 26.1462a11–18).

9. *Pistis apodeixis tis (tote gar pisteoumen malista hotan apodedeichthai hypolabōmen), esti d' apodeixis rētorikē enthumēma, kai est touto ōs eipein haplōs kuriōtaton tōn pisteōn.*

10. For further consideration of the relation between internal and external ends, see chapter 3. But at this point I should point out one of the oddities of Aristotle's presentation

of rhetoric: throughout the *Rhetoric* he sees argumentation directed by a speaker to an audience, with the competitive relations between speakers as a very secondary matter. Therefore he does not face the issue of what happens when two artistic arguments clash and only one can win. There is another oddity worth mentioning here. When he says that *ēthos* is the most authoritative source of belief, he immediately insists that the kind of *ēthos* that is persuasive, and which falls within the art of rhetoric, is limited to trust in character produced by the speech itself and not by preexisting reputation (I.2.1356a5–13). This has the advantage of making what is persuasive coincide with what ought to persuade. It has the drawback that each piece of persuasion must in this sense start from scratch. The contrast between a form of character that must be made each time by argument and the continuities of virtue established through habituation form one unbridgeable gap between rhetorical manifestations of character and the true character described in the *Ethics*.

11. Charles Fried, "Constitutional Doctrine," *Harvard Law Review* 107 (1994): 1145–46. See too Paul Ricoeur, *Oneself as Another* (Chicago and London: University of Chicago Press, 1992), 155: "Constitutive rules are not moral rules. They simply rule over the *meaning* of particular gestures. . . . To be sure, constitutive rules point the way toward moral rules to the extent that the latter govern conduct capable of conveying meaning. But this is only a first step in the direction of ethics. Even the constitutive rule of promising . . . has not as such a moral signification, although it contains the reference to an obligation. It is confined to defining what 'counts as' a promise, what gives it its illocutionary 'force.' The moral rule, which can be termed the rule of faithfulness, according to which one must keep one's promises, alone has a deontological status."

12. Christine M. Korsgaard, "Aristotle and Kant on the Source of Value," *Ethics* 96 (1986): 497–98: "Performing a certain process can be an activity. The notion of activity, *energy*, is closely associated with the notion of *ergon*, function. . . . One can make a certain process one's activity. And this is in a sense what Aristotle envisions for the political life. For moral actions are in a sense processes: they have an aim outside themselves, and their occasions should not be created, though the political person seeks them. As long as there is occasion for them, they can be the activity of someone's life, just as architecture can, as long as there is a need for houses. But just as the architect's life and activity are only possible as long as someone—not necessarily the architect herself—needs and will enjoy the house, so the statesperson's life and activity are only possible as long as someone—the citizens—enjoy the benefits in the form of the different sort of happiness. And in general, for any activity that is also a process there will be this dependence: the possibility of its being an activity will depend upon someone's benefiting from the results of the process."

13. Sarah Broadie, *Ethics with Aristotle*, 195.

14. D. F. Pears, "Aristotle's Analysis of Courage," *Midwest Studies in Philosophy* 3 (1978): 273–85, reprinted in *Essays on Aristotle's Ethics*, ed. Amélie Oksenberg Rorty (Berkeley and Los Angeles: University of California Press, 1981), 171. The distinction between behavioral and emotional senses of fear and confidence occurs on 185. For a similar yet subtler distinction, see Edward Halper, "Unity of the Virtues," 121: "Courage is both a capacity for particular actions and a characteristic arrangement of parts of the soul."

15. Alasdair MacIntyre, *Whose Justice? Which Rationality?* (Notre Dame, Ind.: University of Notre Dame Press, 1988), 113: "It is in part in this aristocratic carelessness about consequences that the nobility, the fineness of the exercise of such virtues resides." Compare Plato, *Theaetatus* 184c: "The easy use of words and phrases and the avoidance of strict precision is in general a sign of good breeding; indeed, the opposite is hardly worthy of a gentleman."

16. Arendt often reduces virtue to virtuosity, equating political action with "an excellence we attribute to the performing arts . . . where the accomplishment lies in the performance itself and not in an end product which outlasts the activity that brought it into existence." Hannah Arendt, *Between Past and Future* (New York: Viking, 1968), 153.

17. Georg Henrik von Wright:, *The Varieties of Goodness* (New York: Routledge and Kegan Paul, 1963), 139: "A virtue is neither an acquired nor an innate skill or any particular

*activity.* 'To be courageous' or 'to show courage' do not name an activity in the same sense in which 'to breathe' or 'to walk' or 'to chop wood' name activities. If I ask a person who is engaged in some activity, 'What are you doing?' and he answers, 'I am courageous; this is very dangerous,' he may be speaking the truth, but he is not telling me what he is doing.

"The lack of an essential tie between a specific virtue and a specific activity distinguishes virtue from that which we have called technical goodness. We attribute technical goodness or excellence to a man on the ground that he is *good* at some activity. But there is no specific activity at which, say, the courageous man must be good—as the skilled chess player must be good at playing chess and the skillful teacher must be good at teaching, There is no art of 'couraging,' in which the brave man excels."

Similarly, 141: "The results of all courageously performed acts need not have any 'outward' features in common. Killing a tiger and jumping into cold water can both be acts of courage, though 'outwardly' most dissimilar. No list of achievements could possibly exhaust the range of results in courageous action."

18. D. F. Pears, "Aristotle's Analysis of Courage," 278.

19. Richard Bodéüs, *Le philosophe et la cité* (Paris: Les Belles Lettres, 1982), trans. as *The Political Dimensions of Aristotle's Ethics,* trans. Jan Edward Garrett (Albany, SUNY Press, 1993), 51: "Strictly speaking, the acquisition of the moral virtues owes little to teaching as we understand it: it rests upon habit, which perfects or corrects nature. However, once acquired, the moral virtues allow one to know the human good and this knowledge belongs to the prudent person, who uses it for the premises of his deliberation. In a sense the Socratic thesis is inverted: knowledge is no longer the condition of virtue but virtue is the condition of knowledge."

20. Thinking of self-knowledge as the center of virtue can nicely capture many of the differences between Plato and Aristotle. Much of what Hadot says about Socrates can also be said of the *Ethics,* but with a radically different meaning. "It is very interesting to state that here [in the *Apology*] knowledge and non-knowledge apply not to concepts but to values: the value of death on the one hand, the value of moral good and evil on the other. Socrates knows nothing of what value he should attribute to death, because it is not within his own power, because the experience of his own death escapes him by definition. But he knows the value of moral action and intention, because they depend on his choice and his decision, his engagement. They have their origin in him. Here then knowledge is not a series of propositions, an abstract theory, but the certainty of a choice, a decision, an initiative: knowledge is not a knowledge as such, but a knowledge of what one must prefer, and so a knowledge of how to live (*un savoir-vivre*)." Pierre Hadot, *Qu'est-ce que la philosophie antique?* (Paris: Gallimard, 1995), 62. Translation mine.

21. See *NE* III.8.1117a17–22. For the rhetorical connection between believing *in* a speaker and believing *that* something is the case, see my *Aristotle's Rhetoric: An Art of Character* (Chicago: University of Chicago Press, 1994), and *For the Sake of Argument: Practical Reasoning, Character and the Ethics of Belief* (Chicago: University of Chicago Press, 2004).

22. In the final chapter, I will show how *theōria,* contemplation, is also a kind of self-knowledge. Alan Code argues that all human contemplation, including metaphysics, is really self-knowledge. "The ultimate goal of First Philosophy is to systematically understand our nature as systematic understanders." Alan Code, "The Aporematic Approach to Primary Being in *Metaphysics* Z," *Canadian Journal of Philosophy* 10 (1985): 1–20, at 2.

23. Irwin, "Unity of the Virtues, 373: "It is not immediately evident why an account of happiness should help us to find an account of the virtues. The recognized virtues seem to be those that benefit other people. . . . Aristotle, quite legitimately, presents another conception of virtue that is derived directly from his claims about happiness. He has argued that happiness is the good performance of the human function, and that therefore it is the realization of the soul in accordance with complete virtue in a complete life. . . . Further argument is needed to show that the reference to human function explains the nature of the moral virtues as well."

24. See too *NE* IX.7.1167b32–1168a9, IX.9.1169b28–1170a4, 1170b1–5, *EE* VII.12. 1244b29–1245a1, *Rh.* I.11.1371a31–b12.

25. *NE* I.7.1097b1–5, 1099b2–8, 1140a26–30, VII.4.1147b29–31, *EE* VIII.2. 1248b27–30, 1249b16–19, *Pol* II.9.1271b7–10, VII.1.1323a36–b21.

26. For just of few of the commentators who consideration deliberation about ends, see Richard Sorabji, "Aristotle on the Role of Intellect in Virtue," in *Essays on Aristotle's Ethics,* ed. Rorty, 201–20; Norman O. Dahl, *Practical Reason, Aristotle, and Weakness of the Will* (Minneapolis : University of Minnesota Press, 1984); Troels Engberg-Pedersen, *Aristotle's Theory of Moral Insight* (Oxford: Clarendon Press, 1983).

27. Speaking about those who distinguish means/end deliberations and rule/case deliberations, David Wiggins says: "I think that those how employ these or similar terms usually intend the distinction of two kinds of reasoning, and the two distinct kinds of nontheoretical syllogism allegedly recognized by Aristotle, to correspond in some way to Aristotle's distinction of production (*poiēsis*) and practice (*praxis*). David Wiggins, "Weakness of Will, Commensurability, and the Objects of Deliberation and Desire," in *Essays on Aristotle's Ethics,* ed. Rorty, 241–65, at 238, n. 2.

28. For this sense of *energeia* to work, Aristotle will have to assume that things conventionally thought good really are good. I will consider ways in which *phronēsis* would have to be reconceived today in chapters 3 and 4. For now, consider the following citation from Habermas: "The concept of practical reason as a subjective capacity is of modern vintage. Converting the Aristotelian conceptual framework over to premises of the philosophy of the subject had the disadvantage of detaching practical reason from its anchors in cultural forms of life and sociopolitical orders. It had the advantage, though, of relating practical reason to the 'private' happiness and 'moral' autonomy of the individual. That is, practical reason was thenceforth related to the freedom of the human being as a private subject who could also assume the roles of member of civil society and citizen, both national and global." Jürgen Habermas, *Between Facts and Norms: Contributions to a Discourse Theory of Law and Democracy* (Cambridge, Mass.: MIT Press, 1996), 1.

29. David Wiggins, "Incommensurability: Four Proposals," in *Incommensurability, Incomparability, and Practical Reason,* ed. Ruth Chang (Cambridge, Mass., and London: Harvard University Press, 1997), 62: "*Pace* the received misinterpretations of Aristotle, the main business of practical reason is ends and their constituents, not instrumental means. For an Aristotelian, the idea that a self-contained part of the concept of rationality can be bitten off and studied in value-free fashion as the rationality of means, leaving the rest, that is ends, to the taste or formation of individual agents, is a delusion, and a gratuitous delusion at that." Wiggins attaches a footnote that blames "the received misinterpretations" on mistranslating *pros ta telē* as means. But the rationality of means is not value-free. Ends can be rational without being subject to deliberation, while Wiggins seems to assume that only if we choose our ends can they be rational.

Nicholas White, *Individual and Conflict in Greek Ethics* (Oxford: Clarendon Press, 2002), 281: "Modern philosophy has been actively concerned with problems about the dynamic ways in which people might rationally adjust aims to each other over time in the light of improved information, changed circumstances, and the like. . . . On the whole Greek ethics is inattentive to problems about action under imperfect information and to the diachronic adjustment of aims. The same is true of Aristotle."

30. My Aristotelian distinction of ends *haplōs* and *pros ti* corresponds to Christine M. Korsgaard's distinction between conditional and unconditional ends in her "Aristotle and Kant on the Source of Value," 491–92: "If we suppose that Aristotle is giving a rationalist account of the good, his three categories are means, conditional ends, and unconditional ends. Conditional ends, for Aristotle, are ends valued for their own sake, given that we are human beings living in human conditions—among friends, in the city, with a nature both animal and rational to cope with. They 'befit our human estate' (10.8.1178a). The unconditional end plays a different role: it is what makes it worth it to be a human being and to live in human conditions.

"It will be the mark of a conditional end that it is also a means. But this 'also' is not merely conjunctive; rather, its being a 'means' or constituent of a worthwhile life will be what makes it possible to choose it as an end. The fact that something plays a certain instrumental or constitutive role in human life makes it worthy of choice. Its instrumentality may be regarded as essential to what it is; this is true of artifacts which are made for certain purposes and for activities understood as instances of, say, 'recreation' or 'exercise.' When something which is essentially an instrumental or a constitutive activity is also interesting or beautiful or pleasant it may be chosen as an end under the condition of its utility."

David Wiggins, "Deliberation and Practical Reason," *Proceedings of the Aristotelean Society* 76 (1975–76): 50, n. 5: "See *Politics* 1332b6 and *Metaphysics* 1072a20: 'We desire it because it seems good to us, it doesn't seem good to us because we desire it.' It is the beginning of wisdom on this matter, both as an issue of interpretation and as a philosophical issue, to see that we do not really have to choose between Aristotle's proposition and its apparent opposite (as at e.g., Spinoza *Ethics* III.9). We can desire because it seems good and it seems good because we desire it." My argument has been an explication of the conditions under which the two relations of good and desire become indifferent.

31. See Henry Richardson, *Practical Reasoning About Final Ends* (Cambridge: Cambridge University Press, 1994). Where Richardson talks about "specification" as a way of deliberating about ends, I have internalization as a way of apprehending ends rationally and being rationally committed to them. That there is more at stake than the translation of *pros to telos*, or a difference between specification and internalization as competing descriptions, see Nicholas White, *Individual and Conflict in Greek Ethics* (Oxford: Clarendon Press, 2002), 76: The Greeks "tended to think of such [extended] plans not as dynamic or evolving over time, but as static, as made during youth and then simply followed out. Greek philosophical discussions do not deal in any substantial way with questions about how a life plan might rationally be revised at later stages." I will return to that contrast in chapter 5.

32. Lon Fuller, *The Morality of Law*, 97.

33. A. D. Smith, "Character and Intellect in Aristotle's *Ethics*," *Phronesis* 41 (1996): 67: "Whenever we are not motivated by what is fine or what is good, we are pursuing pleasure."

34. Therefore virtue is transformed when God guarantees that it will be rewarded, as Locke clearly notes. "God, having, by an inseparable connexion, joined *Virtue* and public Happiness together; and made the Practice therefore, necessary to the preservation of Society, and visibly *beneficial* to all, with whom the Virtuous Man has to do; it is no wonder, that every one should, not only allow, but recommend and magnify those Rules to others, from whose observance of them, he is sure to reap Advantage to himself." *Essay concerning Human Understanding*, ed. Peter H. Nidditch (Oxford: Oxford University Press, 1975), 1.3.6, p. 69. See too *The Reasonableness of Christianity*, ed. I. T. Ramsey (Stanford: Stanford University Press, 1958), 70: "That [virtue] is the perfection and excellency of our nature; that she is herself a reward, and will recommend our names to future ages, is not all that can now be said for her. 'Tis not strange that the learned heathens satisfied not many with such airy commendations. It has another relish and efficacy to persuade men, that if they live well here, they shall be happy hereafter. Open their eyes to the endless unspeakable joys of another life; and their hearts will find something solid and powerful to move them. The view of heaven and hell will cast a slight upon the short pleasures and pains of this present state, and give attractions and encouragements to virtue, which reason and interest, and care of ourselves, cannot but allow and prefer. Upon this foundation, and upon this only, morality stands firm, and may defy all competition. This makes it more than a name, a substantial good, worth all our aims and endeavours; and thus the gospel of Jesus Christ has delivered it to us." But see *NE* X.9.1179b21–23: "The good that is ours by nature clearly does not depend on us but comes from certain divine causes to beings that are truly fortunate." I will return to this question in chapter 3.

35. See too *NE* VII.13.1153b7–25, VIII.2.1155b21–27, VIII.13.1162b35–37, *De An.* 431b10–13, *Met.* VII.3.1029b6–7, *EE* I.1.1214a30–b5, I.4.1215b1–5, I.5.1216b18–25, I.5.1216a10–37, VII.1.1234b23, VII.1.1237b37–1238a8, VIII.3.1249a4–7, *Rh.* I.7. 1364b. For Platonic antecedents see *Republic* 331c1–9, *Statesman* 294a10–b6, *Laws* II. 661b. See also *Pol.* VII.13.1332a21–25: "A truly good and happy man, as we have stated elsewhere in our arguments on ethics, is one who by the nature of his goodness [which is *absolute*] has advantages at hand which are *absolute* advantages." And *Pol.* 1332a30: "We

pray that the composition of the state be lucky enough to be supplied with the goods which depend on fortune, for we posit fortune as being sovereign over them. The virtue of the state, on the other hand, is the work not of fortune, but of knowledge and intention."

36. Sarah Broadie, "Introduction" to Aristotle, *Nicomachean Ethics,* trans. Christopher Rowe, philosophical introduction and commentary by Sarah Broadie (Oxford: Oxford University Press, 2002), 82, n. 49: "The good 'which all things seek' of *NE* I.1, 1094a3 turns out, on the next page, to be the political objective, where 'political expertise' is explained as authoritative over production and use of the other *goods* (2, 1094a35–b11), not as laying down right *action* for everyone concerned."

37. Broadie, *Ethics with Aristotle,* 209. "Although any given production must as a matter of fact *be* particular if it occurs at all, its particularising conditions are external and accidental to its *nature* as a that-sort-of-production. But the particulars of an action belong to its essence as action, since these are features of *what* it is that is judged good or not. The verdict depends on the when, the where, the agent's relations with those affected, the forseeable consequences, the cost, the alternatives sacrificed, etc."

38. Theoretical science cannot know the individual because for theory, the individual is the accidental (*Met.* VI.2.1027a19–21).

39. See, among many others, Christopher Gill, "The Character-Personality Distinction," in Cristopher Pelling, ed., *Characterization and Individuality in Greek Literature* (Oxford: Clarendon Press, 1990), 1–31, and idem, "The Question of Character and Personality in Greek Tragedy," *Poetics Today* 7 (1986): 251–73. See too my "The Rhetoric of Friendship in Plato's *Lysis*," *Rhetorica,* forthcoming.

## Chapter Two

1. "The word actuality has two senses corresponding respectively to the possession of knowledge and the actual exercise of knowledge. It is obvious that the soul is actuality in the first sense, viz., that of knowledge as possessed, for both sleeping and waking presuppose the existence of soul, and of these waking corresponds to actual knowing, sleeping to knowledge possessed but not employed, and in the history of the individual, knowledge comes before its employment or exercise. That is why the soul is the first *energeia* of a natural body having life potentially in it" (*De An.* II.1.412a22–27; see II.5.417a21–b2).

2. Immediately we see one complication that I will have to postpone examining until my final chapter. Not only virtuous activity but happiness are both fairly called second actualities of the virtues: happiness is *energeia kat'aretēn,* and Aristotle contrasts happiness as an activity with virtue as a first actuality that one can have while asleep (*NE* I.5.1095b31–1096a2, I.8.1098b31–1099a3), which is the same analogy he uses in *De Anima* II.1 to show that the soul is a first actuality. The final chapter will explicate the relation between happiness and virtuous activity.

3. John McDowell, *Mind and World* (Cambridge, Mass.: Harvard University Press, 1994), 79: "Modern readers often credit Aristotle with aiming to construct the requirements of ethics out of independent facts about human nature. This is to attribute to Aristotle a scheme for a naturalistic foundation for ethics, with nature playing an archaic version of the role played by disenchanted nature in modern naturalistic ethics. But I think this kind of reading is a historical monstrosity. This reassuring role for nature can seem to make sense only as a response to a kind of anxiety about the status of reasons—ethical reasons in this case—that is foreign to Aristotle. What underlies the anxiety is precisely the conception of nature that I have represented as distinctively modern."

Ronald Beiner, *What's the Matter With Liberalism?* (Berkeley and Los Angeles: University of California Press, 1992), 54–55. "One of the most familiar objections to Aristotelian practical philosophy is that it depends upon a set of metaphysical and cosmological doctrines that are today highly implausible, or even unintelligible. Stoic ethical theory is indeed so dependent, with frequent appeals to the rational structure of the universe, the moral intentions of the gods, and cosmic providence. In Aristotle, by contrast, the whole stress is on the inner structure of the virtues, with only minimal reference to metaphysical or cosmological assumptions. . . . What is striking is the autonomy of the ethical world in relation to cosmological doctrines."

4. I will revisit this list in the last section of chapter 4.

5. Of course, the relation of reason and emotion is much more complicated than this formulation allows. While the scientific practitioner might do a better job when her knowledge is accompanied by appropriate emotions, the scientific reasoning itself is distinct from its emotional charges in a way not true for practical reason.

6. W. F. R. Hardie, *Aristotle's Ethical Theory*, 101. The literature on the *energeiai/kineseis* and *praxis/poesis* distinctions is huge. I have found most helpful J. L. Ackrill, "Aristotle on Eudaimōnia," *Proceedings of the British Academy* 1974, 339–59, and his "Aristotle's Distinction Between *Energeia* and *Kinēsis*," in *New Essays on Plato and Aristotle*, ed. R. Bambrough (New York, 1965), 121–41; Timothy C. Potts, "States, Activities, and Performances," *Proceedings of the Aristotelian Society*, Supplement 39 (1965), 65–84; Terry Penner, "Verbs and the Identity of Actions—A Philosophical Exercise in the Interpretation of Aristotle," *Ryle*, ed. Oscar Wood and George Pitcher, 393–404. Also L. A. Kosman, "Substance, Being, and Energeia," esp. 135: "The distinction between two sorts of potentiality is thus more generally and importantly a distinction between two modes of relation between potentiality and actuality, or perhaps we should say a distinction between two fundamental pairs of potentiality and actuality." In addition, a different but useful account of the relation between *eudaimōnia, energeia,* and *hexis* can be found in A. W. H. Adkins, "*Theoria* versus *Praxis* in the *Nicomachean Ethics* and the *Republic*," *Classical Philology* 73 (1978): 297–312.

7. See too Hamlyn's note on *De Anima* II.1.412a3 in his commentary: "The distinction between the two ways in which form can be actuality is the distinction between *hexis* (state or capacity) and *energeia* (activity or actuality, cf. 412a22ff.), as the two forms of what is actual; a *hexis* must be distinguished from mere potentiality (*dynamis*) which manifests itself in movement or change (*kinēsis*) not activity (v. *Metaphysics* IX.6). *Hexis* is, though, actual, potential in relation to *energeia*, since it is dispositional." D. W. Hamlyn, trans. and notes, *Aristotle: De Anima Books II and III* (Oxford: Clarendon Press, 1993) 82. I will consider the contrast between *dynamis* and *hexis* in *NE* V.1.1129a11–17 later in the chapter.

8. I am temporarily ignoring the way incontinence can interrupt the transition from decision to action. *Akrasia* is a puzzle precisely because it is the interruption of what looks like a practically necessary connection.

Marcia Homiak, "Aristotle on the Soul's Conflicts: Toward an Understanding of Virtue Ethics," *Reclaiming the History of Ethics: Essays for John Rawls*, ed. Andrews Reath, Barbara Herman, and Christine Korsgaard (Cambridge: Cambridge University Press, 1997), 27: "The brave person's confidence is continuous. It is not upset by failure of some planned action, by the recognition of the enemy's superior numbers, and so on. Now the brave person's confidence can be continuous if it is derived from an enjoyment taken in the expression of his human powers, for the expression of these powers is not a contingent feature of the agent who expresses them. That it is so derived is our best way of understanding why Aristotle emphasizes the brave person's love of life at 1117b10–15. And it is this love of life, that is, a love of what is essential to a human life, that carries him forward to defend his city against attack."

Broadie, "Introduction" to Rowe's translation of the *Ethics*, 19 (see chap. 1, n. 1): "What distinguishes human excellence from expertise is that the former is an *unconditional preparedness* to act, feel, and in general respond in the ways typical of the human excellent person, whereas the latter is only an *ability* to act and respond (and perhaps, in some sense, to feel) in the ways typical of the sort pf expert in question."

9. *Phronēsis* seems to fit neither category here: it is an intellectual virtue, but not "produced and increased by instruction." I will return to questions of how *phronēsis* is acquired at several points in the coming argument.

10. Joachim is wrong to say that a virtuous action is always the "realization of a *dynamis ton enantion,* and therefore implies a strain and an effort" (H. H. Joachim, *Aristotle, The*

*Nicomachean Ethics* [Clarendon Press, Oxford, 1951], 281). We learn in II.3 that actions done by a virtuous man differ from those same acts done by someone else precisely because they do involve not strain and effort but pleasure. Joachim's conclusion comes from taking two true premises, that virtuous actions are the realization, (*energeia*), of virtuous habits, and that virtuous habits are the realization of some *dynamis ton enantion,* and wrongly inferred that therefore the virtuous actions are a realization of that original *dynamis:* the potency/act distinction is not transitive.

There are special problems with courageous action being pleasurable. I tried to address those problems in "Aristotle on Virtue and Pleasure," in *The Greeks and the Good Life,* ed. David Depew (Indianapolis: Hackett, 1980), 157–76.

11. "Pain destroys the sufferer's nature; whereas pleasure has no such effect. . . . [Therefore] it is easier to train oneself to resist the temptations of pleasure, because these occur frequently in life and to practice resistance to them involves no danger, whereas the reverse is true with the objects of fear" (*NE* III.12.1119a23–28). See Plato, *Laws* I.643b–d, 650a, VIII.830d–831b. It might be easier for us if Aristotle had contrasted erthical virtue with continence here, or claimed that continence is a stage on the way toward virtue. But his discussion of continence is limited to Book VII and he does not develop his understanding of virtue through contrasts with continence.

12. Joachim is alive to this distinction between the virtues and the arts: "The relation of a *hexis* to its expressions, of a moral habit to its single acts, is therefore determinate. You can infer from effect to cause in this case with complete security, and from cause to its own determinate kind of effect" (*Aristotle,* 127). Because the kinds of potency and act help to structure the available forms of inference for a given field, the distinction between rational and irrational *dynameis* also appears at *Int.* 13.22b36–23a6, when Aristotle is talking about the logical meanings of possible and necessary. There the distinction is a *logical* one because the two kinds of potencies differ in the kinds and directions of reliable inference they permit.

See also Richard McKeon, "Dialectic and Political Thought and Action," *Ethics* 65 (1954): 26: "Like the use of reason in the natural sciences, its use in practical affairs is an inference. . . . The inference is not from a proposition to a prediction, however, except in an analogical sense. Principles, theories, and statements are only one ingredient in the premises from which a practical inference proceeds. They are made precise, in so far as they enter serious consideration, not by their truth but by their reliability as statements of intention, granted the circumstances, history, and character of their proponents. . . . Reason in application to practical questions therefore has, in addition to its direct inferential function of relating assumptions to conclusions [the function assumed in the so-called practical syllogism and in productive action], an inverse inferential or imputative function of relating proposals to the character and attitude form which they flow."

See, too, Sarah Broadie, *Ethics with Aristotle* (New York and Oxford: Oxford University Press, 1991), 230: "The original scientist shares his explanation . . . with others who, it is assumed, desire to understand the same thing. If they absorb the explanation presented, they are now able themselves to explain the phenomenon. The argument which passes from mind to mind in this way is primarily the explanatory one, in which the cause figures in the premises. . . . Practice, however, is different, because the primarily practical argument cannot be generally shared. For grasping *how* to realise O in C is primarily a matter of being ready to become, oneself, the vehicle of a causal first premise displaying the answer to that practical question. . . . The argument is a *logos,* a communicable structure; but to whom can it be communicated in this primary form? Only to someone in the same position as the agent. Then communicating it is giving advice. But in practical life, arguments are not communicated only in order to bring others into the same practical position as oneself. Nor are others interested only with that in view.

"The scientist's followers are chiefly interested in external nature . . . but the practical agent's fellows are interested in *him* as a moral agent and in his action as issuing from one who is expected to take responsibility. This is not the deliberator's immediate interest; as such he is more concerned with solving the practical problem than with what the solution says about *him.* But he is also an essentially moral and social being, dependent for his development and well-functioning on the interest in him as such by others of his kind; thus it is natural even to the deliberator himself to see his choice not merely as the yet-to-be determined answer to his own practical question . . . but also as externalised into a public phenomenon (an observable action) which he needs others to understand and which they cannot understand unless they know his reasons for it, reasons which explain more fully its direction and justify what can be publicly seen. Therefore the practical argument forged in deliberation naturally assumes the reverse form: the choice appears as conclusion, being for others an explanandum, and the practical problem . . . figures in explanatory premises."

13. There is a complication. In the first chapter I pointed to some examples where we shouldn't complain because someone chose a strategy that did not require virtue, such as Odysseus not acting temperately in resisting the Sirens by being tied up. Examples such as these certainly look like someone deciding not to act virtuously. In chapter 5 I will ask what in Aristotle is equivalent to the categorical nature of modern morality, so the discussion of this complication will have to wait until then. Being able to count on the virtuous person doesn't make him infallible. For a discussion, see Shane Drefcinski, "Aristotle's Fallible Phronimos," *Ancient Philosophy* 16 (1996): 146–53.

14. Whether *technē* is a virtue is not a simple question. Aristotle says that it is one of the "states in which the soul grasps the truth in its affirmations and denials" (*NE* VI.3.1139b15–16). Therefore it should be a good condition of one part of the soul. And it produces good results. On the other hand, of the things mentioned in Book VI, only *phronēsis* and *sophia* are explicitly called virtues.

15. Passion here does not have the logical or metaphysical meaning of being acted upon—passion is one of the ten categories in the *Categories*—or of affective quality, like the passions which are one type, alongside *dynameis* and *hexeis*, within the category of quality. For details on passion taken metaphysically and ethically, see Amélie Rorty, "Aristotle on the Metaphysical Status of Pathe," *Review of Metaphysics* 38 (1984): 521–46. Aquinas notes the connection between persuasion and the fact that action, while always a response to an external object of desire, is voluntary. "The proximate moving cause of the will is the apprehended good, which is its object, and the will is moved by it as sight is by color. Therefore no created substance can move the will except by means of the apprehended good—in so far, namely, as it shows that a particular thing is good to do; and this is *to persuade*. Therefore no created substance can act on the will, or cause our choice, except by way of persuasion." *Summa Contra Gentiles*, III, chap. 88. Similarly, there is nothing specifically moral about *hexis* in *Met*. V.20.1022b10–12: "A *hexis* also means a disposition in virtue of which the thing disposed is well or ill disposed, either in itself or with respect to something else—e.g., health is a kind of *hexis*, for it such a disposition." Fortenbaugh, 1969, 178, n. 3: "There is, of course, a general usage of pathos such that all psychic phenomena may come under the label of pathos. See *De An*. 430a3, 409b15. . . . It is not with pathe in this wide sense that moral virtue is concerned but rather with that class of psychic phenomena which Plato had distinguished from itches and tickles, hungers and thirsts (*Phil*. 47e1–2) and which Aristotle distinguished from dynameis and hexeis and explained by means of an illustrative enumeration (*NE* 1105b21–23). There are still wider meanings found in the Categories, first of passion as one of the categories and in addition as one, along with shape, dynameis and hexeis, of the kinds of quality. Neither of those is at work here either."

16. Since this text is so important to my understanding of the *Ethics*, I need to point out that Rackham's "twofold effect" is an overtranslation. It is such a useful phrase that I will continue to use it. Irwin translates it this way: "Every virtue causes its possessors to be in a good state and to perform their functions well." Barnes's revision of Ross renders it: "Every excellence both brings into good condition the thing of which it is the excellence and makes the work of that thing be done well." *The Complete Works of Aristotle: The Revised Oxford Translation*, trans. W. D. Ross, rev. Jonathan Barnes (Princeton: Princeton University Press, 1984). Tricot has: "Toute 'vertu,' pour la chose don't elle est 'vertu,' a pour effet à la fois de mettre cette chose en *bon* état et de lui permettre de *bien* accomplir son oeuvre propre." Rowe says: "One should say that every excellence, whatever it is an excellence of, both gives that thing the finish of a good condition and makes it perform its function well." Broadie's commentary sees the double claim as a trivial one. "Since excellence *is* the good condition,

236 • Notes to Pages 63–68

not a distinct source of it, excellence 'gives' it something only in a logical sense ('having only three angles gives this figure triangularity'); similarly for 'the eye's/horse's excellence makes it excellent' (1106a17–20)." They seem to be trivially identical at *EE* II.1.1220a22–24. Irwin himself overtranslates at *NE* II.6.1107a8, signaling his own additions by brackets. "As far as its substance and the account stating its essence are concerned, virtue is a mean; but as far as the best [condition] and the good [result] are concerned, it is an extreme." See chap. 1, n. 1 for the translations of the *Ethics* mentioned in this note.

17. For more of such a trivial sense of virtue, see *Rh.* I.6.1362b, *Pol.* I.13.1259b10, 22–23, III.13.1283a37, *EE* II.1.1218b36–1219a5, *NE* I.12.1101b15–17, II.6. 1106a15–20, *Ph.* VII.3.246b6–10. Relating this meaning of virtue to the more narrowly ethical will be the subject of chapter 4.

18. "Praise is for virtue . . . encomia for deeds (*tōn ergōn*)" (*NE* I.12.1101b31–32). *Rh.* I.9.1367b: "Praise is language that sets forth greatness of virtue . . . but encomium deals with achievements (*tōn ergōn*)—all attendant circumstances, such as noble birth and education, merely conduct to persuasion; for it is probable that virtuous parents will have virtuous offspring and that a man will turn out as he has been brought up. Hence we pronounce an encomium upon those who have achieved something (*praxantas*). Achievements (*erga*) are signs of habits; for we should praise even a man who had not achieved anything, if we felt confident that he was likely to do so." See too *Cat.* 10b7–9, *EE* II.1.1219b16–17.

19. John Cooper, *Reason and Human Good in Aristotle* (Cambridge, Mass.: Harvard University Press, 1975), 145, n. 2: "The biological function of the soul . . . seems much too weak a basis on which to establish a conception of human flourishing. For just as a knife's excellence guarantees only efficient cutting, and does not control whether the product it helps to produce will be good or not, so (on Aristotle's analogy here) the soul's excellence ought only to ensure abundant vitality and ought not to determine the goodness or badness (satisfactoriness or the opposite) of what is made of this vitality." See too Gary Watson, "On the Primacy of Character," in Daniel Statman, ed., *Virtue Ethics* (Washington: Georgetown University Press, 1997), 67: "Many of our modern suspicions can be put in the form of a dilemma. Either the theory's pivotal account of human nature (or characteristic human life) will be morally indeterminate, or it will not be objectively well founded. At best, an objectively well founded theory of human nature would support evaluations of the kind that we can make about tigers—that this one is a good or bad specimen, that that behavior is abnormal. These judgments might be part of a theory of *health,* but our conception of morality resists the analogy with health, the reduction of evil to defect. (This resistance has something to do, I suspect, with a conception of free will that resists all forms of naturalism.)"

20. There are many praiseworthy *ēthē* that are not virtues because they are "means, but towards emotions (*mesotētes pathētikai*)" (*EE* III.7.1234a24). None of these emotional means, however praiseworthy, is a virtue, because they are without *prohairesis.* Because they are natural (*to physika*) they contribute to natural virtues. True virtues differ from natural virtues because they are *meta phronēsis.* In addition, the list of the virtues and vices in the *EE* contains another hint that there is something far from trivial in the claim that the virtues are themselves means as well as aiming at means. Justice is not listed as a mean, but the just is. The just (*dikaion*) is a mean between gain and disadvantage (*EE* II.2.1221a4; see Plato, *Republic* 359a). But it does not follow that justice is a mean. And that list in the *EE* also contains the claim that *phronēsis* is a mean between "unscrupulousness" and "unworldliness," a suggestion that Aristotle does not follow up. Generally, *mesotēs* refers to the mean state of character and *to meson* to actions that lie between extremes. There are exceptions, where *mesotēs* refers to actions: *NE* II.2.1104a25–27, II.6.1106b11–12, *EE* II.10.1227b8–9, III.6.1233a36–38. I am grateful to Dan Devereux for the complication.

21. There is a huge contemporary literature on whether belief is voluntary. See, for one seminal example, Bernard Williams, "Deciding to Believe," in *Problems of the Self: Philosophical Papers, 1956–1972* (Cambridge: Cambridge University Press, 1973), 136–51.

22. For more on the difference between reasoning and using reasoning, see chapter 2 of *For the Sake of Argument: Practical Reasoning, Character and the Ethics of Belief.*

## Chapter Three

1. See Michelle Gellrich, *Tragedy and Theory: The Problem of Conflict Since Aristotle* (Princeton: Princeton University Press, 1988). I am not going to argue here against the imputation of tragedy, moral luck, and moral conflict to Aristotle. I want instead to present what I see as his own sense of the main barriers to human flourishing. I do in fact think that the discovery of Aristotle's anticipations of our own moral concerns is mistaken. Tragedy and moral luck both come from apolitical conceptions of morality that worry about theodicy, while the interest in moral conflict is a function of the belief-desire model of practical reason, with its own interpretations of the practical syllogism and deliberation. Theodicy might be an issue raised in some Greek tragedies, but not in Aristotle's own treatment of them or of ethics. Theodicy has no place because, as I will argue in chapter 5, there is no extrapolitical measure of desert. "There is no call whatever to think that Aristotle made a *special point* of either denying or asserting the existence of conflicts within ethical virtue. . . . Most of the time . . . his attitude towards question about conflicts among ethical virtues seems to be one of indifference." Nicholas White, *Individual and Conflict in Greek Ethics* (Oxford: Clarendon Press, 2002), 239. See also Julia Annas, "Ancient Ethics and Modern Morality," *Philosophical Perspectives* 6 (1992): 126: "It is certainly true that in some ancient texts we find reflected a belief in 'moral luck'—in tragedy, for example. But it is striking that we do not find it in ancient moral *theory*. The main reason for this seems to be that ancient moral theory is centrally concerned with the virtues."

2. *NE* I.4.1095a1–3: "Each person judges well what he knows, and is a good judge about that; hence the good judge in a particular area is the person educated in that area. . . . This is why a youth is not a suitable student of political science; for he lacks experience of the actions in life which political science argues from and about." Also *NE* I.4.1096b7–8: "The *archē* is the fact that a thing is so (*to hoti*); if this be satisfactorily ascertained, there will be no need also to know the reason why it is so." And *NE* I.7.1098a34–b3: "Nor again must we in all matters alike demand an explanation (*aitia*) of the reason why things are what they are, in some cases it is enough if the fact (*to hoti*) that they are so is satisfactorily established. This is the case with principles; and the fact is the primary thing—it *is* a first principle." See also *An. Post.* II.2.90a24–29: "That the object of our inquiry is the middle term can be clearly seen in cases where the middle term is perceptible by the senses. We ask our question when we have not yet perceived whether there is a middle term or not, e.g., in the case of an eclipse. If we were on the moon, we should ask neither whether nor why it was taking place; the answers to both questions would be simultaneously obvious, because from the act of perception we should be able to apprehend the universal."

But see *EE* I.6.1216b35–37: "The political man should also not regard as irrelevant the inquiry that makes clear not only the *that*, but also the *why*. For that way of proceeding is the philosopher's way in every discipline." And for the relation between knowing and knowing that we know, see *NE* IX.10.1170a26–34, *De An.* III.2.425b12–25, *De Somno* 2.455a15.

3. The distinction between individual and historical-political causes of success and failure has also been drawn by Michael Slote, "Is Virtue Possible?" *Analysis* 42 (1982): 70–76, reprinted in *The Virtues: Contemporary Essays on Moral Character,* ed. Robert B. Kruschwitz and Robert C. Roberts (Belmont Calif.: Wadsworth, 1987), 100–105. The section on friendship contains the closest Aristotle comes to addressing things like moral conflict and moral dilemmas, precisely because friendship, unlike virtue, demands a treatment that looks at the individual agent rather than the structure of practices (e.g., *NE* IX.2.1164b23–29). The discussion of friendship supplements that of virtue just as a complete account of individual moral failure would complement this treatment of more structural sorts of failures.

Of course on many conceptions of tragedy, the tragic hero, or tragic situation might represent the universal human condition, but Aristotle's location of the genesis of tragedy in a mistake by an individual makes tragedy, although more philosophical than history, not a source of such generalizations. Although tragedy is the imitation of a serious action, it is not the imitation of tragic actions. Tragedy is a term restricted to works of art. Tragic imitations are not imitations of tragedies.

4. Compare *De An.* II.3.414b20–22, along with II.2.413a22, for the need for species of psychic functioning rather than a single definition of soul. Sarah W. Broadie, "Nature and Craft in Aristotelian Teleology," *Biologie, Logique, et Métaphysique Chez Aristote,* ed. Daniel Devereux and Pierre Pellegrin (Paris: Éditions du CNRS, 1990), 396: "The world of craft is divided into craftsmen of *various kinds,* each qua craftsman seriously dedicated to his own specialty. So it is with the world of natural substances. For each individual there is the circumscribed end proper to its specific definable essence, and for each an equivalently circumscribed range of means. There are no amateurs here, or dilettanti." See too Michael J. Loux, "Aristotle on Matter, Form, and Ontological Strategy," *Ancient Philosophy* 25 (2005): 81–124.

5. Alasdair MacIntyre, "A Partial Response to My Critics," in *After MacIntyre: Critical Perspectives on the Work of Alasdair MacIntyre,* ed. John Horton and Susan Menus (Notre Dame: University of Notre Dame Press, 1994), 283–304, at 284.

6. I criticize MacIntyre for assimilating arts and virtues under his idea of practices in "The Human Function and Aristotle's Art of Rhetoric," *History of Philosophy Quarterly* 6 (1989): 133–46.

7. *Pace* John Cooper, "Aristotle on the Goods of Fortune," *Philosophical Review* 94 (1985): 177–91. For the place of external goods in happiness, see too *Rhetoric* I.5. 1360b19–29.

8. So Aristotle explains in lines reminiscent of the *Symposium:* "The proper method of proving the good itself is the contrary of the method now adopted. At present it is from things not admitted to possess goodness that they prove the things admitted to be good, for instance, they prove from numbers that justice and health are good. . . . But the proper method is to start from things admitted to be good, for instance, health, strength, sobriety of mind, and prove that beauty is present even more in the unchanging; for all these admitted goods consist in order and rest, and therefore, if that is so, the things unchanging are good in an even greater degree, for they possess order and rest in a greater degree" (*EE* I.8.1218a17–24).

9. Herodotus, *The History,* trans. David Grene (Chicago: University of Chicago Press, 1987), I.33. This is also the theme of Jonathan Shay, *Achilles in Vietnam: Combat Trauma and the Undoing of Character* (New York: Atheneum, 1994). Paul Rahe, "The Primacy of Politics in Classical Greece," *American Historical Review* 89 (1984): 265–93 at 272 quotes a Euripedean fragment that says: "The race of slaves is ignoble (*kakon*). They observe everything from the perspective of the stomach." The reference is to Euripides fr. 49 (Hauck²).

10. See, similarly, Xenophon, *Memorabilia* 1.3.3: "Life would not be worth living for human beings if what came from the wicked were more gratifying to the gods than what came from the good."

11. Edward Morgan, *Inventing the People: The Rise of Popular Sovereignty in England and America* (New York and London: W. W. Norton, 1988, 306): "The word 'leader' is old, but 'leader*ship*' was a term that no one seems to have felt a need for as long as the qualities it designates remained an adjunct of social superiority. The decline of deference and the emergence of leadership signaled the beginnings not only of a new rhetoric but of a new mode of social relations and a new way of determining who should stand among the few to govern the many. It signaled not only the rise of the professional politician and the religious hero but the vulnerability of any institution that denied the equality in which men and women had been created."

12. In *Politics* I Aristotle lists master/slave, marriage, and parenting as the three relationships constituting the household. He talks about the science of mastery and says that mastery is more a matter of character than knowledge (I.7.1255b21). However, he never considers that issue for either being a spouse or a parent.

For a further example, in Ronald Dworkin, *Law's Empire* (Cambridge, Mass.: Harvard University Press, 1986), Dworkin uses "courtesy" as the paradigm for a practice. Courtesy is neither a virtue nor a skill. There are standards of excellence for courtesy. It is a practice with a purpose. It is, as Dworkin says, possible to be reflective about courtesy. Even so, courtesy, like leadership, does not fit Aristotle's criteria for arts and virtues.

13. "It is possible to create [urbanities and well-liked expressions] by natural talent or practice, but to show what they are belongs to the art of rhetoric" (*Rh.* III.10.1410b7–8).

14. The "virtues stand in a different relationship to external and to internal goods. The possession of the virtues—and not only their semblance and simulacra—is necessary to achieve the latter; yet the possession of the virtues may perfectly well hinder us in achieving external goods." Alasdair MacIntyre, *After Virtue: A Study in Moral Theory* (Notre Dame, Ind.: University of Notre Dame Press, 1984), 196. For a version of virtue as contrary to nature giving rise to a modern sense of moral failure, see Charles Taylor's account of Locke's "hyper-Augustinianism." Charles Taylor, *Sources of the Self: The Making of the Modern Identity* (Cambridge, Mass.: Harvard University Press, 1989), 248: "God's law is doubly external to us fallen creatures. First, we cannot identify the good with the bent of our own natures; we have rather to discover what God's sovereign decrees are in relations to us (although Locke thought that the actual tendency of our nature to preservation gives us a shrewd hint about God's intentions . . . ). And second, this law runs against the grain of our depraved wills. It has to be imposed on an unwilling nature, if it is to be followed at all, until we are fully sanctified by grace."

15. "It often happens that purity of purpose is in inverse ratio to the goodness of the cause, and that candor and honesty are perhaps more likely to be found among the assailants [of God, freedom and immortality] than among its defenders." Kant, *Critique of Pure Reason*, B778. Commenting on what happens to Philoctetes, and why Sophocles' play is a tragedy, James L. Kastely comments: "In an environment that does not properly nurture heroic virtue, that virtue does not simply disappear but rather becomes distorted, and energy that might have been directed to a common good is instead diverted into an intractable private hatred that makes the recovery of a noble public existence even more difficult." *Rethinking the Rhetorical Tradition: From Plato to Postmodernism* (New Haven: Yale University Press, 1997), 100.

16. Lenn Goodman, *On Justice* (New Haven: Yale University Press, 1991), 154: "It is not true that in all possible worlds actions would have consequences; nor it is true that in all causal worlds the consequences of actions would be such as to visit good or ill, wisdom or unwisdom of an act upon the agent. For beings might be insulated so as to be capable of inflicting evils they did not reap, or they might suffer only capriciously or accidentally." See also Robert Audi, "The State, The Church, and the Citizen," in *Religion and Contemporary Liberalism*, ed. Paul J. Weithman (Notre Dame, Ind.: University of Notre Dame Press, 1997), 49, for a similar comment on what the world must be like for religion to be a moral teacher: "If God has created an ambiguous world in which evil looms so large that even many theists are tempted to conclude that this sorry world could not have been created by *God*, it would seem possible that there is no secular path to moral truths. But it is one thing for God to test us and provide conditions for our freely choosing to become children of God; it is quite another thing to make it virtually impossible for those who do not so choose, even to be moral in non-theological matters." Thus Luther says that "the whole Aristotelian ethic is grace's worst enemy." Quoted in Joseph Owens, *Some Philosophical Issues in Moral Matters: The Collected Ethical Writings of Joseph Owens*, ed. Dennis J. Billy and Terence Kennedy (Rome: Editiones Academiae Alphonsianae, 1996), 43, n. 18.

17. Charles L. Black Jr., *The Humane Imagination* (Woodbridge, Conn.: Ox Bow Press, 1986), 29.

18. H. Jefferson Powell, *The Moral Tradition of American Constitutionalism: A Theological Interpretation* (Durham and London: Duke University Press, 1993), 119. See too Thomas C. Grey, "Cover Blindness," in *Prejudical Appearances: The Logic of American Antidiscrimination Law*, ed. Robert C. Post et al. (Durham and London: Duke University Press, 2001), 85–98, at 95. Within our "legal practices is a complex of traditions that constitute the political ideal we call 'the rule of law,' the notion that coercive state power should be limited so that we may have a government of laws. . . . When the set of traditions constituting the rule of law create barriers to our most worthy strivings for social change, we are likely to condemn them as 'legalism.' Legalism and the rule of law are not easily separated from each other, perhaps because they are two sides of the same coin."

19. Jeremy Waldron, "Humility and the Curse of Injustice," in *Race and Representation: Affirmative Action*, ed. Robert Post and Michael Rogin (New York: Zone Books, 1998), 388.

20. See Locke's similar remark: "Whoever goes beyond this measure of assent [i.e., entertaining a proposition with the degree of assurance that the proofs on which it is built warrant], it is plain receives not truth in the love of it, loves not truth for truth sake, but for some other by-end." *Essay concerning Human Understanding,* ed. Peter H. Nidditch (Oxford: Oxford University Press, 1975), 4.19.1, p. 697.

21. Georg Henrik von Wright, *The Varieties of Goodness* (New York: Routledge and Kegan Paul, 1963), 148. "The course of action, which is the virtuous man's choice in the particular case, is not necessarily that which we call *a virtuous act* or *an act of virtue*. A man of courage, for example, may sometimes rightly choose to retreat from danger rather than to fight it. . . . Such choices, however, do not terminate in acts called after the virtues. To retreat from danger is never an act of courage. . . . [This] shows a new sense in which a virtue is an 'inward' trait of character rather than an 'outward' feature of conduct. The *right choice* in a situation, when a virtue is involved, need not be the choice of a so-called *virtuous act.*" See Charles Young, "Aristotle on Liberality," *Boston Area Colloquium on Ancient Philosophy* 10 (1994): 317, n.9: "We may distinguish between actions that express a given virtue and actions that one would expect from someone who has that virtue: Thus one would expect a courageous person to behave well in a prisoner of war camp, even though on Aristotle's official account of courage such behavior is not itself courageous."

22. MacIntyre, *After Virtue,* 215: "In a society where there is no longer a shared conception of the community's good as specified by the good for man, there can no longer either be any very substantial concept of what it is to contribute more or less to the achievement of that good. Hence notions of desert and honor become detached from the context in which they were originally at home. Honor becomes nothing more than a badge of aristocratic status, and status itself . . . has very little to do with desert."

23. Hannah Arendt, *The Human Condition* (Chicago: University of Chicago Press, 1958, rpt. Garden City, New York: Anchor Books, 1959), 159.

24. For details of such an indictment, see Anthony Kronman, *The Lost Lawyer: Failing Ideals of the Legal Profession* (Cambridge, Mass., and London: Harvard University Press, 1993). To continue the case of Machiavelli, without a polis to make evident the connections between being good and doing well, Machiavelli's student must learn virtue and *phronēsis* from history instead.

25. "The honor of combat consists in rivalry of heart and not of expertise; that is why I have seen of some of my friends who are past masters in [fencing] choosing for their duels weapons which deprived them of the means of exploiting their advantage and which depend entirely on fortune and steadfastness, so that nobody could attribute their victory to their fencing rather than to their valor." Montaigne, *The Complete Essays of Montaigne,* trans. Donald M. Frame (Stanford: Stanford University Press, 1958), 2.27, p. 527.

"Those who praise or blame do not consider whether someone has done actions that are advantageous or harmful [to himself] but often they include it even as a source of praise that he did what was honorable without regard to the cost to himself" (*Rh.* I.3.1358b38–1359a2). See too *NE* IV.3.1125a11–12, X.7.1177b1–4, *Pol.* II.5.1273a21–38, VII.9. 1329a30–33, VIII.3.1338b2, and the description of the young man in *Rh.* II.3. David Landes, *The Wealth and Poverty of Nations: Why Some Are So Rich and Some So Poor* (New York and London: W. W. Norton, 1998), 235: "Idealism is the affectation of those who feel they have less than they deserve in the presence of those who have more." Jean-Jacques Rousseau, *Emile, or On Education,* trans. Allan Bloom (New York: Basic Books, 1979), 186: "There is a public esteem attached to the different arts in inverse proportion to their real utility. This esteem is calculated directly on the basis of their very uselessness, and this is the way it ought to be. The most useful arts are those which earn the least, because the number of workers is proportioned to men's needs, and work necessary to everybody must remain at a price the poor man can pay. On the other hand, these important fellows who are called artists instead of artisans, and who work solely for the idle and the rich, set an arbitrary price on their baubles. Since the merit of these vain works exists only in opinion, their very price constitutes a part of that merit, and they are esteemed in proportion to what they cost. The importance given them by the rich does not come from their use but from the fact that the poor cannot afford them."

26. Learned Hand, "On Receiving an Honorary Degree," in *The Spirit of Liberty*, 3d ed., ed. Irving Dillard (Phoenix, 1960), 138, quoted in Philip B. Kurland, "The True Wisdom of the Bill of Rights," in *The Bill of Rights in the Modern State*, ed. Geoffrey R. Stone, Richard A. Epstein, and Cass. R. Sunstein (Chicago: University of Chicago Press, 1992), 8. I cannot resist offer another quotation to match that of Hand's from Philippa Foot, "Moral Realism and Moral Dilemma," *Journal of Philosophy* 80 (1983): 379. "The far more difficult thought is that [a person] can only become good in one way by being bad in another, as if e.g., he could only rein in his ruthless desires at the cost of a deep malice against himself and the world. Or as if a kind of dull rigidity were the price of refusing to do what he himself wants at all costs."

27. For similar reasons, there is no pathway from the friendships of utility and pleasure to virtue friendship. The only way to be part of a virtue friendship is to be virtuous and to have a friendly relationship with another virtuous person. Doing as well as possible at a friendship of utility or pleasure will not help us to approach virtue friendship.

28. Kant, "Observations on the Feeling of the Beautiful and Sublime," excerpted in Isaac Kramnick, ed., *The Portable Enlightenment Reader* (London: Penguin, 1995), 341.

29. Benjamin Constant, "Principles of Politics," in *Political Writings*, trans. and ed. Biancamaria Fontana (Cambridge, Cambridge University Press, 1988), 280. Compare: "It is very proper that in England, a good share of the produce of the earth should be appropriated to support certain families in affluence, to produce senators, sages, and heroes for the service and defense of the state; or in other words, that a great part of the rent should go to opulent nobility and gentry, who are to serve their country in Parliament, in the army, in the navy, in the departments of science and liberal professions. The leisure, independence and high ideals which the enjoyment of this rent affords has enabled them to raise Britain to pinnacles of glory. Long may they enjoy it. But in India that haughty spirit, independence and deep thought which the possession of great wealth sometimes give ought to be suppressed. They are directly averse to our power and interest. The nature of things, the past experience of all governments, renders it unnecessary to enlarge on this subject. We do not want generals, statesmen, and legislators; we want industrious husbandmen. If we wanted restless and ambitious spirits there are enough of them in Malabar to supply the whole peninsula." William Thackeray, *Madras Civil Servants* (London: Longman, Orme, Brown and Co., 1839), quoted in Robert Kanigel, *The Man Who Knew Infinity: A Life of the Genius Ramanujam* (New York: Charles Scribner's Sons, 1991), 64. Later Kanigel quotes the mathematician E. H. Neville as saying that Ramanujam "'entered the Presidency College in Madras to practice as a virtue that singleminded devotion to mathematics which had been a vice in Kumbakonam nine years earlier" (179).

30. Oliver Wendell Holmes Jr. articulated the idea of "living nobly in the law." But Holmes in saying this meant to deny a conflict between "professional ethics" and "personal ethics" and indeed between craft values and moral values. For Holmes, my third kind of moral failure does not exist. See Oliver Wendell Holmes Jr., *The Essential Holmes: Selections From the Letters, Speeches, Judicial Opinions, and Other Writings*, ed. with an introduction by Richard A. Posner (Chicago: University of Chicago Press, 1992), 79: "The rule of joy and the rule of duty seem to me all one. I confess that altruistic and cynically selfish talk seem to me about equally unreal. With all humility, I think 'Whatsoever thy hand findeth to do, do it with thy might,' infinitely more important than the vain attempt to love one's neighbor as one's self. If you want to hit a bird on the wing, you must have all your will in a focus, you must not be thinking about yourself, and, equally, you must not be thinking about your neighbor; you must be living in your eye on that bird. Every achievement is a bird on the wing." For an argument about the place of the skills and virtues of adversarial justice in a community, see David Luban, *Lawyers and Justice: An Ethical Study* (Princeton: Princeton University Press, 1988).

31. "With such a robust confidence both in the very existence of truths (in general and in ethical and political matters) and in the human capacity to reach them, Aristotle felt no

need to develop a substantive understanding of human nature to serve as the foundation for whatever conception of justice he might present." Troels Engberg-Pedersen, "Justice at a Distance—Less Foundational, More Naturalistic: A Reply to Pierre Aubenque," in *Aristotle and Moral Realism,* ed. Robert Heinaman (Boulder and San Francisco: Westview, 1995), 49. "There can be no conception of human function or human nature specified independently of the views of the practically wise, and no set of morally neutral desires whose satisfaction constitutes wellbeing for us." David Charles, "Aristotle and Modern Realism," in ibid., 137, n. 3.

32. Susan D. Collins, "Justice and the Dilemma of Moral Virtue," in *Aristotle and Modern Politics: The Persistence of Political Philosophy,* ed. Aristide Tessitore (Notre Dame, Ind.: University of Notre Dame Press, 2002), 122, formulates "the dilemma of moral virtue: as justice, it looks to the good of the community, and as virtue, it looks to the good of the virtuous individual, yet these are different ends and different perfections." When these are different ends and different perfections, we have the fourth kind of moral failure.

33. Benjamin Constant, "The Liberty of the Ancients Compared with that of the Moderns," in *Political Writings,* 308–28, at 313. Paul Rahe, "The Primacy of Politics in Classical Greece," *American Historical Review* 89 (1984): 265–93, at 266: "Benjamin Constant hinted at the source of our difficulty [in understanding Greek civic life] when he pointed out that modern circumstances deny us many of the pleasures associated with participation in public affairs while multiplying and invigorating those derived from attentiveness to matters lying outside the political realm. As the economy has expanded, shattering the relationship between *oikonomia* and the simple management of a household and its attached estate, the polity has contracted."

34. Constant, 315.

35. Constant, 317.

36. Tocqueville shows what happens to aristocratic virtues when they are no longer functional. Alexis de Tocqueville, *Democracy in America,* trans. Arthur Goldhammer (New York: Library of America, 2004), vol. 2, part 3, chap. 11, 703–4: "Nothing is more wretchedly corrupt than an aristocracy which retains its wealth when it has lost its power, and which still enjoys a vast deal of leisure after it is reduced to mere vulgar pastimes. The energetic passions and great conceptions which animated it heretofore leave it then; and nothing remains but a host of petty consuming vices, which cling about it like worms upon a carcass." Lee C. Bollinger, *The Tolerant Society: Freedom of Speech and Extremist Speech in America* (Oxford and New York: Oxford University Press, 1986), 238–39: "The ordering of the several virtues will vary from society to society, depending on the conditions prevailing. For a culture threatened by external aggression or bent on conquest, courage and honor will be the most prized. For a country like the United States, tolerance appears have to assumed a leading position. . . . The containment of belief, and the impulses associated with it, and of the fears of the thought processes of others, serves a variety of important social functions. To these might be added the consideration that a capitalist economic system requires a broad capacity for self-containment. . . . A strong capacity for tolerance is also required for a society with pervasive bureaucratic and professional systems. The performances of tasks within each of these sectors of society requires the ability to submerge the self. One's own values are not to be introduced into one's performance."

37. Alasdair MacIntyre, "After Virtue and Marxism," *Inquiry* 27 (1984): 252. When the relation of the virtues to happiness is an external one, everything about practical reason changes, starting with what is better known to us to what is better known as such, and so the relations among Aristotle's four questions that I use to structure this essay. Charles Taylor rightly expresses the internal relation between the virtues and happiness this way in "A Most Peculiar Institution," *World, Mind, and Ethics: Essays on the Ethical Philosophy of Bernard Williams,* ed. J. E. J. Altham and Ross Harrison (Cambridge: Cambridge University Press, 1995), 149: "Aristotle sees us pursuing a number of goods, and our conduct as exhibiting a number of different virtues. We can speak of a single 'complete good' (*teleion agathon*), because our condition if such that the disparate goods we seek have to be coherently combined in a single life, and in their right proportions. But the good life as a whole

does not stand to the partial goods as a basic reason. There is no asymmetrical conferral of their status as goods. A good life should include, *inter alia,* some contemplation, some participation in politics, a well-run household and family. These should figure in their right proportion. But we cannot say informatively that contemplation is a good because it figures in the good life. It is much more that this life is good because, in part, it includes contemplation. This drive towards unification, far from being an essential feature of morality, is rather a peculiar feature of modern moral philosophy."

### Chapter Four

1. Christine Korsgaard, "Aristotle on Function and Virtue," *History of Philosophy Quarterly* 3 (1986) 259–79, at 262.

2. For a historical account of how virtues become generally useful traits, see Charles Taylor, *Sources of the Self: The Making of the Modern Identity* (Cambridge, Mass.: Harvard University Press, 1989), 153: "Strength, firmness, resolution, control, these are the crucial qualities, a subset of the warrior-aristocratic virtues, but now internalized. They are not deployed in great deeds of military valor in public space, but rather in the inner domination of passion by thought. This explains the crucial place that Descartes gives to the motive of 'generosity.' This was the frequently used term of the central motive of the honour ethic. Although the word was already beginning to take on its modern meaning of open-handedness, it mainly referred to that strong sense of one's own worth and honour which pushed men to conquer their fears and baser desires and do great things. We might say that the generous man was a 'great soul' (cf. 'les grandes âmes' of the letter to Elizabeth), except that the term for this—'magnanimous'—has gone through an analogous slide since the seventeenth century towards its modern meaning; something like a being ready to forgive, to make allowances to others."

3. Jennifer Whiting, "Eudaimōnia, External Results, and Choosing Virtuous Actions for Themselves," *Philosophy and Phenomenological Research* 65 (2002): 270–90: "The virtuous agent performs generous actions for the sake of benefiting others; she does not benefit others for the sake of performing generous actions or even for the sake of exercising her generosity." See too Charles Larmore, *Les pratiques du moi* (Paris: Presses Universitaires de France, 2004), 209–10: "De l'intention de bien faire, on passe aisément à l'intention d'être bon. . . . L'homme courageux ne cherche pas à deployer son courage, pas plus que l'homme généreux ne s'applique à être généreux. Ceux qui agissent avec de telles intentions sont trop égocentriques pour être en mesure de manifester les vertus en question. Le courage consiste à soutenir une cause malgré le coût."

4. Oliver Wendell Holmes Jr., *The Essential Holmes: Selections From the Letters, Speeches, Judicial Opinions, and Other Writings,* ed. with an introduction by Richard A. Posner (Chicago and London: University of Chicago Press, 1992), 105. For a contemporary variation on the idea that someone may live nobly anywhere, even in the law, see Anthony T. Kronman, "Living in the Law," *University of Chicago Law Review* 54 (1987): 835–76.

5. Troels Engberg-Pedersen, *Aristotle's Theory of Moral Insight* (Oxford: Clarendon Press, 1983), 3: "*Praxeis* are often understood as identical with what we should call moral acts. This is false, I believe: *praxeis* form a wider class of acts, which *includes* Aristotelian moral acts, whether good or bad." Aristotle himself notes that there are other things, beyond the amusements mentioned in *NE* X.6 that are choiceworthy in themselves (e.g., *EE* VIII.3.1248b23–24, where the list includes honor, wealth, bodily excellences, goods of fortune, and capacities). See also *NE* V.2.6.1130b2–3, *Rh.* I.6.1362b9–23. See also David Depew, who in discussing *Politics* VII says that "if the political man is genuinely *right,* as Aristotle says he is, in holding that the best life for states as well as individuals is an active life, the term activity (*praxis*) must means something recognizably and genuinely active—and not just 'actualization.'" David Depew, "Politics, Music, and Contemplation in Aristotle's Ideal State," *A Companion to Aristotle's Politics,* ed. David Keyt and Fred D. Miller Jr. (Oxford and Cambridge, Mass.: Blackwell, 1991), 346–80, at 352.

6. In the first chapter I drew an analogy between Aristotle's practices with their internal ends and Lon Fuller's idea of the internal morality of law. H. L. A. Hart attacked Fuller by

raising the possibility of the internal "morality of poisoning." Hart wondered whether Fuller's principles were principles of efficiency, to which I would add principles of virtuosity, rather than of morality. H. L. A. Hart, Book Review, *Harvard Law Review* 78 (1965): 1286.

7. Michael Slote, "Law in Virtue Ethics," *Law and Philosophy* 14 (1995): 91–123, at 104: "Even if the better off do give to charity, they evince a less long-range and confident sense of having enough or more than enough, if they insist on always keeping the prerogative of charitable giving or non-giving in their own hands and, by contrast, a greater self-sufficiency if they are wiling to tie their own hands through legislation or constitutional provisions that mandate welfare benefits, progressive taxation, and the like."

8. To anticipate a possible objection: the philosophical significance of the phenomenon of *akrasia* for Aristotle lies precisely in the fact that the connection between reasoning well about what to do and feeling the right amount of some passion is a very tight connection, so tight that its separation is a puzzle.

9. Thomas Hobbes, *Leviathan,* ed. Richard Tuck (Cambridge: Cambridge University Press, 1991), 131.

10. Deborah K. W. Modrak, *Aristotle: The Power of Perception* (Chicago: University of Chicago Press, 1987), 140–41: "An emotion is a pleasure or a pain experienced with respect to a particular type of object under particular circumstances. Each type of emotion is defined in relation to its object and the circumstances of its occurrence. . . . Aristotle's strategy for dealing with emotions and desires of all sorts is to reduce them to the experience of pleasure or pain in relation to a particular object or situation and to treat the awareness of pleasure and pain as a kind of perceptual activity (cf. *De Anima* 431a12–14). . . . Since the object as presented is a component of the desire (there is no desiring without an object), the desire is itself a particular way of apprehending an object as well as an impulse to pursue or avoid that object." See also David Furley, "Self-Movers," first published in *Aristotle on Mind and the Senses,* ed. G. E. R. Lloyd, and G. E. L. Owen (Cambridge: Cambridge University Press, 1978), rpt. in *Essays on Aristotle's Ethics,* ed. Amelie O. Rorty (Berkeley and Los Angeles: University of California Press, 1980), 55–68.

11. Noticing that passions have objects, and that therefore the fulfillment of a passion is the *energeia* of the object, and not just a satisfying feeling regarding the passion, is a difference between James and Dewey. Diggins's analysis in *The Promise of Pragmatism* describes Dewey in terms I would use for talking about Aristotle. While James "maintained that inquiry arises from a state of psychological tension and culminates in a new state of belief, Dewey insisted that inquiry aims to alter not only mental states but actual conditions, and it does so by rendering an 'indeterminate situation' determinate in order to achieve not only emotional comfort but intelligent control. Unlike James, Dewey became interested in knowledge that could contribute to a public good and not only individual success; unlike Peirce, he saw the thinker moved to inquiry not only by an 'irritation of doubt' but also by an encounter with a 'problematic situation' whose resolution required cooperative effort." John Patrick Diggins, *The Promise of Pragmatism: Modernism and the Crisis of Knowledge and Authority* (Chicago: University of Chicago Press, 1994), 227. See Henry S. Richardson, "Desire and the Good in *de Anima,*" in *Essays on Aristotle's de Anima,* ed. Martha C. Nussbaum and Amélie Oksenberg Rorty (Oxford: Clarendon Press, 1992), 381–99, esp. 385.

12. See Anthony Duff, "Aristotelian Courage," *Ratio* 29 (1987) 2–15, at 12: "Our *pathe* embody our understanding of the good; the acquisition of practical wisdom is not a matter of subordinating our *pathe* to the dictates of a separate reason, but of so structuring and ordering them that they embody a concern for what is good and noble, not for what is evil and base. Our understanding of the good is not a function of pure practical reason, separate from our emotions; it is through coming to care for the right things, and to feel the appropriate kinds of emotion, that we come to understand what is good."

13. Many modern commentators do not take this narrowing seriously, and want, for example, to extend the scope of temperance, both in III and VII, to pleasures in general, instead of one subset of the pleasures of taste and touch, assimilating Aristotle's problem of incontinence to Plato's. But if the passionate material for the virtues does the work I have

been ascribing to it in Aristotle's argument, such an extension is far from innocent, and Aristotle's narrowing and broadening of the passions deserves more attention. For a more cautious sorting out of the role of temperance, not only as a limited virtue in Book III, but in the *Ethics* as a whole, see L. H. G. Greenwood, *Aristotle: Nicomachean Ethics, Book Six* (1909; rpt. New York: Arno Press, 1973), 53. "It is perhaps possible to distinguish two views of sophrosyne. . . . Sophrosyne may be regarded as that hexis in which a man never allows his moral action to be influenced either by desires of pleasure or by avoidance of pain: or it may be regarded as that hexis in which he takes pleasure and pain in the right things, at the right time, to the right amount, and so on. It is when looked at in the former way that sophrosyne bears its peculiar relation to phronesis, and so to moral virtue generally, including itself looked at in the latter way: and it is in the former way that it is looked at in this passage, 1140b11–20. It is then not a mean but an absolute state: not depending on phronesis, but securing room for the activity of phronesis. Viewed in the second way, sophrosyne simply takes its place along with the other moral virtues, is like the others a means state, is subject to the determination of the orthos logos, and refers more especially to the bodily pleasures and pains, whereas in the first view it seems to refer to all pleasures and pains. In the same way akolasia has the double meaning of 'consistent pleasure-seeking' (the absolute vice, opposed to the absolute virtue which is sophrosyne in the former sense, that which prevents the activity of phronesis and destroys all conception of the true end) and 'bodily intemperance' (one of the extremes corresponding to the meson which is sophrosyne in the latter sense)."

14. The distinction between the trivial way in which any desire is the *energeia* of the passion and the peculiar way in which only the desire equated with choice and following from the virtuous *hexis* is the *energeia* of the passion is elucidated in L. A. Kosman, "Aristotle's Definition of Motion," *Phronesis* 14 (1969): 40–62, at 58: "In the case of motion, the actuality, because it is the actuality of a potentiality toward some other entity, remains incompleted even in its actuality. But in the case of energeia proper, the actuality has no other end than itself. Consequently, in being actualized qua potentiality, it is at one and the same time actualized qua the actuality which that potentiality is a potentiality toward. There is, in other words, an entity in the case of motion which is intermediate, namely, the motion itself. But in the case of what I have called energization, what is analogous the motion is one and the same entity as what is analogous to the resultant state toward which the motion is directed. There is therefore, no distinction between actuality qua potential and qua the actuality of that potential."

15. Compare *Rh.* I.9.1367b5–6: "For if a person meets danger unnecessarily, he would be much more likely to do so where the danger is honorable." See Edward Halper, "The Unity of the Virtues in Aristotle," *Oxford Studies in Ancient Philosophy* 17 (1999): 115–43.

16. Anthony Kronman, "Practical Wisdom and Professional Character," *Social Philosophy and Policy* 4 (1986): 219: "A judicial decision which possess the property of suitability or fit has a self-strengthening integrity like that of a work of art. It is this relational property—and neither the outcome nor the argument of a case considered by itself—to which we are referring when we say that a decision is sensible or prudent or practically wise."

17. For further elaboration of the difference between these two kinds of regularities, which seem to me parallel to the difference between the dependability of the virtuous man and the predictability of the vicious one, see David Hull, "The Metaphysics of Evolution," *British Journal for the History of Science* 3 (1967): 309–37. In both the ethical and the biological cases, the regularities that are not *energeiai* in the full sense come from the dominance of the matter rather than form, and when I claim that in a vice such as cowardice it is not the passion whose actualization is courage, fear of death on noble circumstances, but a more general passion, death as such, one could also say that it is not proximate matter that is actualized but a more generic matter. See *Gen. An.* IV.1.766a18.

Parallel to my idea that only in the virtues are the potencies of the passions and nothing but them realized is the infallibility of the senses (*De An.* II.6.418a14–16). Later in the *De Anima* he instead says that the perception of proper objects is "true or rather subject to a minimum of error" (III.3.428b18, see 427b13, 428b25–30). Bolton explains the difference this way: Aristotle "means that, when our powers or capacities of perception are *absolutely in act,* our perceptions are always true. It is only when we do not happen to actualize completely our sense that our perceptions can be false." Imagination, "or thought in general or opinion," is not veridical in this way "even when they are fully actualized." See Robert Bolton, "Scepticism et véracité de la perception dans le *de Anima* et la *Métaphysique* d'Aristote," in *Corps et Âme: Sur le de Anima d'Aristote,* ed. Gilbert Romeyer Dherbey and Cristina Viano (Paris: Vrin, 1996), 295–330. The quotations are from 305 and 306. Translations are mine.

18. J. L. Ackrill, "Aristotle on Eudaimonia," *Proceedings of the British Academy* 60 (1974): 339–59, and reprinted in *Essays on Aristotle's Ethics,* ed. Rorty, 15–33, at 15, says that in Book VI Aristotle "recalls that moral virtue (or excellence of character) was defined as a mean determined by the rule or standard that the wise man would employ, and now says that this statement though true was not clear: we need also to discover what *is* the right rule and what *is* the standard that fixes it. Unfortunately he does not subsequently take up this question in any direct way." Since the history of ethics contains numerous attempts to say what the right rule is, we have sufficient evidence that Aristotle's "failure" might not be unfortunate.

19. Bernard Williams, *Moral Luck: Philosophical Papers 1973–1980* (Cambridge University Press, 1981), 18, talks about having "one thought too many." The idea that only the virtues are the *energeia* of the passions fits the claim in *Metaphysics* IX.9 that *energeia* is better than a *dynamis* (1051a4–5). If the vices were *energeiai* of the passions, this would be false.

20. On this point I think Kosman goes wrong: "Throughout his discussion of the moral virtues, and particularly in his earlier account of them in Book II, Aristotle makes clear that the activities for which virtues are dispositions are of two sorts, actions and feelings, *praxeis kai pathe.*" L. A. Kosman, "Being Properly Affected: Virtues and Feelings in Aristotle's Ethics," in *Essays on Aristotle's Ethics,* ed. Rorty, 103–16, at 104.

21. The potency/act distinction I am attributing to Aristotle here is in one respect parallel to that found in the practical syllogism. To oversimplify a great deal of the secondary literature—although perhaps not the text itself—the conclusion of a practical syllogism is an action. The reasoning does not represent an event prior to the action, but is the structure of the action itself. Still, in cases where there is a slip between cup and lip, where an intended action is prevented, either by internal or external interference, including the time not being right, and including *akrasia,* the practical syllogism can lead to a conclusion that is a decision rather than an action. Similarly here: the actual desire, or the actualization of the passions, is, in potentia, the good action, but there can be circumstances in which it is instead the decision rather than the actual act.

22. Kosman, "Being Properly Affected," 106: "Aristotle's claim that virtues are dispositions toward feeling as well as action can be seen, in light of our recognition that feelings are passions, to rest upon a theory of potentiality which recognizes the existence of passive as well as active powers." See also Richard McKeon, "Rhetoric and Poetic in Aristotle," in *Aristotle's Poetics and English Literature,* ed. Elder Olson (Chicago: University of Chicago Press, 1965), 226: "Habit may be defined in terms of the two pairs of distinctions thus far employed: it is midway between activity and power, partaking of certain aspects of both, and it is midway between action and suffering. Like power it is a cause of action, but unlike a power a habit is not productive of contrary results; like actuality it is the principle and end of actions, for habits are the result of prior activities that are in turn the principles from which actions originate."

23. I take the following remarks to be a gloss on this meaning of *atechnia:* "The condition that seems essential to judge a work as 'bad' is . . . not incomprehension but comprehending only too well, seeing *through* it; we perceive enough formal combination to account for the parts that the poet has assembled and failed to integrate, and we understand the extrinsic social and psychological pressures that have made him attempt much and achieve little." Paul Goodman, *The Structure of Literature* (Chicago: University of Chicago Press, 1954), 11.

24. See also *Pol.* V.1.1301a27, in which everyone makes a mistake about proportionate equality. "Not all errors are crimes or sins, but any crime or sin can be called 'error' (*hamar-*

*tia*) in Greek." K. J. Dover, *Greek Popular Morality in the Time of Plato and Aristotle* (Oxford, 1974), 152, quoted in Stephen Halliwell, *Aristotle's Poetics* (Chapel Hill: University of North Carolina Press, 1986), 220, n. 26. See too Halliwell's comment on the following page: "The word-group to which *hamartia* belongs not only carries . . . a wide range of meanings in Greek generally, but within Aristotle's own ethical philosophy covers virtually the whole gamut of moral failure and error, from voluntary wickedness at one extreme to innocent mistakes at the other." See too Richard Sorabji, *Necessity, Cause and Blame* (Ithaca, N.Y.: Cornell University Press, 1980), and Elizabeth Belfiore, *Tragic Pleasures: Aristotle on Plot and Emotion* (Princeton: Princeton University Press, 1992), esp. 166–70.

25. See John M. Cooper, "Reason, Moral Virtue, and Moral Value," in *Rationality in Greek Thought,* ed., Michael Frede and Gisela Striker (Oxford: Clarendon Press, 1996), 81–114. Cooper notes that *boulesis* is a specifically rational form of desire, connected somehow to *thumos*. But, he argues, where *logos* and *phronēsis* aim at the good, and *epithumia* at pleasure, there is no special object for *thumos*. There is, though, a special object for the *thumos* of the good man, namely the noble, *to kalon*. See esp. 110: "Spirited desires in general are competitive in character; they aim at self-assertion as an agent, as a person to be taken serious practical account of, in comparison and in competition with other agents. It is for this reason that Plato in the *Republic* made victory or honour the immediate object of this kind of desire, parallel to pleasure (or money, the means of obtaining it) as object of appetitive desires, as such. But we have seen evidence that Aristotle refused to follow him in this. So far as I can see, Aristotle nowhere offers a replacement for Plato's rejected specification(s) as to the objects of spirited desires in general. My suggestion is not that Aristotle proposes the noble or fine or beautiful as the immediate object of spirited desires in general—for such desires of non-human animals, or children, or even all adult human beings. It is only for the ethically virtuous person, and only after a certain stage is reached on the special course of moral development and self-discipline that leads a person to the possession of virtues of character, that I want to claim that this is Aristotle's view." Other considerations of *thumos* appear in Laurence Berns, "Spiritedness in Ethics and Politics: a Study in Aristotelian Psychology," *Interpretation* 12 (1984): 334–48, W. V. Harris, *Restraining Rage: The Ideology of Anger Control in Classical Antiquity* (Cambridge, Mass.: Harvard University Press, 2001), and Barbara Koziak, *Retrieving Political Emotion: Thumos, Aristotle, and Gender* (University Park: Penn State University Press, 2000).

26. Some of the difficulties with the meaning of *thumos* are indicated in Angela Hobbs, *Plato and the Hero: Courage, Manliness and the Impersonal Good* (Cambridge: Cambridge University Press, 2000), 3: "At first sight the *thumos* of the *Republic* seems one of the more bizarre creations of an already bizarrely creative period in Plato's life. At different points it is connected with a very wide range of characteristics, not all of which obviously cohere: anger, aggression and courage; self-disgust and shame; a sense of justice, indignation and the desire for revenge; obedience to the political authorities though not necessarily to one's father; a longing for honor, glory and worldly success; some interest in the arts but a fear of intellectualism; a preference for war over peace and increasing meanness over money." See also P. A. Vander Waerdt, "The Political Intention of Aristotle's Moral Philosophy," *Ancient Philosophy* 5 (1985): 83, where he says that Aristotle's "account of moral education in the *EN* abstracts from the forms of regime and from the natural role of thumos in education—from the political face of virtue, as it were." In Christian moral psychology, to oversimplify, *thumos* is replaced by the will as the supplement to reason and passion. In modern moral psychology, *thumos* is replaced as the supplement to reason and passion by interest. The virtues, especially temperance, are radically transformed under these newer psychologies.

Important reflections on the meaning and nature of *thumos* can be found in Jonathan Shay, *Odysseus in America: Combat Trauma and the Trials of Homecoming* (New York: Scribner, 2002). Discussions with Shay, as well as Betty Belfiore and David O'Connor, have helped me formulate the argument in this section.

27. Charles Taylor, *Sources of the Self,* 22: "With the decline of the specifically theological definition of the nature of a transformed will, a formulation of the crucial distinction of higher and lower in terms of altruism and selfishness comes to the fore."

28. W. V. Harris, *Restraining Rage,* 158: "Athenians seem to a large extent to have internalized the notion that their freedom would survive only if they were able to limit the action of their own passions, including especially their own anger. For there to be courage, there had to be *thumos,* spirit, passion, but on the other hand if there was too much *thumos*—anger, terrible civil conflict (*stasis*) was a likely consequence." That the human *thumos* realized in love for the noble is not the same as animal *thumos* is explicitly remarked at *Politics* VIII.3.1338b24–38 (cf. 1271a10–18):"Even the Spartans, although so long as they persisted by themselves in their laborious exercises they surpassed all other peoples, now fall behind others both in gymnastic and in military contests: for they used not to excel because they exercised their young men in this fashion but because they trained and their adversaries did not. Consequently honor and not animal ferocity (*to kalon all' ou to thēriōdes*) should play the first part; for it is not a wolf nor one of the other wild animals that will venture upon any noble hazard, but rather a good man. But those who let boys pursue these hard exercises too much and turn them out untrained in necessary things in real truth render them vulgar, making them available for statesmanship to use for one task only."

29. "The frequency with which speakers narrate feuds and disputes reveals not only that orators *were* usually *personally involved* in the case at bar, and not only that they felt *obliged to be personally* involved in the case at bar, but also, and more importantly, that they felt obliged *to show* their audiences that they were personally involved." D. S. Allen, "Angry Bees, Wasps, and Jurors: The Symbolic Politics of *orgē* in Athens," in *Ancient Anger: Perspectives from Homer to Galen,* ed. Susanna Braund and Glenn W. Most (Cambridge: Cambridge University Press, 2003), 76–98, at 80–81.

30. Michael Slote, "From Morality to Virtue," in *Virtue Ethics,* ed. Daniel Statman (Washington: Georgetown University Press, 1997), 128–44, suggests that self/other asymmetry in commonsense morality makes behavior in which an agent pointlessly sacrifices her own good "stupid, absurd, or irrational" but not vicious, while the same sacrifice would be vicious if it is another's good that is in question. "If one could easily *prevent* pain to another person, it is typically thought wrong not to do so, but not to avoid similar pain to oneself seems crazy or irrational, not morally wrong" (129).

31. "What is most opposed to pity is what people call being indignant; for it is in some way opposed to feeling pain at undeserved *misfortune* and, being pained at undeserved *good* fortune, arises from the same moral character, and both emotions are characteristic of a good character, for it is right to sympathize with and pity those who suffer undeservedly and to feel indignation at those who [undeservedly] fare well; for what takes place contrary to desert is unjust, and thus we attribute being indignant to the gods" (*Rh.* II.9.1386b9–16).

Alasdair MacIntyre, *Dependent Rational Animals: Why Human Beings Need the Virtues* (Chicago and LaSalle, IL: Open Court, 1999), 119: "Adam Smith's contrast between self-interested market behavior on the one hand and altruistic, benevolent behavior on the other, obscures from view just those types of activity in which the goods to be achieved are neither mine-rather-than-others' nor others'-rather-than-mine, but instead are goods that can only be mine insofar as they are also those of others, that are genuinely common goods. . . . If we need to act for the sake of such common goods, in order to achieve our flourishing as rational animals, then we also need to have transformed our initial desires in a way that enables us to recognize the inadequacy of any classification of desires as either egotistic or altruistic. The limitations and blindness of merely self-interested desire have been catalogued often enough. Those of a blandly generalized benevolence have received too little attention."

32. For important parts of this history, see Albert O. Hirschman, *The Passions and the Interests: Political Arguments for Capitalism Before Its Triumph* (Princeton: Princeton University Press, 1977), and Stephen Holmes, *Passions and Constraint: On the Theory of Liberal Democracy* (Chicago: University of Chicago Press, 1995). Locke still recognizes the importance of *thumos* even as liberalism, capitalism, and modern morality begin to denigrate it in favor of acquisitiveness: "Extravagant young fellows that have liveliness and spirit come sometimes to be set right, and so make able and great men; but *dejected* minds, timorous and tame, and *low spirits* are hardly ever to be raised and very seldom attain to anything." John Locke, *Some Thoughts concerning Education,* in *Some Thoughts concerning Education*

*and Of the Conduct of the Understanding,* ed. Ruth W. Grant and Nathan Tarcov (Indianapolis: Hackett, 1996), 33. Catherine H. Zuckert, "On the Role of Spiritedness in Politics," in *Understanding the Political Spirit: Philosophical Investigations from Socrates to Nietzsche,* ed. Catherine H. Zuckert (New Haven and London: Yale University Press, 1988), 18: "Where Aristotle sought to domesticate the desire for preeminence and conquest by attaching it primarily to love of one's own (constraining the scope or space in which the desire for preeminence is to operate), Locke attempts to civilize the tyrannical desire for gaining mastery over others by transforming it into the civil desire to have one's rights recognized by others." See too Michael Stocker, "Affectivity and Self-Concern: The Assumed Psychology of Aristotle's *Ethics,*" *Pacific Philosophical Quarterly* 64 (1983): 211–29.

## Chapter Five

1. Elizabeth Anscombe, "Modern Moral Philosophy," *Philosophy* 33 (1958): 1–19.

2. Daniel Statman, "Introduction to Virtue Ethics," in *Virtue Ethics,* ed. Daniel Statman (Washington: Georgetown University Press, 1997), 21: "According to most versions of VE [virtue ethics], act-appraisals are reducible to, or replaceable by, agent-appraisals, which means that actions are evaluated only as manifestations of character." For another example, see Gregory Trianosky, "What Is Virtue Ethics All About?" *American Philosophical Quarterly* 27 (1990): 335–46; reprinted in *Virtue Ethics,* ed. Statman, 43–44: "A pure ethics of virtue makes two claims. First it claims that at least some judgments about virtue can be validated independently of any appeal to judgments about the rightness of actions. In Plato's *Republic* for example it appears to be simply the harmonious order of the just person's psyche which makes it good, and not, say, its aptness to produce right actions. . . . Second, according to a pure ethics of virtue it is this antecedent goodness of traits which ultimately makes any right act right. For instance, Plato says that just actions are those which produce and maintain that harmonious condition of the psyche; and Aristotle might be read as saying that what one ought to do is what the virtuous person, or the person of practical wisdom, would do. In both these cases the rightness of action supervenes on some appropriate relation to what is antecedently established as virtue." I would have thought that this was an opportunity to contrast Plato and Aristotle. And one more statement about virtue ethics that I believe disqualifies Aristotle's *Ethics* from counting as an instance of it: Gary Watson, "On the Primacy of Character," in *Virtue Ethics,* ed. Statman, 64: "A concern for outcomes will be internal to certain virtues. For instance, the benevolent person will be concerned that others fare well. But the moral significance of this concern stems from the fact that it is part of virtue, not from the fact that misery and wellbeing are intrinsically or ultimately bad and good respectively. To put it another way, it will follow from an ethics of virtue that virtuous people care about certain things (and outcomes) for their own sakes (as final ends in themselves). There is no further commitment, however, to the idea that these concerns are virtuous ones because their objects are inherently valuable or desirable for their own sakes."

3. John Stuart Mill, *The Subjection of Women,* in *Essays on Politics and Society,* ed. J. M. Robson (Toronto: University of Toronto Press, 1977), chap. 2, 95.

4. Harry Frankfurt, "The Importance of What We Care About," *Synthese* 53 (1982): 257. For an earlier modern contrast, see Hobbes, *De Homine* 13:9: "All moral virtue is contained in [justice and charity]. However, the other three virtues (except for justice) that are called cardinal—courage, prudence, and temperance—are not virtues of citizens as citizens, but as men, as these virtues are useful not so much to the state as they are to those individual men who have them." Thomas Hobbes, *Man and Citizen: Thomas Hobbes' De Homine,* trans. Charles T. Wood, T. S. K. Scott-Craig, and Bernard Gert, and *De Cive,* trans. Thomas Hobbes, ed. Bernard Gert (Garden City, NY: Anchor Doubleday, 1972), 69. The expression "peculiar institution" applied to morality is from Bernard Williams, *Ethics and the Limits of Philosophy* (Cambridge, Mass.: Harvard University Press, 1985). Placing the good life outside morality has been a theme of the work of Charles Taylor. See, especially, *Sources of the Self: The Making of the Modern Identity* (Cambridge, Mass.: Harvard University Press, 1989).

5. For the idea that morality becomes one form of good among others, see, e.g., Kant, *Critique of Practical Reason,* trans. Lewis White Beck (Indianapolis: Bobbs-Merrill, 1956),

61–62 (*Kants gesammelte Schriften*, 23 vols., ed. the Prussian Academy of Sciences and the Berlin Academy of Sciences [Berlin: Reimer, 1900–1955], 5:59–60): "The German language has the good fortune to possess two very different concepts and equally different expressions for what the Latins named with the single word *bonum*. For *bonum*, it has *das Gute* and *das Wohl;* for *malum*, *das Böse* and *das Übel* or *das Weh*. Thus there are two very different judgments if in an action we have regard to its goodness or wickedness or to our weal or woe (*ill*)."

It is also a commonplace of the criticism of modern morality that privacy removes central parts of our lives from the reach of significant languages of assessment. See, e.g., Onora O'Neill, "Children's Rights and Children's Lives," *Ethics* 98 (1988): 445–63, at 450: "Liberal theorists who allow space for imperfect obligations but then allocate that space to the pursuit of personal preferences do not offer *any* account of imperfect obligations. It is no wonder that some of them characterize action that might traditionally have been thought a matter of (imperfect) obligation in jocularly trivializing terms, for example, as 'frightfully nice,' 'a matter of decency' or of being 'morally splendid.' Sometimes such action is seen as a matter of individual preference or style; sometimes it is promoted as supererogatory and so (once again) not obligatory. Recent rights-based thinking, whether libertarian or nonlibertarian, obscures the differences between mere expressions of individual style or preference, ordinary kinds of kindness and consideration which may (in a given context) be matters of imperfect obligation, and truly saintly or heroic action. Without an account of imperfect obligation all of these may seem no more than ways in which we have a right to act, since others' rights are not constraint." For a defense of the removal of goods from the reach of morality, see Susan Wolf, "Above and Below the Line of Duty," *Philosophical Topics* 14 (1986): 131–48. As one reader pointed out, this topos is arguably not the case for all modern moral theories; in particular some versions of consequentialist ethics leave nothing outside the sphere of morality.

Julia Annas, "Prudence and Morality in Ancient and Modern Ethics," *Ethics* 105 (1995): 242: "In ancient theories rational reflection on one's life as a whole leads the agent to reason morally, and no distinct competing role is left, within the theory, for prudential reasoning." For part of the story of how prudence becomes distinguished from morality, see my *Machiavelli and the History of Prudence* (Madison: University of Wisconsin Press, 1987).

6. David L. Norton, "Moral Minimalism and the Development of Moral Character," *Midwest Studies in Philosophy* 13 (1988): 183. See also 180: "Modern ethics is typically minimalist (a) with respect to the kinds of situations and choices that count as moral, and (b) in its conception of moral character, and . . . its minimalism in these respects removes from moral consideration factors that cannot be disregarded without the dilution of moral thought and moral life." See also John Dewey, *Human Nature and Conduct: An Introduction to Social Psychology* (New York: Modern Library, 1930), 4: "Morals cut off from positive roots in man's nature is bound to be mainly negative. Practical emphasis falls upon avoidance, escape of evil, upon not doing things, observing prohibitions." The connection between a morality of categorical requirements and a heterogeneous society is also remarked by William H. Simon, *The Practice of Justice: A Theory of Lawyers' Ethics* (Cambridge, Mass.: Harvard University Press, 1998), 72: "The choice between categorical and contextual norms turns most importantly on, first, the costs of discrepancy between a norm's prescriptions and its goals (high costs cut in favor of contextual norms), and second, confidence in the capacities for judgment of the people applying the norms (high confidence cuts in favor of contextual norms)."

7. Bernard Williams, *Ethics and the Limits of Philosophy*, 14.

8. I am going to use the contemporary topos of contrasting ancient vs. modern moral theory to concentrate on Aristotle, not on the ancients in general. In addition, I note that the ancient/modern contrast ignores many other, including intermediate, possibilities. For example, the demands of virtue are higher than the demands of justice and law-following. But the demands of ancient virtue are low compared to Machiavellian *virtù* battling and seducing *fortuna*. Greek ethical virtues may seem heroic to us, at least if we stop at the first virtue in Aristotle's list, courage, but in relation to Machiavelli, Aristotle's virtues are quite

routine. That is Nietzsche's point in seeing everything going downhill from Socrates and Jesus instead of making Hobbes or Kant the turning point as so many of the contrasts of ancient and modern do. Great philosophers such as Kant are too nuanced to fit simply into my contrasts, but my topoi still mark off the distance between Aristotle and most modern moral thought. The apolitical understanding of morality begins with the eclipse of the polis that Aristotle witnessed. See Alasdair MacIntyre, *A Short History of Ethics* (New York, Macmillan, 1966), 100: "In Greek society the focus of the moral life was the city-state; in the Hellenistic kingdoms and the Roman empire the sharp antithesis between the individual and the state is inescapable. The question now is not In what forms of social life can justice express itself? or What goods can I achieve as a private person? The human situation is such that the individual finds his moral environment in his place in the universe rather than in any social or political framework. . . . The individual who is situated in a well-organized and complex community, and who cannot but think of himself in terms of the life of that community, will have a rich stock of descriptions available to characterize himself, his wants, and his deprivations. The individual who asks, What do I desire, as a man, apart from all social ties, in the frame of the universe? is necessarily working with a meager stock of descriptions, with an impoverished view of his own nature, for he has had to strip away from himself all the attributes that belong to his social existence." For the contrast of ancient and modern, see Quentin Skinner, "Modernity and Disenchantment: Some Historical Reflections," in *Philosophy in an Age of Pluralism: The Philosophy of Charles Taylor in Question,* ed. James Tully (Cambridge: Cambridge University Press, 1994), 45: "It was obviously in the interest of aspiring absolutist rulers to insist that, as Hobbes puts it in *De cive,* a citizen's primary duties lie not in the public but entirely in the private and familiar spheres. The prize for winning this argument was to permit the concentration of more and more political power in fewer and fewer hands." And see the footnote to that passage: "Although [Hobbes's] book is entitled *The Citizen,* part of his aim is to show citizens that they ought to think of themselves as subjects." Along similar lines to the present inquiry, Peter Simpson, "Contemporary Virtue Ethics and Aristotle," *Review of Metaphysics* 45 (1992): 503–24, at 504, claims that this nonpolitical nature of contemporary virtue ethics makes it non-Aristotelian: "The work of Aristotle that is most used and referred to by these theorists is the *Nicomachean Ethics.* The *Politics* is seldom if ever mentioned. This is not because such theorists are unaware of the connection between the *Nicomachean Ethics* and the *Politics;* rather they do not pay it much attention."

9. Benjamin Constant, *Political Writings,* trans. and ed. Biancamaria Fontana (Cambridge: Cambridge University Press, 1988), 104.

10. *NE* I.3.1095a2–3, I.4.1095a4–17, 1095b4–6, I.9.1099b29–32, I.13.1102a7–9, 1102a18–21, II.3.1105a10–12, VII.11.1152b1–2, X.9.1179a33–118b23. For a useful argument that there is only one study, *hē politikē,* which studies both ethical and political matters, see Max Fisch, "Poliscraft," in *Philosophy and the Civilizing Arts,* ed. Craig Walton and John P. Anton (Athens: Ohio University Press, 1974), 24–48. One of the few writers I have found who sees that Aristotle's ethical virtues are political finds that a ground for criticizing Aristotle: "Obviously there is a strong moral element in Aristotle's theory of ethical virtue; but he did not succeed in distinguishing moral virtue as such, the virtue of a man as a man, from political virtue, the virtue of a citizen of a good city." Alan Donagan, *The Theory of Morality* (Chicago: University of Chicago Press, 1977), 4. On the other side Barker rightly says that the *Ethics* is "a treatise discussing the moral life of a *polites.*" Ernest Barker, *The Political Theory of Plato and Aristotle* (New York, Dover, 1959), 240. In *Rhetoric* I.2 Aristotle says that "the concern about character can justifiably be called political" (1356a26). Richard Bodéüs, *Le philosophe et la cité* (Paris: Les Belles Lettres, 1982), trans. as Richard Bodéüs, *The Political Dimensions of Aristotle's Ethics,* trans. Jan Edward Garrett (Albany, SUNY Press, 1993), 44–45: "One must observe that the principal moral virtues analyzed by the philosopher, even without considering justice and friendship, are essentially virtues of the public man. Courage, displayed in the dangers of war, is a virtue of the citizen-soldier and particularly of the military leader (who is a prudent person). Liberality and magnificence engage the noble citizen respectively in the domain of small expenses vis-à-vis his fellow citizens or his

friends and in the domain of great expenses for the benefit of the entire state, for example in the practice of the liturgies. . . . Honors, large or small, are also the subject of two virtues (magnanimity and an anonymous virtue, the just mean between ambition and the lack of ambition), which are virtues of the citizen who exercises a magistracy. Thus are thus the virtues only the politician can aspire to. Temperance and mildness—as well as other minor virtues 'concerned with conversations and interactions in common life' (truthfulness, humor and friendliness)—are no more virtues of the private person than the other virtues are; they attach to the citizen either in his life of leisure (let us think of the symposia!) or in the meetings or assemblies where, directly or indirectly, the affairs of state are discussed and negotiated."

11. Bernard Yack, *Problems of a Political Animal: Community, Justice, and Conflict in Aristotelian Political Thought* (Berkeley and Los Angeles: University of California Press, 1993), 168: "Although Aristotle seeks determinate and certain knowledge of the human good, he denies the existence of comparable standards of justice. As a result, he rejects a perfectionist understanding of human justice, even while advocating a perfectionist understanding of the human good. . . . [Aristotle] differs from modern defenders of liberal distinctions between the right and the good in thinking that it is standards of justice, rather than standards of goodness, that must be left indeterminate and open to a variety of interpretations."

12. Stuart Hampshire, "Two Theories of Morality," *Morality and Conflict* (Cambridge, Mass.: Harvard University Press, 1983), 43: "There have been changes both in knowledge and in ways of life, which have the effect of making Aristotle's construction of moral and particularly political thought seem incorrigibly incomplete. The succinct phrase for the barrier, and for the missing element, is the concept of freedom, which is applied in individual psychology and politics."

13. Alasdair MacIntyre, "Social Structures and Their Threats to Moral Agency," *Philosophy* 74 (1999): 315.

14. For important considerations of the connection between citizenship and sacrifice or risk, see Paul W. Kahn, "Speaking Law to Power: Popular Sovereignty, Human Rights, and the New International Order," *Chicago Journal of International Law* 1 (2000): 1–18, and idem, "Nuclear Weapons and the Rule of Law," *NYU Journal of International Law and Politics* 31 (1999): 349–415.

15. "Callipus was one of your citizens and, therefore, a man able to do both well and badly (*poiesai kakos*) to someone, while Cephisiades was a metic and was not able to do anything." Dem. 52.25, quoted in Danielle S. Allen, *The World of Prometheus: The Politics of Punishing in Democratic Athens* (Princeton: Princeton University Press, 2000), 108. See too *NE* VIII.14.1163b13: "This is how we should treat unequals. If we are benefited in virtue or in money, we should return honor, and thereby make what return we can. *For friendship seeks what is possible, not what corresponds to worth*, since that is impossible in some cases. e.g., with honor to gods and parents. For no one could ever make a return corresponding to their worth, but someone who attends to them as far as he is able seems to be a decent person."

16. For the difference between ancients and moderns on the self/other distinction, see Christopher Gill, "The Character-Personality Distinction," in *Characterization and Individuality in Greek Literature*, ed. Christopher Pelling (Oxford: Clarendon Press, 1990), 1–31, and idem, "The Question of Character and Personality in Greek Tragedy," *Poetics Today* 7 (1986): 251–73.

17. Thucydides describes as virtuous those who died of plague because they helped their friends and thereby got infected (*Peloponnesian War* 2.51.5). Aristotle is not then somehow relying on ordinary Greek usage of the time. See too Plato, *Laws* 1.646e–647b.

18. William Ian Miller, *The Mystery of Courage* (Cambridge, Mass.: Harvard University Press, 2000), 157–58: "I wonder if the modern philosophic discourse hasn't shifted courage from the grit of battle to primarily noncontentious settings, the dangers that threaten threaten abstractly or hypothetically; they aren't felt. Neither the dangers nor the fears they engender are sufficiently particularized. And they seldom involve facing off against another human being rather than against the weather; and though facing a hostile Mother Nature

surely requires courage, it does not do so in quite the same way as with fighting a human. Nature doesn't need courage to pose a threat to you; a human enemy, however, will be drawing on reserves of the same virtue you are drawing on, and one of the things that is being contested is who has the most of it. Being rash might be as helpful against a storm as against a human, but against only one of these adversaries will your rashness or prior reputation for it have an effect. A storm doesn't care one bit about your virtue. A human, though, will sit up and take notice when you burn your bridges, when you forgo, riskily, the ability to deliberate further."

19. For details on Aristotle's virtue of temperance, see Charles Young, "Aristotle on Temperance," *Philosophical Review* 97 (1988): 521–42. See also Joseph M. Bryant, *Moral Codes and Social Structure in Ancient Greece: A Sociology of Greek Ethics from Homer to the Epicureans and Stoics* (Albany: SUNY Press, 1996), 90–91: "The adoption of close-formation tactics coincides with a significant shift in the meaning of one of the major virtues in the Greek moral code, *sophrosune,* a word originally meaning 'prudence' and 'shrewdness of mind' but that henceforth came to mean 'self-control' and 'moderation'—precisely the traits a man hoped to find in the hoplites who stood beside him in the line, since it was their composure that literally shielded his life." Bryant gives a political reason Aristotle should put courage and temperance together.

20. Paul Kahn, *Law and Love: The Trials of King Lear* (New Haven: Yale University Press, 2000), 147: "Sacrifice is an affirmation to the other that the body continues to maintain the common meaning. To see sacrifice as only a burden or even an injury is to act as if the body has some meaning in and of itself. Sacrifice is the vehicle of transubstantiation by which the flesh takes on a meaning. A love or a state that cannot call upon its members for sacrifice has no historical presence. It is an idea without force in the world."

21. I suspect that some of the difficulty in seeing temperance as a virtue comes from a modern assumption that there are marked differences in temperament that make some of us more sensible to these pleasures than others, while Aristotle maintains that we are only praised and blamed for our habits. For Aristotle to make that claim, he must think that there are no moral differences among our natural endowments (e.g., *NE* III.4.1114a31–b25).

22. A sign of temperance's political nature comes from Aristotle's complaint that Socrates, when he makes the polis too much of a unity, destroys the virtues as well. "Those who make the city too much of a unity . . . eliminate temperance concerning women (it being a noble deed to abstain through temperance from a woman who belongs to another)" (*Pol.* II.5.1263b6–11).

23. James N. Davidson, *Courtesans and Fishcakes: The Consuming Passions of Classical Athens* (New York: St. Martin's, 1997), 142–43: "The Greeks, in contrast [to us], distinguished no special category of consumables as particularly open to abuse, but considered a fierce struggle against desire a normal state of affairs. They saw themselves as exposed to all kinds of powerful forces. The world's delights were lying in wait to ambush them around the next corner. The pleasures of the table, eels and fried tuna-steaks, fragrant wine, and above all human beauty naturally exerted a strong influence on all those who came within their gravitational field. There was not special mechanism at work to produce a particular addiction. People naturally wanted to indulge as much as possible in things that were enjoyable— the rhetoric of orators, the delights of theatrical spectacle, the pleasures of the flesh. This led to a prevailing model of addiction that looks like an exact inversion of our own. People who overindulged in something had not developed an abnormal dependency on it, driven by unique compulsions. It was simply that their capacity to resist the regular, natural, insistent pleasures of the world was lower. Compulsion was seen as a function of enjoyment."

24. At the start of chapter 3 I rejected the modern suggestion that Aristotle was concerned with moral luck. This picture of the ethical virtues concerned with inequality could be the beginning of an argument that shows the distance between Aristotle's ethics and ours. Thus I see no evidence at all for Aubenque's claim that the function of justice is to modify given inequalities: "The virtue of justice is not satisfied with a situation in which we are born furnished with goods or noble titles; or in which we benefit, thanks to the wealth or culture of our family, from an education which renders us capable of exercising 'honours,' i.e. politi-

cal functions; or in which, on the contrary, we are deprived of these advantages. By proposing to distribute these goods in an 'equal' fashion, the virtue of justice works in opposition to the chance inequalities that randomly result from our birth and social situation. The virtue of justice, as is said of Greek ethics in general, is a means for rationalizing chance and, thus, suppressing it up to a certain point." Pierre Aubenque, "The Twofold Natural Foundation of Justice According to Aristotle," in *Aristotle and Moral Realism,* ed. Robert Heinaman (Boulder and San Francisco: Westview, 1995), 36–37.

For one explanation of why *megaloprepia* is a difficult virtue, see Adam Smith, *Wealth of Nations,* III.ii.7: "It seldom happens . . . that a great proprietor is a great improver. . . . To improve land with profit, like all other commercial projects, requires an exact attention to small savings and small gains, of which a man born to a great fortune, even though naturally frugal, is very seldom capable. The situation of such a person naturally disposes him to attend rather to ornament. . . . The elegance of his dress, of his equipage, of his house, and household furniture, are objects which from his infancy he has been accustomed to have some anxiety about. The turn of mind which this habit naturally forms, follows him when he comes to think of the improvement of land. He embellishes perhaps four or five hundred acres in the neighborhood of his house, at ten time the expense which the land is worth after all his improvements."

25. This brief section does not purport to offer a full understanding of the virtue of justice. I simply want to show what justice looks like as an example of fleshing out Aristotle's thesis that the ethical virtues are political virtues. A fuller account of justice can be found in Charles Young, "Aristotle on Justice," *Southern Journal of Philosophy* 27 (1988): 233–49.

26. Love within the family might be an initial experience in disinterested action, but it cannot be the source of a love for the noble. For friendship within the family, see Elizabeth Belfiore, "Family Friendship in Aristotle's *Ethics,*" *Ancient Philosophy* 21 (2001): 113–32.

27. Julia Annas, "Ancient Ethics and Modern Morality," *Philosophical Perspectives* 6 (1992): 120: "The most prominent feature of modern moral theories that we fail to find in the ancient ones is the thought that moral and non-moral reasons are different in kind. Moral reasons have a special, compelling force, for when properly appreciated they have a special status in our deliberations: they override or silence all non-moral considerations." Danielle S. Allen offers an account of corrective justice that fits my thesis perfectly: "In corrective justice it is the good of 'agency' that matters. Both parties start out with an equal amount of agency, but a violation of justice disturbs that equality. In an involuntary transaction, one party has suffered or been subject to the violation. The other has done it. The violation of voluntarism undoes the equal distribution of agency between citizens. Corrective justice is therefore concerned with maintaining the equality of citizen interaction. Citizens are not to be made into 'subjects' nor are they to make one another into subjects or into those who are acted upon. Justice works to establish the principle that the relationships between citizens must consist not in involuntary interactions but only of voluntary interactions. This idea coincides with an idea that is central to Aristotle's understanding of how a just politics will work. In the just city, citizens live in a regime where they are always able to act voluntarily (cf. esp. *Politics* 3.4.7, 3.9–10). Corrective justice helps to maintain the social structures necessary for the citizens to live as voluntary actors. The focus of corrective justice is not so much on the people involved in any given situation of wrongdoing and punishment or on their specific emotions or desires (their personal characteristics are to be ignored) but on the wrongdoing itself and its subversion of the conditions necessary for agency. It is not the anger of the victim that motivates the punishment but the general need to maintain a context in which citizens can live as agents rather than as subjects." Danielle S. Allen, *The World of Prometheus,* 288.

28. John Stuart Mill, *On Liberty* (Indianapolis: Library of Liberal Arts, 1956), 60.

29. See too *NE* X.9.1179a33–1181b23, *Pol.* 1280b1–12, 1281a4–8, 1340b41–1341a3.

30. At the beginning of *NE* III.8 Aristotle announces that there are five "tropes," or forms of courage that fall short of true courage (1116a17). He does not tell us how to count off the five forms. There seems to be unanimity among translators and editors that the first inferior form, the citizen soldier, includes those who are compelled. The professional soldier

then is the second trope, the angry man third, the hopeful man fourth, and the ignorant fifth. I see a significant difference between the citizen and the compelled soldier, and so would like to renumber the tropes, putting the hopeful and the ignorant together. There is some textual support for my position. First, he says that "the courage of troops forced into battle by their officers may be classed as of the same type, though they are inferior as their motive is not a sense of shame but fear, and the desire to avoid not disgrace but pain" (*NE* 1116a30–32). Since those motives seemed to define political courage, the change in motives could indicate a different type. There is little to choose between that distinction and that between the hopeful and the ignorant. "Those who face danger in ignorance also appear courageous; and they come very near to those whose bravery rests on a sanguine temperament, though inferior to them inasmuch as they lack self-confidence, which the sanguine possess" (1116b23–24). However the kinds are numbered, the difference between the citizen soldiers motivated by shame and those who are compelled seems to me ethically significant. For more on shame as a moral emotion, see Elizabeth Belfiore, *Tragic Pleasures: Aristotle on Plot and Emotion* (Princeton: Princeton University Press, 1992), esp. 196–99.

Another passage makes a distinction like that between true courage and political courage, and so challenges my thesis that the ethical virtues are political. "Political friendship (*politikē*) looks at the agreement (*homologia*) and to the thing (*to pragma*), but moral friendship (*ethikē*) at the decision (*prohairesis*); hence the latter is more just—it is friendly justice (*dikaiosynē philikē*)" (*EE* VII.10.1243a32–34). Here again the difference is the absence of decision in political friendship, and so the absence of doing things for their own sake and for the sake of the friend. True friendship looks to *prohairesis* by treating others as engaged in action for its own sake.

31. I cannot develop the point here, but that remark from *Politics* III.5 recalls Aristotle's observation in *Politics* I that in women the deliberative part of the soul is *akurios*.

32. Lynn Holt notes that the distinction between function and virtue, between doing something and doing it well, seems to break down for the intellectual virtues. "If the *excellent* function, the virtue, of this part of the soul is to achieve the truth (1139b15), then its function is to do what? This is a difficult problem: a) if the non-virtuous function of this part of the soul is to grasp what is not true, then one grasps a falsehood, but this clearly cannot be the function of thought; b) perhaps the function is to grasp propositions, either true or false, but this is highly un-Aristotelian, and there is no good solution for the psychological source of said propositions." Lynn Holt, *Apprehension: Reason in the Absence of Rules* (Aldershot: Ashgate, 2002), 24, n. 30.

"Someone who possesses the *that* is not devoid of the *because;* full-blown possession of the *because,* the intellectual virtue of practical wisdom, is no more than possession of the *that* in a reflectively adjusted form." John McDowell, "Eudaimōnism and Realism in Aristotle's Ethics," in *Aristotle and Moral Realism,* ed. Robert Heinaman, 218: "Everything that *phronēsis* has to offer the ethically virtuous person already has (VI.12.1143b24–33, I.4.1095b2–13, VI.13, 1144b30–32)."

33. On the issue of whether the *orthos logos* is to be identified with *phronēsis* or not, see Sandra Peterson, "*Horos* in Aristotle's *Nicomachean Ethics,*" *Phronesis* 33 (1988): 233–50.

34. Those who practice virtue in their private affairs are not apolitical or antipolitical, however. They are acting as ruled citizens rather than rulers. For a similar analysis, see Lloyd Gerson, "Why Ethics Is Political Science for Aristotle," *Proceedings of the American Catholic Philosophical Association* 68 (1994): 93–107, esp. 99: "Private *phronēsis* . . . cannot exist apart from moral virtue which is public or political. There is no such category as that of *idia arēte* for Aristotle, although he speaks often of the *arēte* of the members of the household which is itself a constituent of the polis." Right before Aristotle says that *phronēsis* is the only virtue peculiar to a ruler, he says that it is "the work of the man to acquire and of the women to guard" household property (*Pol.* III.4.1277b24–25).

35. William Ian Miller, *The Anatomy of Disgust* (Cambridge, Mass.: Harvard University Press, 1997), 184: "Without hangmen and lawyers the judicial system cannot carry out its mission; without politicians public order seems largely unachievable and only imaginable as utopian fantasy. I call these people *moral menials;* they perform functions in the moral order

similar to those played by garbagemen and butchers in the system of provisioning, by hod carriers in building, by scavengers and bottom feeders in various ecosystems. Moral menials deal with moral dirt, or they have to get morally dirty to do what the polity needs them to do. And despite the fact that we need to attract people to this kind of labor, we still hold them accountable for being so attracted." Academic administrators seem to me to fit in the third sort of "superintendents" that Aristotle lists at *Pol.* IV.15.1299a20–25, not political or economic but menial. "To these, if they are prosperous, they appoint slaves."

36. In the line immediately before he says that only rulers have *phronēsis,* Aristotle contrasts the household virtues of men and women: "The duty of the one is to acquire, and the other to preserve." This fits my claim that rulers are concerned with providing the means to virtue, while ruled citizens use those means. See too *Pol.* I.13.1260a13: "The courage of a man is shown in commanding, of a woman in obeying."

37. John Dewey, *Freedom and Culture* (New York: Capricorn Books, 1939), 103. See also Isaiah Berlin, "European Unity and Its Vicissitudes," *The Crooked Timber of Humanity,* ed. Henry Hardy (London: Fontana, 1990), 179: "The division of mankind into two groups—men proper, and some other, lower order of beings, inferior races, inferior cultures, subhuman creatures, nations or classes condemned by history—is something new in human history." For an account of these changes, see Judith Shklar, *Ordinary Vices* (Cambridge, Mass.: Harvard University Press, 1984). See also Taylor, *Sources of the Self,* 284: "The new place of sentiment completes the revolution which has yielded a modern view of nature as normative, so utterly different from the ancient view. For the ancients, nature offers us an order which moves us to love and instantiate it, unless we are depraved. But the modern view, on the other hand, endorses nature as the source of right impulse or sentiment. So we encounter nature paradigmatically and centrally, not in a vision of order, but in experiencing the right inner impulse. Nature as norm is an inner tendency; it is ready to become the voice within, which Rousseau will make it, and so be transposed by the Romantics into a richer and deeper inwardness."

38. Alasdair MacIntyre, *After Virtue: A Study in Moral Theory* (Notre Dame, Ind.: University of Notre Dame Press, 1984), 148. See too David Luban, "The Self: Metaphysical Not Political," *Legal Theory* 1 (1995): 401–37; John McDowell, "Eudaimōnism and Realism in Aristotle's Ethics," in *Aristotle and Moral Realism,* ed. Robert Heinaman, 201–18, esp. 216–17.

39. This contrast of senses of nature seems to me at the heart of Larmore's contrast between ancient and modern morality as "attractive" vs. "imperative." Charles Larmore, *The Morals of Modernity* (Cambridge: Cambridge University Press, 1996). That distinction apparently derives from Henry Sidgwick, *Methods of Ethics,* 7th ed. (London: Macmillan, 1907), 105–6.

40. Thus in Rousseau's second *Discourse,* in the state of nature man has neither reason nor *thumos.* The invention of the competitive emotions that Aristotle situates in the *thumos* causes the development of reason and civilization. Instead of the natural pleasure of sex, I seek the unnatural pleasure of possessing a beautiful woman, where the sense of beauty is a comparative emotion and the desire for beauty a competitive one. Comparisons give rise to abstractions and so to reasoning. In nature, there is neither spirit nor reason nor community. See too Thomas Hobbes, *Leviathan,* ed. Richard Tuck (Cambridge: Cambridge University Press, 1991), 119: "Man, whose joy consisteth in comparing himselfe with other men, can relish nothing but what is eminent."

41. Harry Frankfurt, "Freedom of the Will and the Concept of a Person," *Journal of Philosophy* 68 (1971): 5–20. David A. J. Richards, *Conscience and the Constitution: History, Theory, and Law of the Reconstruction Amendments* (Princeton: Princeton University Press, 1993), 71: "Reason—epistemic and practical—can have the power that it does in our lives because it enables us to stand back from our ends, to assess critically how they cohere with one another and with the ends of others, and to reexamine and sometimes revise such judgments in light of new insights and experience and to act accordingly. Reason can only reliably perform this role when it is itself subject to revision and correction in light of public standards open, accessible, and available to all." Since Aristotle would reject such a

conception of reason, he is often thought to be on the side of "communitarians" in a debate against "liberals." If, though, Aristotle presents the moral psychology of rulers, his alternative to liberalism is far more radical than the communitarian vision. The liberal/communitarian opposition presupposes that individual moral subjects are legal subjects, not rulers.

42. For this rhetorical adaptation of prudence, in which seeing both sides of an issue becomes central to the development and exercise of prudence, see my *Machiavelli and the History of Prudence* (Madison: University of Wisconsin Press, 1987), and Victoria Kahn, *Rhetoric, Prudence, and Skepticism in the Renaissance* (Ithaca: Cornell University Press, 1985). For one of many possible examples of "liberal virtues" that differ from Aristotle's on just this point, see this list presented by Stephen Macedo: "broad sympathies, self-critical reflectiveness, a willingness to experiment, to try and to accept new things." Stephen Macedo, *Liberal Virtues: Citizenship, Virtue and Community in Liberal Constitutionalism* (Oxford: Clarendon Press, 1991), 271. None of these would be a virtue for Aristotle. See too F. H. Bradley, *Ethical Studies* (London: Oxford University Press, 1927), 197n: "Practical morality means singlemindedness, the having one idea; it means what in other spheres would be the greatest narrowness. Point out to a man of simple morals that the case has other sides than the one he instinctively fixes on, and he suspects you wish to corrupt him. And so you probably would if you went on. Apart from bad examples, the readiest way to debauch the morality of anyone is, on the side of principle, to confuse them by forcing them to see in all moral and immoral acts other sides and points of view, which alter the character of each."

43. Michael Stocker, "Some Problems with Counter-Examples in Ethics," *Synthese* 72 (1987): 281. "Some think that it is conceptual of the notion of *intrinsic value* that if a value *v* is intrinsic anywhere, it is intrinsic everywhere. Some also think that what is not good just everywhere is, therefore, only instrumentally good where it is good. But these are simply confusions of *intrinsic* value with *absolute* or *unconditional* value." Terence C. Irwin, *Aristotle's First Principles* (Oxford: Oxford University Press, 1988), 413: "While we want rational agency to be exercised in our lives, some types of exercise are preferable to others. We may exercise it even when we decide to make the best of a bad job, and when a less virtuous person would make the same choice. But we prefer the exercise of reason when we are free to do more than adapt ourselves to disagreeable conditions that we would rather avoid. We prefer the exercise of rational agency in conditions that allow its maximum extension and development in forming the character of our lives."

44. *An. Post.* II.11.94b27, *Met.* 2.982b19–27, V.5.1015a23–25, XII.7.1072b10–11, *NE* I.7.1097a34–b6, X.7.1177b15, *Pol.* 1254a20–21, VII.14.1333a7–11, VIII.2.1337b4–17, *Part. An.* 658b2–663b12, *Gen. An.* II.4.739b20–28, II.6.743a36–b5.

45. This transformation sometimes forces modern commentators are to assimilate the entire field of the practical to Aristotle's category of mixed actions. I am indebted to Norman Dahl for discussion on this point.

The idea that because something is merely best in the circumstances, it therefore isn't really good, is responsible for the idea that Aristotle's virtues are "corrective." See Philippa Foot, "Virtues and Vices," in *Virtues and Vices and other Essays in Moral Philosophy* (Berkeley and Los Angeles: University of California Press, 1978). For a useful refutation, see Paula Gottlieb, "Are the Virtues Remedial?" *Journal of Value Inquiry* 35 (2001): 343–54.

Since tragic plots depend on a *hamartia*, which consists in choosing and acting in partial ignorance, tragic actions do fit the mixed voluntary and involuntary. All the more reason not to assimilate the realms of the ethical and the tragic. Aristotle had the opportunity, in *Ethics* III.1 and in the *Poetics,* to draw explicit connections between the mixed and the tragic, and he never does so. Here I oppose Christine M. Korsgaard, "Aristotle and Kant on the Source of Value," *Ethics* 96 (1986): 486–505, at 491–92, which seems to me to argue for such an assimilation of praxis to the realm of the mixed. The realm of the practical is governed by what she calls "conditional ends, [which], for Aristotle, are ends valued for their own sake, given that we are human beings living in human conditions—among friends, in the city, with a nature both animal and rational to cope with. They 'befit our human estate' (10.8.1178a)." See also Irwin, *Aristotle's First Principles,* 412: "Occupations involve some 'mixed' actions that are a mixture of voluntary and involuntary elements; and though these allow choice and decision, the difference between the virtuous and the vicious decision is not as clear here as elsewhere (cf. *NE* 1110a11–19, 1115b7–10, 1116a29–b3)." On my side is Michael Stocker, *Plural and Conflicting Values* (Oxford: Clarendon Press, 1990), esp. 59–66.

46. Christine M. Korsgaard, "Aristotle and Kant on the Source of Value," 494. "The exercise of the moral virtues in a morally motivated project can be the final good of an individual's life. One can center one's life around, say, justice in fighting for oppressed people or courage in a military life or political and practical wisdom in making laws for the city. For an individual such an activity is a final good, for the virtuous person does these things for their own sake. But this sort of life is conditioned in a particular way, namely, on something being wrong or imperfect." Richard Kraut too notes that the conditional/absolute distinction employed in the *Politics* does not occur in the *Ethics*. See Aristotle, *Politics: Books VII and VIII*, trans. with a commentary by Richard Kraut (Oxford: Clarendon Press; New York: Oxford University Press, 1997), 25.

47. *Pol.* VII.4.1326b3–5: "A city made up of too many persons is with respect to the necessary things self-sufficient like a nation, but it is not a polis, for it not easy for a constitution to be present."

48. For more on Aristotle's idea of slavery, see my "Aristotle's Natural Slaves: Incomplete *Praxeis* and Incomplete Human Beings," *Journal of the History of Philosophy* 32 (1994): 1–22.

49. W. F. R. Hardie, *Aristotle's Ethical Theory* (Oxford: Oxford University Press, 1968), 231, 335.

50. "Against those who are one's match and not very superior numerically it is not noble to try to defend oneself through the security provided by walls. But it can turn out that the superiority of the attackers surpasses human virtue and the virtue of a small number, and if the city must be preserved and avoid ill-treatment and arrogant insult, then one should realize that the highly secure defense provided by walls is quite an appropriate military measure, particularly in light of recent discoveries about the accuracy of missiles and devices used in sieges" (*Pol.* VII.11.1330b35–1331a1).

51. John Stuart Mill, *Utilitarianism*, in *Collected Works of John Stuart Mill*, vol. 10: *Essays on Ethics, Religion, and Society*, ed. J. M. Robson (Toronto: University of Toronto Press, 1969), 305.

52. See too *NE* IV.2.11228–10, VIII.14.1163b15, *Top.* IV.6.141b36–142a2, *Met.* II.3.994b32–995a17, *Pol.* I.11.1258b37–38, *Rh.* I.10.1369b31–32, II.22.1395b28–1396a1, III.12.1414a7–18, 17.1418a2–4, III.17.1418b1–3. Similarly we are told at *Republic* VI.486a that petty thinking (*smikrologia*) is incompatible with a philosophical nature. See also *Republic* I.340e, where Thrasymachus accuses Socrates of such excessive precision: *su akribologei*. Shorey's note for the Loeb edition on this passage is instructive: "For the invidious associations of *akribologia* (1) in money dealings, (2) in argument, cf. Aristotle, *Metaphysics* 995a11, *Cratylus* 415a, Lysias vii.12, Antiphon B3, Demosth. xxiii.148, Timon in Diog. Laert. ii.19." In addition, we are told in *De An.* II.9 that smell is less *akribē* than hearing and sight because we do not sense smells without either pleasure or pain (421a11–13); presumably those senses are more precise which can experience objects as they are apart from their causing pleasure and pain. For the later history of the contrast between precision and truth, see Wesley Trimpi, *Muses of One Mind: The Literary Analysis of Experience and Its Continuity* (Princeton: Princeton University Press, 1983).

53. Jonathan Shay, *Achilles in Vietnam: Combat Trauma and the Undoing of Character* (New York: Atheneum, 1994), 197. See too George Kateb, "*Brown* and the Harm of Legal Segregation," in *Race, Law, and Culture: Reflections on Brown v. Board of Education*, ed. Austin Sarat (New York: Oxford University Press, 1997), 101: "The law of a constitutional democracy can never rightly expect of people the amount of *civil* courage require to rise Stoically above a system meant to degrade, and having behind it the full authority of the law. . . . The extent of *political* courage required of blacks to test the system of segregation and challenge it and try to circumvent it was too much to require by any government, that,

as a constitutional democracy, claimed to be legitimate. That eventually black resistance to legal segregation came is a heroic fact. But one of the defining traits of constitutional democracy is that political courage—the willingness to risk legal punishment as well as social penalty—is not a daily necessity, is not needed to claim or exercise one's rights." At *NE* V.10.1137b34–1138a3 Aristotle says that the good man will take less than his share. *Brown* asked the victims of injustice to claim less than they deserved. Rosalind Hursthouse, "Virtue Theory and Abortion," in *Virtue Ethics,* ed. Statman, 227–44, at 238: "To go through with a pregnancy when one is utterly exhausted, or when one's job consists of crawling along tunnels hauling coal, as many women in the nineteenth century were obliged to do, is perhaps heroic, but people who do not achieve heroism are not necessarily vicious."

See too: "The bravest seem to be those who hold cowards in dishonor and do honor to brave people" (*NE* III.8.1116a21–22). The heroic actions that go beyond the law are called excessive or hyperbolic in *Rhetoric* I.13.1374a21–25. Aristotle's examples are acknowledging one's benefactors and supporting one's friends. Such actions get praise, honors, and decorations (a22–23). Contrast, too, the thesis that the virtues and vices are the subject of both praise and blame with Adam Smith's comments that prudence warrants only "cold esteem" and his contrast between the rules of justice and those of the virtues, which are "loose, vague, and indeterminate." Adam Smith, *Theory of Moral Sentiments,* ed. D. D. Raphael and A. L. Macfie (Oxford: Clarendon Press, 1976), 263.

54. Charles Larmore, *Patterns of Moral Complexity* (Cambridge: Cambridge University Press, 1987), 12: "By overlooking the importance of judgment, modern moral theories have presented a dessicated view of virtue. . . . [This view] fails to capture the way in which the exercise of virtue, through imagination and judgment, is an organ of moral discovery." Nicholas White, "Conflicting Parts of Happiness in Aristotle's Ethics," *Ethics* 105 (1995): 258-283, at 269: "Aristotle treats opportunities for virtuous action as potentially scarce, as not always present in abundance, as moderns are usually disposed to think that they are."

55. John Stuart Mill, *On Liberty* (Indianapolis: Library of Liberal Arts, 1956), 60.

56. There is no becoming of an *energeia*. See *Ph.* VII.3.247b2–13, V.2.225b15–226a17, *De An.* II.5.417b2–9, *NE* X.4.1174b9–14.

## Chapter Six

1. For nature doing nothing in vain, see *De An.* II.4.415b16–20, *Caelo* 288a2–3, 290a31, *IA* 2.704b1–17, *Part. An.* II.14.658a10, III.1.661b4–5, IV.12.694a15, IX.13. 695b19–20, *Pol.* I.2.1253a9–10, I.8.1254b20-26.

*Pol.* VI.2.1319b31–32: "Living in a disorderly way is more pleasant to the many than living with moderation." VII.13.1332b3–8: "The other animals live by nature above all, but in some slight respects by habit as well while man lives also by reason (for he alone has reason); so these things should be consonant with the other." *NE* X.5.1176a3–10: "Each kind of animal seems to have its own proper pleasure, just as it has its own proper function to have the same pleasures also. In fact, however, the pleasures differ quite a lot, in human beings at any rate." See also *NE* II.4.1104b30-1105a1, IX.8.1168b15–19, X.9.1179b10-16, *Pol.* VI.4. 1319b31–32, VII.1.1323a35–b1, VII.13.1331b39–1332a3, VII.14.1333b10–18.

That people do not reliably do what is best is also seen in the case of natural slaves who wrongly think they are better off free instead of enslaved. See *Pol.* I.8.1256b20–26, VII.1333b38–1334a2. "People generally wrong others if they can" (*Rh.* II.5.1382b8–9).

Julia Annas, "Aristotle on Human Nature and Political Virtue," *Review of Metaphysics* 49 (1996): 731: "Aristotle gives us an account of *physis* or nature in the *Physics* which is adequate for his immediate purposes there, but gives little indication of his broad deployment in the ethical and political works of the concept of the natural. He never systematically investigates nature as an ethical or political concept. Had he done so, he could not have failed to see that there are some tensions within the roles he assigns to the natural. He might thereby have avoided several problems, including one of his most unfortunate legacies, that of reactionary political attitudes which have appeals to nature, often in Aristotle's name, to uphold existing inequalities in society, such as slavery and the subordination of women. . . . Aristotle's own lack of precision about the role of nature in his ethical and political arguments must bear some of the responsibility."

Sarah Broadie, *Ethics with Aristotle* (New York and Oxford: Oxford University Press, 1991), 382: "It is an ironic fact of the human condition that the things whose use it matters most to get right are those general resources which do not come to us with their correct use stamped on their conceptual faces. All this is as much as to say that practical wisdom is not a craft; which is why practical wisdom is necessary as well as the crafts, and also why an ethical inquiry such as Aristotle's is necessary." Broadie, "Nature and Craft in Aristotelian Teleology," *Biologie, Logique, et Métaphysique Chez Aristote,* ed. Daniel Devereux and Pierre Pellegrin (Paris: Éditions du CNRS, 1990), 402: "*Reflective* rationality . . . is the means by which human nature compensates for its own failure to provide genetically all that it needs in order to flourish and continue. Non-human natures, on the other hand, are genetically adequate for their own needs, including the need to reproduce in kind."

2. See, e.g., *Pol.* I.13.1260a7ff, 1260b35, VII.13.1332a40–42. Jonathan Lear, *Aristotle: The Desire to Understand* (Cambridge: Cambridge University Press, 1988) reads this problem, for the *Politics* at least, as a "tension between Aristotle's role as descriptive biologist and his role as teleological biologist" (203). David Keyt, "Distributive Justice in Aristotle's *Ethics* and *Politics,*" *Topoi* 4 (1985): 33. "A polis with a deviant constitution differs from a freak of nature in the animal kingdom in one important respect. A freak of nature in the animal kingdom is an anomaly, a deviation from what happens for the most part (*epi to polu*) (*G.A.* IV.4.770b9–13). That which is contrary to nature is the complement of that which is according to nature; and that which is according to nature, Aristotle holds, is that which happens always of for the most part (*Physics* II.8.198b35–36; *Gen. Corr.* II.6.333b4–7, *et passim*). Hence that which is contrary to nature is that which happens on those rare occasions when what happens for the most part does not happen (*Physics* II.6.197b34–35, 8.198b36; and see *Met.* E.2.1026b27–1027a17). In Aristotle's political philosophy this situation is reversed. The best polis, the only one that strictly speaking is according to nature, occurs rarely, if ever, whereas polises that deviate from this norm and are contrary to nature are the rule." For a refutation of Keyt on just this point, see Bernard Yack, "A Reinterpretation of Aristotle's Political Teleology," *History of Philosophy Quarterly* 12 (1991): 15–33. See also Stephen G. Salkever, *Finding the Mean: Theory and Practice in Aristotelian Political Philosophy* (Princeton: Princeton University Press, 1990), 82: "The curious and decisive fact about human life is that we have a profound biological need for an institution that will shape our desires into healthy patterns, but a relatively weak natural impulse (*hormē*) toward institutions of that sort (as opposed to our powerful natural impulse to form families or clans). Such political inclinations as we do inherit need to be supplemented by our much stronger social inclinations toward institutions that provide security or company rather than *paideia*. Thus it is not surprising that most existing cultures are not well designed for the purpose that justifies them, but are instead promiscuous or random heaps of ad hoc custom and legislation (*Pol.* 7, 1324b5–6). Such cities are *poleis* in name only (as a corpse is a human body in name only) and may in fact be nothing more than concealed forms of despotism, the rule of the master over slaves." L. P. Gerson, *God and Greek Philosophy: Studies in the Early History of Natural Theology* (London and New York: Routledge, 1990), 283, n. 82: "An organic individual strives to become what it is." I believe that this failure of nature also accounts for the fact that nature fails to make apparent the distinction between natural slaves and natural masters.

Jonathan Lear, *Happiness, Death, and the Remainder of Life* (Cambridge, Mass.: Harvard University Press, 2000), 56: "All the rest of animal nature is basically able to fulfill its nature unproblematically. . . . For humans, happiness *is* human flourishing, yet happiness by and large eludes them. Thus by injecting 'happiness' as the organizing goal of human teleology, Aristotle manages to disrupt the teleological structure itself. For he has made it virtually impossible for humans to fulfill their nature. Although the teleological worldview is used to give content to what happiness consists in, once the picture is filled out it puts pressure on the teleological world-view itself." And 57: "The human race is the only species in nature almost all of whose members are failing to flourish. This disruption of the harmonious order is caused precisely to the introduction of 'happiness' as the purported concept by which we should evaluate our lives. It is usually assumed that it is because Aristotle was an aristocrat that he was attracted to such a teleological worldview. The question now arises whether to hold onto his teleology he had to be an aristocrat."

3. Donald Morrison, "Some Remarks on Definition in *Metaphysics* Z," *Biologie, Logique, et Métaphysique Chez Aristote*, ed. Devereux and Pellegrin, 141–42: "The primary substances of the natural world are not just enmattered forms; they are *souls*. And those substances which are prior to the substances of the natural world are not only immaterial forms; they are also souls. But the souls of mortal substances are rather complicated: they must extend throughout the matter of their substance, and they must care for nutrition and growth; in some cases they originate motion, have memories, make plans, and even philosophize. Even the souls of the heavenly bodies, which are enmattered but eternal, are complicated to this extent, that they originate motion and have a desire for something different from themselves. But immaterial substances are souls which are as simple as a soul can get: all there is to them, so to speak, is the thought of their own essence."

4. I am assuming that "seeing" here is purely psychic and not necessarily practical, not seeing what is right or anything similarly sophisticated. If Aristotle means something specifically human or practical by sight here, my case is easier and simpler. The kind of seeing Aristotle refers to is not all that passive. Consider, for example, *NE* IX.12.1171b30–32: "What the erotic lover likes most is to see his beloved, and this is the sort of perception he chooses over the others, supposing that this is above all what makes him fall in love and remain in love." The pairing of *nous* and perception as perfect *energeiai* also occurs in *NE* IX.9.1170a16–19: "For animals life is defined by the capacity for perception; for human beings it is defined by the capacity for perception or understanding. Every capacity refers to an activity, and a thing is present to its full extent in its activity. Hence living to its full extent would seem to be perceiving or understanding." *EE* II.1.1219a16 also pairs sight and *theōria:* "The work of sight is the act of seeing, that of mathematical science the contemplation of mathematical truths" (1219a16–17). See too *EE* VII.12.1244b23–29: "It is manifest that life is perception and knowledge, and that consequently social life is perception and knowledge in common. But perception and knowledge themselves are the thing most desirable for each individual (and it is owing to this that the appetition for life is implanted by nature in all, for living must be deemed a mode of knowing)." We should compare this list in the *Metaphysics* to the set, "honor, pleasure, intelligence (*nous*) and every virtue" which we choose for themselves even if nothing else resulted from them (*NE* I.7.1097b2).

Charles Young, in response to a draft of this chapter, noted that there is another prime example of *energeia* which Aristotle does not use in *Met.* IX—pleasure, which is listed in I.6. It is difficult to say what its *dynamis* is, and so difficult to fit it in with many of the claims about *energeia* in *Met.* IX. Here I simply acknowledge the problem and leave it for another time. However, it is worth noting that when Aristotle considers pleasure as an *energeia* or as the completion of an *energeia* in *Ethics* X the examples he appeals to are perception, thought, and life itself, before moving on to happiness.

5. The gods might be the purest case of activity, but not the most useful case for us to learn about activity in general. The association of praxis and *energeia* is the most useful guiding thread through metaphysics. One apparent counterexample to this relation between ethics and metaphysics is *NE* I.9.1099b11–14: "If anything that men have is a gift of the gods, it is reasonable to suppose that happiness is divinely given. . . . This subject however may perhaps more belong to another branch of study." To say that human praxis is the paradigm of substance and activity is, of course, to raise questions for the *Metaphysics* concerning the relation between *Met.* IX and XII. Ethically, those questions are the subject of my next chapter, where the issue is whether the best life for humans is a divine life or a human life.

Unlike Aristotle, Plato offers extensive answers to my question, "How does knowing man's place in the universe help us know how to live?" In the *Phaedo,* knowing that the gods' life is best means that we should at least prepare, and maybe hurry up, to live a divine life of contemplation. Platonic ethics is impossible without a prior metaphysics. Thus Socrates criticizes Callicles for neglecting geometry, since "geometrical equality is all powerful among the gods as among men" (*Gorgias* 508a). Aristotle does not even acknowledge the question.

6. Terence C. Irwin, *Aristotle's First Principles* (Oxford: Clarendon Press, 1988), 587, n.1. "In Aristotle's repeated formula, *hē phusis outhen poiei matēn,* we should understand *matēn* to refer to pointless activity, aiming at no end, rather than unsuccessful activity—Aristotle does not claim that nature is always successful in achieving the ends it tends towards. In most contexts nature's way is contrasted with something done pointlessly, or for no reason, or superfluously (*periergon*)." But see *De An.* II.12.434a30–b1: "Animals must be endowed with sensation, since Nature does nothing in vain. For all things that exist by nature are means to an end, or will be concomitants of means to an end. Every body capable of forward movement would, if unendowed with sensation, perish and fail to reach its end, which is the aim of Nature." For an even stronger claim, see III.9.432b21–23: "Nature never makes anything without a purpose and never leaves out what is necessary (except in the case of mutilated and imperfect growths)."

7. For details see my "Aristotle's Natural Slaves: Incomplete *Praxeis* and Incomplete Human Beings," *Journal of the History of Philosophy* 32 (1994): 1–22.

8. "The question of moral choice in the deepest sense finally concerns questions of creating the conditions in which our actions and our feelings may be as we would wish them." L. A. Kosman, "Being Properly Affected: Virtues and Feelings in Aristotle's *Ethics,*" in *Essays on Aristotle's Ethics,* ed. Amélie Oksenberg Rorty (Berkeley and Los Angeles: University of California Press, 1981), 115. See also Amélie Rorty's description of a magnetizing or tropic disposition as one which "promotes and even constructs the occasions that require its exercise." Amélie Oksenberg Rorty, *Mind in Action* (Boston: Beacon Press, 1988), 301.

9. Sarah Waterlow Broadie, "The Problem of Practical Intellect in Aristotle's *Ethics,*" in *Proceedings of the Boston Area Colloquium in Ancient Philosophy,* vol. 3, ed. John Cleary (Washington, D.C.: University Press of America, 1988), 250: "The fundamental difference between the reasoning of the craftsman and of the ethical agent is not that the former is concerned only with means, but rather that there is a limit in the case of craft, but not in the ethical case, to the kinds of consideration that might reasonably claim the agent's attention. The fact that a certain drug has unhealthy side effects is a relevant consideration for the physician *qua* physician; the fact that it is expensive is not."

10. On this reading, Aristotle does not have an ethical sense of the tragic which is featured in the tragedians. For example, among many others, Jonathan Shay, *Achilles in Vietnam: Combat Trauma and the Undoing of Character* (New York: Atheneum, 1994), 37: "Homer and the Greek tragic poets held the terrifying view that apparently stable adult character *continues* to be dependent and vulnerable, even after if has been established by good nurturing in childhood. According to these tragic poets, good character is dependent on good-enough stability and reliability of *thémis* and remains vulnerable to high-stakes betrayal of *thémis* by power holders. The moral dimension of trauma destroys virtue, undoes good character."

11. Nicholas White, *Individual and Conflict in Greek Ethics* (Oxford: Clarendon Press, 2002), 100.

12. L. P. Gerson, *God and Greek Philosophy,* 279, n. 51: "Active potencies are present in substances wherever there is growth towards the fulfillment of a nature or decay leading to its destruction." Active potencies belong to living things alone because, as *Ph.* VIII.4 shows, only they are capable of self-motion. This is an example of the correlation between properties of potencies and properties of activities that I find lacking in *Met.* IX.

13. Sarah Waterlow, *Nature, Change, and Agency in Aristotle's Physics* (Oxford: Clarendon Press, 1982), 41: "The nature of a natural substance is uniquely related to one particular in a way not paralleled by the principle of artifice that defines an artificer. Both nature and artifice are embodied in particular agents, and in this respect Aristotle's anti-Platonism is impartial between the two kinds of cause. But they differ in that a particular exemplifier of skill (i.e. a particular artificer) stands to its effect as a Platonic 'one over many,' whereas the opposite holds true of nature. . . . The Aristotelian artificer can realize the same form in any num-

ber of particular subjects, and its realization in one in no way limits this agent's power to produce it again in others. Whereas the relation between the natural substance and the particular subject in which the natural form is to be realized is to be realized is necessarily one-one, since they are necessarily the same individual."

14. Charlotte Witt, *Ways of Being: Potentiality and Actuality in Aristotle's Metaphysics* (Ithaca and London: Cornell University Press, 2003), 64: "In *Metaphysics* IX, chapter 2, Aristotle distinguishes powers that inhere in things with souls from powers that inhere in things without souls. But, he does not develop a systematic distinction between powers on that basis." See also the way Aristotle jumps over the intermediate stage of the animate but nonrational in the ergon argument: "Living is apparently shared with plants, but what we are looking for is the special function of a human being; hence we should set aside the life of nutrition and growth. The life next in order is some sort of life of sense-perception. . . . The remaining possibility is some sort of life of action of the [part of the soul] that has reason" (*NE* I.7.1097b33–1098a3). That the animate might be a separate stage could be argued on the basis of *Ph.* VII.2.244b1–15, which concludes: "Thus the animate is capable of every kind of alteration of which the inanimate is capable, but the inanimate is not capable of every kind of which the animate is capable, since it is not capable of alteration in respect to the senses." D. W. Hamlyn senses something odd in commenting on *De An.* II.1.412a6–10 when he says: "*Metaphysics* IX.2. says that things which have a rational part of the soul have a potentiality for opposites; in these the development of a *hexis* is possible, and there is a general implication in Aristotle that this comes about by practice. To apply this notion in the present case would restrict the soul to rational creatures, which Aristotle never intends." Aristotle, *De Anima, Books II and III,* trans. D. W. Hamlyn (Oxford: Clarendon Press, 1968), 82–83.

Terence C. Irwin, *Aristotle's First Principles* (London: Oxford University Press, 1988), 598, n. 28: "*Met.* 1046a36–b13 contrasts non-rational potentialities of inanimate things with the potentialities involving reason in animate things. 1047b31–1048a11 contrasts the congenital potentialities, e.g. perception, with the potentialities acquired 'by habit and reason,' 1047b34. Aristotle has no clear place for potentialities that are acquired by training in non-rational subjects (or by non-rational training in rational subjects)." See too *De An.* III.3.427b8–15: "Thinking is distinct from perceiving—I mean that in which we find rightness and wrongness—rightness in prudence, knowledge, true opinion, wrongness in their opposites; for perception of the special objects of sense is always free from error, and is found in all animals, while it is possible to think falsely as well as truly, and thought is found only where there is discourse of reason as well as sensibility."

15. Are all rational powers active? Here Aristotle's sliding through the animate to the rational asks for trouble. The power to see is a power of being affected, but it is arguably rational: it is a power to receive form (*logos*) apart from matter and to be actualized in many ways, as rational powers are. My skin can either be burned or not, and in that trivial sense Aristotle says that all potencies are powers for opposites (*Met.* IX.8.1050b28–35). But my eyes can see either light or dark.

16. "Hume cannot . . . distinguish someone's character from other durable elements of him. He does not think ends can be chosen by rational deliberation and decision; for Hume, deliberation and practical reason are never practical except when they discover means to ends pursued by nonrational desires. For Aristotle it is important to distinguish character traits, the product of deliberation, from other constant features; Hume cannot draw this distinction." Terence C. Irwin, "Reason and Responsibility in Aristotle," in *Essays on Aristotle's Ethics,* ed. Rorty, 135.

17. It is for this reason, as I argued in chapter 5, that while *phronesis* and *sophia* are activities, *energeiai,* they are not the activity of separately specifiable *dynameis.*

18. "A science is a rational formula (*logos*), and the same rational formula explains a thing and its privation, only not in the same way; and in a sense it applies to both, but in a sense it applies rather to the positive fact. Therefore such sciences must deal with contraries, but with one in virtue of their own nature and with the other not in virtue of their nature; for the rational formula applies to one object in virtue of that object's nature, and to the

other, in a sense, accidentally" (*Met.* IX.2.1046b7–13). See *An. Pr.* I.1.24a21, 36.48b5, *Top.* I.14.105b5, VIII.1.155b31, *Met.* IV.2.1004a9, *Pol.* V.8.1307b27–30.

19. I skip chapters 3 and 4 in this exposition. Ethics does not dictate the conclusions of metaphysics, but there are some metaphysical theses incompatible with a happy life in which our actions have consequences. The conditions ethics places on metaphysics are violated in the options Aristotle refutes in *Met.* IX.3–4.

20. One reason for the hedge is that in nature there are continua from the inanimate to the most animate and rational, continua that are hard to maintain while one is establishing the sorts of distinctions through contrariety of *Met.* IX. See, e.g., *HA* VIII.1.588b4–10: "Nature moves on little by little from soulless things to animals in such a way that because of the continuity we cannot discern the border between them. . . . After soulless things plants is first, and of these one differs from another in seeming to be more alive, but all plants, although relative to the other bodies appears quite as if ensouled, relative to animals plants appear soulless."

21. Charles Taylor, "Justice After Virtue," in *After MacIntyre: Critical Perspectives on the Work of Alasdair MacIntyre,* ed. John Horton and Susan Mendus (Notre Dame, Ind..: University of Notre Dame Press, 1994), 24.

22. Alasdair MacIntyre, *After Virtue: A Study in Moral Theory* (Notre Dame, Ind.: University of Notre Dame Press, 1984), 219.

23. For example, contrast these lines from Rawls with *NE* VIII.9.1160a10–24. First, Rawls: "Within a Kantian view there is no place for the idea of an individual's contribution to society that parallels that of an individual's contribution to associations within society. Insofar as we compare the worth of citizens at all, their worth in a just and well-ordered society is always equal." "Inequalities do not arise form unequal moral worth; their explanation lies elsewhere." John Rawls, *Political Liberalism* (New York: Columbia University Press, 1993), 279–80, with 280, n. 16. Now Aristotle: "People make their way together on the basis that they will get some advantage from it, and so as to provide themselves with some necessity of life; and the political community too seems both to have come together in the beginning and to remain in place for the sake of advantage, since this is what is aimed at by the legislators too, and people say that what is for the common advantage is just. . . . The political community does not seek the advantage of the moment, but takes regard to the whole of life."

24. Immanuel Kant, *Grundlegung zur Metaphysik der Sitten* (1785), Ak. 437; *Fundamental Principles of the Metaphysics of Morals,* trans. Thomas K. Abbott (Indianapolis: Library of Liberal Arts, 1949), 42.

25. Immanuel Kant, *Metaphysik der Sitten,* Teil II, *Tugendlehre* (1797), Ak. 392 (Einleitung zur Tugendlehre, VIII.i.a.); *The Metaphysics of Morals,* trans. Mary Gregor (Cambridge: Cambridge University Press, 1991), 195.

26. Unlike the divine activity of thinking about thinking, all human activities involve motions, and these *kinēseis* take time. But while it takes time for me fully enjoy listening to Beethoven's Piano Sonata in C minor, that pleasure itself isn't half finished at the end of the second movement.

27. The final chapter will elaborate on this point, but for now please note that I am claiming on the one hand that *theōria* reflects on man's place in the universe, and so *theōria* completes ethics, but on the other that nature would be incomplete and imperfect without the existence of the perfect and complete *energeiai* which happy humans display, that is, without *practical,* not theoretical, *energeiai.* Man does not complete nature by knowing it but by being leading a *eudaimōn* life. For a similar idea, see Immanuel Kant, *Critique of Judgment,* trans. Werner S. Pluhar (Indianapolis: Hackett, 1987), 442–43: "Without men the whole creation would be mere waste, in vain, and without final purpose. But it is not in reference to man's cognitive faculty that the being of everything else in the world gets its worth; he is not there merely that there may be someone to contemplate the world. . . . It is that worth which [man] alone can give to himself and which consists in what he does, how and according to what principles he acts. . . . That is, a good will is that whereby alone his being can have an absolute worth, and in reference to which the being of the world can have a final purpose."

28. Sarah Waterlow, *Nature, Change, and Agency in Aristotle's Physics,* 208: "It appears from [*Phys.*] VIII.2 and 6 that the self-changes of living things are even more dependent on external conditions than are the natural movements of fire and earth. The latter presuppose only (a) generation of the substance in question, and (b) conditions that make or keep the pathway clear; but the former require not only these but also (c) environmental stimuli that trigger the changes although without enforcing their pattern (2.253a9–20), and (d) certain physiological conditions of the living substance which it owes to earlier interactions with the environment (such as the ingestion of food) (6.259b6–16)."

"What distinguishes self-change for Aristotle is not superior self-sufficiency, but the logical complexity of that which has the change. A self-changer, i.e. a substance that changes (transitive), or is changed by, itself comprises in itself both agent and patient of the same change; and this agent and patient, Aristotle insists, are in some way distinct from one another. Supplementing this, Aristotle's account (since he himself seems resolved to say as little as possible about self-change) we can state the following analytic difference between the case of a self-change externally obstructed and then released, and that of a change that is merely natural and not self-instigated: in the latter case, what is repressed is simply a change in the object; while in the former, not only is the *change* first prevented, then permitted, but something else too, namely the effective exercise of agency by the agent-element 'within' the object."

Edward Halper, "The Substance of Aristotle's Ethics," in *The Crossroads of Norm and Nature: Essays on Aristotle's Ethics and Metaphysics,* ed. May Sim (Lanham, Md.: Rowman and Littlefield, 1995), 16: "The activity of the citizens aims to preserve the continued common activity of the citizens. This is, I think, still another sense in which the activities of decision and rule are their own ends; decisions made for the sake of the common good aim to preserve conditions in which there can be other such decisions, decisions that are generically the same insofar as they too are for the common good. Indeed, a decision is for the common good precisely when it aims at preserving the possibility of other such decisions."

See too Aryeh Kosman, "Aristotle on the Desirability of Friends," *Ancient Philosophy* 24 (2004): 143: "Consciousness as a capacity for objective determination characterizes living substances specifically by virtue of their being substances. For it is the capacity for further determination—a capacity belonging to substances by reason of their determinate nature—that characterizes them in the first instance as substance. It is because substances are what they are that they are capable of exhibiting the feature identified in *Categories* 5.4a10–21 as most characteristic of substance: they are able to take on further determination without being overwhelmed by it and so are able to remain one and the same individual while undergoing a variety of accidental affections. This fact about substance is the source of a central tenet of a5.4a10–21 as most characteristic of substance: they are able to take on further determination without being overwhelmed by it and so are able to remain one and the same individual while undergoing a variety of accidental affections. This fact about substance is the source of a central tenet of Aristotle's ontology: the codependency of determinacy and openness to determination. Determinacy, as we learn in the *Metaphysics,* is a condition of the possibility for further determinability; the essential nature of substances is thus a condition of their ability to constitute ultimate subjects of predicates."

29. Bernard Yack, *Problems of a Political Animal: Community, Justice, and Conflict in Aristotelian Political Thought* (Berkeley and Los Angeles: University of California Press, 1993), 273: "If we thought these specific actions fully desirable in themselves, we would seek them as occasions to display our virtue. Without war, for example, we lack the opportunity to display courage in the manner that Aristotle associates with moral virtue. Nevertheless, Aristotle warns us against the conclusion that wars are therefore desirable, even as means to virtuous actions. 'For no one chooses to make a war for the sake of being at war, nor aims at provoking such a war; a man would seem absolutely murderous if he were to make enemies of his friends in order to bring about battles and slaughter' (*NE* 1177b9). Yet if acts of courage were wholly choiceworthy for their own sake, and we were not provided with opportunities to perform them, it would be hard to avoid concluding that we should seek to create these opportunities, even if it meant making enemies of friends."

30. David Berlinski, *A Tour of the Calculus* (New York: Pantheon Books, 1995), 131–32.

31. The gods, we will see, are called happy by extension from the human case because they do well what we are trying to do.

32. My thesis that the virtues create their own enabling conditions is as far as possible from Nussbaum's claim that virtue contains the "seeds of its own disaster." Martha Nussbaum, *The Fragility of Goodness* (Cambridge: Cambridge University Press, 1986), 338–39.

33. Amelie Rorty, "The Two Faces of Courage," *Philosophy* 61 (1981): 151–71, rpt. in her *Mind in Action*, 300–301: "When a virtue is central to a person's character—when its exercise is organizationally dominant—the thoughts and categorical preoccupations that are central to that virtue form interpretations of situations: they focus attention and define what is salient. It is not enough that the virtuous person acts and reacts in specific ways when the occasion arises. She must also have a certain cast of mind. This is not primarily a matter of purity of heart or intention, not a matter of nobility or disinterest: it is the very practical matter of seeing situations in such a way as to elicit actions and reactions. A virtue of action is worthless without sensitivity to the conditions that require it."

34. But see *Pol.* VII.13.1331b39–1332a3: "That everyone strives for living well and for happiness is evident. It is open to some to achieve these things, but to others not, on account of some sort of fortune or nature; for living nobly requires a certain equipment too—*less of it in a better state, more for those in a worse one.*" The contradiction here between the claim in the text that better the virtue, the more equipment it takes, and the claim in this quotation that the better the polis, the less equipment virtue needs, is parallel to the contradictory claims about how easy and available, and how difficult and rare, virtue is.

35. F. H. Bradley, *Appearance and Reality: A Metaphysical Essay* (London, Oxford, and New York: Oxford University Press, 1893, rpt., 1969), xiv.

36. "All essences are by nature first principles of a certain kind, owing to which each is able to generate many things of the same sort as itself, for example a man engenders men, and in general an animal animals, and a plant plants. And in addition to this, obviously man alone among other animals initiates certain conduct, for we should not ascribe conduct to any of the others" (*EE* II.6.1222b15–20). For the biological equivalent of artisans both producing and teaching, and praxis both acting and creating the conditions for its own success, see David Depew, "Etiological Approaches to Biological Aptness in Aristotle and Darwin," *Aristotelische Biologie: Intentionen, Methoden, Ergebnisse*, ed. Wolfgang Kullman and Sabine Föllinger (Stuttgart: Franz Steiner Verlag, 1997), 215: "Organic processes—the orderly articulation of parts and the development and exercise of a specific array of apt behavioral capacities—typically occur in sites where like produces like, that is, in systems that have highly faithful replicating capacities. This coextension between living entities and things that come to be from entities like themselves, and in the course of their own life-cycles generate 'another like themselves, an animal [of a certain kind] producing an animal, a plant a plant' (*De An.* II.415a27–b7, *Part. An.* I.1.640a25–27, I.1.640b1–4, *Ph.* II.1.193b8, II.2.194b13) suggests to Aristotle that deployment of materials and their dispositional properties to generate living things is normally achieved in and through this reproductive cycle, and indeed that it is the *function* of reproduction to orchestrate an apt deployment of materials that will not normally occur in any other way." See also *Met.* IX.9.1049b24–7: "From the potential the actual is always produced by an actual thing, e.g., man by man, musician by musician; there is always a first changer, and the changer already exist actually."

## Chapter Seven

1. Martha Nussbaum, *The Fragility of Goodness* (Cambridge: Cambridge University Press, 1986), 373–77; J. Donald Monan, *Moral Knowledge and its Methodology in Aristotle* (Oxford: Clarendon Press, 1968), 108–11; Jon Moline, "Contemplation and the Human Good," *Nous* 17 (1983): 37–53. Urmson says that Aristotle's "enthusiasm" for his own scholarly life temporarily got the better of him. J. O. Urmson, *Aristotle's Ethics* (Oxford: Blackwell, 1988),

125. Aristotle "vacillates" according to J. L. Ackrill, "Aristotle on Eudaimonia," *Proceedings of the British Academy* 60 (1974): 339–59, rpt. in *Essays on Aristotle's Ethics,* ed. Amelie Rorty (Berkeley and Los Angeles: University of California Press, 1981), 15–33, at 31; W. F. R. Hardie, *Aristotle's Ethical Theory* (Oxford: Clarendon Press, 1980), 299–300; and K. V. Wilkes, "The Good Man and the Good for Man in Aristotle's Ethics," *Mind* 87 (1978) 533–71, rpt. in *Essays on Aristotle's Ethics,* ed. Rorty, 341–58, at 341.

2. Sarah Broadie, *Ethics with Aristotle,* 370: "If the *Nicomachean Ethics* had come down to us minus Chapters 7 and 8 of Book X, our overwhelming impression from the work would be that Aristotle means to define the essence of happiness in terms of morally virtuous activity informed by practical wisdom." Bernard Yack, *Problems of a Political Animal: Community, Justice, and Conflict in Aristotelian Political Thought* (Berkeley and Los Angeles: University of California Press, 1993), 269: "If Aristotle really believes in the superiority of the contemplative life, then it is hard to understand why he devotes almost all of the *Nicomachean Ethics* to exploring the practical life of active virtue. Our picture of the Aristotelian good life would be considerably clearer—although ultimately less intriguing—if we could find some reason to discount his praise of one of these two lives."

3. *NE* I.2.1094a22–24, 1095b5–6, 1099b29–32, 1103b26–31, 1143a6–10, 1146a7–9, 1151a15–17, 1152a8–9, 1179a35–b4; *Pol.* I.11.1258b9–10; *Met* II.1.993b20–21.

4. There is no deliberation, thus, when he compares living the life of ethical virtue with the competing lives of pleasure or money-making or honor. We don't deliberate in order to see that the political life is better than the others. We simply correct misunderstandings and clarify what we all mean by happiness. At *NE* I.5.1095b20 he does talk about most men choosing a life fit only for cattle, but in the comparison of different kinds of lives in I.5, he does not talk about deliberating among the options. But see *EE* I.2.1214b7–12, I.4.1215a35–b14. See too *NE* I.7.1097b14–19: "We think happiness the most desirable (*hairetōtatēn*) of all good things without being itself reckoned as one among the rest; for if it were so reckoned, it is clear that we should consider it more desirable (*hairetōteran*) when even the smallest of other good things were combined with it, since the addition would result in a larger total of good, and of two goods the greater is always the more desirable (*hairetōteron*)."

Commentators without argument frequently represent the question of the two lives as an issue for choice. For just one recent example, see Richard Kraut, *Aristotle on the Human Good* (Princeton: Princeton University Press, 1989), 44: Aristotle "sees the political and contemplative lives, each with its own conception of happiness, as alternatives between which we must choose." The only place I have been able to find where Aristotle explicitly talks about choosing between the two lives is *Pol.* VII.2.1324a25–29. *Politics* VII begins with the question of the most choiceworthy way of life, saying that determining it is necessary in order to say what is the best constitution, and that same expression is repeated a few lines later (VII.1.1323a16, 20). There is one more passage from the *Politics* that is relevant: VII.13. 1333a41–b3, in which Aristotle says that the statesman has to legislate in regard "to modes of life and choices of conduct man should be capable (*dynasthai*) of engaging in business and war, but still more capable of living in peace and leisure, and he should do what is necessary and useful, but still more should do what is noble." Apart from these passages, I do not think Aristotle talks about choosing a life. Certainly Aristotle can use the words *haireses* and *prohairesis* to talk about something being better without a choice being involved. See, for example, "in *technē* voluntary error (*ho hekōn hamartia*) is not so bad as (*hairetōteros*) involuntary, whereas in the sphere of *phronēsis* it is worse, as it is in the sphere of the virtues" (*NE* VI.5.1140b21–24). I have also discussed the idea of choosing ends in "Choosing the Good in Aristotle's *Topics*," *Aristotle on Dialectic,* ed. May Sim (Lanham, Md.: Rowan and Littlefield, 1999), 107–24. There is one more place where Aristotle talks about choosing a life. It is in *Metaphysics* IV: "Sophistic and dialectic treat the same *genos* as philosophy, but philosophy differs from sophistic by the kind of *dynamis,* and from dialectic in its *prohairesis* of a way of life. Dialectic treats as an exercise what philosophy tries to understand (*gnoristike*), and sophistic seems to be philosophy, and is not" (IV.2.1004b23–26). I discussed this passage in *Aristotle's Rhetoric: An Art of Character,* 213.

5. There is a parallel in the *Metaphysics*. At VI.1.1026a28–30 we learn that unless there is a god, metaphysics will be physics. In the same way here, unless man is not the best thing in the universe, *sophia* will be *phronēsis*. Ultimately, I will show, unless man is not the best thing in the universe, not only will philosophy be reduced to politics, but politics will in turn be reduced to economics.

6. Anaxagoras reappears once in *NE* X.8, paired this time with Solon to agree that only moderate possessions are needed for virtue, and not as a philosophical paradigm.

7. "He who is without a city through nature rather than chance is either a mean sort or superior to man . . . for the one who is such by nature has by this fact a desire for war, as if he were an isolated piece in a game of chess" (*Pol.* I.2.1253a3–7). The naturally apolitical person is not the person of godlike virtues in *NE* VII, who is not a contemplator anyway. There are those who are apolitical by nature and those who are by chance, but none are by choice and praxis. For one example of someone who claims that the isolated individual of *Pol.* I.2 lives the life of contemplation, see R. G. Mulgan, *Aristotle's Political Theory: An Introduction for Students of Political Theory* (Oxford: Clarendon Press, 1977). For one who thinks that *theōria* is prepolitical, see Judith A. Swanson, *The Public and the Private in Aristotle's Political Philosophy* (Ithaca: Cornell University Press, 1992). For a refutation along the lines of my argument, see David Depew, "The Inscription of Isocrates into Aristotle's Practical Philosophy," in *Isocrates and Civic Education,* ed. Takis Poulakos and David Depew (Austin: University of Texas Press, 2004), 157–85. See also Depew's unpublished paper, "The Primacy of Theoria Over Praxis in *Politics* 7.1–3," 32: "Indeed, while it is true that from the point of view of its content and value the *bios theoretikos* can be described as a share in the apolitical divine, from the point of view of Aristotle's practical philosophy, and thus of the sort of society in which a contemplative life is even conceivable, eligible, or physically livable, this way of life looks like nothing so much as a hypertrophied case of the *bios politikos,* depending not only on the resources that city life provides, but on the friendship proffered by leisure." But see *Pol.* VII.2.1324a15-17. Depew's entire article as almost as great a help to me as a long series of personal conversations with him.

8. Someone might object—Edward Halper has on an earlier draft of this chapter— that no substance can be made of substances (*Met.* VII.16.1041a3–5, 1040b14, VII.13. 1039a3ff), and so no *energeia* can be made of *energeiai*. Certainly no *energeia* can be made of *energeiai* that are independent of each other and of the unifying *energeia*. As we will see, the relation of happiness as an *energeia* to the *energeiai* that make it up is like the relation of a soul to its organic body, and so of a polis to its citizens. Neither exists, and is fully substantial or actual, without the other. For more on the idea of a substance made of substances, see Pierre Pellegrin, "Taxonomie, moriologie, division: réponses à G. E. R. Lloyd," *Biologie, Logique, et Métaphysique Chez Aristote,* ed. Daniel Devereux and Pierre Pellegrin (Paris: Éditions du CNRS, 1990), 37–48. See too Edward Halper, "The Substance of Aristotle's Ethics," in *The Crossroads of Norm and Nature: Essays on Aristotle's Ethics and Metaphysics,* ed. May Sim (Lanham, Md.: Rowman and Littlefield, 1995), 7–8: "Insofar as it consists of a plurality of faculties united by their form or actuality, a happy life is a quasi-substantial entity. In contrast, the life of a person whose faculties do not function together lacks this substantial character. I contend that the happy life is the best life precisely because it is substantial. To function well is simply to use one's faculties in such a way that they constitute a substantial whole, and virtue lies in the faculties' being capable of such unified functioning."

9. In the *Poetics,* Aristotle describes the plot both as the imitation of action and as the synthesis of actions. Plot must be both made up of *praxeis* and be itself a single *praxis*. This isn't just a linguistic puzzle or a matter of squaring the facts with Aristotelian doctrine. The poet has to solve the problem of creating a unity which has magnitude and significance. A plot made up of incidents that are not actions is an inferior plot, a tragedy of suffering. A plot made up of actions but without its own unity as an action is an episodic plot (*Poet.* 9.1451b34–35). The successful poet makes one action out of many. For a different reading of this double demand, see Elizabeth Belfiore, *Tragic Pleasures: Aristotle on Plot and Emotion* (Princeton: Princeton University Press, 1992), 83–84.

10. It is obviously paradoxical to say that *the political life is also theoretical,* although in a secondary way. Without the paradox, there are anticipations of my view in other commentators. Sarah Broadie, *Ethics with Aristotle,* 413: "If *theōria* were, so to say, subtracted from the best human life, what remains would be a life of practical virtue, and it would not be best since what remains would be truncated. It may seem to follow that a life characterised as a life of practical virtue is not the best, on the ground that a life so characterised is inferior to the combination of itself with *theōria.* But that does not follow. Aristotle can hold, and, I believe, does hold, that the life of practical virtue is as such the best; the mere description 'practical' says less than everything about it." On the political life pointing beyond itself to the theoretical life, see Harold H. Joachim, *Aristotle, The Nicomachean Ethics: A Commentary* (Oxford: Clarendon Press, 1951), 242: "The life of action contains in itself . . . features which point onwards to their own more perfect fulfillment in the life of thought, . . . [and] the life of thought admits of being exhibited as the extension and fuller realization of some leading characteristic or characteristics in the life of action."

Nicholas White, "Conflicting Parts of Happiness in Aristotle's Ethics," *Ethics* 105 (1995): 279, n. 45. "When Aristotle says that we desire everything for the sake of happiness, does he mean—when it all comes out in the wash in *Ethics* 10.6–8—that we desire everything for the sake of *theōria,* or that we desire everything for the sake of the life that is dominated by *theōria?* The answer is, I think, some of both. Aside from being valuable for themselves, other activities contribute causally to the activity of theorizing." Amélie Oksenberg Rorty, "The Place of Contemplation in Aristotle's *Nicomachean Ethics,*" 388: "Contemplating the essential energeiai that define the species realizes our formal identity as the species. The contemplator of Humanity becomes a unified whole, a self-contained, self-justified, actualized Humanity, his essential and perfected life." Michael Woods, "Intuition and Perception in Aristotle's Ethics," *Oxford Studies in Ancient Philosophy* 4 (1986): 145–66 at 165: "Aristotle does not envisage that the virtuous life, in the ordinary sense, is one sort of *alternative* to the life of contemplation; rather, Aristotle is now taking it for granted that one will need to be a good person, having the virtues of character, and he asks which, given that, of the alternative kinds of life available is the best one." Woods goes on to claim that Aristotle does make the life of *theōria* and of politics into alternatives, but presents no evidence that that is the case. He assumes that the political life is only one way that the virtues can be exercised, while I claim, and have argued for it earlier, that the political life is the life of ethical virtue and so the only possible contrast to the theoretical life.

11. Aristotle says that animals have no reason but only perception at *De Anima* 414b1–9, and that they have only perception and memory of particulars, not universals at *NE* VII.3.1147b3–5. Note also that slaves are not happy, and engage in neither praxis nor *theōria.* See *NE* X.6.1177a6–9. At *EE* VII.2.1236b6, only man is capable of true friendship, because only he has *aisthanetai prohaireseōs.* See also *EE* VII.6.1240b33–34. In *EE* VII.6, only mature humans, who have *prohairesis,* and not animals or children, are capable of self-love (1240b31–33).

12. The story I trace differs from Aristotle's own history of philosophy at the start of the *Metaphysics* in which the first philosophers concerned themselves with natural science and Socrates brought philosophy down from the skies into the homes of men. I think there is no contradiction because of the findings of chapters 2 and 6 that metaphysics is incomplete without praxis. The idea that scientific rationality develops out of political rationality is somewhat easier to swallow on Aristotle's understanding of both kinds of rationality than on ours, though, because science is a system of purposes as much as human action is. See also *Pol.* VII.15.1334a26–34 in which leisure requires both philosophy and the virtues of justice and temperance. "The life expressing *nous* is not the life expressing only it; and the life expressing *phronēsis* . . . is not the political life. What are being compared . . . is the part of (what we would call) a person's life that expresses the merely human thing in him and the part that expresses the divine thing in him." C. D. C. Reeve, *Practices of Reason: Aristotle's Nicomachean Ethics* (Oxford: Clarendon Press, 1992), 159.

13. Richard Kraut, *Aristotle on the Human Good,* 49–53; John Cooper "Contemplation and Happiness: A Reconsideration," *Synthese* 72 (1987): 186–216, at 207, n. 14. See also

Charles Taylor, "Leading a Life," in *Incommensurability, Incomparability, and Practical Reason*, ed. Ruth Chang (Cambridge, Mass.: Harvard University Press, 1997), 183: "Some people have objected that Aristotle seems to fall into a confusion—or perhaps pulls a fast one on us—in the discussion of the supreme good in *Ethics* I.vii. He talks first as though there might be one, but there might also be several such ends. Later he seems to slip into assuming that there is just one final aim.

"I am suggesting that some move of this kind has to be made. There are in fact two separable stages of reflection, which Aristotle perhaps does not separate here: We can determine what we think the goods are that we seek 'for their own sakes' and also their relative ranking, if any. But even if we see a plurality of final ends of equal rank, we still have to *live* them; that is, we have to design a life in which they can be somehow integrated, in some propositions, since any life is finite and cannot admit of unlimited pursuit of any good. This sense of life— or design or plan, if we want to emphasize our powers of leading here—is necessarily one. If this is our final end, there can be only one."

14. Compare *EE* I.4.1215a33–b2: "There are three ways of life in which those to whom fortune gives opportunity invariably choose (*prohairountai*) to live, the life of politics, the life of philosophy, and the life of enjoyment."

15. "It is not necessary that an active life be in relation to others, as some people think, nor is that thought alone practical which is for the sake of the consequences of the action, but much more so are the studies and thoughts that are their own ends and for their own sakes" (*Pol.* VII.3.1325b16–21).

Therefore, I offer a hypothesis why Aristotle talks about choosing between praxis and *theōria* in *Politics* VII and only there, not elsewhere in the *Politics* and never in the *Ethics*, and why *Politics* VII contains far more detailed assertions about the nature of the gods than anything found elsewhere in Aristotle's practical writings. *Politics* VII is concerned with the best state absolutely. He begins the treatment of that best state by posing the choice between the two happy lives because he will go on to show that, the better the state, the less difference there is between praxis and *theōria*. The better the polis, that is, the more we can live by the Two End interpretation. It is a mistake, as I have already quoted him saying, to think that only the philosopher engages in *theōria*. That is a mistake which is true for inferior states, in which one must indeed sometimes choose between two lives. But the better the state, the less episodic and circumstantial the practical life and so the easier it is to lead that life as a unity and so as an object of *theōria*. That is why we should pray that we live in such a polis. The difference between happiness as "a whole composed of elements that are activities, and . . . the elements (activities) comprising the whole," and the consequences of ignoring the difference, are stressed by Robert Heinman's Review Article of John Cooper's *Reason and Emotion, Polis* 17 (2000): 161–85 (quotation at 182).

16. My Two Act and Two End interpretations are prefigured in *Met.* XII.10.1075a11– 18: "We must consider in which of two ways the nature of the universe contains the good, that is, the highest good, whether as something separate and in itself, or as the order of the parts. Probably in both ways, as an army does. For the good is found both in the order and in the leader, and more in the latter; for it is not because of the order that he exists, but the order exists because of him. And all things are ordered together somehow, but not all in the same way—fishes, birds, and plants; and the universe is not such that one thing has nothing to do with another, but they are connected. For all are ordered together to one end."

17. Plato, *Laws* 803b–c: "The affairs of human beings are not worthy of great seriousness; yet it is necessary to be serious about them. . . . What is serious should be treated seriously, and what is not serious should not, and that by nature god is worthy of a complete, blessed seriousness, but that what is human . . . has been devised as a certain plaything of god, and that this is really the best thing about it. Every man and woman should spend life in this way, playing the noblest possible games."

18. Nicholas White, "Good as Goal," *Southern Journal of Philosophy* 27 (1988): 169–93, at 171: "By contrast with standard intellectualist and mixed-life accounts [i.e., the only possibilities under the Two Act interpretation], my own position will be that Aristotle ascribes to

*theōria* a kind of preeminence in the best life to which mixed-life accounts do not do justice, but not the kind of preeminence that maximizing intellectualist accounts say that he ascribes to it. . . . The special kind of preeminence that Aristotle attaches to *theōria* . . . is the role, which is foreign to recent ethical theorizing, of being a certain particular kind of '*focus*'— as I shall call it—of a person's life."

19. Richard Kraut, *Aristotle on the Human Good*, 6. See also L. P. Gerson, *God and Greek Philosophy: Studies in the Early History of Natural Theology* (London and New York: Routledge, 1990), 137: "Organic individuals are never all at once what they strive to be. Perfect actuality is available to an organic individual such as a human being only in those rare moments when they step outside themselves, as it were, in contemplative thinking. Understanding the being of a sensible substance would be understanding the undivided unified activity it strives to attain."

20. From this perspective, I understand the conflict between the "inclusive end" and "dominant end" interpretations of happiness as two varieties of Two Act interpretations, differing in whether philosophy is the only content of the philosophic life or whether that life includes other things too. This pair of interpretations of happiness and *theōria* was first laid out in W. F. R. Hardie, "The Final Good in Aristotle's *Ethics*," *Philosophy* 40 (1965): 277–95.

21. As noted in John Cooper, "Contemplation and Happiness: A Reconsideration," and in idem, *Reason and Emotion: Essays on Ancient Moral Psychology and Ethical Theory* (Princeton: Princeton University Press, 1999), 212–36, at 227–29.

22. Jonathan Lear, *Happiness, Death, and the Remainder of Life* (Cambridge, Mass.: Harvard University Press, 2000), 54.

23. Aryeh Kosman, "*Metaphysics* Λ: Divine Thought," *Aristotle's Metaphysics Lambda*, ed. Michael Frede and David Charles (Oxford: Clarendon Press, 2000), 311: "We need to understand Aristotle's attribution of thinking to the divine in light of what is essentially a reverse attribution: the attribution of divinity to thinking. The claim that God thinks turns out to mean that since the activity of thought is divine, it may therefore be the clearest icon we have of the being of the divine principle whose essential nature is activity, and on which depend heaven and earth. We say that God thinks because we want to understand the self-directed pure activity that is the activity of the divine, and thinking is the best way to do so, since it most powerfully figures this activity.

"We may recall that Aristotle employs a similar strategy in the *Nicomachean Ethics* when arguing that active thought—*theōria*—is the critical element in a happy life. There the revelation of *theōria* as the activity of the divine (*Nicomachean Ethics* X.8.1179b21–24), which justifies the claim that in such an activity is our highest happiness, is established by a process of elimination. No constructive argument establishes thinking as what a god does; that fact emerges only dialectically in the course of an argument designed to show what is most divine in our life."

24. See too *Met.* XII.9.1074b16: "Thought seems to be the most divine of phenomena." And see as well *NE* X.8.1177b31–34: "We should not follow those who exhort us, being human, to think human thoughts and, being mortal, to think mortal thoughts, but, as far as is possible, we should make ourselves immortal (*athanatizein*) and do everything in life in accord with the most powerful thing in us."

25. Roberto Calasso, *The Marriage of Cadmus and Harmony* (New York: Vintage, 1994), 102: "When Homer gives the epithet *dîos* to his characters, the word does not refer first of all to what they may have of 'divine,' but to the clarity, the splendor that is always with them and against which they stand out." See also *Pol.* III.16.1287a28–31. Lenn Goodman, *God of Abraham* (New York and Oxford: Oxford University Press, 1996), 88: "Human holiness begins with human nature, and the call to emulate God's holiness contains no paradox, so long as we recall that what we seek is our perfection, not God's. God's transcendence would make divinity irrelevant only if we had no idea of the human good. . . . The nexus of morality to divinity is the plainest conceptual shift we know, since it is from our highest values that our idea of divinity takes its rise. It would be a poor thinker indeed who

could not rederive morality from the Ideal that has morality at its source. The emulation called for by God's perfection . . . means pursuit of human perfection."

26. Eternal beings can be *energeiai* without being the *energeia* of any *dynamis* (*Met.* IV.8.1050b6–8, 1050b22–28). All human activities are the *energeia* of some *dynamis,* which is why we cannot engage in contemplation continuously. *Theōria,* though, can be understood without our needing to think of it as the *energeia* of any *dynamis.* We can't say anything informative about the human powers that make *theōria* possible.

27. "The description of consciousness and self-consciousness expresses the fact that the awareness implicit in all perception and cognition must be understood as a kind of transparency, intentionality whose being is . . . determined objectively, that is, by what it is the consciousness of. This transparency is revealed to us in the fact . . . that *nous,* thought that is for Aristotle the sheerest mode of consciousness, is not in and of itself anything." Aryeh Kosman, "Aristotle on the Desirability of Friends," *Ancient Philosophy* 24 (2004): 135–54, at 141.

28. For analogous Platonic paradoxes about "becoming immortal," see my "Immortality and Ethical Argument in Plato's *Phaedo,*" in *A Companion to Rhetoric and Rhetorical Criticism,* ed. Walter Jost and Wendy Olmsted (Malden, Mass.: Blackwell, 2004), 206–20.

29. Thus I think David Charles gets the argument backwards. "One of [Aristotle's] major strategies in the *Ethics* is to argue that since intellectual contemplation has a paradigmatic role in wellbeing (and human wellbeing), practical knowledge, which is strongly analogous to theoretical contemplation, must also be an element in human wellbeing. Thus, theoretical contemplation is the focal case of human wellbeing, and practical knowledge is itself an element in human wellbeing because it closely resembles theoretical contemplation." David Charles, "Aristotle and Modern Realism," in *Aristotle and Moral Realism,* ed. Robert Heinaman (Boulder and San Francisco: Westview, 1995), 159, n. 19. See *An. Post.* I.27.87a31–35: "A science which is knowledge at once that something is true and why it is true, and not of the fact itself without the reason why, is the more exact and prior science." The life of *theōria* gives the "why" to the political life. It is not the *energeia* of a particular *dynamis* or "underlying subject." It depends not on fewer hypotheses but on fewer external resources.

30. See too *Pol.* VII.13.1332a1–2: "The aim of all men is living well or happiness. But, through luck or nature, some men have the requirements to attain this aim, others do not; for to live well a man needs also external goods, fewer if he has a superior disposition but more if he has an inferior disposition."

31. Alasdair MacIntyre, "Bernstein's Distorting Mirrors: A Rejoinder," *Soundings* 67 (1984): 38–39. "Bernstein seems to believe that ancient and medieval beliefs, including Aristotelean beliefs, in the objectivity of the moral order required as a 'foundation' or were 'based upon' theories about human nature and the nature of the universe. This is an important, although a common misreading of the structures of ancient and medieval thought which projects back on to that thought an essentially modern view of the ordering of philosophical and scientific enquiries. On this modern view, ethics and politics are peripheral modes of enquiry, dependent in key part on what is independently established by epistemology and by the natural sciences. . . . But in ancient and medieval thought, ethics and politics afford light to the other disciplines as much as vice versa. Hence from that standpoint, which I share, it is not the case that *first* I must decide whether some theory of human nature or cosmology is true and only *secondly* pass a verdict upon an account of the virtues which is 'based' upon it. Rather, if we find compelling reasons for accepting a particular view of the virtues and the human telos, that in itself will place constraints on what kind of theory of human nature and what kind of cosmology are rationally acceptable."

32. From the fact that *theōria* is the best way to live, it does follow that whatever the content of first philosophy, it will not affect the practical truth. There are certainly some possible things that first philosophy could find that would be incompatible with what *phronēsis* has determined. That there are gods who behave as the Olympian gods are supposed to, intervening in human affairs without regard for ethical excellence, for example, would have implications for how we are supposed to live and would therefore be excluded from what

metaphysics could come up with. Gods who listened to prayer and rewarded something other than good works would be incompatible with Aristotle's account of virtue. Divine perfection cannot require human imperfection. Aristotelian human autonomy does not require a single perfect, not capricious, god, but it still requires gods who are better than people.

33. Sarah Broadie, *Ethics with Aristotle,* 418–19: "If [happiness is *theōria*] means . . . that the happy life is one in which *theōria* occupies most of the time or is pursued even at the cost of good practical dealings, the message, though shocking, is simple: so why was it not made clear before? . . . The more he expatiates on practical excellence in the meantime, the more illogical such a message, when it came, would seem. But if *theōria* contributes to the happy life by essentially being the leisure-activity of those whose practical excellence deserves no less (no less, that is, than to be set off by leisure devoted to the activity in which we are most like gods), then the order of Aristotle's exposition makes methodical sense."

David Depew, "Politics, Music, and Contemplation in Aristotle's Ideal State," in *A Companion to Aristotle's Politics,* ed. David Keyt and Fred D. Miller Jr. (Oxford and Cambridge: Blackwell, 1991), 346–80, at 354: "Self-sufficiency does not consist only in the *de facto* achievement of material plenty, but in a condition where the attitudes of political associates are not longer dominated or distorted by a means-oriented mentality—a mentality that, having inevitably arisen in a world of scarcity, can live on even in a world of great abundance, as it does in deviant states."

Depew, 362: "A state living on the ragged edge of material sufficiency may look adequate to the exclusively contemplative man, whose material needs are minimal. But the fact is that this condition will generate a state always threatening to regress into a vulgar and debilitating concern with basic necessities."

34. In addition to these ways in which the political life is a necessary condition for *theōria,* the possession of ethical virtue for the individual is a necessary condition for *theōria. Phronēsis* and ethical virtue are necessary for the individual because uncontrolled passions will make *theōria* impossible. See for example *EE* VIII.2.1249b16–19: "Whatever selection and possession of thing naturally good will most produce the contemplation of god, this is best, and this is the finest standard." A few lines later he says: "This is the best standard for the soul; when it least perceives the irrational part of the soul as such" (1249b21–23). See too *NE* VI.13.1145a6–9, X.8.1178b5–6.

35. The claim that friends help us to contemplate makes more sense if, as I have been arguing, we contemplate our own good activities than if we contemplate the gods. Friends could help us *learn* about the gods, as they could be instrumental in our learning about all kinds of things, but why should they make it easier for us to *think* about the gods? On the other hand, friends can help us *know* ourselves and the goodness of our activities as well as simply learn about them.

36. "Pleasure should be called not perceived, but unimpeded" (*NE* VII.12.1153a13). See Sarah Broadie, *Ethics with Aristotle,* 402n: " 'Perceived' is eliminated presumably because, given 'activity,' or 'unimpeded activity,' it is redundant—although the reason for this becomes clear only from IX.9.1170a13–1170b10, and X.4–5 (especially 5.1175b33–35): activities that are pleasures (according to the doctrine of *NE* VII) are cognitive ones—perception, sensation, and intellection—and they are necessarily self-aware."

37. Hence I reject John Cooper's interpretation which claims that someone "ultimately concerned only with his own intellectual accomplishments would . . . surely on occasion find it rational at least to neglect to do some positive act of virtue, if not actually do something immoral, as a means to the furtherance of his consuming interest" in *theōria.* John Cooper, *Reason and Human Good in Aristotle* (Cambridge, Mass.: Harvard University Press, 1975), 149.

38. See Cynthia Farrar, *The Origins of Democratic Thinking: The Invention of Politics in Classical Athens* (Cambridge: Cambridge University Press, 1988).

39. Nicholas White, "Conflicting Parts of Happiness in Aristotle's Ethics," *Ethics* 105 (1995): 282, n. 53: Aristotle "ends up saying that *theōria,* not virtuous activity, appeals to

the element that is most truly oneself (Aristotle *Ethics* 1178a2–7, 1166a17–18). . . . Modern morality, e.g., Kant or Bradley, will argue that virtue is the true self in opposition to egoism, evil, or sensuality. But Aristotle argues that *theōria* is the true self not to defeat egoism but to rebut the idea that *theōria* imposes an alien, divine, standard on human excellence." Someone could object that to make that application extends Aristotle's point against his own boundary condition that it applies not to "all goods, but only with those involved in good and bad fortune, goods which are, [considered] unconditionally, always good, but for this or that person not always good." But Aristotle himself extends the good *haplōs*/good-for-me distinction more broadly in way that is just what I want when he turns from discussions of virtue (including justice) to considering friendship. *NE* IX.8.1169a32–b2: "The good man may even give up actions to his friend; it may be nobler to be the cause of his friend's acting than to act himself. In all actions, therefore, that man are praised for, the good man is seen to assign himself the greater share in what is noble." Cf. *EE* VII.2.1236b27–1237a10: "Since the same thing is absolutely good and absolutely pleasant at the same time if nothing interferes, and the true friend and friend absolutely is the primary friend, and such is a friend chosen in and for himself (and he must necessarily be such, for he for whom one wishes good or his own sake must necessarily be desirable for his own sake), a true friend is also absolutely pleasant; owing to which it is thought that a friend of any sort is pleasant. . . . The absolutely good is absolutely desirable, but what is good for oneself is desirable for oneself; and the two ought to come into agreement. This is effected by virtue; and the purpose of politics is to bring it about in cases where it does not yet exist. And one who is a human being is well adapted to this and on the way to it (for by nature things that are absolutely good are good to him), and similarly a man rather than a woman and a gifted man rather than a dull one; but the road is through pleasure—it is necessary that fine things should be pleasant. When there is discord between them, a man is not yet perfectly good; for it is possible for unrestraint to be engendered in him, as unrestraint is caused by discord between the good and the pleasant in the emotions." See too the analogous references to prayer in the *Politics,* e.g., II.6.1265a19, VII.3.1325b37, and 13.1332a29–35.

40. Anthony Kronman, *The Lost Lawyer: Failing Ideals of the Legal Profession* (Cambridge, Mass.: Harvard University Press, 1993), 72: "The sort of imaginative sympathy that deliberation requires combines two opposite-seeming dispositions, that of compassion on the one hand, and that of detachment, on the other. . . . It is difficult to be compassionate, and often just as difficult to be detached, but what is most difficult of all is to be both at once." See too Plato, *Laws* 803b3–804b4.

41. David Depew, "Politics, Music, and Contemplation in Aristotle's Ideal State," 361. "A stronger sort of inclusivism asserts that the contemplative virtues serve as an ordering principle, according to which contemplation is to be pursued as vigorously as possible within the bounds of social obligations, which must be met first. 'Moral virtue comes first,' writes John Cooper, 'But once moral virtue is securely entrenched intellectual goods are allowed to predominate.' This has been called [by Keyt] the 'superstructure view.' . . . This account has the disadvantage of suggesting that practice of the moral or social virtues is a constraint on time that would be better spent contemplating."

42. Depew, "Politics, Music, and Contemplation in Aristotle's Ideal State," 346.

43. White ("Good as Goal," 184) notes that "Aristotle never says anything to suggest what would in any case be entirely unbelievable, that a life of *theōria* will never contain occasions in which the passions associated with the virtues arise, and so where virtuous actions are called for. He makes clear that such a person will be a normal human being with normal tendencies with regard to the passions, and will live in society in a normal way (1178b5–7)." I believe that my interpretation is superior to White's because I see no need for the hesitation expressed in the note attached to the passage I quoted. In the note he says: "There is room for uncertainty about whether such a person could be said to act virtuously in the full sense that Aristotle stipulates. He would not be acting for the sake of moral virtue or *to kalon* taken as his final end, because *ex hypothesi* his final end is *theōria* and so his action is partly for the sake of it." I claim that only such a person is acting virtuously in the fullest sense, just because his final end is *theōria*. I do not think it follows from the fact that *theōria*

is the final end means that such a man's "action is partly for the sake of it." On the final conclusion of the note, though, I am in complete agreement. "Someone who makes *theōria* his primary goal . . . can attach intrinsic value to morally virtuous activity, and can engage in it without thinking of its value as merely its conduciveness to *theōria*" (193).

44. My conclusion about the relation of the political to the theoretical life is similar to that found in F. H. Bradley's *Ethical Studies* (Oxford: Oxford University Press, 1927), in which for similar reasons the moral life points beyond itself, as the morality of my station and its duties is succeeded by an ideal morality. This movement is a movement toward the infinite or unlimited, toward the fully comprehensive. Aristotle's argument for the superiority of *theoria* is matched, at the end of Bradley's chapter on Ideal Morality, by the assertion that advance consists in greater specification and more intense homogeneity (249). The chapter ends: "Whatever evolution may be, Ethics is confined within it. To ask what it is, is to rise above it, and to pass beyond the world of mere morality." The reader can decide whether that similarity is a point in my favor or not.

*Rhetoric*